Dimensions. Journal of Architectural Knowledge
03/2022

Species of Theses
and Other Pieces

Issue Editors
Meike Schalk, Torsten Lange, Andreas Putz,
Tijana Stevanovicé, Elena Markus

Issue Editors
Meike Schalk, Torsten Lange, Andreas Putz,
Tijana Stevanović, Elena Markus

[transcript]

This journal is published bianually (in spring and autumn) and printed editions are available for annual subscription directly from the publisher. The retail price for an annual subscription to the print issue incl. shipment within Germany is 75,00 € and for international purchases 85,00 €. The electronic version is available free of charge (Open Access).

All information regarding notes for contributors, subscriptions, Open Access, back volume and orders is available online at:
https://www.transcript-publishing.com/dak

Additional information on upcoming issues, calls for contributions and the options for partaking as contributors, editors or members of the peer review procedure can be found at the journals website: www.dimensions-journal.eu
If you have any further questions please contact us, addressing Katharina Voigt, at: mail@dimensions-journal.eu

Bibliographic information published by the Deutsche Nationalbibliothek

Dimensions. Journal of Architectural Knowledge

Lead Editors
Katharina Voigt, Uta Graff, Ferdinand Ludwig

Advisory Board
Isabelle Doucet, Susanne Hauser, Klaske Havik, Jonathan Michael Hill, Wilfried Kühn, Meike Schalk

Editorial Context
BauHow5
Bartlett University College London, Great Britain
Chalmers University Gothenburg, Sweden
Delft University of Technology, Netherlands
Swiss Federal Institute of Technology Zurich, Switzerland
Technical University of Munich, Germany

Associated Institutions
Royal Institute of Technology, Stockholm, Sweden
Technical University of Vienna, Austria
University of the Arts Berlin, Germany

The initial funding to this journal is provided by the Department of Architecture at the TUM School of Engineering and Design in Munich, Germany. Additional funding for this issue is provided by the Federal Ministry of Education and Research (BMBF) and the Free State of Bavaria under the Excellence Strategy of the Federal Government and the Länder, as well as by the Technical University of Munich – Institute for Advanced Study.

First published by 2022 transcript Verlag, Bielefeld
© transcript Independent Academic Publishing

Cover layout: Uta Graff, Technical University of Munich
Copy-editing: Elena Markus, Technical University of Munich
Proofreading: Lisa Goodrum, London
Typeset: Fabius Kossack (Studio Fabius Kossack), Berlin

ISSN 2747-5085
eISSN 2747-5093
Print-ISBN 978-3-8376-5920-7
PDF-ISBN 978-3-8394-5920-1

Contents

Dimensions of Architectural Knowledge, 2022-03 ∂
https://doi.org/10.14361/dak-2022-0301

Editorial

Meike Schalk, Torsten Lange, Andreas Putz, Tijana Stevanović, Elena Markus

This issue entitled »Species of Theses and Other Pieces« is concerned with practice-oriented research. It responds to the growing interest in questions concerning architectural practice and the forms of representation that such research efforts can take. The issue began with the international doctoral workshop »Approaching Research Practice in Architecture: Five Questions« on October 8–9, 2020, followed by five further course modules for early career researchers between December 2020 and April 2021, and consequently concluded with this publication.

For this issue, consisting of 21 contributions, we have invited the participants and guest speakers from the course to contribute works about or for, and reflections through, a format; meaning a genre, form, style, media, or mode of representation for practice-oriented research and its implication for knowledge creation in architecture. With practice-oriented research we approach the broad field of artistic research, research by design, practice-based and practice-led approaches, research through practice, mixed-mode research, and broadly, practice-oriented methods and methodologies that have come to enter long-established architectural research areas such as history and theory, heritage studies, technology, and urban and rural studies among others.

The international doctoral workshop that began the program was a joint venture between the BauHow5 Alliance[1] and ResArc, the Swedish research school in architecture. We are indebted to Martin Luce and Yolande Schnei-

---

1 BauHow5 Partners are The Bartlett Faculty of the Built Environment of the University College London, the School of Architecture of Chalmers University of Technology, the Department of Architecture of the Swiss Federal Institute of Technology Zurich, the

Corresponding authors: Meike Schalk (Royal Institute of Technology, Sweden/Technical University of Munich - Institute for Advanced Study, Germany), Torsten Lange (Lucerne University of Applied Sciences and Arts, Switzerland), Andreas Putz, Elena Markus (Technical University of Munich, Germany), Tijana Stevanović (Royal Institute of Technology, Sweden); meike.schalk@arch.kth.se; https://orcid.org/0000-0002-1744-6776; torsten.lange@hslu.ch; https://orcid.org/0000-0002-5737-0876; putz@tum.de; https://orcid.org/0000-0002-7612-9893; elena.markus@tum.de; https://orcid.org/0000-0002-6119-4270; tijana.stevanovic@arch.kth.se; https://orcid.org/0000-0002-0697-846X

der of TU Munich, and Frank van der Hoeven of TU Delft for inspiring the idea for an open digital platform for doctoral education, which was launched by the partners and offered to all interested research students in architecture across institutions and national borders. This initiative fell precisely at the outbreak of the Covid-19 pandemic and made the program a useful and desirable opportunity for doctoral students to meet once a month for two days online to exchange research and connect. Following this, not only did doctoral researchers from the partner universities sign up, but so did participants from other institutions in Europe, South Africa, Syria, and Lebanon. This broadened geographical reach was particularly valuable for us to expand and diversify our range of topics, methods, and methodology, and our view on the histories, theories, and ways of regarding research ethics.

»Approaching Research Practice: Five Questions« was organized online at TUM with keynote addresses from the faculty of the partner universities and a guest. It included talks by Isabelle Doucet (CTH) on »Thinking and Writing Through Practices«, Momoyo Kaijima (ETHZ) on »Architectural Ethnography«, Jane Rendell (UCL) on »Practicing Ethics«, and Bryony Roberts (WIP – Work in Progress | Women in Practice design collective, New York) on »Expanding Modes of Practice«. Participants were asked to address one or more of the five research questions that all pointed at a component that theses traditionally develop, such as:

- A research interest: What do I want to know and why?
- Paths for learning: What do I need to know to pursue my research?
- Practical knowledge: What do I know through my practice and experience?
- Knowledge in a field: What is already known about my topic?
- Relevance: What would the effects of my intervention be?

The five research questions posed to everyone at the beginning of the doctoral program were repeatedly addressed in each module. The answers to these questions are implicitly provided by the authors in the resultant essays.

We wish to thank all of the amazing presenters and the chairs of the eight workshop sessions: Ute Besenecker; Irina Davidovici; Dietrich Erben; Janina Gosseye; Carola Hein; Tanja Herdt; Jonathan Hill; Ulrika Karlsson; Emma

Department of Architecture of the Technical University of Munich and BK Bouwkunde of Delft University of Technology.

Nilsson; Christina Pech; Barbara Penner; Hilde Remoy; Amy Thomas, and Miloš N. Mladenović for his input into the participant-organized session on mobility, as well as the panelists in the concluding conversation on current doctoral research: Benedikt Boucsein; Isabelle Doucet; Jonathan Hill; Hannah Le Roux; Sophia Psarra, and Alain Thierstein.

The conference was the first module of the doctoral program, followed by a second module on methods using the example of oral history, with talks by Janina Gosseye, Hannah Le Roux, and Jennifer Mack; module three was on histories of research by design with Ole W. Fischer, Jonathan Hill, and Helena Mattsson; module four was on theoretical positionings with Tom Avermaate, Hélène Frichot, and Peg Rawes, module five was on ethics with Nishat Awan, Aya Musmar, and David Roberts, and module six was on modes of representation of practice-oriented research with readings of distinguished dissertations by Martin Ávila, Emma Cheatle, Nicholas Drofiak, and Mohamad Hafeda, and discussions with the authors.

The research training program and this resulting publication was made possible through the TUM Department of Architecture, KTH ABE School and School of Architecture, and above all through the generous support of the TUM Institute for Advanced Study's Anna Boyksen Fellowship. Thank you![2]

This issue would not have been at all possible without the invaluable advice of colleagues: Matthias Ballestrem; Anders Bergström; Camillo Boano; Katarina Bonnevier; Benedikt Boucsein; Marianna Charitonidou; Emma Cheatle; Kathrin Dörfler; Isabelle Doucet; Dietrich Erben; Catharina Gabrielsson; Katja Grillner; Susanne Hauser; Klaske Havik; Maria Hellström Reimer; Sophie Hochhäusl; Ebba Högström; Janna Holmstedt; Heidi Kajita Svenningsen; Irene Kelly; Behzad Khosravi Noori; David Kiss; Daniel Koch; Elke Krasny; Mona Livholts; Daniel Lohmann; Ferdinand Ludwig; Charlotte Malterre-Barthes; Helena Mattsson; Ramia Mazé; Anna-Maria Meister; Torsten Meyer; Kryzstof Nawratek; Anna Maria Orrù; Julieanna Preston; Sophia Psarra; Patrícia Joao Reis; Karin Reisinger; Svava Riesto; Jonas Runberger; Gabrielle Schaad; Susanne Schindler; Gerhard Schubert; Rainer Schützeichel; Dubravka Sekulić; Jan Silberberger; Erik Stenberg; Alain Thierstein; Taguhi Torosyan; Stephanie van der Voorde; Christiane Weber;

---

2 Thank you also to the focus group around the Anna Boyksen Fellowship »Rethinking Patterns of (In)equity and Diversity in Architecture« including the chairs and professorships of Benedikt Boucsein (host), Dietrich Erben, and Uta Graff at TUM, and Paula-Irene Villa Braslavsky at Ludwig Maximilian University, in Munich.

Ines Weizman; Stefanie Wuschitz; Malin Zimm, and Daniel Zwangsleitner. Great thanks to you all! Last and not least we thank *Dimensions. Journal of Architectural Knowledge*'s main editors, Uta Graff, Ferdinand Ludwig, and Katharina Voigt for their patience!

Dimensions of Architectural Knowledge, 2022-03 ౩
https://doi.org/10.14361/dak-2022-0302

Species of Theses and Other Pieces

Meike Schalk, Torsten Lange, Andreas Putz, Elena Markus

Practice-oriented thesis

The term »thesis« derives from the Greek θέσις, meaning »something put forth«, and refers to a proposition. How we know is mediated as much through the form of the thesis as it is through its content. While traditionally a thesis takes the format of a written treatise and follows specific conventions that guide and limit its structure, content, and language, research through practice is more often »an epistemic inquiry, directed towards increasing knowledge, insight, understanding, and skills« that challenges accepted epistemic norms, research processes, and outcomes (The Vienna Declaration on Artistic Research 2020).

Practice-oriented research is thus characterized by a level of freedom to invent its own formats, methods, and visual and written languages in line with the requirements of the research endeavor. It often »connects to a variety of professional fields and communities« (The Vienna Declaration on Artistic Research 2020), may address audiences beyond academia, and focuses on the inspiration of novel research questions for creative development in, for example, education, societal and environmental debate, and innovative technology. Consequently, practice research or practice as research does not only exist in the arts, design, and architecture but in most practical fields such as clinical medical research, research related to care practices, and learning sciences, etc. This opens up the possibility of new trajectories and exciting collaborations between the arts and design, and natural and social science research.

Species of Theses and Other Pieces

The title of this issue is borrowed from, and is a variation on *Species of Spaces and Other Pieces* (in French, *Espèces d'espaces*, 1974) by Georges Perec. In refer-

Corresponding authors: Meike Schalk (Royal Institute of Technology, Sweden/Technical University of Munich - Institute for Advanced Study, Germany), Torsten Lange (Lucerne University of Applied Sciences and Arts, Switzerland), Andreas Putz, Elena Markus (Technical University of Munich, Germany); meike. schalk@arch.kth.se; https://orcid.org/0000-0002-1744-6776; torsten.lange@hslu.ch; https://orcid. org/0000-0002-5737-0876; putz@tum.de; https://orcid.org/0000-0002-7612-9893; elena.markus@ tum.de; https://orcid.org/0000-0002-6119-4270

ence to Perec's writings, »Species of Theses and Other Pieces« takes the love of playing with forms, genres, and arrangements as its program. Initially, an architect friend had commissioned Perec to write *Species of Spaces*. This may explain the subject of the book as it starts from the space of a page that expands to regard domestic objects and spaces that employ lists, timetables, and the instructions for inhabiting them, and the characters of urban and rural spaces that include exercises for observing and describing what one sees in the street, to the world with its continents, and back to the specificities of space again.

Perec was part of OuLiPo (*Ouvroir de littérature potentielle*/Workshop for Potential Literature), a group of writers and mathematicians who were interested in using word games and formal constraints in writing. He enjoyed the prolific opportunities presented by formats such as lists, inventories, classifications, dictionaries, and the alphabet in his works. While he applied them as forms, at the same time, he was also calling them into question as a way of trying to set things in order. Rather, the use of such formats can encourage the writers to leave established paths and think beyond normativity. This issue demonstrates that the appropriation of specific formats or modes of representation such as the atlas, diary, graphic novel, metalogue, performance, score and storyboard for example, can prompt the imagining of other ways to perform research and communicate findings to various audiences.

Glossary and Heteroglossia

The Glossary-format of this issue is inspired by Rosi Braidotti and Maria Hlavajova's *Posthuman Glossary*. It employs Braidotti's knowledge cartographic method for an assemblage of contributions that are connected and related without suggesting any form of hierarchy. Contributions by researchers at the beginning of their careers appear here side by side with works by distinguished architectural theorists and historians, critical studies scholars, and artistic researchers. Together, they provide a momentous overview of what research oriented toward practice might look like today. A glossary is hereby understood as an open and loosely structured collection. Items can be added, and meaning is created by the dialogue of the present entries. It includes well-known research formats as well as more experimental ones that challenge the conventions of the research article.

Overall, research attempts to order phenomena and findings to explain the world. Like Perec, the Russian literary theorist Mikhail Bakhtin questioned the possibility of imposing order upon a life that he deemed as too complex, unexpected, subjective, and uncontainable to be dominated by unifying explanatory systems. He distinguished the ideal of disciplines striving for unity from disorderly reality and called for awareness of the fact that any systematic explanation was forced upon it arbitrarily. For Bakhtin then, scientific activity was not an objectification and an abstraction from reality into stable and universal sets of rules, and conventions of structure, form, and language. Rather, languages and formats of theses needed to be recognized in their multiplicities as different forms that conceptualize the world in words that spring from different ideologies – a »heteroglossia« (Bakhtin 1981 [1934]).

These various modes of reflection are expressions of the diversity of social contexts and experiences, and any force of uniformity would move research activity toward cultural and socio-political centralization in which certain forms preside over others and make the plurality of ways of speaking invisible. It is precisely this heteroglossia that ensures the dynamics of thinking that widen and deepen, and develop languages and formats that do not exclude each other but can interact dialogically. In this sense, this issue includes a number of contributions that focus on broadening the possibilities for how we can conduct and communicate research, and what formats we can imagine and invent for this.

Situated and Multi-dimensional Perspectives in Architectural Research

The authors in this issue contribute via their backgrounds, experiences, and knowledge of various contexts to submit examples of formats of practice-oriented research. Their research practices are situated within the different research cultures and traditions of three continents. Although research conventions have been built upon the seeming »neutrality« of language and styles of presentation, and research outputs striving for »objectivity« are predominantly seen as the center of scientific credibility and legitimacy, critical research practices that question this one-dimensional perspective have emerged, and they have encouraged a range of approaches for performing research.

An early, powerful critique was introduced by Donna Haraway in 1988, with »Situated Knowledges: The Science Question in Feminism and the Privilege of Partial Perspective«, which followed Sandra Harding's influential and contested book, *The Science Question in Feminism* (1986), which examined the practices and cultures of dominant research institutions, from which marginalized groups have often been excluded. Harding's standpoint theory and methodology, and Haraway's situated knowledges creating »partial objectivity« have since evoked an opening to acknowledge a multiplicity of ways of conducting research which have led to the inclusion of a variety of voices and experiences that have previously not been recognized as subjects, and objects of, research.

With growing criticism of the Eurocentrism of Western-oriented research institutions, and an awareness of the necessity of decolonizing research and curricula, many research contexts have come to employ languages and styles that acknowledge the situatedness of the researchers and their research subjects. This involves the undoing of frameworks that cut to the heart of many disciplines, including architecture and design. As historian Dipesh Chakrabarty noted in his *Provincializing Europe* (2000), universally applied theories of historical development (historicism) grounded in 19th-century Europe are in fact, highly specific and should thus no longer be viewed as the model for the transition to modernity on a global scale. What the European historicist tradition actually does is to extend colonial power relations into the present by means of its logic of »not yet« which denies non-European experiences and knowledge formations any relevance. Countering this »political-epistemic violence of modernity«, decolonial thinkers such as Walter D. Mignolo and Catherine E. Walsh (2018) put forth the concept of relationality to avoid the creation of new abstract universals, and to recognize and value local differences and embodied experiences within a wide range of decolonial practices. A pluriversal conception of knowledge, of which Western thought is only a part but not the center, comes to replace the totality of European universality. Achille Mbembe (2016) uses these ideas of decolonial pluriversality and applies them to the university, which consequently must become a critically cosmopolitan »pluriversity« open to multiple geographies – the opposite of the current reproduction of Eurocentric knowledges within the global academy. Practicing such a pluriversity, albeit with limitations, through the digital platform's open structure has been one of our key ambitions for the doctoral program.

Contributions
This issue is organized as a glossary, or an inventory of forms of theses, reaching from »Atlas« to »Metalogue« and to »Website«. Contributors have employed formats that practice-oriented research might take and have reflected upon how to think about research methods deliberately as a form, as

well as a tool or »device« (Lury/Wakeford 2013). The formats contributed can then be roughly grouped by the approaches they use.

Some of them such as Site-Writing, workshops, or experiments use »live« methods, or performative methods. **Jhono Bennett**, through »Reflective Animation« of writing and drawing, explores their complex situatedness and positionings, navigating between the multiple voices of the global South and northern forms of knowledge generation. Reflective Animation employs a *What-What* approach that the author borrows from the South, and which allows them to dwell in »the trouble« (Haraway 2016) as a way to discuss the ethics of such multi-identities and multi-locationality and the repercussions for research. **Santosh Kumar Ketham** suggests »Speculative Design Workshops« as a collective forum to bring multiple actors into the conversation on climate change and flooding cities by the example of Hyderabad. This format aims to create the conditions that enable more climate-responsive policy-making by involving a broader section of society. **Jane Rendell**, through her »Website« Site-Reading Writing Quarterly, offers a platform for invitees to »review« each other's recently published works by performing mutual readings and conversations. These acts spring from a feminist critique of the conventional form of a review essay. They foreground the dialogical qualities of Site-Reading Writings through the presentation of a number of experiments and approaches, and the theoretical reflections they have generated. In »Prototype«, **Rasha Sukkarieh** explores the aspect of waste reduction and material technology within the design processes, and specifically addresses concrete molding. In her practice-based research, she presents the possibility of rethinking the relation between design, material performance, and construction techniques by means of experimental investigations developing physical prototypes and a digital model, as well as a 1:1 demonstrator. **Ina Valkanova's** essay focuses on the interdependence of global production and local actors. Through »Collective Workshop«, she introduces a method of action research to initiate openings for the meaningful transformation of post-socialist industrial development.

In practice-oriented research in architecture, established historical methods are applied and adapted to understand historic architectural practice, and to reintegrate them to meet today's requirements. **Gabriel Bernard Guelle**, in »Textbook«, relays the personal discovery of a formerly influential French construction textbook that causes him to reflect on the importance of formalized architectural education, the role of construction, and the textbook to the profession and its academic self-image 100 years ago and today.

Rachel Győrffy, in »Miniatures«, takes us to the late modernist architectural heritage of Central and Eastern Europe and its peculiar transformation in recent years. By applying a two-fold conceptual framework, projection as a discursive method and Mark Cousins's theory of ugliness, she reflects upon the current trend toward architectural reconstruction. In »Research by Design«, **Jonathan Hill** rediscovers the design process as a present reinterpretation of the past. However, in a conscious deviation from historical objectivity, just like fiction, the method of design allows for free movement in time. Such temporal understanding of design, he concludes, is a means by which to learn from the past, reassess the present, and speculate on future models of practice and discourse.

Other contributions use drawing as a method for the purposes of documenting, comparing, analyzing, de-constructing, narrating, gathering, and organizing evidence. **Davide Franco** employs »Brick by Brick Redrawing«: façade constructions of 1920s industrial buildings in Berlin to simulate the historical building process and to reconstruct the physically built structure in digital drawing. A critical redrawing hereby represents a synthesis of the theoretical and practical studies undertaken by the author. An inversion of drawing from a planning and design tool to epistemological means was possible thanks to digital modeling. **Janina Gosseye** and **Meitar Tewel** challenge the genre of architectural historiography with a ficto-critical short story presented as a »Graphic Novel« by Meitar Tewel. In their conversation the student and the instructor reflect on conventional modes of writing history versus the visual narrative, and ask whether a shift of modes of representation enabled new knowledge in architectural and urban design history. **Walaa Hajali** applies the tool of »Diary« to collect information on (dis)comfort and use patterns from the inhabitants of a Syrian multi-family building. A visual essay makes residents' experiences tangible and serves as an argument for a paradigm change in the current model for affordable housing in Syria, which would also consider the inhabitants' social and cultural needs. **Anna Keitemeier** explores elements of the enclosure of urban green spaces in Paris through collecting and representing them in the format of »Atlas«. In her contribution, she proposes atlas as an epistemic genre to visually create knowledge. The collection of enclosure typologies in the atlas serves for the comparison and critical discussion of a range of Parisian urban landscape projects from the last 40 years. **Anita Szentesi** employs the methods from film production, screenwriting, and »Storyboard« in architectural pedagogy, to discuss design through the lens of particular characters and their experiences. She has explored these methods together with students who were asked to produce stage sets in which architecture became a character as well as a product. Her work aims to generate knowledge in teaching and architectural theory.

Considering, and in some cases re-enacting, the materiality of language and the spatiality of writing are a fourth set of contributions. In »Unseen Acts«, **Yara Al Heswani** utilizes the format of dialogue as in the medium of the stage play to reflect and make tangible what she describes as the »Polyphonic Morphology« of Jaramana, a dense city district in the metropolitan area of Damascus, whose material fabric is significantly shaped by informal construction in the wake of displacement and migration due to military conflict. **Hélène Frichot** and **Therese Keogh** in their »Metalogue« seek to open up a space between and across different bodies (student and teacher) and matters (conceived and concrete) through an open-ended conversation. In doing so, they not only question, and ultimately abandon, established hierarchies between who teaches and who is being taught in favor of a more relational setting, but also critique the extractivist logic which underpins the mobilization of concepts and the flux of materials in the present. As well as attending to the texture/textuality of the text, highlighting the former's relationship to textiles while exploring connections between writing and weaving, **Anna Odlinge's** work reflects on the spatial dimension of writing through the placing of, and spacing between, letters and text passages on the page, in particular commentaries, or »Catena and Glosses«. In creating these architextual configurations, she seeks to rupture the text's linearity and actively engage the reader in a way that destabilizes the author's own authoritative position, akin to the critical drawing practice championed by architect Lebbeus Woods. **Emma Cheatle's** contribution speculates on the non-binary entanglement of »Writing-Drawing« and builds on the work of Hélène Cixous, as employed in her doctoral dissertation on the Maison de Verre by Pierre Chareau in Paris (1928–1932). While partial, yet inseparable, she argues that together, the line of drawing and that of writing allowed her to draw out/forth hidden stories using the materiality of the building – glass, dust, and air – as an archive.

A group of contributions apply mixed practice methods, often between visualization and ethnographical approaches. **Dirk Bahmann**, in »Sculptural Artifact«, studies, together with students, atmospheres of sacral architecture and explores ways to express experiences from such powerful and emotive spaces via the making of embodied sculptural work. **Nicholas**

Drofiak explores »Score« as a creative work and a research tool. When examining the implications of scoremaking between anticipation and performance, the real encounters between stories and actors on the Enisej river come to the fore. Drofiak is particularly interested in the tension, or collision, between these two conditions and what knowledge relations they generate. In »Performance«, **Amina Kaskar** observes the articulation of a performative soft spatiality that represents migrants' cultural practices and everyday rituals involving textiles in Johannesburg. These improvised forms emerging in urban spaces disrupt rationalized and oppressive built forms. Her research explores soft spatialities as soft systems developing their own visual language and allows for a representation of architecture that captures the performative nature of buildings, sites, and design processes. **Natalia Petkova's** »Ethnography of Stone« focuses on her fieldwork around the construction of the Swiss collective-housing project Plan-les-Ouates that employs stone as a load-bearing material. Petkova traces the mining of the limestone from two sites with different geological formations. She discusses their application through three concepts of key phases in stone formation: gathering, layering, and cementing, which she relates to different encounters with multiple actors exploring what working with a geo-sourced material means for professional architectural practice.

Concluding Remarks

The contributions in this issue stem from a research training program offered by the BauHow5 Alliance and ResArc through TU Munich and KTH Stockholm. Postgraduate architectural research has become a topical question in university departments in recent years, in Germany and beyond. While for a long time, a doctorate was rather the exception for architects, the regained prominence of research points to a current transformation of the profession. The modernist ideal of an architect as a creator and designer-artist is expected to decline in favor of a more complex, but also more demanding professional model, that of an expert on the human-made environment; who considers a wide range of social, theoretical, cultural, artistic, technical, and environmental aspects, and is capable of analyzing, communicating, and making design and planning decisions. For such a professional profile, postgraduate programs will become more and more relevant in the future, and provide the intellectual stimulation, freedom, and structure for the individual pursuit of artistic or scientific research questions. Such programs will have the task of tying academic perspectives back to the practice of architecture.

During our training program, we were able to gain insights into a variety of different academic contexts in which doctorates in architecture are currently being pursued around the world. For the participants, it was a welcome opportunity to connect with an international network, especially during the Covid-19 pandemic. In many cases there is a lack of a critical mass of similar doctorates in architecture departments. Funding and institutional structures for cooperation and doctoral education are often lacking. The exchange and collaboration necessary for the subject's further development must take place beyond such institutional boundaries. Initiatives such as BauHow5 are likely to become more important in the future. Sketching out an alternative for doctoral training, our course, which we were able to repeat in the academic year 2021/22, also showed how precarious postgraduate education in architecture often is and how much it relies on the initiative, idealism, and commitment of those involved. These external conditions for postgraduate research training in architecture are significant, as they also determine the forms and species of the theses.

References

Bakhtin, Mikhail Mikhailovich (1981): *The Dialogic Imagination: Four Essays*, Michael Holquist (ed.) and transl. by Caryl Emerson and Michael Holquist, Austin/ London: The University of Texas Press.

BauHow5, http://www.bauhow5.eu. (Accessed: July 4, 2022).

Braidotti, Rosi/ Hlavajova, Maria, eds. (2018): *Posthuman Glossary*, London: Bloomsbury.

Chakrabarty, Dipesh (2000): *Provincializing Europe: Postcolonial Thought and Historical Difference*, Princeton: Princeton University Press.

Haraway, Donna (1988): »Situated Knowledges: The Science Question in Feminism and the Privilege of Partial Perspective«, in: *Feminist Studies* 14/3, 575–599.

Haraway, Donna (2016): *Staying with the Trouble: Making Kin in the Chtulucene*, Durham, NC: Duke University Press.

Harding, Sandra (1986): *The Science Question in Feminism*, Ithaca, NY: Cornell University Press.

Lury, Celia/ Wakeford, Nina, eds. (2013): *Inventive Methods: The Happening of the Social*, London: Routledge

Mbembe, Achille (2016): »Decolonizing the University: New Directions«, in: *Arts and Humanities in Higher Education* 15/1, 29–45.

Mignolo, Walter D./Walsh, Catherine E. (2018): *On Decoloniality: Concepts, Analytics, Praxis*, Durham, NC: Duke University Press.

Perec, Georges (1997): *Species of Spaces and other Pieces*, edited and translated by John Sturrock, London: Penguin Books.

Perec, Georges (1997) [1982]: »Think/Classify«, in: *Species of Spaces and Other Pieces*, edited and translated by John Sturrock, London: Penguin Books, 184–201, first published in *Le Genre humain*.

ResArc, resarc.se. (Accessed: July 4, 2022).

The Vienna Declaration on Artistic Research (2020): https://societyforartisticresearch.org/wpcontent/uploads/2020/10/Vienna-Declaration-on-Artistic-Research-Final.pdf. (Accessed July 4, 2022).

GLOSSARY

The following Glossary is arranged alphabetically according to the »Species of Theses« employed by the authors, from ATLAS to WRITING-DRAWING. The contributions appear here side by side, without suggesting a hierarchy or thematic boundaries. Together, they provide a broad overview of what practice-oriented research looks like in different contexts today. Among them are well-established research formats as well as experimental ones that challenge the conventions of the scientific article. The glossary is intended as a loosely structured collection that emphasises the multiplicity of approaches, and their open-ended possibilities in research concerned with practice.

Dimensions of Architectural Knowledge, 2022-03 ⧏
https://doi.org/10.14361/dak-2022-0303

ATLAS
Comprehending Enclosures of Urban Nature

Anna Keitemeier

Abstract: The enclosing of spaces of nature in urban contexts is today again a common practice in Paris. Whereas modern planning produced open green spaces, multiple changes in the
late 20th century resulted in the revival of the *urban park*, which refers again to the traditional
element of structural enclosing. After defining the enclosing of spaces of nature in Paris as a
research object and situating the genre of atlas in research practice, this article elaborates upon
the *atlas* as an epistemic genre and a visual form of knowledge production. Urban landscape
projects realized in previous decades are presented while critically discussing the applicability
of the atlas to urban and landscape design research.

Keywords: Altlas, Design Research Methodologies; Urban Landscape Design.

The Enclosing of Spaces of Urban Nature in Paris as Research Object

In France it is common to enclose urban parks and public gardens. Elements
of enclosing are particularly present in the Parisian urban space and they
manifest spatially in different forms, as walls, fences, and ditches, often
equipped by street furniture and technical devices. As this form of separation is an element of the everyday urban landscape, it does not usually receive closer attention from the locals. For me, a person socialized in Germany,
where parks are commonly open green areas, these borders in urban space
are still remarkable elements, and the further I investigated the types of enclosure, the more I was intrigued. Etymologically, the terms *garden* and *park*
derive from the act of enclosing a plot of land (Turner 2005: 1; Vernhes 2015).
Accordingly, the enclosing is an inherent element of these outdoor spaces,
which not only fulfill a functional and protective role but also a symbolic one
(Berque 2011). The structural enclosing separates the garden from the surrounding rural or urban territory and it is only through this element that the

Corresponding author: Anna Keitemeier (École nationale supérieure d'architecture Paris-la Villette,
Conservatoire national des arts et métiers, France, and Karlsruher Institut für Technologie, Germany);
annakeitemeier@gmx.de; https://orcid.org/0000-0001-6769-5175

garden is individualized and autonomous (Mosser/Brunon 2007: 59). As a spatial configuration specific to urban landscape design, the enclosing intervenes into human-dominated spaces of nature and highlights a historically specific and culturally determined element of separation. In differencing and connecting at the same time, the enclosing constitutes in itself a space where different gestures and activities of control are performed. It is the aim of my doctoral thesis to situate the contemporary practice of enclosing in a *longue durée* (Braudel 1958) – the term anchored in the French Annales School – giving priority to long-term historical structures –and to question its spatiality and materiality as a manifestation of epistemic views, notably the human/ non-human relation.

The Ontological Ambiguity of the Garden

Foucault describes the garden as the most original form of *heterotopia*. According to him »heterotopias always presuppose a system of openings and closings that makes them at once isolated and penetrable« (Foucault 1984 [1967]). Consequently, an ontological ambiguity is touched upon here: The garden as an *other place* is defined through its border and at the same time necessarily transcends it (Mosser/Brunon 2007: 66).

From the Jardin à la française to the Retour au Jardin at the End of the 20th Century

In order to comprehend today's role of enclosing spaces of nature, the element has to be investigated in a *longue durée* of French landscape design. In this context, the baroque *jardin à la française* has to be underlined, being characterized by the principle of imposing order on other living entities. The overarching symmetry is one manifestation of the human ambit of control over nature (Haubl 1999: 48–49; Turner 2005: 292–295).

Further, the »Transformation de Paris«, mainly directed by George Eugene Haussmann was a vast public works program executed between the 1850s and 1870s that completely changed the city's morphology and image. Within this transformation, the creation of a modern system of public green open spaces played a major role. The engineer Adolphe Alphand realized squares, parks, and forests, in which English landscape architecture and notably the residential squares of London served as references (Alphand 1867–1873; Lawrance 1993: 114). Whereas the large forests at the periphery of the city remained mainly open, squares and urban parks in Paris were explicitly subject to regulation and guarding, which manifested in the installation of

1.

Emile Adolphe Hochereau (1867–1873): »Bois de Boulogne. Portes, grille, bank«,
engraving in: Adolphe Alphand: Les Promenades de Paris. Public Domain.

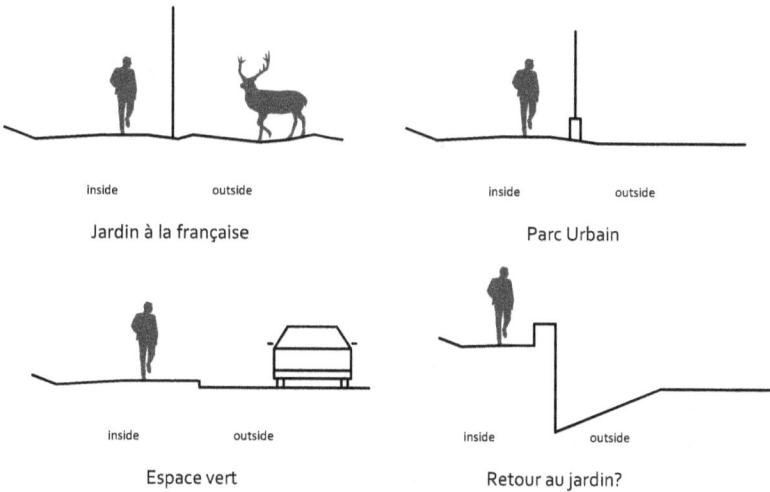

2.

Enclosing spaces of naturein longue durée of French landscape design.
Drawing: Anna Keitemeier.

fencing (Santini 2021: 252–256). These elements used were part of the uniformity of street furniture (fig. 1).

The post-war period in France, characterized by economic boom – *Les Trentes Glorieuses* – is known to go hand in hand with the urban planning goals of functional separation, declared in the Charter of Athens (CIAM/Le Corbusier 1946 [1943]). The notion of »espace vert« (Mosser/Brunon 2006: 19; Mehdi et al. 2012) prevailed in this period and the identity or aesthetic quality of »green space« was most often not the center of attention. It was considered that there was a qualitative and figurative crisis of the urban landscape design project (Cortesi 2000: 37–40).

Multiple turning points set in motion a reversed trend in France starting from the 1970s on: First, a growing awareness of ecological concerns (Charvolin 1997), second, an increasing attention towards the social aspects of the built environment (Ministre de l'aménagement du territoire 1973), third, transformations in academia and in the training of landscape architects (Dubost 1983; Blanchon-Caillot 2007), and fourth, a renewed regard for the past and understanding the city through its morphology, namely its buildings and spaces (Lucain 1981).

As new urban landscape projects were installed on the conversions of former industrial facilities located in the central districts, these designed spaces emerged once again as an independent element of the urban morphology. The competition of the Parc de la Villette in Paris is considered as a key event with international significance that launched a revival of the »urban park« and set in motion a shift in urban landscape architecture This is debated in French art history discourse as the »Retour au jardin« (Mosser/Brunon 2006: 21), referring to the work of Rossario Assunto.

After having sketched these key developments in the enclosing of spaces of nature in French landscape design history, fig. 2 aims to give a visual overview of this evolution. Short hand sections are used, as this type of drawing is not only demonstrative, but is also a key tool in the process of landscape design (Bava/Hössler/Philippe 2021: 5).

The Atlas as Tool to Think through Urban and Landscape Design Research

The atlas as a time-honored genre has recently been rediscovered in architectural design research. In the tradition of the 16th-century geographer, Gerardus Mercator, the notion of atlas became associated with cartography, which in the following centuries aimed to show the word as it *really* was and to produce *true* knowledge about the surface of the earth (Halder/Michel 2018: 12). Especially with the rise of modern nation states, atlases were seen as a medium of power, they became tools of education and everyday objects. Today, many alternative approaches have emerged (Kollektiv Orangotango+ 2018). The following references show how the atlas has become an evolving epistemic genre.

The Atlas as a Processual Work Approach

One inspiring case of the notion atlas is the *Bilderatlas Mnemosyne* by the historian of art and culture Aby Warburg from the 1920s. Although this work was never finished and only published in a book posthumously, the way that Warburg conducted his analyses had a significant impact on research methods in various disciplines, launching an »iconic turn / pictural turn« (Bachmann-Medick 2016: 232, 250–252). Moreover, the *Bilderatlas* has been called an »Organon« of transdisciplinary visual studies (Diers 2006: 185).

In this research Warburg conducted a form of media archeology, referring to an immense archive of visual material that he pinned on different thematic panels (fig. 3). As he continually reorganized his material and made photos of the different states of configuration, Warburg followed a processual work approach. The research process is thus an activity in situ and in actu, resulting in a spatial constellation and a common site for contemplating and reflecting (Weigel 2013: 4–5).

Contemporary Forms of Atlases in Spatial and Urban Design Research

The atlas has been rediscovered as a concept in architectural research and collaborative design practice in recent years. Other than the approach from Warburg, these atlases usually contain visual material that is not only collected, but also created by the researchers. Producing these forms of atlases follows at least two scopes: First, they are a tool for knowledge production in research as they bring together different visual media, and second, they aim to classify existing (built) phenomena in order to serve as a reference system and handbook for practice. In the following, three publications of this type of atlas are presented.

The publication *Squares. Urban Spaces in Europe* (Wolfrum 2015 [2014]) compares different squares in Europe. The projects investigated are made comparable by using the method of drawing, namely redrafting (ibid.: 310). Consequently, all projects are drawn in the same scale and manner, namely

4.
Wolfrum, Sophie (ed.) (2015, 175):
Squares. Urban spaces in Europe, Basel:
Birkhäuser, Place Georges-Pompidou.
Drawing: Francesca Fornasier
and Heiner Stengel.

3.
Panel B of the final version of Warburg's
Bilderatlas, 1929.
Courtesy: The Warburg Institute.

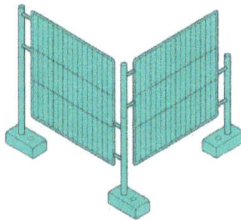

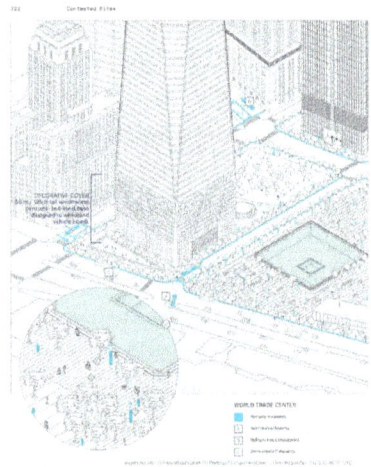

5.
ARCH+ 191/192: Schwellenatlas –
Von Abfallzerkleinerer zu Zeitmaschine
(2009, 26), Laurent Stalder/Elke Beyer/
Kim Förster/Anke Hagemann (eds).
Absperrgitter (barrier grid).
Drawing: Katja Gretzinger.

6.
Deane Simpson/Vibeke Jensen/
Anders Rubing (eds)(2016, 223):
The City between Freedom and Security.
Basel: Birkhäuser. World Trade Center
74°W. Drawing: Line Myhre, Anders
Sletten Eide.

black line graphics (ground plans, views, sections, and axonometric draw-ings). In the introduction, Wolfrum points to the axonometric projection as a »three-dimensional, immediately understandable image« (ibid.: 9). More-over, the elements that are presented in public space are very simplified, for example there is only one type of tree and human figures are absent.

The project »*Schwellenatlas*« (threshold atlas), published in the architec-ture magazine *ARCH+* (Stalder/Beyer/Förster/Hagemann 2009), investigates 45 everyday elements of threshold. In adding photos and texts, and especially in developing their own drawings, all elaborated in the same manner to make them suitable for comparison – namely simple graphic isometrics – this research aims to make the different elements comparable. Placing these line graphic isometrics over a plain background, the focus is on the struc-tural character of the element. No human or other living form is represented in the axonometries.

A third reference to be mentioned in this context is the publication *The City between Freedom and Security* (Simpson/Jensen/Rubing 2016). Although the notion of atlas is not mentioned, the book follows a similar approach to the other ones, that is collecting and elaborating visual material: »Isometric drawings, maps, analytical diagrams, and timelines are used to describe the composition, organization, and disposition, as well as the consequences, of the securitization of space in different settings« (ibid.: 177). Here again, axo-nometric drawings of the situations and the color-coding of different ele-ments are used as a method for comparison. Human beings are presented – as crowds and not as individuals – in a simplified manner.

You Never Read It, You Consult It: The Power of the Atlas
What these three publications have in common is that their predominant vi-sual elements are line drawings, especially axonometric projections. These forms of illustration – as every form of graphical representation – contain an inevitable abstractness. They are the result of selection, omission, isola-tion, distance, and codification – and are never neutral or passive. Whereas in former times axonometric projections served as tools in the design pro-cess and as a method for documentation and comparison, they have progres-sively become an analytical tool, as shown in the work *Histoire de l'Architecture* (Choisy 1899).

As manual drawing has shifted to digital models in recent decades, the practice of drawing in planning disciplines has again profoundly changed. Being extracted from digital models, today axonometric drawings are rather *demonstrative* and not *generative* (Lucas 2020: 164). It is particularly these architectural representations that lead to a dry and factual style of visual storytelling. As the juxtaposition of these drawings suggests connections that cannot be represented in pure text form, these collections create their own powerful form of narrative, focusing on the structural, and apparently *objective*, configuration of space.

The Atlas as Method for Understanding the Enclosing of Spaces in Four Examples over Four Decades

Tracing the Development of Urban Landscape Design

Four parks, designed in the last four decades in Paris and the *Métropole du Grand Paris* in the context of urban redevelopment projects of former industrial sites, are used in this article to show the latest developments in urban landscape design and serve as examples of the atlas applicability: Parc de la Villette (1980s), Parc André Citroen (1990s), Jardins d'Éole (2000s), and Parc de Billancourt (2010s).

Parc de la Villette was part of a transformation project located on the periphery of the 19th arrondissement. »Le Parc - Espace ouvert« was at the center of the competition program (APUR 1975), inviting the participants to orientate their proposals toward the more traditional functions of a park, while also aiming to realize an open park without a fence (APUR 1975: 19). The competition entries changed the discipline of landscape architecture and the urban landscape project on an international level (Barzilay/Hayward/Lombard-Valentino 1984), declaring the park once again as a structural element of the city. As the project was ultimately directed by Bernard Tschumi, the design is mainly characterized by an architectural vision over space, considering landscape secondary. The park opened in 1983 and was realized without structural enclosing. In keeping an openness toward the urban surroundings and in placing some building structures on the green space, the Parc de la Villette marks the shift from the former modernist »green space« to qualitative elements in urban landscape projects (Cortesi 2000: 41–44).

The international competition for the Parc André Citroën in 1985 (Garcias 1993: 100), located on the banks of the Seine at the 15th arrondissement are in line with what is declared »retour au jardin« (Mosser/Brunon 2006). Realized by an interdisciplinary team of landscape architects, that is to say, Gilles Clément and Alain Provost, and architects, namely Patrick Berger with Jean-

François Jodry and Jean-Paul Viguier, the Parc André Citroën opened in 1992 (Starkman 1993: 88). The project transgresses the disciplinary boundaries between architecture and landscape and rethinks the human – nature relation. Furthermore, it remakes traditional elements of the garden, such as structural spatial and material enclosing. A broad variety of enclosure typologies are realized, leading from hedges, walls, and fences to haha-ditches.

The Jardins d'Éole in the 18th arrondissement was installed on a former railroad wasteland, the so- called Cour du Maroc, and was the result of a long history of political mobilization from the 1990s onward. As the site was formerly a place of conflict between drug dealers and residents, the competition, launched in 2003, was accompanied by sociologists (Renaud/Tonnelat 2008). The winning project of Claire and Michel Corajoud is characterized by green spaces on different topographical levels in the north and a more mineral space in the south. Whereas the initial request was to create a park open and accessible to all without constraints, there was a public fear that the park would be taken over again by drug addicts (Renaud/Tonnelat 2008: 62). Finally, when the project was realized in 2007, it contained structural enclosures on different levels that separated several spaces for different uses. The enclosing elements were mainly designed as simple vertical wire elements which still allowed a visual permeability.

The final project to be discussed is the Parc de Billancourt in Boulogne-Billancourt, a suburb in the Métropole du Grand Paris, characterized by its recent high densification due to the urban redevelopment of the former Renault industrial sites. The site's redevelopment program, the so-called Trapèze, foresees an ecological transformation of the terrain with a park in the center, which is again defined as a constituting element of the urban fabric, serving simultaneously as the main flooding area when the Seine is at high tide (Elsea 2018). Agence TER won the 2006 competition with a design that integrates a surrounding water trench as a constitutive element of the project, serving as a reservoir during high water and concurrently fulfilling the function of enclosing this urban space of nature. The designers aimed to »reinvent the landscape park of the 19th century, where the landscapes are given to see« (Agence TER 2022: own translation). Finally, the realization in 2017 was characterized by different heights, namely the park being on a topographical lower level than the surroundings, thus resulting in a visual permeability from the outside to the inside, even during times when the park is closed.

7.
Parc de la Villette, Paris. Entry from Avenue Jean Jaures.

8.
Parc André Citroën, Paris. Haha-ditch, Rue de la Montagne de l'Esperou.

9.
Jardin d'École, Paris. Entry from Rue d'Aubervilliers.

10.
Parc de Billancourt, Boulogne-Billancourt. Entry from Avenue Pierre-Lefaucheux to the Parc Est. Photography and post-production (2018- 2021): Anna Keitemeier.

The Making of an Atlas: Collecting Data and Elaborating Visual Material
In regard to these different types of enclosed spaces of urban nature in Paris, the method of atlas is used as a processual work. The data that constitutes the atlas consists of my own visual material collected and elaborated from site visits. By (post-) producing it in a similar manner, the aim is to make the different sites comparable. Thus, in bringing these different elements together and rearranging them again and again, the aim of my atlas is to carve out differences and commonalities between the design projects, and to reveal hidden linkages.

The investigation of the projects in situ and in actu is a fundamental research practice of my study. I am hereby inspired by the *Mouvance de la Vilette* movement with its *approche sensible*, which declares the sensual experience as a central element in the construction of spatial entities (De Marco 2016). This research takes the human body as an agent of knowledge production, viewing especially the body's movement in public space as active research practice (Luxembourg 2019: 14).

Photography and Cartography as Tools to Catch the Present
A first group of visual material is formed by photography and cartography. While strolling around on site, snapshots of various situations along the peripheral margins of the parks are taken (figs. 7-10, left column). Holding the camera at a level of about 1.60 meters, these photos aim to mirror the eye-level of the researcher walking upright on the terrain. Then, in the post-production process, the images are transformed into black and white, and the elements and devices that constitute the enclosure of the spaces of nature are color-coded in red (figs. 7-10, right column). This step aims to work out the constitutive elements of the enclosing.

Second, maps form another group of images to reveal the movement on site. The background layer of these cartographies are satellite pictures from Google Maps. In showing the spatial situation from above, these images reveal how the urban park is situated in the adjacent and larger urban morphology. Emphasis is put on the horizontal spatial configuration of the enclosure. To show these spatial organizations of the park, its surface is also marked in the post-production process in red. Thus, the physical demarcation between the space of nature and the surrounding urban fabric is highlighted with a red line, and entries and threshold zones are respectively tagged. This form of cartography also contains an inevitable abstraction, as the verticality of the enclosing elements cannot be represented.

The Production of Isometric Projections

In the third step, the observations on site led to the production of my own orthographic isometries. In aiming at the comparability of the different spatial configurations, all drawings are developed in the same scale and in the same manner, more precisely as architectural line drawings, carried out with computer-aided design software. By color-coding in red the specific architectural elements that compose the enclosure and inking in green the »nature«, the representations make it possible to discuss differences and commonalities in the types of enclosing. As already emphasized in the previous paragraph, this form of graphical representation also contains an inevitable abstractness. The focus of these images is on the spatial composition and highlighting of enclosing devices. In this case, the way human beings and other living entities interact with these built elements and how they make these spaces their own is not emphasized. People are inserted as black silhouettes, serving only as an approximate scale. The diversity of the vegetation on site is reduced to one type of tree which is presented in green lines and green surfaces.

Types of Enclosing Spaces of Urban Nature

The analysis of the different examples in a similar manner by using the method of atlas identified three main types of structural enclosure. fig. 13 shows the three examples drawn as short-hand sections, the same type of drawing used in fig. 2. The first one reveals an open configuration, where the boundary between the inner and outer space is dispersed. It is demarked only by some single elements like pillars. This form of threshold, when understanding it as a space of transition in itself, is found mainly in the Parc de la Villette. The second type, which is predominant in the design of the Jardins d'Éole and in some parts of the Parc André Citroën, is a form of border that articulates mainly vertically, in that it permits visual permeability due to the use of translucent material such as wire with open meshes. The third type is the most complex figuration of enclosing as it expands spatially on different levels and is composed of different materials, such as concrete and stone, but also living and fluid elements like vegetation and water. The natural elements in particular are not static and thus difficult to grasp and represent in the graphic representation chosen, namely line drawings. In this overview, only green lines represent the border's natural component and a grey horizontal line indicates the water's constantly changing height. This last type of border is found mainly in the Parc André Citroën and the Parc de

11.
From top-left to bottom-right: Parc de la Villette, Parc André Citroën, Jardins d'Éole,
Parc de Billancourt. Satellite images: Google Maps. Post-production: Anna
Keitemeier.

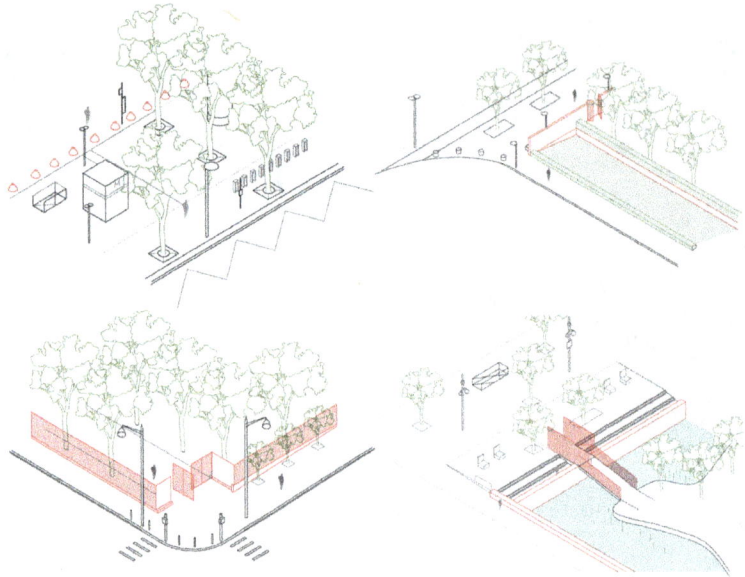

12.

Isometric projections of situations of park enclosings. From top-left to bottom-right:
Parc de la Villette, Parc André Citroën, Jardins d'Éole, Parc de Billancourt.

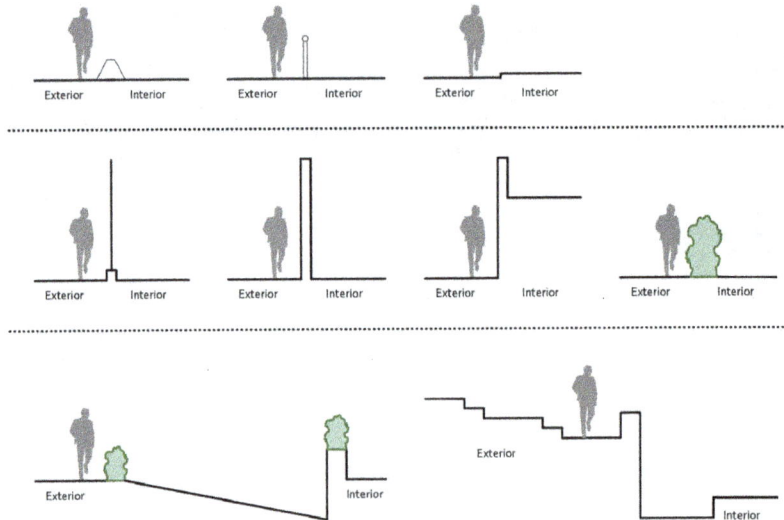

13.

Types of enclosings of nature in contemporary urban landscape designs.
Drawings: Anna Keitemeier.

Billancourt, both containing deeper reflections on ecology and the human relationship to nature. This last example in particular shows that the applicability of the chosen approach has to be critically reflected as it cannot convey the vegetative component of enclosures as changing entities.

Concluding Reflections: The Atlas as a Process in Urban and Landscape Design Research

In following a processual approach, Aby Warburg comprehends the atlas as a dynamic tool of knowledge production that is able to reveal hidden linkages and enduring cultural structures. In aiming to point out these lasting connections between the research material, Warburg's objective is similar to the interest of the *longue durée* (Braudel 1958). The former's novel approach, namely the construction of the atlas as a visual memory bringing into motion a paradigm shift, shows that epistemic reference systems and methodologies – in short, ways of knowledge production – are constantly evolving.

I also understand my research practice as an open process of collecting, reorganizing, and producing knowledge. With reference to three examples of atlases in architectural and urban design research, I stress that the epistemic significance of confronting and the dialoging of different factual visual material is to animate reflections on the underlying linkages. Furthermore, I consider my atlas as a snapshot of an open processual approach of broader methodological investigations in urban and landscape design research. As »openness« is also an intrinsic characteristic of the research object –urban spaces of nature, being under constant transformation – an adaptive method is required to provide answers to further emerging questions.

Taking into account my atlas's intrinsic characteristics of openness and constant renewal, the visual material collected has to be examined critically. Whereas photos and cartographies can be seen as being able to catch the present in a (more or less) neutral way, the line graphics and their interpretive character are of another quality. Coming from a background of architecture and urban design, my perception is trained for the static dimension of the built environment, resulting in the ambit of clean representations of line graphics, such as the descriptive axonometries of the references discussed and those elaborated in this research. These forms of representation, playing mainly a demonstrative role, are one-sided reductions of the public space as they can only illustrate the *factual elements* of spaces, omitting the transformative and living character of the landscape projects. Indeed, they are not able to demonstrate moving entities, such as humans and other forms of the living like vegetation in public space. These representations remain silent on how different living entities interact with these spaces.

In taking the creation of the atlas as a processual approach of collecting, reorganizing, and producing knowledge, my dissertation project keeps exploring the integration of the visual material that is capable of better understanding the living character of public spaces.

References

Agence TER (2022): *Boulogne-Billancourt, Parc de Billancourt.* https://agenceter.com/projets/parc-du-billancourt/ (Accessed: March 7, 2022).

Alphand, Adolphe (1867–1873): *Les promenades de Paris: Histoire, description des embellissements*, Paris: Rothschild.

Atelier parisien d'urbanisme (APUR) (1975): *Concours pour l'aménagement du secteur de la Villette.* https://50ans.apur.org/data/b4s3_home/fiche/69/05_concours_amenagement_la_villette_apapu79-2_1dea6.pdf (Accessed: July 30, 2021).

Atelier parisien d'urbanisme (APUR) (1976): *Aménagement des terrains Citroën.* https://50ans.apur.org/data/b4s3_home/fiche/83/04_citroen_amenagement_memoire_conseil_paris_applan97-1_e6c45.pdf (Accessed: July 30, 2021).

Bachmann-Medick, Doris (2016): *Cultural Turns. New Orientations in the Study of Culture*, Berlin/Boston: De Gruyter.

Barzilay, Marianne/Hayward, Catherine/Lombard-Valentino, Lucette (1984): *L'invention du parc. Parc de la Villette, Paris, concours international*, Paris: Graphite.

Bava, Henri/ Hössler, Michel/ Philippe, Olivier (2021): *Sols vivants. Socles de la nature en ville*, Paris: Agence TER.

Berque, Augustin (2011): »Pourquoi les jardins sont-ils clos?«, in: *Mésologiques, Études des milieux*, May 5. https://ecoumene.blogspot.com/2011/05/pourquoi-les-jardins-sont-ils-clos.html (Accessed: July 30, 2021).

Blanchon-Caillot, Bernadette (2007): »Pratiques et compétences paysagistes dans les grands ensembles d'habitation, 1945–1975«, in : *Strates* 13 doi : 10.4000/strates.5723.

Braudel, Fernand (1958): »Histoire et Sciences sociales. La longue durée«, in: *Annales* 13/4, 725–753. doi: 10.3406/ahess.1958.2781.

Charvolin, Florian (1997): »L'invention du domaine de l'environnement. Au tournant de l'année 1970 en France«, in: *Strates* 9 doi: 10.4000/strates.636.

Choisy, Auguste (1899): *Histoire de l'architecture*, 2 volumes, Paris: Gathier-Villars.

Congrès Internationaux d'Architecture Moderne (CIAM)/Le Corbusier (1946 [1943]): *The Charter of Athens*, translated by Jaqueline Tyrwhitt, Paris: The Library of the Graduate School of Design, Harvard University.https://www.getty.edu/conservation/publications_resources/research_resources/charters/charter04.html (Accessed: April 19, 2022).

Cortesi, Isotta (2000): *Parcs publics. Paysages 1985–2000*, transl. from Italian by Marguerite Pozzoli, Arles: Actes Sud.

De Marco, Rosa (2016): »Du paysage aux ambiances successives. La contribution de la Mouvance de la Villette au devenir de l'ambiance, des ambiances demain«, in: Nicolas Tixier/Nicolas Rémy (eds.), *Ambiances, tomorrow*. Proceedings of 3rd International Congress on Ambiances, Volos: International Network Ambiances, 135–140.

Diers, Michael (2009): »Atlas und Mnemosyne. Von der Praxis der Bildtheorie bei Aby Warburg«, in: Klaus Sachs-Hombach (ed.), *Bildtheorien. Anthropologische und kulturelle Grundlagen des Visualistic Turn*. Frankfurt/ Main: Suhrkamp, 181-213.

Dubost, Françoise (1983): »Les paysagistes et l'invention du paysage«, in: *Sociologie du travail* 25/4, 432 – 445. doi: 10.3406/sotra.1983.1947

Elsea, Daniel (2018): »Parisian Accents/La touche Parisienne«, in: *Landscape Architecture Magazine. The Magazine of the American Society of Landscape Architects*, April, 120–137.

Foucault, Michel (1984 [1967]): »Of Other Spaces: Utopias and Heterotopias«, transl. by Jay Miskowiec, in: *Diacritics* 16/1, 22-27. https://doi.org/10.2307/464648 (Accessed: July 30, 2021).

Garcias, Jean-Claude (1993): »Un lustre après. Le concours Citroën revisité«, in: *Paris Projet, Espaces publics* 30/31, 100–118.

Halder, Severin/Michel, Boris (2018): »Editorial – This Is Not an Atlas«, in: Kollektiv Orangotango+ (ed.), *This is not an Atlas: A Global Collection of Counter-cartographies*, Bielefeld: Transcript, 12–25.

Haubl, Rolf (1999): »Angst vor der Wildnis. An der Grenze der Zivilisation«, in: *Bayrische Akademie für Naturschutz und Landschaftspflege* 2, 47–56.

Haussmann, Georges-Eugène (1890–1893): *Mémoires du Baron Haussmann*, 3 volumes, Paris: Victor-Havard.

Kollektiv Orangotango+ (ed.) (2018): *This is Not an Atlas. A Global Collection of Counter-cartographies*, Bielefeld: Transcript.

Lawrance, Henry (1993): »The Greening of the Squares of London. Transformation of Urban Landscapes and Ideals«, in: *Annals of the Association of American Geographers* 83/1, 90–118.

Lucain, Pierre (1981): »Art urbain, urban design ou urbanité?«, in: *Architecture d'aujourd'hui* 217, 2–7.

Lucas, Ray (2020): *Drawing Parallels: Knowledge Production in Axonometric, Isometric and Oblique Drawings*, London/New York: Routledge.

Luxembourg, Corinne (2019): *Habiter aux intersections*. Postdoctoral Thesis (Habilitation à diriger des recherches), Université d'Artois. https://hal.archives-ouvertes.fr/tel-02398066 (Accessed: March 7, 2022).

Mehdi, Lotfi/Weber, Christiane/Di Pietro, Francesca/Selmi, Wissal (2012): »Évolution de la place du végétal dans la ville, de l'espace vert à la trame verte«, in: *VertigO – la revue électronique en sciences de l'environnement* 12/2. doi : 10.4000/vertigo.1.

Ministre de l'aménagement du territoire (1973): «Circulaire du 21 mars 1973. Relative aux formes d'urbanisation dites grands ensembles et à la lutte contre la ségrégation sociale par l'habitat». https://www.legifrance.gouv.fr/jorf/id/JORFTEXT000000661400 (Accessed: March 7, 2022).

Mosser, Monique/Brunon, Hervé (2006): *Le jardin contemporain. Renouveau, expériences et enjeux*, Paris: Editions Scala.

Mosser, Monique/Brunon, Hervé (2007): »L'enclos comme parcelle et totalité du monde. Pour une approche holistique de l'art des jardins«, in: *Ligeia, dossiers sur l'art* 73–76 Janvier-Juin, 59–75, https://halshs.archives-ouvertes.fr/halshs-00167922 (Accessed: July 30, 2021).

Renaud, Yann/Tonnelat, Stéphane (2008): »La maîtrise d'œuvre sociologique des Jardins d'Éole. Comment construire une gestion publique ?«, in: *Les Annales de la recherche urbaine* 105/1, 55–65, doi: 10.3406/aru.2008.2763.

Santini, Chiara (2021): *Adolphe Alphand et la construction du paysage de Paris*, Paris: Hermann.

Simpson, Deane/Jensen, Vibeke/Rubing, Anders, eds. (2016): *The City between Freedom and Security: Contested Public Spaces in the 21st Century*, Basel: Birkhäuser.

Stalder, Laurent/Beyer, Elke/Förster, Kim/Hagemann, Anke, eds. (2009): *Schwellenatlas. Von Abfallzerkleinerer zu Zeitmaschine*, Arch+ 191/192.

Starkman, Nathan (1993): »Deux Nouveaux Parcs à Paris«, in: *Paris Projet, Espaces publics* 30/31, 88–89, https://www.apur.org/fr/nos-travaux/paris-projet-30-31-espaces-publics# (Accessed: July 30, 2021).

Turner, Tom (2005): *Garden History, Philosophy and Design, 2000 BC–2000 AD*, London/New York: Routledge.

Vernhes, Jean-Victor (2015): »Une étymologie pour ὁ κῆπος?«, in : *Connaissance hellénique*, Billets 141, https://ch.hypotheses.org/1309 (Accessed: March 7, 2022).

Weigel, Sigrid (2013): »Epistemology of Wandering, Tree and Taxonomy«, in: *Images Re-vues. Histoire, anthropologie et théorie de l'art* (Hors-série 4), doi : 10.4000/imagesrevues.2934.

Wolfrum, Sophie (2015 [2014]): *Squares. Urban spaces in Europe*, Basel: Birkhäuser.

Dimensions of Architectural Knowledge, 2022-03 ᑐ
https://doi.org/10.14361/dak-2022-0304

BRICK BY BRICK REDRAWING
A Digital Approach to Dismantling and
Reconstructing a Historical Building

Davide Franco

Abstract: This article reflects upon the methods I used to investigate the relationship between the structure and the facade construction of industrial architecture. In Berlin in particular, iron and brick have been a constructive characteristic of the first third of the 20th century. The tool of technical drawing proved particularly effective in the preliminary investigation. After choosing to investigate buildings that still exist today by means of a critical redrawing, fragments were gradually dismantled and the construction hypotheses took on the character of a redesign of the elements. With the help of recent drawing technologies it was possible to reconstruct a »technical style«, obtained by comparing different fragments represented in the same way. Three-dimensional modeling allowed the physical reconstruction of portions of the buildings digitally, brick by brick.

Keywords: Redrawing; Iron Architecture; Brick Architecture; Construction Techniques.

Introduction

In September 2019, I was traveling to Berlin for the first time as part of my doctoral research whose theme is the construction techniques of industrial architecture that was built between 1913 and 1926. It would give me the opportunity to compare the work carried out up to that point by analyzing historical and bibliographical sources with the buildings object of my case studies. The relationship between two materials, iron and bricks, is expressed in different ways in the period that goes from the construction of the Loewe *Maschinenhalle* by Alfred Grenander (1906), to the completion of the *Wernerwerk Hochhaus* Siemensstadt by Hans Hertlein (1928). Anyway, the hybridized grammars of the constructive system find their synthetic expression in the AEG *Großmaschinenhalle*, built in 1911 by Peter Behrens (Buddensieg

Corresponding author: Davide Franco (Politecnico di Bari); franco.davide@poliba.it; http://orcid.org/0000-0002-4647-037X

1978: D76–81) or the *Umspannwerk* Kottbusser Ufer, built in 1924 by Felix Thümen and Hans Heinrich Müller.[1]

From a theoretical and constructive point of view, the German experience at the turn of the 19th and 20th centuries has contributed significantly to a more precise definition of the issues in the relationship between form and construction. Although the topic has been the subject of several publications, analytical studies concerning the construction of these buildings are still missing. Identifying the characteristics of industrial construction in Berlin, I focus deeply on the study of the techniques and technologies employed. Exhaustive introductory research into Berlin's industrial architecture has already been carried out by Julius Posener (1979) and Miron Mislin (2002).[2]

The industrial building represents an interesting form of architecture stretched between the abstract and the functional space. The construction associated with it is often elaborated on principles of economy and functionality, as well as on experimental choices, and is sometimes influenced by the work machines that are placed inside. Starting from the 1910s, industrial architectures built in Berlin became a way to research a valid alternative to the historicist facades that were prevalent in industrial design during the 19th century (Mislin 2002: 249). Until the beginning of the 20th century, industrial buildings were composed of two parts: the structure, generally designed and built for functional purposes only, and conceived by engineers; and the shell, often full of decorations, with the sole purpose of presenting the building in an aesthetic form, often designed by architects (Mislin 2002: 201–228). The change in the sensibility of the architectural context generated a different approach to industrial architecture. Architects and engineers worked simultaneously, influencing each other. In this way, the engineering struc-

---

1 The following buildings should also be mentioned: the *Schaltwerk Hochhaus* Siemensstadt, built in 1926 by Hans Hertlein (Hertlein/ Schmitz 1927; Hertlein 1928; Ribbe/Schäche 1985: 657); the *Großkraftwerk Klingenberg*, built in 1925 by Waltar Klingenberg and Werner Issel and the AEG construction department (Klingenberg 1926; Laube 1927; Rein 1928; Lorenz/ May/Staroste 2020: 294–297).

2 The latter in particular has provided a classification of construction techniques by comparing the different types of buildings and inserting the technical problem in a broader system of historical and theoretical knowledge. A few researchers have recently addressed specifically the evolution of the historical and technical context after 1910, among them the contributions on Berlin »Elektropolis« (Dame 2011; Dame et al. 2014), on iron structures techniques (Prokop 2012), the compendium of structures »Ingenieurbauführer« (Lorenz/ May/Staroste 2020), and the study on the brick construction techniques (Potgeter 2021).

tures acquire an architectural value with proportional and volumetric studies, while using the engineering knowledge to express the new »technical
form« (Poelzig 1911).

In Berlin, the introduction of iron as a fundamental element for the
load-bearing structures of large-scale industrial buildings is dated to the
first half of the 19th century (Mislin 2002: 158). The ability of this material to
respond statically to various stresses and the practicality of its use during
construction had accelerated experimentation in the technical field. This
technological push had created a fracture between the structure of technical
buildings and the envelope (Posener 1979: 369): the former was conceived and
built with the sole purpose of serving its function; the latter, on the other
hand, had an aesthetic function. The design of the latter was for a long time
the only field of action of architects in the industrial context (Lindner 1978;
Poelzig 1911). A change in sensibility, mainly due to the desire to move beyond
the styles, occurred at the end of the 19th century when some attempts to
synthesize the structural and facade systems began to be made (Posener
1979: 387). Most of Berlin's industrial buildings produced between 1898 and
1928 consist of a masonry structure and an iron structure, which, depending
on the case, are built subordinately or coordinated in static operation. Given
the need to free up space for production, the element of synthesis of the relationship between form and structure is identified in the facade. Attempts to
codify a language led to the spontaneous emergence of a style in industrial
architecture. This »technical style« owes its grammar to structural and functional needs. Recent research on the subject has demonstrated a continuity
in the constructive conception of these industrial buildings, which also suggests the existence of a sort of »collective design« obtained with the contribution of several professional figures and the fruitful collaboration of
different technicians (Dame 2011). The cooperation of architects, engineers,
and construction firms, coordinated through the work of their technical offices, caused the language of industrial construction to develop from certain
recurring characteristics in the designs of Berlin's technical architectures.

In order to understand the dynamics that led to the construction of these
buildings, I set myself the goal of disassembling them, in digital drawings,
and analytically studying their individual technologies and materials to reconstruct the architectural artifact starting from a »ground zero« of the construction. The disassembly of these buildings is carried out through the
description of the individual parts and, as a whole, the return to drawings
that allow us not only to understand and study the problem of the relation-

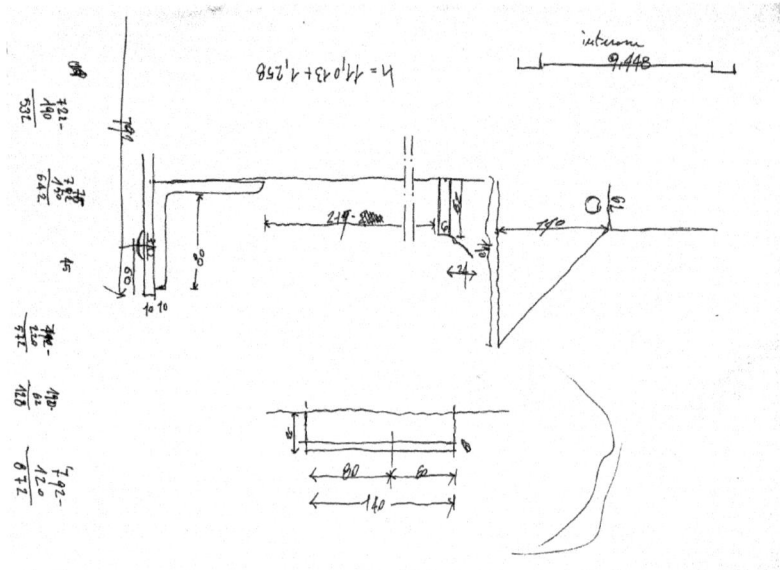

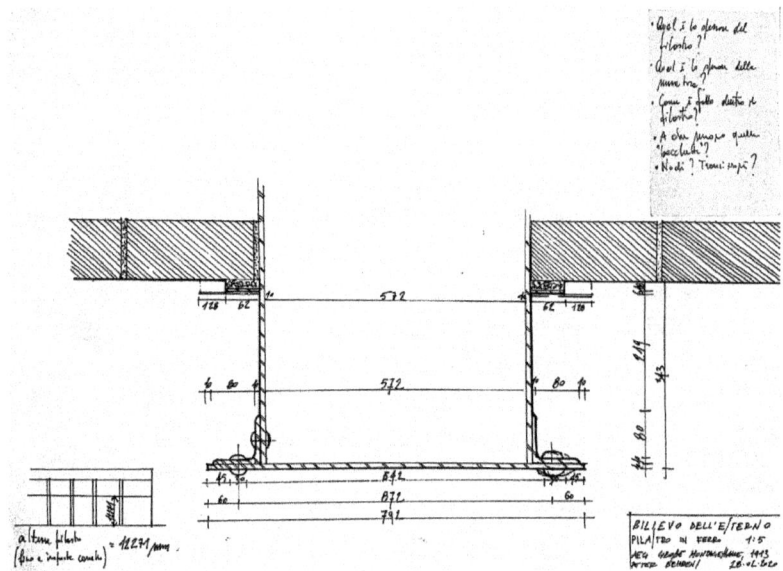

1.
Survey sketches of the 1913 AGE Große Montagehalle by Peter Behrens: Franco
Davide, 2020.

ship between technique and technology, but also to present it and make it intelligible.

Research Focus

To understand the relationship between technique and construction, it is necessary to investigate its material components. Through the comparison of technological systems and building techniques it is possible to frame the state of construction in an epoch. A possible method to investigate a building has been codified over time in a process that begins with finding sources and represent them as evidence through an architectural survey, in a drawing of the situation present to the researcher (Schuller et al. 2017: 14–15). In the archaeological field, traces of building bodies are detected and studied in order to understand the construction techniques and return the shape of a building, often through hypotheses (De Mattia 2012: 134–138). These are supported by comparisons with the current theoretical knowledge and with similar buildings (chronologically or stylistically) of which certain details are better known (Gruben 2007: 32–37). Similarly, in the case of these industrial architectures, it was necessary to survey the contemporary situation and compare it with the original one through the building plan, in order to understand the evolution of design and the motivation that might have led to a different realization of the work.

Therefore, in order to understand how a certain building was constructed and with which technologies, it would have been useful to go through the archaeological method. However, what in archaeology is carried out as a re-assembly of parts through the study of fragments, in my case has turned into a disassembly of parts and the comparison of fragments that I considered significant. Although the fundamental part of the work was the survey, the aim of the study was still the abstraction of building techniques and their comparative analysis.

A general survey began with a complete cataloging of the state of the knowledge, gathering information mainly on buildings still existing today. The information came from various sources: bibliographical and archival. In the first case, the considerable production of publications, manuals, and material published in the form of books at the beginning of the last century, made it possible to trace many buildings and their descriptions. The archival material, on the other hand, consisting of project reports, drawings, and

4.
Detail of the main elevation of the
Kleinturbinenhalle, Heizkraftwerk
Klingenberg.
Photographer: Franco Davide, 2020.

2.
Using a photo editing program, bricks
can be counted easily.
Photographer: Franco Davide, 2020.

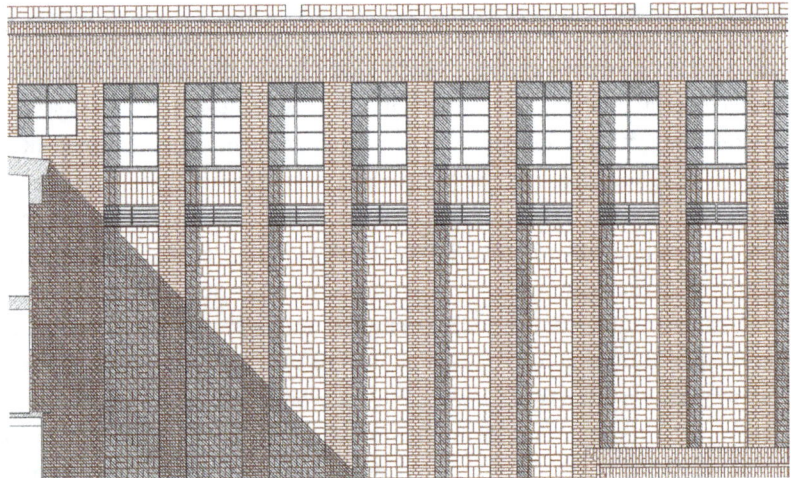

3.
Photo of the north elevation, 1927. Every brick layer is clearly visible.
Courtesy: Vattenfall Historical Archive (BEWAG).

photographs, suffered damage during the two world wars and material was lost due to the relocation of offices.

The collection of this material served as support for the metric and photographic survey of the building. Among the most important material found, there are some technical drawings and high-resolution site photographs. Other technical drawings, used as references, were commonly published in trade journals and, in the case of Hertlein's work for Siemens and the Klingenberg power plant, were published in books introducing the building (Ribbe and Schäche 1985). The AEG buildings (Buddensieg 1978; Rogge 1983) and the Klingenberg power plant, were extensively documented in individual construction phases as one of the largest infrastructure constructions of public interest (Dame 2011: 269).

The metric survey, I carried out on my own in several tranches from September 2019 to January 2022. The difficulty in obtaining permits for access to the various parts of the buildings for measuring it, meant that the resources to be employed would have been great and accurate preliminary planning work would have been fundamental. In addition, the lack of technical support for the survey had proved decisive (Krautheimer/Corbett/Frankl 1937: XV). Therefore, the use of the laser detection and ranging technology (LIDAR) had to be excluded. The only inexpensive tools at my disposal were a flexible and a rigid meter, a 20-meter roll, a laser distance meter, and my camera. In order to always have the buildings close by, I moved my residence to Berlin for the duration of my PhD.

The Process of Redrawing

The operation of »critical redrawing« constituted one of the principles of philological investigation of the building in the 19th century (De Mattia 2012) for researchers called »Bauforscher«. These were architects particularly interested in the archaeological field. With their experience as builders, they were able to reconstruct the buildings of antiquity and, at the same time, retrieve from them important information for designing from scratch. Schinkel is generally referred to as the first »Bauforscher«, although he never attended an archaeological site (Gruben 2007: 50).[3]

3 »Critical redrawing« is one of the research tools used by the technology department of the Faculty of Architecture at the Politecnico di Bari (Ardito 2014). It is rooted in a

An important design feature of industrial buildings is their vocation for seriality which, in the case of mixed iron and brick structures, is amplified. The brick used in a building can be of a few different sizes; the structures almost always have a regular pitch; the iron elements are designed to be assembled in an elementary way and have a tendency toward the simplification of geometries and thickness which corresponds to an ease of redesign. Considering these elements, the survey activity was divided into two parts. The first one was the analysis and metric survey of the single portions reachable and measurable with a laser disto or a metric roll (fig. 1). A second one consisted of an accurate general, and detailed, photographic campaign which allowed for the reconstruction of entire portions of the building using computer software. Not having the possibility to work in a prolonged manner in the field, the work done later at home became decisive.

The first phase of the survey involved the recognition of homogeneous structures in terms of materials and construction. Of these, portions of approximately one square meter were photographed and the size of individual elements was noted. Iron structures often had replicated dimensions or standardized elements (Büttner 1928; Müller 1928; Herbst 1930; Prokop 2012). The masonry structures, almost always in clinker, presented hand-baked bricks whose dimensions had deviations of +/- 5 millimeters and irregular mortars, but were still traceable to an ideal average size of 10 millimeters. In order to understand the starting size of the element, that is the one chosen by the designer, it was necessary to compare the dimensions detected, and the material, with those present in the catalogs and manuals of the time. The brick-building system also has the advantage of having portions of the structure that are multiples of the size of the bricks themselves: the interaxis of the openings, pillars, and pilasters, etc. The survey of these portions for obtaining the dimensions consisted of counting the bricks that were visible on the facade (fig. 2).

This operation, however, needed to be deepened by analyzing the statics of the masonry construction in the case of the *Prüßwand* (Schumacher 1985: 136–137), whose structure is understood to be an iron lattice simply infilled with two facings, divided by a layer of air. The masonry texture of the nucleus almost constituted a separate investigation: to the same appearance on the facade, corresponded different possible internal dispositions of the ash-

---

well-established method that is the basis of important publications, such as the *Corpus Basilicarum Christianarum Romae* (Krautheimer/Corbett/Frankl 1937).

lars. These have been recovered from the manuals of the time. Some dispositions are traditional and well known to masons, others have instead an
experimental nature and serve to solve the problem of structural hybridiza-
tion. The iron parts with riveted box structures have a sheet thickness of 10
millimeters and a rivet diameter of 20 millimeters. The technology, which is
consistently repeated, is for example used by the AEG construction department in the buildings they design and construct: the journal *Der Stahlbau* in
the 1928 presented many buildings designed by them in which the same patterns of structure are used. Buildings that use profiled iron structural elements instead are easily traceable to the dimensions given in the manual.
Some buildings have constantly been compared with design reports and specific drawings, published mainly in the form of demonstration pamphlets or
in articles from specialized magazines (Rudolf Laube 1928). The elements
embedded in the masonry, undetectable by an external survey, could be re-
designed thanks to a comparison and a positioning given by the contingency
of the space necessary to the construction of the organism.

The process of reconstructing the nucleus started therefore from a plan
design of several overlapping rows (fig. 3). Subsequently, this drawing was
implemented through the design of a »by handbook« configuration. Finally,
the »critical redrawing« obtained was again compared with the actual state
to understand if it was a plausible and functional solution in all parts of the
building. Thanks to the available site photographs it was possible to draw the
construction of the structural cores with more accuracy and to establish the
relationships between the different techniques and technologies (fig. 4).

Since the survey and redesign were carried out at a scale that tended
from the detailed to general, the final drawing also absorbed this characteristic. The portions of the building were redrawn at a scale of 1:20, preferring
the restitution of the parts that constituted »constructive modules«. Subsequently, with the help of photographs, the missing parts of the buildings
were saturated, obtaining the overall drawings of the fronts in scale 1:50 (fig.
5). The peculiarity of this process lies in the fact that the drawings could be
performed away from the building without necessarily being able to reach all
parts of it. Thanks to the use of photographic and historical documentation,
it was possible to count the rows of bricks, obtain the apparent textures, and
establish with sufficient approximation the dimensions of the structures.
For example, the north face of the *AEG Großmaschinenhalle* has 251 rows of
bricks measuring 65 x 115 x 240 millimeters with a »*Kreuzverband*« texture.
The pilasters of the tower of the Klingenberg power station are built with 425

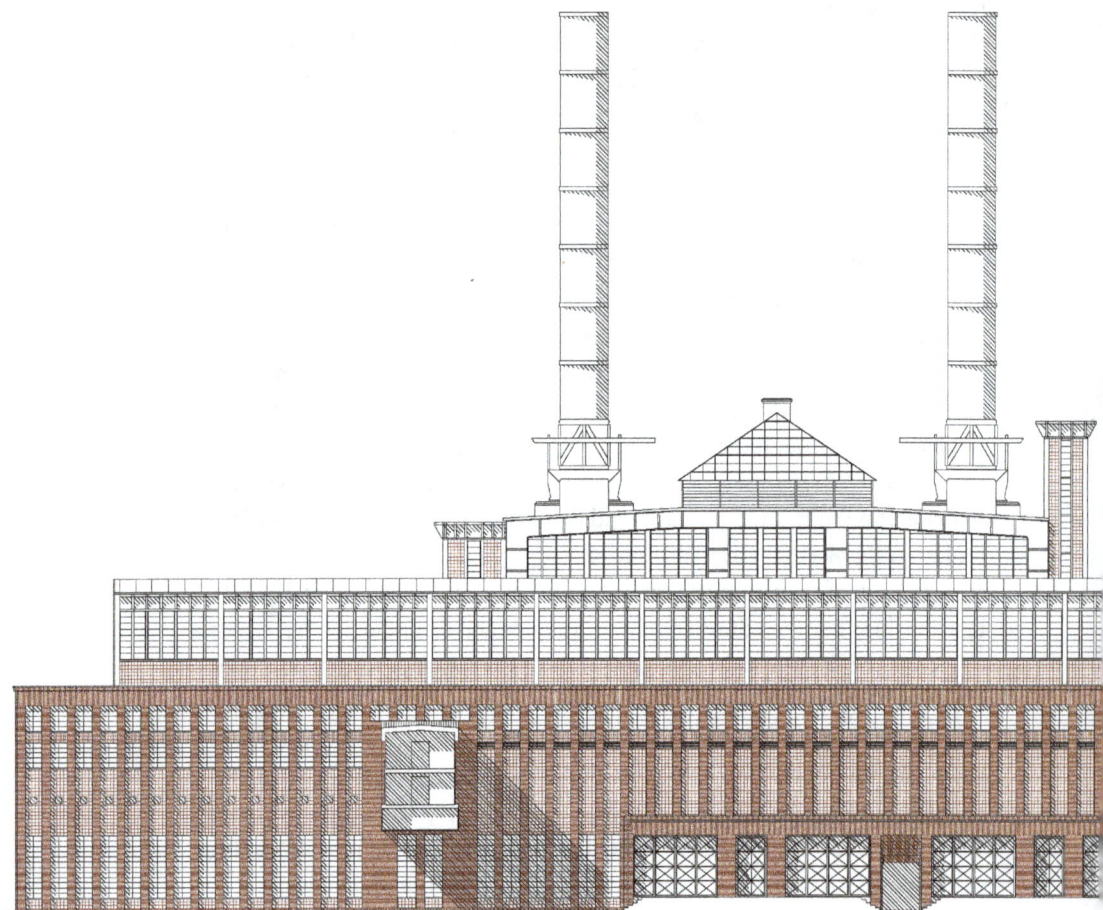

5.
Main elevation of the Kleinturbinenhalle, Großkraftwerk Klingenberg.
Drawing: Davide Franco, 2020.

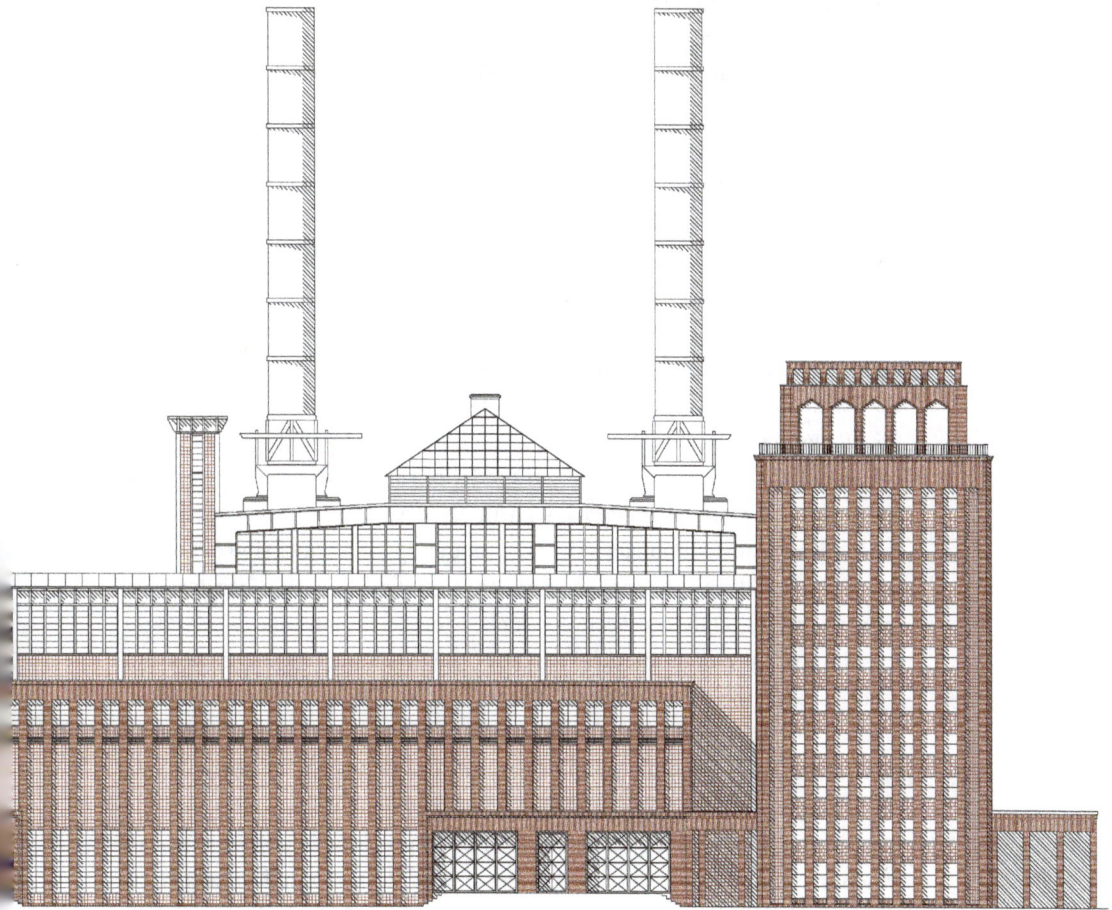

rows of bricks measuring 65 x 120 x 250 millimeters. In this way I could also reconstruct the height of the buildings.

However, the replicability of the construction remained at the stage of appearance. The redesign of the *Umspannwerk* Kottbusser Ufer building is a case in point. The structure expresses the use of large masses and a distinct boxiness. However, bibliographical sources indicated the presence of predominantly iron-frame buildings with a secondary masonry system concealing the load-bearing part in the work of the architects Felix Thümen and Hans Heinrich Müller (1879–1951), all designed for the *Berliner Städtische Elektrizitätswerke Aktien Gesellschaft* (BEWAG) between 1922 and 1930. No historical photographs were found. The initial survey was therefore performed assuming a frame system concealed by the two-face masonry thickness. The external face is composed of violet clinker measuring 52 x 105 x 220 millimeters and the internal one of yellow clinker 65 x 120 x 250 millimeters.

My photographs showed some incongruities between the rules of frame construction — which is presumed to be made of discrete and punctual elements generally aligned up to the foundations — and the actual construction of the building. The most obvious detail was the thin thickness of the *Schalthaus's* mezzanine floor facings which prevented the placement of the steel mullions. A three-dimensional model of the portions of the building was created on computer-aided design (CAD) software. The model replicated the masonry construction on a 1:1 scale, modeling each dimension of the ashlar, and rebuilding the masonry portion digitally but with a handcrafted process (fig. 6). Only the accurate replication of the masons' work could somehow suggest the structural syntax of the masonry. Despite the possibility of reading the dimensions of the steel parts — reported on an original plan kept in the Vattenfall archives[4] — five different models were made, one after the other, each with small variations: the arrangement of the lintels, the arrangement of the ashlars, the relation between the iron parts, and the masonry ones. A further question was raised by the thickness of the masonry, which in the drawing's reported dimensions of 510 x 640 millimeters, actually found in the dimensional survey of the building. Only the last model definitively agreed that the thing detected corresponded with the thing guessed, and coherently explained the different parts of the building: these are load-bearing wall boxes resting on linear steel elements. The floors are

---

4 Part of the BEWAG Archive has been absorbed by the Vattenfall and is currently stored in a building next to the Klingenberg power plant.

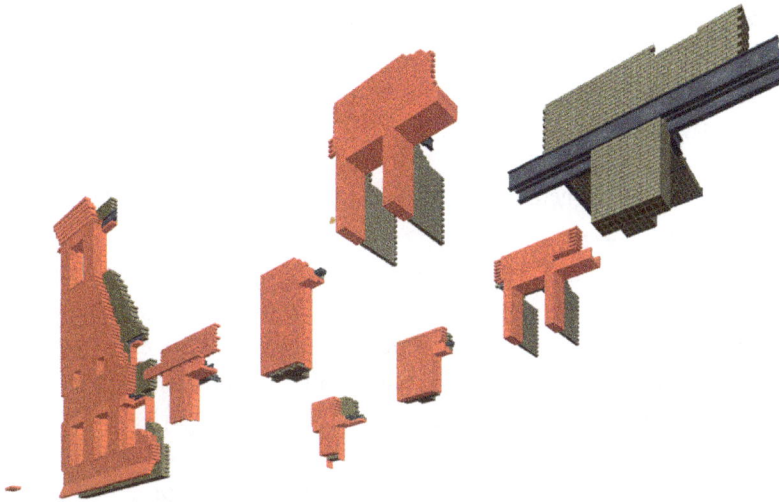

6.
Constructive fragments seen on CAD 3D modeling.
Drawing: Davide Franco, 2020.

7. – 8.
Schalthaus Kottbusser Ufer. First (left) and last (right) hypothesis.
Drawings: Davide Franco, 2020.

made with a steel structure embedded in concrete resting on the wall box: in this way, there is no need for the beam to correspond to a solid, to a pillar in the facade. The holes are obtained by means of flat bands that hide steel girders (figs. 7 and 8).

Aesthetics of Redrawing

The critical redrawing carried out at such a detailed scale allowed for an understanding of the experimental techniques that were avant-garde elements of industrial design in the 1920s. Moreover, the disassembly of each part of the buildings returned a picture of the overall situation of the construction that allowed the introduction of the concept of »technical style«.

In the choice of the graphic expression to be used, two drawings fascinated me: the first is the ideal construction site of a Greek propylaea (fig. 9), made by Karl Friedrich Schinkel (Schinkel 1821: 63), the second is the collection of detailed axonometries (fig. 10) made by August Choisy (Choisy 1873). In both cases the organic idea of the building passed through the ideal representation of one of its constructive fragments. Schinkel's drawing represents the elements of the propylaea construction (elevation and roof) in a way that suggests the process of building the individual elements, as »unfinished« that aims to describe how the building is made and the logical sequence that unites the various technological elements. Choisy's axonometries, on the other hand, have the aspect of a fragment, that is, a portion of the organism considered by the author to be significant enough to constitute a drawing. In contrast to Schinkel, this type of representation does not aim to describe the construction phases, but is rather a, so to speak, anatomical dissection: the single parts of the construction are clear, but they are always traced back to the unitary and whole idea of the building.

My intuition that guided the initial categorization of the case studies was then confirmed by the empirical activity of survey and redesign. Those architectures that at the beginning were interesting from a historical-critical point of view proved to be milestones in the process of consolidation and diffusion of a constructive thought concerning technical buildings in the Berlin context. The two-dimensional redrawing carried out with an initial 1:50 scale detailed and then deepened or simplified, that means brought between the scales 1:200 and 1:10, showed the material continuity and allowed me to understand the design and construction phases of each building and to compare them, obtaining an overall picture of the construction technique. For example, the clinker wall construction of the *Umspannwerk* Kottbusser Ufer reveals the dualism between structure and tectonics (Frampton 2005). The drawing in the masonry core would show that the building was conceived with a single clinker dimension like the other pre-1924 buildings designed by Felix Thümen. A hypothesis for the difference in the treatment of the facings can be then explained with the chronological coincidence of the construction of the building and the architect Hans Heinrich Müller joining the BEWAG's technical office, whom might have suggested the introduction of purple clinker out of a need for the appropriateness of language in the urban context (Hoffmann-Axthelm 1986; Potgeter 2021).

The analysis and hypotheses concerning the building cores made it possible to make explicit the relationships between different architectures. The tower structure of the Klingenberg power station is directly comparable to that of the *Schaltwerk Hochhaus* in Siemensstadt. The system of two profiles joined by a steel sheet is described by Hertlein (1928) and can be seen in the site photos (Hertlein 1928, 23; Vattenfall Archives). The *Kleinturbinenhalle* of the Klingenberg power plant, apparently consisting of only six-headed pillars, conceals an iron structural system. In this case, the discretized masonry becomes an unprecedented element of mediation between the language of the discrete and the continuous system. Again, the critical redrawing provided the basis for reading the building and revealed the complexity of the designers' thinking.

Since my research had initially assumed traits of continuity within the study of historical architectures, I decided to rely completely on a graphic restitution as close as possible to that of my references. This feature was extremely efficient since the same »skeletal« drawing, which I had used for the study of the building, presented itself in the printing phase with a bare and technical aesthetic. The presentation of general elements was enriched with information and contingencies in the drawing of the details. The substantial difference between the drawing elaborated on CAD and the drawing executed in an »analogical way« is found in the infinitesimal precision of the vectorial drawing and in the possibility of multiplying the elements with a single command. The construction of the drawing itself is more mechanical, but the restitution is obviously more precise. The digital instrument also allows an immediate interscalarity.

The line drawing has meant for me the instrument of study and presentation at the same time. An immediate passage from the photograph and the hand-drawn eidotype to the publication. The final drawings are divided for

9.
Karl Friedrich Schinkel, Vorbilder für Fabrikanten und Handwerker. Steinkonstruktion des Gesims- und Deckenwerks bei den Propyläen zu Eleusis, 1821-1830, 63.

10.
Auguste Choisy, L'art de batir chez les Romains (1873, 237). Public Domain Mark 1.0, https://digi.ub.uni-heidelberg.de/diglit/choisy1873 (accessed: July 2021).

the different chromatic treatments: the sections and the axonometries are simple, in gray tones and the elevations are in color, following the constructive chromaticism. Each chromatic difference owes its reason to a communicative necessity. The plan and the sections show the relationship between the elements and the space they build and sometimes describe. The gray tones give back a difference necessary for the legibility of the various parts of the building, making the representation homogeneous at the same time. Similarly, axonometries tend to describe the portion of the building element in its unity, although composed of different parts and studied in an analytical way. Elevations, on the other hand, use lines in color. Red or yellow represent the clinker parts, those in dark gray the metal parts. The choice of color representation comes from a desire to suggest materiality. The burgundy-colored rectangle drawn on the screen, if composed with other rectangles, becomes immediately intelligible as a brick in the reader's mind.

The three-dimensional digital model assumes peculiar characteristics in the work of investigating the construction of these industrial buildings. The original file can be explored and rotated in space for further analysis, but the entire portion is consistent and detailed in all its parts. This means that the constructive details represented in axonometry are the result of a reasoning also applied to the parts hidden in the drawing, i.e., those that are behind the shown object. In this case, the use of the exploded view as a mode of representation has the will to return the complexity, not only of the original element, but also of the work done for the digital reconstruction. The planimetric axonometry returns an overall view of the object by altering the perceptual relationships between the parts and giving a more descriptive view. As it is composed of a plan that shows the elevated in a 1:1:1 ratio, it is possible to measure the parts on the printed drawing and immediately understand their mutual relationship.

The method of modeling »brick by brick« was not only useful to understand similarities and differences, and to identify the structural essence but also as a simulation of the craftsmanship: stacking, joining, and juxtaposition had to be done in an elementary way, based in each case on principles of practicality and economy: of construction site, of finances, of time. The model, though detailed, was voluntarily left as a »snapshot« of the construction process in the making to contribute to the understanding of the architecture represented as derived from a physically constructed architecture. And, as with Schinkel's drawing, to restore constructive relationships and subordination between the various parts of the architectural structure.

The redrawing method described above has shown its validity but also its weaknesses. Critical redrawing, used as a graphic synthesis of theoretical and practical study assumes the contours of an essential and decisive tool in my training as a researcher, but above all as an architect. The redrawing of all the parts that can be seen and the drawing of the hidden parts force me to think in terms of the re-design of the building. The activity of restitution of the single parts of the building is supported by an accurate bibliographical and archival investigation in order to decipher the signs of the construction and endorse possible hypotheses. The nature of the instrument is not simply inventive but advances and is refuted in a scientific way (De Mattia 2012: 28). It is possible that the hypotheses described and represented are re-discussed, but the very construction of the drawing provides a logical reading of the parts that make up the building. The redrawing has helped frame the language of these architectures and to suggest their ways of being constructed. More in-depth studies may reveal more precise solutions, but these are alternatives to already valid hypotheses.

The investigation of an existing building carried out by means of an inverse archaeological method and through redrawing, reveals the validity of a traditional method that, thanks to the recent technologies of vector drawing and digital modeling, offers an easily employable working tool without the need to resort to extraordinary resources.

References

Ardito, Vitangelo (2014): »La Baukunst ed il progetto della forma della Costruzione. Ricerche e didattica«, in: *Techne* 8, 271–281

Buddensieg, Tillmann (1978): *Industriekultur. Peter Behrens und die AEG. 1907-1914*, Milan: Gruppo Editoriale Electa

Büttner, Wilhelm (1928): »Die Stahlbauten für das Kraftwerk Schulau der Elektrizitätswerk Untreibe A.-G. ›Altona‹«, in: *Der Stahlbau* 11/1

Choisy, Auguste (1873): *L'art de bâtir chez les Romains*, Paris. DOI: https://doi.org/10.11588/DIGLIT.2380.

Dame, Torsten (2011): *Elektropolis Berlin: Die Energie der Großstadt; Bauprogramme und Aushandlungsprozesse zur öffentlichen Elektrizitätsversorgung in Berlin*, Berlin: Mann

Dame, Torsten et al. (2014): *Elektropolis Berlin: Architektur- und Denkmalführer*, Petersberg: Imhof

De Mattia, Daniela (2012): *Architettura antica e progetto: dalla Bauforschung al progetto architettonico in area archeologica*, Roma: Gangemi

»Die Stahlkonstruktion für das Schaltwerk-Hochhaus der Siemens-Schukert-Werke in Berlin-Siemensstadt.« (1928), in: *Der Stahlbau* 15 (1), 177-180

Frampton, Kenneth (2005): *Tettonica e Architettura. Poetica della forma architettonica nel XIX e XX secolo*, Milano: Skira editore.

Gruben, Gottfried (2007): *Klassische Bauforschung*, Munich: Hirmer.

Herbst, Friedrich (1930): »Stahlskelettbau des neuen Umspannwerks ›Schnarhorst‹ der Bewag zu Berlin«, *Der Stahlbau* 3 /9, 97-101

Hertlein, Hans (1928): *Das Schalwerk Hochhaus in Siemensstadt*, Berlin: Ernst Wasmuth Verlag

Hertlein, Hans/Schmitz, Hermann (1927): *Neue Industriebauten des Siemenskonzerns: Fabrik-und Verwaltungsgebäude, Wohlfahrtsanlagen*, Berlin: Ernst Wasmuth.

Hoffmann-Axthelm, Dieter (1986): »Stadtbild - Baumeister«., in: J. Boberg. (ed.), *Die Metropole. Industriekultur in Berlin im 20. Jahrhundert*, Munich: C.H. Beck'sche Verlagsbuchhandlung

Klingenberg, Georg (1926): *Bau großer Elektrizitätswerke*, Berlin: Springer-Verlag Beling Heidelberg GmbH.

Krautheimer, Richard/Corbett, Spencer/ Frankl, Wolfgang (1937): *Corpus Basilicarum Christianarum Romae*. 1, Città del Vaticano: Pontificio Istituto di Archeologia Cristiana

Kuban, Sabine (2019): »Building Frames: Aspects of the Development of Reinforced Concrete in Berlin«, in: *Informes de la Construcción* 71/553, 284. DOI: 10.3989/ ic.70537.

Laube, Richard (ed.) (1927): *Das Grosskraftwerk Klingenberg*, Berlin: Verlag Ernst Wasmuth.

Laube, Richard (1928): »The Structural Work«, in: *Engineering Progress* 3 »Klingenberg number«, 57-96.

Lindner, Werner (1978): *Le costruzioni della tecnica*, Milano: Franco Angeli Editore

Lorenz, Werner/May, Roland/Staroste, Hubert (2020): *Ingenieurbauführer Berlin*, Petersberg: Michael Imhof Verlag.

Mislin, Miron (2002): *Industriearchitektur in Berlin 1840–1910*, Munich: Ernst Wasmuth Verlag

Müller, Anton (1928): »Kesselhaus für das Großkraftwek Gesteinwerk der Vereinigten Elektrizitätswerke Westfalen in Dortmund«, in: *Der Stahlbau*, 18/1, 209-211

Poelzig, Hans (1911): »Die Moderne Industriearchitektur«, in: *Der Industriebau* 5/2, 100–106

Posener, Julius (1979): *Berlin: Auf dem Wege zu einer neuen Architektur*, Munich: Prestel Verlag.

Potgeter, Wilko (2021): *Backstein-Rohbau im Zeitalter der Industrialisierung. Bautechnik des Sichtbacksteins im deutschen Sprachraum von der Zeit Schinkels bis zum Backsteinexpressionismus*, Zurich: ETH Zurich. DOI: https://doi.org/10.3929/ ethz-b-000475553

Prokop, Ines (2012): *Vom Eisenbau zum Stahlbau: Tragwerke und ihre Protagonisten in Berlin 1850–1925*, Berlin: Mensch und Buch Verlag

Rein, W. (1928): »Die Eisenbauten des Grosskraftwerkes Klingenberg«, in: *Der Bauingenieur* 42, 752–765

Ribbe, Wolfgang/Schäche, Wolfgang (1985): *Die Siemensstadt: Geschichte u. Architektur e. Industriestandortes*, Berlin: Ernst

Rogge, Henning (1983): *Fabrikwelt um die Jahrhundertwende am Beispiel del AEG Maschinenfabrik in Berlin-Wedding*, Cologne: DuMont

Schinkel, Karl Friedrich (1821-1830): *Vorbilder für Fabrikanten und Handwerker. Steinkonstruktion des Gesims- und Deckenwerks bei den Propyläen zu Eleusis*, Kupferstichkabinett, Staatliche Museen zu Berlin. (CC BY-NC-SA 3.0 DE), 63.

Schuller, Tobias et al. (2017): *Bauaufnahme*. mediaTUM - Dokumenten- und Publikationsserver der Technischen Universität München. DOI:10.14459/2016MD1353273.

Schumacher, Fritz (1985): *Das Wesen des neuzeitlichen Backsteinbaues. Repr. d. Originalausg. München 1920.* München: Callwey.

Dimensions of Architectural Knowledge, 2022-03 ∂
https://doi.org/10.14361/dak-2022-0305

CATENA AND GLOSSES
Textualization through Spatial Writing and Materiality

Anna Odlinge

Abstract: Revisiting my research project from 19 years ago, which deals with notions of integrity in architectural creative processes, this article reflects upon the underlying techniques of forms of spatial writing, as part of my ongoing doctoral thesis work. I approach writing now as a process of ordering references and thoughts for inspection, in relation to the textile-like patterns that I created in the previous project and concluded with a licentiate thesis or halfway doctorate. To understand more about the differences between such textile writing versus the gathering of individual threads into the format of a book, I turn to, and use as my method, the medieval arts of memory, ars memoria, specifically with regard to books, textual systems such as catena and glosses, and illustrations, or bas-de-page. I use these formats as both an instruction for making and as a tool for a speculative evaluation of the result. In the center of this article is the question of how to create a book.

Keywords: Spatial Writing and Reading; Text; Book; Ars Memoria; Catena.

Text or book?

The licentiate thesis »Form in the margins« which I finished in 2003, circled around the idea of integrity, or rather variations of integrity, in creative processes, focusing on different forms of creative work but mainly on architecture. With integrity I identified, to name one example, uncompromised work ethics in regard to an exploration of space that attempted to break away from the limits of built architecture for instance, a direction I found in the work of the architect and artist Lebbeus Woods. Woods is known for his complex experimental and visionary drawings (Woods 1992). Just like Woods aimed to find non-established expressions of spatial configurations and non-hierarchical orders, I wanted to explore new ways of arranging texts

Corresponding author: Anna Odlinge (KTH School of Architecture in Stockholm, Sweden); odlinge@kth.se; http://orcid.org/0000-0003-4197-7291

and writing, to involve the reader in new, less hierarchical ways of reading and discovering written thoughts.

At that moment in time, I had three specific aims for the layout of my text. First, I invited the reader to explore my text through a *spatial representation* of my thinking processes. Second, I wanted every spread to offer a continuously developing composition of texts constructed from references gathered in my thesis as in a compilation. Third, I wanted the reader to stay engaged with the reading, in the sense of not falling into reading habits such as reading a text from the left to the right and from top to bottom. I wanted the reader to create their own text(s) and to co-create them together with me while drawing their own conclusions through a spatial form that enabled explorative reading.

To achieve this, I layered texts on top of each other, graphically, creating a spatial depth. My own and most up-to-date text was on top, and my sources and earlier thoughts were in the background, forming a knowledge base and making my own working process transparent. My main text was running on the left-hand page of each spread and on the right-hand side was placed a kind of textual image; a collage of text fragments displaying a reading made by me, hinting at only one possible conclusion. To guide the reader through the layers on the left-hand side, I used images of woven textile to inform the layout; one for each chapter.

The two discussants who were asked to do a reading of my work, one within the field of psychology with a special focus on creativity, and one within the field of architecture, had similar experiences encountering the text; they were lost and frustrated upon first contact with it. As they expressed it, they »knew how to read a dissertation« and »there I was, pulling the carpet away under their feet«. But they had agreed to examine my work so they individually explained how they had then given in and started reading, where they felt that they could enter my thesis. They expressed that finally, they had enjoyed their reading experiences following my journey.

A reviewer of my thesis wrote in a later article that she might indeed not have read the same text as the others did. She pointed out that everyone will create their own text and draw their own conclusions while reading my material. She also described my collection of texts as a book. At that time, I would have been inclined to agree with her, but now I think differently and describe it as a weave of texts that have not been combined or arranged in a way so as to form a book yet. However, in my current work, I am now speculating about the possibility of constructing a book based upon my previous material. With me I bring a few questions, such as: What is a book in contrast to a weave of text? When does text become a book? Could book writing be a method for reframing previous work? These questions will not necessarily be answered in this order in my doctoral thesis, but they are part of the textual explorations that I have begun undertaking.

Spatial Thinking, Reading and Writing in Religious Texts as Precursors

In *Vilém Flusser: An Introduction*, Anke K. Finger et al. give an account of Flusser's thoughts on *pilpul* (2011: 113). Flusser regards pilpul to be both a sophisticated and playful way of studying the Talmud. He likens it to »a dance around a given object, it attacks the object from different vantage points, recedes in different directions only to approach it again and come upon other reflections. This dynamic of reflection, by the way, figures concretely on the Talmud page: the object in the middle of the page, the reflections in converging circles«. This system or structure offers an example of a spatial configuration of text that asks for focus and spatial reading, something that I was aiming for in my own work.

For instance, I understood spatial reading as a challenge to linear reading, from the beginning to the end. For example, my compilation started at the end on page 120 and ran to page 0. In the back of my head, 18 years ago, I was speculating about making it possible to read the work in both directions but in two different ways. Back then, my aim seemed completely unattainable and more like a gimmick than something to be taken seriously. What was clear to me however, when picking up my work again recently, was the necessity to clarify a few things to myself and the reader.

Over the years I have gained an interest in the arts of memory – ars memoria – an interest that grew out of a will to understand more about our perceptions of, and interactions with, spaces. Through studying this technique, I learned more about the creation of texts and gained insight into why medieval illustrated works look the way they do. What fascinates me is the combination of text and images with the contemplation of spaces, architectures, and artifacts as an art of memory (Carruthers 2010: 205–206 and 2013: 2). I learned about the social reading and writing experiences of the time: Medieval texts reflect not only a conscious »handing on« (*traditio*) but also a »chain« (*concatenatio*) of shared and borrowed words and concepts. There was a conscious re-use of complete passages; plagiarism was a foreign concept (Anderson/Bellenger 2003: 2).

Lebbeus Woods produces enormous amounts of drawings for this project with numerous studies of details that would be able to function within these special circumstances, under these particular conditions.

Not only did he make several drawings but also many models and even models[2] scale 1:1 that were shown at the exhibition in the enormous hall of the Pavillion d'Arsenal in Paris.

...this structure was mounted by mountain climbers!

These two projects are part of a series of projects that are referred to as *Terra Nova – the New World*. In this set of projects Woods uses different strategies in different cities and on different sites around the world, and he finally also returns to Berlin after the Wall has collapsed.

Like in the Paris project, fragments arrive in the air above the city of Berlin.

They are *meaningless* – that is, they carry no meaning. Built of very thin and light folded metal sheets they float around without obvious relations to each other.

Materialist Experiments and Experiences...

These structures ingratiate themselves into the existing built structures of Berlin. As they are built of folded metal they are in need of no other structural support, but function like shells to void spaces. They are partly constituted by undefined geometries. Lebbeus Woods calls them *free-spaces*.

The freedom they provide and *intermediate* rises from their characteristics; the characteristics of being very special, very precise and unique in their spatiality, in their form and their tactility. These spaces or structures are not comfortable in themselves but have to be *claimed* by any individual who wants to use them. These individuals have to be inventive to make them habitable.

...For Piranesi and Woods, standing at the beginning and the end of the era of architecture as a profession, the methods of controlling reality through reason are deeply suspect. Rather it is their incompletion, internal contradictions and doomed nature that is rich with possibility, because it presents us with an architecture which we will have to fix, mend, unearth, build, or otherwise participate in.

The result of this romance of the ruin is, as Woods himself has pointed out, a sense of the un-heimlich; that which is strangely familiar, that attracts one because it is made up of the most essential quotidian reality, and then disturbs what one thought was safe haven from the vicissitudes of an unknown world out there. ...

(Betsky, Aaron, 1991, Lebbeus Woods: Materialist Experiments and Experiences, Criticism, p.9, zru, 1991 09, Lebbeus Woods)

All of Lebbeus Woods' projects – in fact his architecture as a whole – has liberated itself from everything that we traditionally regard as architecture.

That is of course not an easy task. He cannot rely on pre-established orders, such as hierarchy, syntax or understandable scale, nor can he use the arguments of functionality or site distinction in any traditional sense. As we see in the Paris project he even distances himself from the need of gravity end of static relationships. What is left is *'nothing else but space'*[4] as Aaron Betsky phrases it.

(Aimsley, Aaron, 1991, Lebbeus Woods, Criticism, p.10, zru, 1991/09, Lebbeus Woods)

The purpose of this, of course, is to come back from the experiment and be able to establish new rules in the reality as we know it; to come back and see the difference between habit and possibility. This architecture establishes a ground for the creation of new confederations of individuals.

These confederations, however, are not static; they are temporary and they will change their configurations continuously. This architecture secures that no static hierarchical structures can exist and it secures that a new world will always be built – again, again and again.

Experimental architecture is a comprehensive, if transitory, form of knowledge, a universal yet personal instrument of experience, a vital tool of human change that changes only itself.

(Woods, Lebbeus, 1991, Terra Nova, p.21, zru, 1991 09, Lebbeus Woods)

1940 born	in Michigan
Studies	at the University of Engineering
	University of Illinois School of Architecture
Featured	in Publications
	at Exhibitions
	through Lectures
	with Work Shops
1988	establishes RIEA with Olive Braun
	Visiting Professor at Cooper Union, New York

He has been teaching Studios and Work Shops and been lecturing all over the world for the last thirty years.

1.

Graphics: Anna Odlinge, 2003.

A further inspiration came from the writing of comments into the margins or between the lines, *catena* and *glosses* in religious texts, which were constantly expanded through adding on passages, a common practice by medieval scholars. Catena denotes authoritative commentary, repeating original sources and older commentaries, meant as an aid to read and interpret the main text (Carruthers 2008: 240). In my earlier licentiate thesis, the texts printed in blue and red are an aid to both orient oneself in the often-dense texts with comments in both the margins and between lines. These two ways of organizing a textual space help a reader *recollect* a larger context when reading a specific selection of thoughts and suggestions, and at the same time offer reading help with the aid of comments or catena.

Material Textualities

In *The Book of Memory* (2008 [1990]: 14), the literature scholar Mary Carruthers writes:

> »The Latin word textus comes from the verb meaning ›o weave‹ and it is in the institutionalizing of a story through memoria that textualizing occurs. Literary works become institutions as they weave a community together by providing it with shared experience and a certain kind of language, the language of stories that can be experienced over and over again through time and as occasion suggests. Their meaning is thought to be implicit, hidden, polysemous, and complex, requiring continuing interpretations and adaptation. In the process of textualizing, the original work acquires commentary and gloss; this activity is not regarded as something other than the text, but is the mark of textualization itself.«

She explains that it is both the gathering of comments that creates the institution, but also the way the material is displayed on a page. The actual authority is formed when the pages carry carefully laid out fragments and reading is made joyful and thorough; that is when the pages have become a book (Carruthers 2008: 14, 323; 2010: 201–203).

It was etymology that helped me see the relationship between text and textile, as is explained above. Fiber crafts of various kinds were an important part of my childhood, so it may not be surprising that textile construction techniques and principles and the metaphor of textile remain present in my spatial explorations.

In medieval times and according to the analysis and theories of Mary Carruthers in respect to works created during that historical period and her studies of the importance and art of memory for medieval culture(s), there is a significant difference between texts and a book.

A book can be seen as an institution and an authority. So, she, too, adheres to the idea of the integrity of a book, as mentioned above. The rebel in me likes that idea. I like it because it allows me to form my own institution with this creation of mine.

The catena in this case is my voice, my word my creation of a possible world. Obviously, there were words spoken before I speak though and so my creation does not come from nothing or pure vibration but from my own reverb.

My voice should rather be compared to a solo in a quire of voices. I believe that this makes this particular catena stronger. It may be compared to chain that is interlaced with other chains. At moments in time, it may even turn into a mail, to then transform back into a fine and thin trace, or possibly a textatile.

This remains to be seen. I will have to re-trace this and the following sections many times over, over the next couple of years. So, dear reader, if you are reading at this specific moment in time (summer of 2021 - spring of 2022), be aware that the landscape you are going to stroll through is an everchanging one. It is new even to me as I have not been here for a very long time.

I will re-start here because this is where I describe the work and creative processes of Lebbeus Woods, which are crucial to my continued work, but also because it is the last chapter of my licentiate thesis that holds the specific definition of integrity that I am underlining above.

If I want to create a book instead of a compilation of texts, this is where I begin. And at the beginning there was the possibility globalization   mondialization

I prefer the later.

Experiments are made. This is our phenomenologist's entire vocation and commentary has infinite possibilities open to it.

But what do innumerable artists do? They are careful not to make pronouncements on the matter. Instead they essay, and so through them we glimpse the importance that must be given to the Essay. Being or beings do not reveal themselves; they present tiny universes with each work. They cram and make micrologies that babble, huff and puff, and are envious of one another. And these essays together constitute satire.

What do we want of art today? Well, for it to experiment. To stop being only modern. By saying this, we're experimenting.

And what do we want of philosophy? For it to analyze their experimentations by means of reflexity.

4

The woman draped in red fabric just enters the room, picks a glass with a drink from the counter next to the entrance and approaches the Japanese man and the guy who watched the basket-ball game, both glasses in their hands – Zaha Hadid, Toyo Ito and Lebbeus Woods. The older man seems to be lingering in the sky still but is also watching the crowd from his seat in the front row – Jean-François Lyotard – he is waiting for the show to start. Frank Lloyd Wright will announce the film and Ayn Rand will lead the following discussion, even though they may not appear in person. What will they say to each other? What will the crowd talk about?

The tube ends next to the outdoor theater where a large screen can be mounted later at night when it is dark enough. While wondering what films are on and what will be shown in the theater, you decide to join them and walk along the wall of the center towards the entrance. The sign reads The Right Stuff, The Good, the Bad and the Ugly and a Surprise Documentary for tonight, only revealing its connection to the other movies but not its exact theme. Sounds of laughter and the murmur of the crowd below meet you upon entering the auditorium high up in the hall, close to the ceiling. - The lightscape in front of you changes and everybody settles down. You are just about to pick a seat next to the people you have met earlier and are curious to what will be discussed later when a hologram enters and walks across the stage ...

But 'WAIT! NO! This does not work! This is not an appropriate space. – I will have to draw a new one!

2.
Graphics: Anna Odlinge, 2021.

For me, the idea of the »line« and the word itself are related to linen threads and the straight lines that occur when one of them is pulled out of a woven fabric. Linen was typically dyed with pigments giving it various blue-colored hues around the world. I was taught to use a fine blue line on the back of pencil architecture drawings as an aid to construct the drawing precisely and a similar blue line can now be found in software for making computer-aided design (CAD) drawings. The blue line is almost ephemeral. My red thread is much more woolly, unruly, and physical. It may be a mix of 90 percent mohair and 10 percent acrylic, but both the precise line and the sprawling thread are equally important to the construction of the text.

In this article, I have tried to perform the retracing of my steps that featured in my earlier work. Initially, I chose a part of my woven textual space and unraveled it. In doing so, I discovered a blue line and a red thread, but I also understood that my action was destroying an essential part of my work. Instead, I now use my line and my thread to start the construction of a book. At this stage, I reread and expanded on my previous material through the spatial writing techniques of ars memoria, paying specific attention to catena or glosses, the reflective comments in the margin, and the bas-de-page, deviations from a strict chain of thought to relax the mind. These are, according to Carruthers, crucial for creating the authority and institution of the book. So far, this reflection on spatial and material text work has helped me to understand my previous explorations within my research and to recollect my thoughts to support the taking-up and reframing of my research project. The working title »Form in the Margins« is beginning to make sense, not least as a spatial writing and reading device. I would like to know, starting the process with this article, how the text format influences the acts of reading, the acts of writing, and the art of recollection. Hopefully, in the long run, that knowledge will also help me understand something more about what occurs in the margins of our creative processes when we make (write, read, and recollect) architectures – »Forms in the Margin«.

References

Anderson, Roberta/Bellenger, Dominic, eds. (2003): »Introduction«, in: *Medieval Worlds: A Sourcebook*, London: Routledge, 2 –27. https://doi.org/10.4324/9781315012803

Carruthers, Mary (2008) [1990]: *The Book of Memory: A Study of Memory in Medieval Literature*, Cambridge: Cambridge University Press https://doi.org/10.1017/CBO9781107051126

Carruthers, Mary (2010): »The Concept of Ductus, or Journeying through a Work of Art«, in: *Rhetoric beyond Words: Delight and Persuasion in the Arts of the Middle Age*, Cambridge: Cambridge University Press, 190 –213.

Carruthers, Mary (2013): »Sensory Complexion and Style«, in: *The Experience of Beauty in the Middle Ages*, Oxford: Oxford University Press. DOI: 10.1093/acprof:osobl/9780199590322.001.0001

Finger, Anke/Guldin, Rainer/Bernardo, Gustavo (2011): Vilém Flusser: *An Introduction*, Minneapolis: Minnesota University Press. https://www.jstor.org/stable/10.5749/j.ctttont

Woods, Lebbeus (1992): *Anarchitecture: Architecture is a Political Act*, New York: Academy Press.

Dimensions of Architectural Knowledge, 2022-03 ᵋ
https://doi.org/10.14361/dak-2022-0306

COLLECTIVE WORKSHOP
Transformational Encounters in the Trakia Economic Zone

Ina Valkanova

Abstract: The following article is a reflection on an action research project with stakeholders of a special economic zone in Plovdiv, Bulgaria. The article describes the process of engagement from the perspective of the workers and the managers of three international factories, with the aim to discover moments and entry points, for the positive social and spatial transformation of a global industrial space.

Keywords: Global Industry; Labor; Practice; Workshop; Urban Transformation.

On building an Active Engagement

I study contemporary global production in the specific case of a post-communist setting – Trakia Economic Zone (TEZ), in Plovdiv, Bulgaria. My initial interest in researching the global dynamics of production was triggered by my first encounter with TEZ in 2016. Trained as an architect, I struggled to make sense of the spatial reality of the zone. It seemed that the large factories, in the form of big boxes scattered around the periphery of Plovdiv, landed in the landscape almost accidentally. Observing the foreign trucks going in and out of the factories, I sensed that the project was a clear articulation of transnational exchange and the distribution of products and people. While TEZ is locally disembedded, it is globally connected.

In my work, I am interested in revealing how the dynamic of global production affects real places and people, and what the possible entry points are to transform those spaces from extractive projects into places with an added social and ecological value to the local community. Since I am interested in urban and social transformation, I naturally adopted a research trajectory focused on introducing change-action research. Action research can hereby be described as »a practice-changing practice« (Kemmis et al.

Corresponding author: Ina Valkanova (ETH Zurich, Switzerland); valkanova@arch.ethz.ch; http://orcid.org/0000-0001-5335-2657.

1.
Visit from the municipality to Kuklen Industrial Park. Photographer: Ina Valkanova.

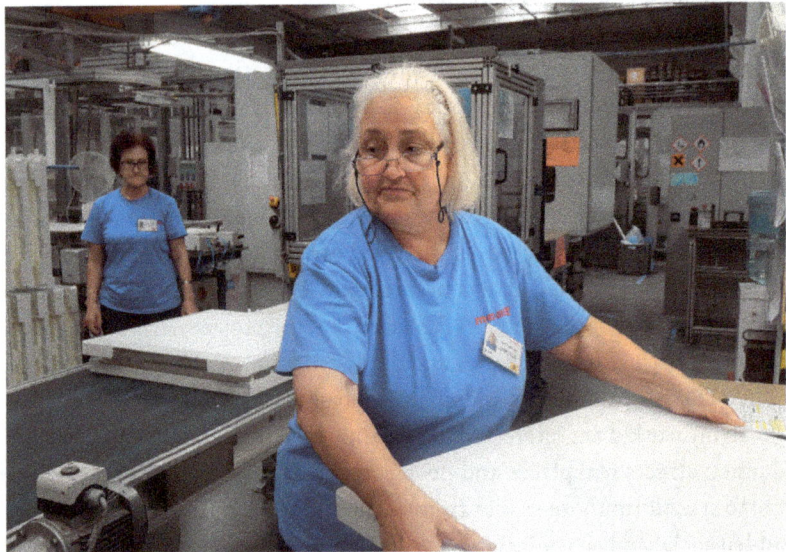

2.
Assembly line workers at Kuklen Industrial Park. Photographer: Ina Valkanova.

2014: 2). Action research is always linked to an existing practice, since it »primarily arises, as people try to work together to address key problems in their communities or organizations« (Reason/ Bradbury 2008: 1). In the case of TEZ I selected the following practices to engage with: International automobile companies in Kuklen Industrial Park, TEZ real-estate management, factory workers, and the local municipality of Kuklen. The selection of actor groups includes the most relevant actors and users of TEZ and is based on the level of influence over the transformation of TEZ, and on their distinct positions and (dis)connections. With the exception of TEZ management, which works closely with most of the actors, the other groups operate in their own distinct areas and rarely interact. The worker's group, for example, although crucial for the future of TEZ, is never included in decision-making processes and is therefore extremely disconnected from the spatial production of TEZ.

My research is a collaborative process that draws on collective knowledge and moves toward a collective goal and practical outcomes for the industrial zone. Such an approach comes with its own set of challenges. First, the research is conducted with various groups with different ambitions and positions. It requires a long-term commitment from each group and the building of trust among participants. Second, my role as a participant in this collective process requires a constant reflection on my own situatedness and agency (Kemmis et. al 2014: 1). Rejecting the subjective view of the researcher as a silent outsider from the beginning, I embraced my own »partial perspective«, (Haraway 1988) by recognizing my own motivation to engage with the process. From my initial observation of the zone, it became clear that the development followed a global set of codes and prescriptions, resulting in a universal architecture of the black box. What I want to find out is whether it is possible to bring in new narratives, such as ecology, landscape, local capacity and care. Therefore, I attempted to create a different configuration between practices where curiosity and experimentation can flourish, and create a space for reflection on the current societal conditions of TEZ.

To understand how to transform the practice of TEZ, I first needed to know how the different actors operate in their everyday conditions. Therefore, I embedded myself within their organizational structure, which naturally led me to adopt various roles. For example, to understand the daily life of a factory worker, I conducted training as an assembly-line factory employee. To understand the dynamics of the local municipality, I worked as an advisor on the region's strategic plan. This role-play process allowed me to

3.
Factory for automobile lights in Kuklen Industrial Park. Photographer: Ina Valkanova.

4. – 5.

Workshop with factory managers. Photographer: Ina Valkanova.

gather knowledge about each actor's mode of operation. Based on this experience, I had a base on which I could challenge the common perceptions of the actors about their own position and agency, and find productive tensions in the system of TEZ.

I chose the joint workshop as a format where the actor groups could collectively rethink their own practice, conditions, and relations. In the article, I will present my reflections on two workshops – with the managers of three international companies and the workers of the same factories. It is important to note that their workshops are not isolated encounters but are formats of continuous reflections that are repeated and enriched throughout the research process.

Encounter 1 – Managers of International Automobile Supply Companies

TEZ is composed of three industrial parks – Maritza, Stryama, and Kuklen, all located on the periphery of Plovdiv. I focus on the park of Kuklen because, in my initial studies, the companies there showed the most interest in the process I aimed to start. The reason for their initiative is that they are part of the newest and smallest park and are still developing their strategy and position within the industrial landscape of Plovdiv. Since my project is goal-oriented and focused on improving the socio-spatial environment of TEZ, they saw the benefits of becoming part of it. The companies were highly interested in the insights on the desires of their employees. Bulgaria's shrinking demographic makes it extremely difficult to find and keep quality workers; therefore, any insight into the labor dynamic and workers' needs and wishes is highly valued by the management. While the managers face the same problems related to lack of roads, technical support, and labor force, they usually deal with them individually. Therefore, they saw my research process as an opportunity to engage and act as a group instead of individual firms. I took these entry points to quickly constitute a collective of four automobile factories, and started working to incorporate myself into their operation.

Within this process, I adopted the role of a consultant to find out how I can improve the general spatial and social environment of industrial park Kuklen. I spent about a week working in the administrative sector of each factory. Finally, I gathered the plant managers in a workshop, where they collectively described and reflected on their problem situation. As with any collaborative effort, this workshop exercise didn't go exactly as planned. One plant manager did not show up and did not respond to my calls; another one also brought his human resources (HR) team, and the third one brought the director of a new factory in the zone, which I was not aware of. These situations and behaviors ultimately led to an inevitable loss of control over the process and revealed the everyday dynamic of the companies. My idea for the workshop was to use my own understanding of the plant managers situation as a basis on which we would include their perspectives and comments. This collaborative effort meant we had to draw on a whiteboard together. This did not happen, as one manager refused to draw, saying how »we will only sit and talk«. The others mimicked his attitude and the whole idea of a collaborative setting turned into a dialogue, which I was schematizing on the board. Even though most of the participants hadn't met before, interestingly, they behaved as a tight collective and acted in support of each other, which clearly showed that they understand themselves as part of the same system and social environment. The exercise consisted of an open dialogue about their most pressing problems, without any pre-given format and structure. All of the participants agreed that the quality of education and the lack of infrastructure are the biggest challenges they face, and painted a rich picture of the fragmentation of systems, activities, and responsibilities.

During the whole process the participants showed a certain attitude of »being in control« and not »taking directions«, but instead giving them. In the same way, this exercise also demonstrated the very decisive nature of the managers in the clear way that they expressed their desired changes for the future, such as the strict monitoring of law implementation, better coordination with educational facilities, and a higher quality of urban and landscape design. But while those managers demonstrated a certain degree of dominance and privilege, they also displayed elements of powerlessness that are being associated with the working class. This tension is primarily a result of the global organization of production. The factories that they operate are all part of a worldwide network and are subordinate to a global western headquarters, which means that the local managers barely influence global decisions. Often, they cannot implement their desired meaningful changes in their operation. Each headquarters has a global marketing strategy and strict rules on material use, space design, and processes that need to be implemented locally.

Additionally, automobile brands use general standards such as International Automotive Task Force IATF, Verband der Automobilindustrie VDA and ASSET, which prescribe operation, spatial, and security rules.[1] Each participant was painfully aware of this precarious position – being in power locally, while being powerless in a global system. This position results in a contradictory worldview which combines the perception of privilege and power with the perception of subordination under a labor system, which is similar to the perception that is often assumed of the workers.

What I was mainly trying to understand with this initial workshop was the personal motivation of the factory managers to participate in the process, and what problems they saw as the most urgent.

As I previously stated, the fight for a qualified labor force was one of the main reasons for the willingness of the managers to create a better working space. Since the managers are also part of the community, they work and live in the region, and there was a genuine interest in improving the space, ecologically, socially, and spatially. Another crucial aspect was the requirements of the global companies' headquarters for green and sustainable local politics. Yet, while the global headquarters demand responsible local actions, they do not provide any knowledge or support to the local industrial plants. The three companies saw the process as a way to experiment with green and socially responsible initiatives. While the willingness for action is there, it is important to note that it remains to be seen to what extent this promise will materialize, or when an action is actually budgeted for and implemented.

Encounter 2 - Factory Workers

The second series of workshops I performed were with the employees of two of the automobile factories I engaged in my research. Initially, while approaching the subject of TEZ, I only had contact with the dominant figures of the zone – plant managers, developers, and mayors, etc. But, due to the nature of the research, it was crucial to include multiple perspectives – and the workers' point of view was one of the most important. I was determined to give them a voice because I assumed they did not have one. Pre-conditioned to think that factories are spaces of mysteries and secrets and that penetrating the closed doors will be difficult, I expected to struggle to gain access to the workers. However, this was not the case. Most factory manag-

---

1   IATF, VDA, and ASSET are the three quality management systems for organizations in the automotive industry. They are used by automotive firms to audit current and potential suppliers.

6. – 7.
Stills from video interviews of factory workers in Kuklen Industrial Park.
Video and stills: Ina Valkanova.

ers were very interested in my research project and provided me with un-
limited access to information, spaces, and people. I quickly realized the
workers (as a group) were a potent fragment and driver of the zone due to
the demographic dynamic of Bulgaria – the country is the fastest-shrinking
nation worldwide (Vollset et al. 2020). This labor dynamic is the reason, I
believe, for the strong commitment of the power players to my research
project and my ability to access the usually closed doors of the factory space.
Each company is trying to attract and keep workers by providing better
working conditions and negotiating with headquarters for higher salaries
while listening to the workers' everyday needs.

However, the workers did not perceive themselves as a dominant influential force. This perception was clearly visible in the way that workers stated
their needs and desired changes. In the interviews I conducted, most of the
factory employees were generally content with their working conditions.
They greatly appreciated a regular salary paid on time, clean spaces such as
bathrooms, and overtime pay for working extra hours. These things should
be considered a standard in a European context and not services with added
value. Although these things should be considered a standard in a European
context and not services with added value, contemporary industrial space is
still understood as a space for the bare minimum that does not need to contribute to the local community and environment. These perceptions are
rooted in Bulgarian industrial history where, under the communist regime,
factories were associated with pollution, dirty spaces, and challenging labor
conditions. The chaotic transition to democracy gave rise to many unregu-
lated informal and corrupted practices, which resulted in insecure payment
and problematic situations.

These accounts from my workshop relate, in a surprising way, to the question Mario Tronti asks in his work on the Fiat Factory in Rome: »What happens when the workers themselves refuse to present demands to capital, in
other words, when they refuse the entire trade-union level, refuse the con-
tractual form of relation to capital?« (Tronti/ Anastasi, 2020: 211). He argues
that the high point of revolutionary struggle in a classically capitalist country
will emerge precisely when the capitalist side proposes improvements and not
the other way around. Surprisingly, this argument means that dismantling
an organizational structure, such as a labor union, actually gives more power
to the workers. This is precisely what is happening in Kuklen, not however, as
a conscious revolutionary act but rather as a result of a failed transition to
democracy. On one side the workers lost faith in the agency of the labor union,

8. – 9.
Outdoor setting of the workshop with factory workers.
Photographer: Ina Valkanova.

due to the corrupted union practices of the 1990s, and on the other side, workers in post-communist countries are not dependent on a work contract, since there are always open positions in many factories in the region. Workers can easily switch to another factory in Plovdiv, or even in Western Europe, since Bulgaria is part of the EU and thus can take advantage of the free labor movement. Therefore, even without the agency of the labor union, workers are treated with care, as a highly valuable resource.

Starting from this understanding of tensions, I conducted a series of workshops with factory workers with a similar initial format to that described in the encounter with the plant managers above – to reflect upon their situation, problems, and desires. The results and environment of the workshops changed as the work progressed. In the first workshop, it became clear that the workers behaved from a position of weakness, doubting the possibility of change or that anyone would finance meaningful interventions. This did not mean that they are actually weak; it only means that they perceived themselves as powerless. Instead of starting from my own understanding of the situation, as in the workshop with the factory managers, I asked them to draw a scheme of their everyday work situation, the places they enjoy most, and the activities they would like to improve. It was the first time that the workers met someone from another factory. There was a clear division between the two groups from the beginning of the workshop, with a strong identification with, and a sense of belonging to, their respective corporations. Each group showed a strong curiosity about the conditions and the working methods of the other, whereby both groups strongly defended their respective companies' policies. Unlike the companies' managers, the workers took my direction to draw and schematize on the whiteboard, even though it was obvious they were not comfortable with this setting. It became evident that, unlike the companies' managers, the workers are used to taking directions and engaging in activities outside of their comfort zone.

I noticed that the participants were not comfortable in the space where we conducted the workshop. It was a corporate room, designed for training and did not provide inviting conditions for creativity and openness. For the second series of workshops, I changed the setting and prepared a breakfast outside in the workers' break space. The fact that we were positioned in an area that the workers related to rest and peace contributed to an informal and vibrant discussion. The initial division between factories was gone and the workers openly shared their struggle with being under pressure to perform and comply with quality standards.

Interestingly, they expressed similar problems, such as the lack of good ventilation, a low quality of machines, and lack of green spaces. Also, in the outdoor breakfast setting, they became creative and radical ideas came to light, such as including animals in the landscapes, creating leisure facilities, dance lessons, and mental health spaces. Interestingly, they made themselves responsible for most of the activities they designed, such as organizing a shared library and planting trees together. While it was initially more challenging to provoke the workers group than the group of managers, the workers engaged in a much more creative process once they opened up.

Crafting the Space for Transformation

The knowledge gathered through this process of engagement reveals on one side, the practical problems of a post-communist industrial development, and on the other, certain relations and behavioral patterns that inform the actions of both groups. This question of what motivates action is the primary concern of Pierre Bourdieu's work (Hillier/Rooksby 2005: 2). In response, he coined the term »habitus« – individual and collective predispositions shaped by past events and structures that shape current practices and systems and, that importantly, condition our very perceptions of them (Bourdieu 2019).

He recognizes social relations among actors as being structured by, and in turn contributing to the structuring of, the social relations of power among different positions. I use the term habitus as defined by Jean Hillier and Emma Rooksby – habitus as social space: as a sense of one's place and a sense of the other's place. They argue that social space is translated in physical space and that a certain world-view may change when physical surroundings are transformed (Hillier/Rooksby 2005: 399).

The presented encounters revealed the participants' specific societal predispositions. When I brought up the results of the worker's workshops to one of the managers, he said that it seemed that he should plant a forest around the factory, but that factories don't plant trees in green spaces. To my question of who determines that industry doesn't create nature, he replied – »we just don't«. Bourdieu's term habitus can be seen as much as an agent of continuity and tradition as it can be regarded as a force of change. To trigger meaningful transformation it is not enough to present specific problem solutions. We need to create a setting where not only physical transformation is possible but where mental change can also occur, and perceptions can be deconstructed to instigate change. In the case of TEZ, this would mean configuring encounters that can deconstruct the perception of what modern production should and can do. As illustrated, sometimes a simple change of spatial environment, such as moving a workshop to an outside, natural environment, can create room for openness and change the perceptions and desires of the actors. The format of a workshop has been a handy tool for creating such a space for dialogue. However, such formats can only be valuable for transformation processes if they are repeated with the same actors, enriched, and adapted as a performance test ground.

References

Bourdieu, Pierre »Structure, Habitus, Practices«. In: James Faubion/Paul Rabinow (eds.), *Rethinking the Subject: An Anthology of Contemporary European Social Thought*, 2019.

Haraway, Donna (1988): »Situated Knowledges: The Science Question in Feminism and the Privilege of Partial Perspective«, in: *Feminist Studies* 14/3, 575–599.

Hillier, Jean/Rooksby, Emma, eds. (2005): *Habitus: A Sense of Place* (2nd ed), Farnham: Ashgate.

Kemmis, Stephen/McTaggart, Robin/ Nixon, Rhonda (2014): *The Action Research Planner*, Singapore: Springer.

Reason,Peter/Bradbury, Hilary (2008) eds. *The Sage Handbook of Action Research: Participative Inquiry and Practice* (2nd ed), London: SAGE Publications.

Tronti, Mario/Anastasi, Andrew (2020): *The Weapon of Organization: Mario Tronti's Revolution in Marxism*, 1959–1967, New York: Common Notions.

Vollset, Stein Emil, et al. (2020) » Fertility, Mortality, Migration, and Population Scenarios for 195 Countries and Territories from 2017 to 2100: A Forecasting Analysis for the Global Burden of Disease Study«, in: *Lancet* 396.

Dimensions of Architectural Knowledge, 2022-03 ᛃ
https://doi.org/10.14361/dak-2022-0307

DIARY
Coping with Discomfort – Use Patterns in a Syrian Home

Walaa Hajali

Abstract: As a result of the Syrian conflict which started in 2011, middle and low-income groups in Syria have been facing difficulties in accessing energy, and left unable to cover their domestic energy expenses. How do these households respond to the low levels of comfort in their homes? In this in-situ study, I seek to investigate the intertwining discourses between domestic space, occupant behavior, and climate. Looking for evidence, I used the diary as a method to investigate the phenomenological experience of inhabiting a building. By collecting the diaries of family members in one flat in a typical domestic block in Damascus, I tell a collective story of the building through the residents. By selecting the stories of three rooms in the flat where the inhabitants felt uncomfortable in summer and winter, I present critical moments of discomfort in a visual essay. This research raises questions about the efficiency of the current model of affordable housing in Syria.

Keywords: Diary; Domestic Comfort; Syrian Housing Model; Practice-based Research; Visual Narrative.

Introduction: The Syrian Context

The enduring situation of power and fuel shortages over the past ten years in Syria has been one of the consequences of the dramatic destruction of the country's infrastructure due to the Syrian conflict, which started in 2011. Chronic electricity cuts have become part of the daily Syrian conversation about inconvenience and discomfort. Moreover, fuel shortages in the four-month heating season in Syria have become a pressing problem. As a result, both low-income and middle-income groups in Syria often have to overlook their level of domestic comfort. Aside from energy services, it can also be argued that the quality of modern housing design in Syria is lacking (Goulden 2011). By looking at the housing supply in Syria, there are three

Corresponding author: Walaa Hajali (Manchester School of Architecture, UK); walaa.haj-ali@stu.mmu.ac.uk; https://orcid.org/0000-0003-1276-3294

main types of housing: public, co-operative, and private housing. Both public and co-operative housing falls under the Syrian definition of social housing, which refers to subsidized housing that is totally or partially supported by public housing institutions for low-income and middle-income groups (Ministry of Housing 2010). Several social housing programs have been set to be implemented in successive five-year development plans (Ministry of Housing 2010). Different social housing schemes cover the two main categories of housing supply. First, public housing built by the General Establishment of Housing, which has several programs to provide subsidized housing projects. These housing units are delivered partially or fully by the construction companies of the General Establishment for Housing.[1] Second, housing built by housing associations, which are private, non-profit organizations that provide low-cost new housing for sale. Overall, social housing accounts for 35 percent of the overall housing production in Syria, while the private and commercial sector provides 65 percent of the housing mass in the country (Ministry of Housing 2010).

Despite the policies and programs made by the public sector to meet the housing needs, the practical operation of these programs has been insufficient. The main obstacle is related to the quality of the housing. The social housing units had minimal design standards and lower quality compared to the private housing (Kassouha 2020), which negatively affected its operational performance. Talking about performance, it should be mentioned that although some energy-efficient building measures (building insulation, solar heating) are considered in the Syrian code for construction and required for getting building permits (Ministry of Local Government, 2008), not all of these measures are implemented in reality. Nearly all social housing in Syria suffers from poor thermal performance. Moreover, according to the researcher Reem Ismail (2015), the current »formal« housing design process (i.e., designed by architects) consequently fails to reflect changes in the cultural and social life of the residents.

As a result, the current Syrian housing model fails to meet the standards of adequate housing supply and so, many questions need to be raised regarding its impact on the occupants. How do residents respond to the spatial dimension of their everyday domestic practices? And how do they respond to the poor levels of comfort in their homes? But first, what is domestic com-

---

1 The General Establishment for Housing was created by the government in 1982 to provide affordable housing for low- and middle-income groups in the Syrian cities.

fort? While occupant comfort demonstrates one of the essential conditions of providing livable indoor environments (Nikkhah 2021), the definition of comfort is usually associated with the physical aspects of thermal and visual comfort, which includes the environmental conditions (air temperature, radiant temperature, air velocity, humidity) and the building properties (Burris et al. 2012). However, domestic comfort seems to have a much wider scope than these thermally based parameters. The occupant's subjective parameters can be a contributing factor to varying states of comfort among occupants in general, including social and psychological factors (Kimpian et al. 2021). But what happens when we turn from comfort to its apparent opposite? Discomfort is usually associated with the concept of the building energy performance gap, which can be defined as the difference between anticipated (designed) and actual performance. This concept suggests that buildings do not perform as they were designed to do and can turn the building into an uncomfortable space. Therefore, people try to shape and influence the space that they live in, looking for comfort (Wilde 2014).

However, by reflecting on the Syrian social housing context, the household's thermal discomfort is related to not only the performance gap, but also to the socio-economic problems, as the ongoing conflict has exacted a heavy burden on the Syrian household. Energy deprivation in Syrian homes has been a significant systemic problem that can be measured in expenditure on domestic energy. While the typical expenditure threshold of measuring fuel poverty is 10 percent of the household income (Boardman 2012), households in Syria need to spend more than 42.5 percent of their average income to maintain an adequate level of warmth and provide energy for cooking (Haddad 2019).[2] More challenges have also arisen since the Syrian conflict started. As a result of these complex political and social issues, the thermal comfort of occupants is completely overlooked and it has become a luxury to talk about the comfort of residents in Syria.

Therefore, in this practice-based research, I seek to explore how a middle-income family in Syria interacts with their residential space in terms of comfort-related behaviors. My desire to examine the occupant's response to discomfort has led me to situate myself as an »Inquisitive Observer« (Bestor 2003) as a first attempt to analyze a one-family flat in a four-story domestic

---

2 Not only the lack of oil and natural gas supply, but also the damage to the domestic electricity infrastructure is very challenging. The daily electricity blackouts have become normal for the Syrian household.

block in Damascus and reflect on its environmental performance after I visited it in August 2020. This study has selected a typical case study dwelling in Syria, which allows to investigate the thermal comfort in more detail and provide insights for further research. The second step in this research was to use the diary research method since it offered a space for discourse and explorative research (Alexander 2015; Livholts 2017). I involved the residents of the flat in my research. As participants, they were asked to record their comfort-related activities in two typical days during the summer and in winter. While the individual diary typically allows one voice to be heard in a story, this research seeks to investigate the (inter)relationship between the various home spaces and several voices of the family members. Therefore, I collected and combined the written material from the diaries of the different family members and represented them in the form of a multi-layered visual narrative. Through this visual narrative, I aim to tell a collective story of the building, not only from the perspective of the researcher as narrator, but also from that of the residents as living characters and co-authors. Finally, I conclude the article with a discussion about the future of the Syrian housing design model in the light of the current debate on reconstruction in response to social and environmental needs.

Designing for (Dis)comfort: A View of an Inquisitive Observer

At a time when »buying an apartment« has become a struggle for many middle- and low-income Syrians in Damascus, the »Youth Housing Project« was one of the most promising cooperative housing programs, which targeted young families (over 18–under 35) to help them secure a home (Khaddour 2021). Yet, what about the quality of these homes? Whereas this program was built by the Public Establishment for Housing in collaboration with housing associations, both the lack of transparency in housing standards and the bureaucratic management of the construction process have led to poor quality houses (Kassouha 2020). The uninsulated walls, poor sanitation, inappropriate orientation, and ventilation have been some negative examples of the poor housing conditions of the Youth Housing Project. »It is cold/hot here«: This sentence probably does not sound surprising to Syrians who experience discomfort in dwellings on a daily basis. Whereas this discomfort is a result of the lack of access to energy services, the occupant also plays an essential role in adapting to this (dis)comfort. The work of C. G. Webb (1964) explains that people are not passive regarding their thermal environment, but ac-

1.

The western facade of the case-study dwelling. Photographer: Walaa Hajali, 2020.

1. Master Bedroom
2. Kitchen
2*. Balcony
3. Girls' Bedroom
3*. Balcony
4. Living Room
5. Boy's Bedroom
5*. Balcony

2.

The sectional perspective shows the case-study flat. Drawing: Walaa Hajali.

tively control it to secure comfort. Human behavior shapes and influences the space we live in. However, discomfort can significantly affect human behavior in the domestic space.

The behavior of discomfort was explored by the researchers Judith Heerwagen, a psychologist of the impacts of building design and operation, and Richard C. Diamond's study (1992) which can be divided into three general types. First, behavior aimed at changing the environment in some way (environmental coping such as opening or closing windows, the use of localized devices including fans or heaters, or spatial arrangements, such as furniture adjustments). Second, changes in one's own behavior (behavioral coping such as changing clothes or moving to another room). And finally, the attempts to adjust to a situation by managing emotions or thoughts about it (emotional/psychological coping such as ignoring the problem) when no environmental manipulations are possible, or the »cost« of appropriate action is too high, which applies to the concept of fuel poverty.

Block 4 in Dahiyat Qudsaya, Damascus is one of these cooperatively built residential blocks built as part of the »Youth Housing Project«, which was launched by the Institute for Public Housing in 2002 (Khaddour 2021). Although the layout of the flats is standardized in the building, the residents have adapted their flats differently. The building facade shows different adaptations of the same balcony design (fig. 1). Some residents opted for closing the balcony and adding it to the interior space, while some added several components such as canopies or extra balustrades in order to have a more comfortable environment, which is applicable to the first type of coping behaviors, »environmental coping«, based on the work of Heerwagen and Diamond (1992).

Inspired by the anthropologist Theodore B. Bestor's study (2003), which stated that »participant observation« can be too vague a term to describe »what actually takes place in ethnographic research«, while »inquisitive observation« can count as an ethnographic technique through which opportunities for the researchers' »real« participation in local social life arises. I positioned myself in this research as an inquisitive observer by visiting one selected flat on the second floor of the dwelling in August 2020, and reflecting on its environmental performance with the aim of investigating the intertwining relationships between domestic space, occupant behavior, and climate in more depth.

The three-bedroom apartment of 105 meters squared is home to a middle-class family of five people, the parents who are in their forties and three children in their early twenties. The two daughters share one room while the son has his own room. Looking at the environmental performance of the flat from the observer perspective leads us to define the climate first. Since the Mediterranean climate of Damascus is characterized by dry, sunny summers and cold winters, the use of passive design strategies that take advantage of climate benefits is recommended in order to provide comfort in the indoor environment.

As an observer, it can be observed that the apartment has been oriented toward east–west, despite the recommended orientation in Damascus being toward the north–south direction in order to reduce heat gains (Edwards et al. 2006). This creates several environmental problems for the family in terms of undesirable solar gains and the adverse effects of ventilation. In addition, the uninsulated concrete walls and low-performance windows contribute to the low performance envelope. Subsequently, the building characteristics are the main contributors to the potential discomfort of the residents. However, it is also interesting to note the spatial response of occupants in searching for comfort. While the flat has three balconies, the family has opted to close two of them, in the daughters' room and in the kitchen, to create more space, which may increase the solar gains in the space and negatively affect comfort. Next, a diary of space use was used as a tool to investigate how the low performance envelope influences the daily domestic comfort.

The Diary as a Research Method

> »The function of a diary is... to build a memory out of paper, to create archives from lived experience, to accumulate traces, prevent forgetting« (Lejeune 2001:99).

In order to capture the Syrians' energy-related actions in dwellings, diary studies can assist as a tool to collect information. As the researchers and educators Alexander et al. (2015) suggest, the diary is an instrument for coping with the unknown. In the Syrian context, the current literature lacks studies about the domestic behavior of the occupants. While a diary is commonly regarded as a text that provides a personal record of various and selective aspects of the diarist's daily life, with each entry self-contained and usually written during or soon after the event (Burt 1994; Cardell 2014), the diary, according to the essayist and specialist in autobiography Philippe Lejeune,

Morning

الجو: صحو | الاستيقاظ | غرفتي | المنزل | الاستلقاء في السرير | قلة الأجهزة | قلة الدفء/البرد | بالورد / البارد

ملاحظات:
مع أنو غرفتي دافئة من الصبح معظم تكون برد بهمن أيام الشتاء مثل اليوم، بس لجردلله اليوم كتير دافئة لعنك فقط و دخلنا الستوناج و غزير
ملاحظة ... الكهرباء هلت من ساعة وصلة !!!
لعنك طلبنا نروح نفطر بالمطبخ بكون كتير برد لأوضاعي بنمسح وسط العادة .. أفرناجه لا
و رجعنا نقعد بغرفة القعدة اللي فيها جو و شمس أكثر .

Afternoon

الوقت: الظهر | النشاط فيه | خارج المنزل غرفتي | المكان | أجهزة صناعية التدفئة والتبريد | قلة الأجهزة | بالبرد/النور | أشعر بشكل قيد

ملاحظات:
معظم وقت الظهر بتمضيه خارج البيت بس لما برجع عالبيت بكون برد شوي وأحياناً كتير بس بلبس أكثر مثل العادة !! بس المطبخ كتير برد بالصبح أما الصبح فبهمني عليهن وبنقدر نتغدى فيه .

Evening

الوقت: المساء | النشاط فيه | غرفتي القعدة | المكان | أجهزة صناعية للتدفئة والتبريد | الدفاية الكهربا - لجلية الكهربا | قلة الأجهزة | بالبرد/البارد | أشعر بشكل مبيد

ملاحظات:
إذا كانت موجودة الكهرباء، فبنشتغل الدفاية والأرضية و صنعدكلا بغرفة النقرة بس المشكلة الرئيسة لما لما تنقطع الكهرباء، وبيجي كتير برد، بنحاول نشعل الأجواء ما في جال وجود الكهربا أو ال ... ميار ثاني .

Do I feel hot/cold	Use of Equipment	Where	What I am doing	When

3.

One example from the diary of the 24-year-old daughter, in summer and winter, which shows her activities in the domestic space at three times of the day, morning, afternoon, and evening, combined with her account of whether she is comfortable.

28 June 2021

٢٨ حزيران ٢٠٢١

هل أشعر بالبرد/بالحر	أجهزة مستخدمة/الأدوات والتجهيزات	المكان	النشاط	الوقت
حبيرة	/	غرفتي	الاستيقاظ	الصبح

ملاحظات:

فضلت عالسنة لأنو عطلة وعندي جامعة بالصيف... لأنو عرفتي مرتبة... نفتح بكير وهلأ الدني بجولي فيق ... نشطة دير المحلة بصير أو الصبح ما بصير... عالمكتب ادام البنالك للساعة ١١ أقل شي ... لبس ما بزعج الشمس ، لهيك أرجح بشتغل عالتخت أو بغرفة المحتمة لأنو المباور بيكون ... مبختون الشمس ، وبرالساعة ١٢ بقدر أشتغل عالمكتب وبكون مرتاحة لأنو بيكون راهتي الشمس ، وبقدر أطمخ الطبخ وافتح البرادي.

هل أشعر بالبرد/بالحر	أجهزة مستخدمة/المرفهة والتجهيزات	المكان	النشاط	الوقت
أشعر بالحر بشكل كبير	المروحة/الحمام!	غرفتي/ المطبخ	الدراسة/ مساعدة ماما	الظهر

ملاحظات:

بعدما أشتغل بغرفتي الظهر، حاول رجع مساعدها بالبيت ويكون جدا ً شوب وب ١١ لهيك ماما بتحاول تغير نشاطها عالصبح ، إذا ً جاية الكهرباء منقعد بالمطبخ وتشتغل مروحة كهرباء ، وبنفتح الشبابك ، لكن إذا كان ماني كهرباء كتير منصوب ومحاول نفتح باب المطبخ وغرفة الفعية بنفس الوقت مشان يجيري تيار هواء.

هل أشعر بالبرد/بالحر	أجهزة مستخدمة/مساعدة للدفء والتبريد	المكان	النشاط	الوقت
حبير نوعا ً ما	مروحة/ولاية	غرفة القعدة	القعدة العيلة	المساء

ملاحظات:

بتبل المساء بدوي ... بيكون لسا شوب و إذا كان في كهرباء بنقعد بغرفة القعدة كلما لأنو هي الغرفة الوحيدة الي فيها تكييف ومادام الطقس شغال كل أفراد البيت بيجتمعو بغرفة القعدة. لهذا إذا قمنا بيكون بكل هذا حتى جا مس بالدور بدسا ً أحيانا ً ممكن نفيق من النوم مرة أو مرتين بالليل أو من هط عك طبيعي بوظ بمل هل لليل هيني وبكون واقد رتام!!

Do I feel hot/cold | Use of Equipment | Where | What I am doing | When

can be also defined as a document that »sculpts life as it happens and takes up the challenge of time« (2009: 173). He outlines three functions of diaries which I relate to my research context. First, to express oneself, which allows one to think and communicate. Second, to reflect, which has an analytical and deliberative effect. Third, to freeze time and build a memory out of paper. Furthermore, the writer and educator Mona Livholts considers diary writing as a form of creative expression in practice-based research (2017).

In order to log the data, diary studies have also been classified into three categories of interval-, signal-, and event-contingent protocols (Wheeler/ Reis 1991). While the interval-contingent design requires participants to report on their experiences at pre-determined intervals, signal-diaries rely on some signaling to provide diary reports at fixed intervals. Lastly, event-contingent diaries require participants to provide a self-report each time the event in question occurs. After visiting the case-study flat in April 2020, I decided to investigate the residents' experience of the domestic discomfort suggested by Lejeune (2001), based on the interval-contingent diary format. The occupants of the case-study flat were asked to record their presence and space-related activities during three main time periods (morning, afternoon, evening). Each participant wrote a paper-based diary for two different days (December 13, 2020 and July 13, 2020), when dwellings in Damascus cannot only rely on passive strategies and rather require active cooling/heating), and then the diaries were shared online with the researcher. Each diary includes the occupants' activities during the day and which space and energy services they used.

By family members recording activities, this diary format acts a form of communication between the researcher and the residents. As mentioned, although diary writing is a common and popular form of writing »to release and communicate« (June et al. 2015), diaries can be a repository for self-reflection »to analyze oneself and to deliberate« (Lejeune 2001: 107). To reflect, the researcher situates herself as a mediator between the residents and the reader by analyzing the residents' diaries and tracing their interrelated behaviors. The third function of the diary format, to freeze time, was accomplished with the help of a collected visual narrative which prompts the readers to discover the domestic Syrian space by themselves through the representation of frozen moments of discomfort that the residents showed in their diaries. These moments act as fleeting glimpses of a visual narrative that shares a story of middle-class family housing in Damascus.

Searching for Comfort: Views of the Co-Authors

The five members of the family wrote their diaries about their daily activities in their home, including their use of equipment in order to feel more comfortable. I selected the stories of three rooms in the flat where the people felt most uncomfortable in summer or winter. In order to present and relate the occupant comfort-related patterns in the case-study flat, a visual narrative of the family members' combined diaries has been drawn as behavioral snapshots for three rooms at different times on typical days during the winter and summer.

The selected snapshots include first, the winter day in the morning in the kitchen when the sunlight and daylight levels are low (west-facing room) and the temperature ranges are also low. Another snapshot was presented in the kitchen in the afternoon in the summer, as most of the family members complained about the extremely hot indoor environment due to the high percentage of solar gains; second, the winter day in the evening in the living room when the temperature can drop to less than 5 degrees Celsius, and third, the summer day in the daughters' bedroom in the morning when there are direct solar gains due to the room's east-facing orientation.

»Oh no! The electricity went out again! It is so cold for the children to eat here without the electric heater« says the 44-year-old mother while she is preparing breakfast for her family in the kitchen when the daylight dims on one of the cold mornings in December 2020.

The problem of electricity rationing has become a daily issue for Syrian families. However, domestic electricity cuts increase dramatically in the coldest and hottest months, which can cause up to 18 hours of blackouts citywide. In the case of not being able to rely on active heating, passive strategies have become essential to reduce cold stress. Despite the availability of sunshine hours in winter in Damascus, the family is not able to benefit from the heat of the sun in the morning due to the western orientation of the kitchen. Moving to another space is one of the discomfort responses to cold stress in the absence of electricity. The family usually moves to the east-oriented living room which has plenty of sun to eat breakfast. Temperature asymmetry is another problem in the kitchen. Due to the low performance of the building envelope, the spaces adjacent to the exterior walls are colder than the rest of the space. Therefore, the family members usually avoid sitting near the windows as a behavioral response to discomfort.

Kitchen

13 December2020 , Morning

Since most of the kitchens in Syria, are not heated, the passive design play an essenial role in residents (dis)comfort. As a result of west-oriented kitchen, the problem arises in the morning in winter season. The kitchen is not only dark, but also very cold, which led the family to use a Portable electric heaters when the electricity is avaiable or move to the living room for the having the breakfast.

while the kitchen is very cold in the mornings in winter season, the cretical problem in summer in the afternoon period because of the unwanted solar gains, which makes the residents uncomfortable in the space especially when the electricity is off, but they have to live with it!

13 July 2020, Afternoon

4.

A visual representation of the family diaries from the kitchen in two seasons and times (winter evening and summer afternoon). Drawing: Walaa Hajali.

Living Room

14 December2020 , Evening

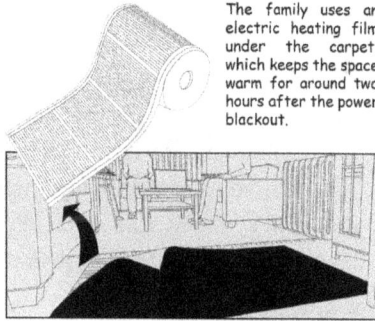

The family uses an electric heating film under the carpet, which keeps the space warm for around two hours after the power blackout.

5.

A visual representation of the family diaries in the living room on a winter evening.
Drawing: Walaa Hajali.

On the contrary, the kitchen witnesses a high risk of heat stress in the summer. A clear expression of overheating is reflected in the afternoon period during lunchtime in summer. On Wednesday July 13, 2021, all the family members complained in their diaries about the high temperatures while they were having lunch in the kitchen. The overheating has been particularly notable in the collected diaries during power blackouts when the family opens the window to cool the space. However, due to the high-speed wind in the west, the inadequate cross ventilation forces the family to close the window. The diaries also revealed the emotional responses to discomfort in the kitchen due to the unavoidable direct solar gains on the refrigerator, as the family members can do nothing about it other than complaining. Whereas the kitchen's original design consisted of a 2-meter-wide balcony, the family has opted to close the balcony and add the extra space to the kitchen due to aforementioned privacy reasons. Therefore, every electric device located in the enclosed balcony is subject to harmful direct sunlight in the afternoon period in summer. This is reflected in the family diaries by the complaints about the location of the refrigerator.

»This is just like a sauna here [...] I am not satisfied with the location of the fridge here! We have to move it somewhere else,« complains the father.

»Most food spoils so quickly, but we don't have enough space in the kitchen. The freezer should have the priority to be in the shaded space!« writes the mother.

It is winter in Damascus by the time the family is gathering in the living room in the afternoon. Due to the characteristics of the climate in Damascus, the temperature decreases at night and reaches its lowest level during December and January. At this time of the day, people may experience greater cold stress, which requires active heating. When the electricity is available, the family uses an electric heater, as a behavior to change the environment, in addition to an electric film on the floor under the carpet. The heating films are a new heating method and are manufactured locally as an alternative because they use less electricity than the air conditioning. Although there is air conditioning in the living room, the family does not use it in order to reduce the electricity costs.

»This air conditioning is for prestige! We only turn it on when we have guests,« says the 21-year-old daughter.

The Daughters' Room

28 June 2021 , Morning

6.
A visual representation of the daughters diaries of their bedroom in winter evenings. Drawing: Walaa Hajali.

However, considering the frequent blackouts, the family spends most winter evenings without any heating utility. The clothing factor acts as one of the main behavioral responses to discomfort to actively control the environment (Brager/de Dear 1998). The only way to get warm is using more blankets and thick carpets in order to increase the heat gains. To further explore the aspects of comfort within the case study, the east-oriented daughters' room is an interesting instance of how environmental conditions affect the occupants' behavior.

»My room gets uncomfortable in summer, especially in the morning when I cannot use my desk because of the sunlight,« writes the 21-year-old daughter.

The daughters' room is like most dwellings in Syria, where overheating and sun glare in south- and east-oriented rooms is a common problem in domestic spaces. While people usually adapt by getting rid of furniture that adds more heat, such as carpets or fabric canopies outside the window (changes in the environment), they sometimes adapt by avoiding the sunny spots in the room (changes in behavior). Similar to the kitchen, the balcony in the daughters' room has been glazed and added to the room because of the lack of space and it is used as a space for the desks. However, since the room has east orientation and no other intervention has been considered, such as adding a shading device, this created overheating in summer due to the direct unwanted solar gains. The problem of intensive solar gains could be observed especially in the morning, when one of the daughters wrote in her diary that she was not able to work because of the sun glare and ultimately had to move to another space (changes in behavior).

Projections: A View of the Inquisitive Observer

This study has investigated how diary research can be used to explore a user-centric approach to architectural research. While active heating/cooling usually acts as a major contributing factor to reach domestic comfort, in this research I tried to look at this comfort in the absence of energy services within the Syrian context where the residents have to adapt their behavior to the resulting discomfort of cold winters and hot summers or adapt their spaces to seek comfort. After visiting a family flat in a typical social dwelling in Damascus, my intention was to understand the domestic space from two perspectives: the users' experiential perspective and the researcher's observational perspective. The diary format was used as a functional tool to involve the residents in framing the problem from the user's perspective, while observation has been actively used to analyze the dwelling performance from the researcher's perspective.

Based on the theoretical framework of the three main responses to discomfort including environmental alterations, changes in behavior, and psychological processes, this study has discussed the written diaries of the inhabitants of a family flat in the Syrian context. It can be agreed that the absence of energy resources, specifically electricity, has significantly contributed to the resultant domestic discomfort. However, by looking at the three domestic spaces studied, the research can distinguish between conditions over which the inhabitants had no control, including the orientation and the intermittent supply of electricity, and over the conditions they could alter, such as adding insulation or enclosing or un-enclosing balcony space, or by using internal or external shutters. However, it is interesting to notice that the residents' daily practices are not an isolated response to thermal conditions. There are other social factors that influenced the residents' decisions, including privacy and the lack of space.

In the context of Syrian reconstruction, this research raises questions about the efficiency of the current model of affordable housing. Is producing the same model of domestic buildings the correct environmental and social answer to the Syrian reconstruction? And can we set standards to build energy efficient homes in Syria that also consider meeting the inhabitants' social and cultural needs? There is limited research on the performance of Syrian dwellings. I argue that in order to shift the current housing model, more studies need to be conducted that are not only concerned with the objective, but also the subjective aspects of comfort and how inhabitants use their spaces on a daily basis. In order to gain a broader insight, the diary study is intended to be expanded to other flats to include other occupants in the residential building and to compare the various responses to discomfort within the same design layout of flats. This research aims to draw attention to the failure of the current model of housing design in Syria, not only as an individual case study but also as a common problem in the domestic space of social housing. While discussing the discomfort associated with one case study, this research is a starting point for further research that aims to implement changes to the current model of social housing in the Syrian context.

References

Alexander, June/ Briene, Donna Lee/ McAllister, Margaret (2015): »Diaries are Better than Novels, More Accurate than Histories, and Even at Times More Dramatic than Plays: Revisiting the Diary for Creative Writers«, in: *TEXT* 19/1, 1–19, https://doi.org/10.52086/001c.25335.

Bestor, Theodore C. (2003): *Inquisitive Observation: Following Networks in Urban Fieldwork: Doing Fieldwork in Japan*, Honolulu: University of Hawaii Press.

Boardman, Brenda (2012): »Fuel Poverty Synthesis: Lessons Learnt; Actions Needed«, in: *Energy Policy* 49, 143–148.

Brager, Gail S./ de Dear, Richard J. (1998): »Thermal Comfort in Naturally Ventilated Buildings: Revisions to ASHRAE Standard 55«, in: *Energy and Buildings* 34, 549–561.

Burris, Andrea/ Mitchell, Val/ Haines, Victoria (2012): »Exploring Comfort in the Home: Towards an Interdisciplinary Framework for Domestic Comfort«, in: *Proceedings of 7th Windsor Conference: The Changing Context of Comfort in an Unpredictable World*.

Burt, C. D. B. (1994): »An analysis of a self-initiated coping behavior: Diary-keeping«, in: *Child Study Journal*, 24(3), 171–189.

Cardell, Kylie (2014): *Dear World: Contemporary Uses of the Diary*, Madison: University of Wisconsin Press, 25–46.

Edwards, Brian/Sibley, Magda/ Hakmi, Mohammad/ Land, Peter (2006): *Courtyard Housing Past, Present and Future*, New York: Taylor & Francis.

Goulden, Robert (2011): »Housing, Inequality, and Economic Change in Syria«, in: *British Journal of Middle Eastern Studies* 38/2, 187–202.

Haddad, Wajeeh (2019): *The Housing Crises in Syria and the Challenges of Housing Sector Reconstruction*, Doha: Harmoon Center for Contemporary Studies.

Heerwagen, Judith/Diamond, Richard (1992): »Adaptations and Coping: Occupant Response to Discomfort in Energy Efficient Buildings« ,in: *Building Technology and Urban Systems Division*, 10, 83–90.

Ismail, Reem (2015): »Adaptation of Housing Design to Culture Change in Syria: Concepts and Practices in the City of Lattakia«, PhD thesis, Edinburgh: Heriot-Watt University.

Kassouha, Sana (2020): »Transferring Experiences of Post-War West Germany in Social Housing to Reconstruction Strategies after The War in Syria«, PhD thesis, Stuttgart: University of Stuttgart.

Khaddour, Lina (2021): »Strategic Framework of Operational Energy Performance Improvement Potential for Damascus Post-War Social Housing«, in: *Intelligent Buildings International*. doi: 10.1080/17508975.2021.1874859

Kimpian, Judit/ Hartman, Hattie/ Pelsmakers, Sofie (2021): *Energy / People / Buildings: Making Sustainable Architecture Work*, London: RIBA Publishing.

Lejeune, Philippe (2001): »How do Diaries End? «, in: *Biography* 24/1, 99–112.

Lejeune, Philippe (2009): *On Diary*, Honolulu: University of Hawaii Press.

Livholts, Mona (2017): »Narrative Writing as Art-Based Practice«, in: *Synnyt: taidekasvatuksen tiedonala*, 10– 29.

Ministry of Housing and Utilities in Syria (2010): »How the General Establishment for Housing Works«, in: The General Establishment for Housing, http://www.escan.gov.sy/laws/1, (Accessed: October 20, 2020)

Ministry of Local Government (2008): »The Syrian Code for Construction and Thermal Insulation«, Damascus: Syrian Engineers Association.

Nikkhah, Saman (2021): »What about Occupant Comfort?«, in: *The Active Building Centre Research*, https://abc-rp.com/what-about-occupant-comfort/ (Accessed: December 6, 2021).

Webb, C. G. (1964): »Thermal Discomfort in a Tropical Environment«, in: *Nature* 202/4938, 1193–1194, doi: 10.1038/2021193a0

Wheeler, Ladd/ Reis, Harry T. (1991): »Self-Recording of Everyday Life Events: Origins, Types, and Uses«, in: *Journal of Personality* 59/3, 339–354.

Wilde, Peter (2014): »The Gap between Predicted and Measured Energy Performance of Buildings: A Framework for Investigation«, in: *Automation in Construction* 41, 40–49.Nikkhah, Saman (2021): »What about Occupant Comfort?«, in: *The Active Building Centre Research*, https://abc-rp.com/what-about-occupant-comfort/ (Accessed: December 6, 2021).

Webb, C. G. (1964): »Thermal Discomfort in a Tropical Environment«, in: *Nature* 202/4938, 1193–1194, doi: 10.1038/2021193a0

Wheeler, Ladd/ Reis, Harry T. (1991): »Self-Recording of Everyday Life Events: Origins, Types, and Uses«, in: *Journal of Personality* 59/3, 339–354.

Wilde, Peter (2014): »The Gap between Predicted and Measured Energy Performance of Buildings: A Framework for Investigation«, in: *Automation in Construction* 41, 40–49.

Dimensions of Architectural Knowledge, 2022-03 ᴓ
https://doi.org/10.14361/dak-2022-0308

ETHNOGRAPHY OF STONE
Gathering – Layering – Cementing

Natalia Petkova

Abstract: This article draws on my ongoing doctoral research on stone and its renewed use as a self-supporting or load-bearing material in architecture today. To complement the existing literature on the subject, which is overwhelmingly quantitative in nature, it discusses the potential, as well as some of the difficulties, of the ethnographic approach I have adopted instead. Focusing on my fieldwork around the construction of a collective housing project in Plan-les-Ouates, Switzerland, one of the case studies in my thesis, it explores the challenges that working with this geo-sourced material poses for the professional practice of actors involved in its production. By taking into account the perspectives of multiple actors across multiple sites, including the stone as found, it aims to contribute to a broader understanding of what its structural use does, and could, imply for architecture.

Keywords: Stone; Geo-sourced; Materials; Actors; Ethnography

Introduction

This article discusses the geological formation of two limestones in Migné-Auxences and Chauvigny in western France and their recent incorporation into a collective housing project for the Swiss municipality of Plan-les-Ouates on the outskirts of Geneva. Structured in three parts that correspond to key phases in the stones' formation, namely those of matter gathering, layering, and cementing, it explores the sedimentary nature of my ongoing doctoral research on the renewed use of stone as a structural, that is to say, self-supporting or load-bearing material in contemporary architecture. In Gathering, I collect historical information and discourses from recent exhibitions. In Layering, I introduce my methodological approach. In Cementing, I reflect on my findings. The paragraphs in italics, which introduce each section, provide descriptions of the material. With reference to existing literature in the fields of social anthropology and oral

Corresponding author: Natalia Petkova (École nationale supérieure d'architecture Paris-Malaquais, Université Paris Est); natalia.petkova@univ-paris-est.fr; http://orcid.org/0000-0003-4784-4414

history, as well as my own trials with ethnographic methods, I will argue that extending our attention beyond architectural objects to the practice of the actors involved in their making provides a broader understanding of what using — or rather working with — a given material can entail.

My curiosity about what stone does to present-day architectural production arises from the growing enthusiasm among professionals of the built environment for this material in particular, and for »natural« materials in general, which are largely portrayed as more sustainable alternatives to their synthetic counterparts. To define »natural«, the distinction between bio-sourced materials that come from plants and animals, such as timber or wool, and geo-sourced, mineral-based materials, such as earth or stone is made increasingly within the building industry. While stone is not considered a renewable resource, owing to the pace of its reproduction, its durability, potential reuse, and high thermal inertia, are commonly cited as low-carbon, energy-efficient attributes.

In order to observe architectural production with stone at first-hand during my doctoral research, I set out to follow a series of ongoing projects in Switzerland, Spain, and England, that employed the material in its structural capacity. The Plan-les-Ouates collective housing project, designed by the office of the French architect Gilles Perraudin and the Geneva-based Atelier Archiplein as part of Les Sciers, a new residential neighborhood, is one of my three case studies. In terms of budget and timeframe, its construction differed little from the other projects being developed on the site. Its use of stone, carrying all the vertical loads of the building down seven storeys, was however, unprecedented within the Swiss context.

I had gone to Switzerland in early 2020 to do fieldwork around the Plan-les-Ouates project, whose construction was underway at that point. My intention to spend two uninterrupted months at each of my case study sites was partially compromised by the outbreak of the Covid-19 pandemic. In the Swiss case, after an initial period spent in situ, I conducted some remote interviews. Several months after my stay in Geneva, I was able to visit one of the French quarries that had supplied stone for the project, as well as a stone-cutting atelier in Chauvigny. I lack the space in this article to address the tension between the long and sited history held within this stone and the apparent lightness of its displacement from the quarry to the construction site, roughly 500 kilometers overland. It is worth pointing out however, that the definition of stone as a local resource is a contested one in practice, and a subject to which a section of my thesis is dedicated.

Be it at the architects' office in Geneva, the construction site in Plan-les-Ouates, the quarry, or the stone-cutting atelier in Chauvigny, my research was guided by one question: Was the structural use of stone challenging the professional practice of diverse actors such as architects, engineers, clients, quarriers and builders, and if so, in what way?

Gathering: Information

In France, it is commonplace to name stones used for construction by the place where they formed geologically. Hence, the two stones that make up the ex-posed load-bearing structure of the Plan-les-Ouates housing project – Migné and Brétigny, otherwise known as Chauvigny – are indigenous to the towns of Migné-Auxence and Chauvigny, a few kilometers from the city of Poitiers. Close relatives geographically, the two stones differ somewhat in age. Migné came into being in the Callovian age of the Jurassic period, around 165 million years ago. Brétigny, dated to the Bathonian age, preceded it by a few million years. Like all sedimentary stones, their formation began with existing matter that had been broken up and displaced by air or water. As limestones, the most common of the sedimentary lot in the world of construction, Migné and Bréti-gny are products of marine environments. Largely composed of the mineral calcite, found in shells, skeletons, and sea water itself, they also contain bio-logical remains of plants and animals that lived therein. The fossil that I would later see in one of the stone blocks on the construction site in Switzerland was thus evidence of life in the warm shallow seas that once covered Poitiers and its hinterlands (fig. 2).

Historically, the structural material of choice for noble buildings and infra-structures, stone saw its place in construction significantly modified with the development of reinforced concrete – and to a lesser extent in Europe, steel frames – in the latter half of the 19th century. Cut into thin slices to finish floors and walls, it became a dressing material. In France, a shortage of energy resources and the difficulty of supplying cement gave stone a new lease of life as a structural material in the aftermath of World War II (Caille 1999). Subject to a mediatic blocus at the time, the vast housing projects de-veloped in load-bearing stone by the architect Fernand Pouillon, predomi-nantly in Marseille and the Paris region, have only recently resurfaced as emblems of an alternative modernism in French architecture (Lucan/Seyler 2003; Caruso/Thomas 2013). An unpublished study of previously undocu-

I.
A block of Migné limestone being squared at a quarry near Chauvigny (FR).
Photographer: Martin Migeon.

mented collective housing projects by largely unknown architects that were built in Paris between 1945 and 1973 (Kurtali/Le Drean 2018) nonetheless hints at the persistent absence of the material used structurally in representations of 20th-century French architecture.

In the 1990s and early 2000s, Gilles Perraudin's experimentations with Cyclopean blocks of roughly sawn limestone stacked without mortar in the south of France, most famously his self-built chai in Vauvert, brought media attention back to stone's load-bearing capacity. Nevertheless, while both private clients and architects eager to employ stone structurally multiplied in France during this period, the material struggled to gain credibility as an affordable component for projects that were larger and more technically complex than single family dwellings or agricultural stores. To remedy this, the stone sector mobilized itself on a national scale to promote the material: Institutions such as the Bureau de Recherches Géologiques et Minières (BRGM), the Centre Technique de Matériaux Naturels de Construction (CTMNC), as well as numerous cultural and commercial actors including the journal Pierre Actual and the Syndicat National des Industries de Roches Ornementales et de Construction (SNROC), collaborated to publish new cartographies of the material and create an online catalog of available stones and their properties, produce construction manuals in line with existing building standards, and establish an annual salon. This concerted effort played into broader societal preoccupations with the depletion of resources, a certain nostalgia for »nature«, notably in urban settings, as well as an aesthetic fascination with geological forms and processes. As a result, in France, the choice of stone as a structural material in architecture has ceased to be the marginal one it was 30 years ago. The exhibition Pierre: Révéler la ressource, Explorer le matériau, curated by the architectural practice Barrault Pressacco and held in the autumn of 2018 at the Pavillon de l'Arsenal, a cultural organ of the City of Paris focusing on contemporary issues of the built environment, represents one of the symbolic milestones in this process of normalization. The apparent difficulties of employing stone from the Paris Basin, the geological basin of sedimentary rocks surrounding Paris, of doing so elsewhere than on building facades and without reinforcement were left unaddressed by the exhibition. However, the ongoing or recently completed collective housing projects in and around the French capital that were presented on this occasion, such as those by Eliet et Lehmann in Bry-sur-Marne and Raphaël Gabrion or Jean-Christophe Quinton in the 15th arrondissement for public clients, or those by Vincent Lavergne with Atelier WOA in

2.

A fossil in a block of Brétigny limestone in Plan-les-Ouates (CH), displaced roughly 500 km from its place of deposit. Photographer: Natalia Petkova.

3.

Blocks of Migné and Brétigny limestone awaiting their incorporation into a housing project in Plan-les-Ouates (CH). Photographer: Natalia Petkova.

Rosny-sous-Bois and Trévelo & Viger-Kohler in the 19th arrondissement for private developers, lent weight to the curators' framing of stone as an »ordinary« material for »ordinary« uses.

More recently, this renewed interest in the architectural potential of stone beyond cladding has manifested in other parts of Europe. The title of the exhibition New Stone Age, held at the Building Centre in London in 2020, and which regrouped projects employing stone structurally in the UK and beyond, playfully overstates its presence on construction sites relative to other materials such as steel and concrete. Curated by the architect Amin Taha, the stone supplier Polychor, The Stonemasonry Company and Webb Yates Engineers, it echoes the mobilization of diverse actors in the French building industry in the early 2000s to see this proportion increase. In Switzerland, a curiosity about the material has emerged predominantly within academic institutions, where the use, though not exclusively structural, of stone has been the object of numerous semester-long design studios such as Multiplicity — Building Material and Material Gesture — Stone respectively led by An Fonteyne and Anne Holtrop at the Swiss Federal Institute of Technology in Zürich (ETH-Z) in 2019/20d as well as Critical Mass at the Laboratory of Elementary Architecture and Studies of Types (EAST) in 2020/21 at the École polytechnique fédérale de Lausanne (EPFL).

Layering: Approaches

In the ground, distinct layers of the Migné and Brétigny stones correspond to periodic deposits left by major changes in sea level. Each layer once covered the lithosphere, the mineral outer part of the planet. Weathering and movements within the lithosphere can cause older layers to re-emerge and younger ones to descend. Such is the case with Migné: resulting from a later deposit than Brétigny stone, it is found deeper and extracted today from an underground quarry. The stratified form of sedimentary stone makes it particularly adapted to construction, as each layer has the same characteristics ensuring a relative homogeneity of its aesthetic and mechanical properties. At the same time, a cross section within a quarry can simultaneously give access to layers of varying qualities that meet differing needs of construction. Within the industry, the layers go by the name of »veins« when thin and unexploitable, and »beds« when above 30 centimetres or so. The incorporation of sedimentary stone into buildings for structural purposes reflects this layered quality. To conserve the stones' strength, blocks are generally stacked on top of one another in the same horizontal orientation that they were formed.

Recent research within and outside academia has addressed the structural use of stone in architecture from an overwhelmingly quantitative perspective. It has sought to measure the availability of the resource in given settings, its thermal performance, or the environmental and economic impact of its extraction, transformation, and transport from quarry to construction site (Zerbi 2011; Ioannidou 2016; Barrault Pressacco 2018). Sensing that the limitations – like the appeal – of using stone in its structural capacity today could not be understood through measurements only, the aim of my research has been to explore it as a social phenomenon, in other words: as a set of practices that result from constantly evolving influences. For methodological guidance, I have looked to ethnography, a form of qualitative research that involves immersing oneself in a particular community or organization to directly observe their behaviour and interactions. With origins in social and cultural anthropology in the early 20th century, the relevance of ethnography for research in architecture has developed significantly in recent decades. Two published ethnographies of architectural practice by Albena Yaneva and Sophie Houdart (with the photographer, film maker, and theorist Minato Chihiro), social anthropologists working in the continuity of the Actor Network Theory (ANT) tradition, in which they follow the day-to-day work of architects at the Office for Metropolitan Architecture in Rotterdam (Yaneva 2009a; Yaneva 2009b) and at the office of Kengo Kuma in Tokyo (Houdart/Chihiro 2009) have proven especially useful in informing my own approach. It is notably Yaneva's sensitivity to the agency of materials used for model making that I tried to develop in relation to the stone in my doctoral research, as well as Houdart's negotiation between the discourses of actors and her own observations. Whereas Yaneva sets out to follow architects »in their daily routines in spite of their interests and theories« (Yaneva 2009: 197), Houdart seeks to gain an understanding of how these operate in practice.

To further investigate the social, collective nature of architectural practice, we might extend our attention to other actors that feature in its making, notably those whose perspectives are often rendered invisible. Research on architecture in the field of oral history offers valuable insights in this regard. Christine Wall's exploration of post-war British brutalism from the perspective of the construction workers who built that style using concrete in unprecedented ways (Wall 2019: 50 –75), was particularly relevant to my research on what using stone structurally implies for masons today. We might also look to spaces of architectural production other than the architect's office and the construction site. In contrast to the foci of Yaneva, Houdart, and Wall on one particular location or group of actors at a time, my doctoral research aims to consider the viewpoints of multiple actors, including engineers, clients, quarriers, and builders gathered across multiple sites like municipal offices, quarries, stone-cutting ateliers, and warehouses.

To facilitate such a multi-actor, multi-site approach, prior to my arrival in Switzerland I had agreed with the Geneva-based architects of the Plan-les-Ouates collective housing project that I could occupy a desk in their office, access related documents, and accompany them to meetings while also being free to organize my fieldwork as I saw fit. Once there, and throughout this residency of sorts, the quantity and variety of potential information available, as well as the organic dimension of the research process was often overwhelming. Sifting through masses of files on the architects' server for instance, how should I decide what to take note of? Sitting in on a construction-site meeting, was I to transcribe the conversations or focus on non-verbal content? My emails asking for interviews were often ignored and questions were dodged, but anecdotes were also shared in unexpected places, and encounters with hitherto unknown people and places were suggested to me. I would argue then, that here lies the primary virtue of using ethnographic methods. By being present in the field and paying attention to what people said or did, alone or when interacting with each other, and the tools and concepts they employed in relation to stone, I gathered fragments of information that I would not otherwise have had access to. Documented as voice recordings, photographs, and observational notes, the significance of these fragments to my inquiry remained unclear to me at this stage. In the final part of this article, I will attempt to demonstrate the passage from a small set of such fragments to a tentative understanding of the professional practices being observed and how they might evolve.

Cementing: Concluding Reflections

Under the weight of new layers piling up above, the particles of matter that had gathered in the geological periods that saw the formation of Migné and Brétigny started to interact. For the sedimentary stones to form, this interaction was necessarily chemical in nature, and the calcite mentioned earlier assures this process of binding, or cementation as geologists call it. Speaking of cement (a key component of modern concrete) and without entering into a demonstration of the energy-intensive process necessary to obtain it, it is worth bearing in mind the indispensable role of limestone therein. In the formation of sedimentary stones, the quantity and distribution of calcite directly informs their structure and as a consequence, their potential use in construction. Migné and Brétigny are both oolitic limestones, made up of tiny spheres of calcite rolled around eclectic remains of the sea. The uniform nature of oolitic limestones makes them well suited for structural use. Comparatively denser – thus better able to withstand horizontal loads – and less porous – thus less accommodating to water – Brétigny was employed for the ground floor of the Plan-les-Ouates collective housing project, as well as all the protruding elements. Migné, lighter, hence easier to transform and lay, was used for the rest of the load-bearing structure.

Before arriving in Switzerland, I was aware that work on the Plan-les-Ouates construction site had come to a complete halt two months prior due to problems with the stone supply. As I exchanged with various actors involved in the production of the project – informally or as part of one to two hour semi-directive interviews – and observed their interactions in meetings or on site visits, multiple reasons for the costly delay were claimed. Some insisted on the disorganization of the quarry, as it had delivered stones for the upper floors while those necessary to complete the ground floors were missing; some pointed instead to the architects' lack of foresight in allowing the necessary time for the freshly extracted blocks to lose their water and gain in strength; while others hinted at the unrealistic expectations of the construction manager and the general contractor, who were responsible for laying the stone, regarding the consistent quality of the blocks that arrived on site (fig. 3).

Reading between the lines of my observation notes and lengthy interview transcriptions, I sensed the actors' frustration about the losses incurred in revenue and sleepless nights as blame was shifted between the architects, the quarry manager, the construction manager, and the general contractor. Yet, also palpable was a sense of pride and achievement in having collectively overcome certain stone-related hurdles. In contrast to building with concrete, where a deficient supplier can be replaced by another, the specificity of the material and the protracted nature of its extraction would not allow that here. Divorce was not an option, as one of my interlocutors put it. Confronted with the physical reality of Brétigny and Migné stones, the actors were thrown out of their habitual practices and into dialogue. During the unplanned interruption of work on site, the clients thus visited the quarry to better understand how it operated, namely the way in which producing blocks of identical dimensions in large batches saved time when recalibrating machines. In parallel, the quarry worked more closely with the general contractor to establish packing lists that sequenced the delivery of stones according to their order of assembly, rather than the logic of their transformation.

It was only a few months after my stay in Switzerland, when I visited the quarry where Brétigny is extracted and squared (fig. 1), as well as the stone-cutting atelier where both Brétigny and Migné underwent some of their transformation, that a further explanation for the delay came to my attention. To one side of the beige open-air pit, the quarry manager gestured at the large void that corresponds to all but the ground floor and the protruding stone elements of the Plan-les-Ouates collective housing project. Highlighting the naturally occurring fractures visible in the hillside, he recalled how the extraction of the larger blocks requested by the architects, all the same height and some measuring more than 2.5 meters, had proved challenging and generated considerable waste. As the quarry manager outlined more easily obtainable block dimensions from the quarry – 30 or 40 centimeters deep, between 30 and 70 centimeters high and up to 1 or 2 meters long – I was struck by the apparent discrepancy between the large standard dimensions of the blocks as they were drawn by the architects and the material as it was found in the ground.

The reflex to standardize building components brings to mind a remark that was echoed by several of the actors that I spoke with in relation to the Plan-les-Ouates project. Independently of one another, and in an unmistakably complimentary tone, they claimed that at a distance, the facades of the project appear to be composed of well-executed pre-fabricated concrete panels. They were referring to the regularity of the assemblage and the texture. Unlike prefabricated concrete however, which all the actors who shared the view above are more familiar with in practice, dimensions of stone elements are far more dependent on the material itself than on the intentions of those who draw them. Herein, I believe, lies one of the largely unexplored challenges of building with stone today: How the intrinsic heterogeneity of the material could be incorporated into architectural production.

Out of necessity, the architects of the Plan-les-Ouates project did, once construction had started, partially adapt the stone layout to the dimensions of the blocks available. The experience showed that using stone in its structural capacity demands a different production process where all of the actors involved – from architects and clients to quarriers and builders – need to invent and abide by new protocols. Drawing on this experience, might the stone layout be designed from the outset according to the formats readily available at a quarry, or provide scope for potential modifications once extraction has begun? Relinquishing this complete control over design a language proper to this material might (re)emerge. It suffices to read Vitruvius' On Architecture (Vitruvius 2009 [c.30–15 BC]): 328) or to look at historic stone buildings with alternating course heights and blocks of differing lengths to see that a more accommodating relationship to the material is not a new, but simply a forgotten, idea.

References

Barrault Pressacco (2018): *Pierre: Révéler la ressource, Explorer le matériau*, Paris: Editions de l'Arsenal.

Caille, Jean-François (1999): »La pierre«, in: *Architecture, Mouvement, Continuité*, 96, 74–75.

Caruso, Adam/Thomas, Helen (2013): *The Stones of Fernand Pouillon*, Zurich: GTA Verlag ETH.

Houdart, Sophie/Chihiro, Minato (2009): *Kengo Kuma, An Unconventional Monograph*, Paris: éditions donner lieu.

Ioannidou, Dimitra (2016): *On sustainability: Aspects through the Prism of Stone as a Material for Construction*, PhD thesis, ETH Zurich.

Kurtali, Jonas/Le Drean, Marie (2018): *La pierre banale. Logements collectifs en pierre massive, Paris, 1945–1973*, Master's thesis, Ecole Polytechnique Fédérale de Lausanne.

Lucan, Jacques/Seyler, Odile (2003): *Fernand Pouillon architecte : Pantin, Montrouge, Boulogne-Billancourt, Meudon-la-Forêt*, Paris: Éditions de l'Arsenal.

Vitruvius, (2009 [c.30–15 BC]): *On Architecture*, London: Penguin Classics.

Wall, Christine (2019): »›It Was a Totally Different Approach to Building!‹: Constructing Architectural Concrete in 1960s London«, in: Janina Gosseye/Naomi Stead/DeborahVan der Plaat, Deborah (eds.), *Speaking of Buildings: Oral History in Architectural Research*, New York: Princeton Architectural Press, 50–75.

Yaneva, Albena (2009a): *The Making of a Building: A Pragmatist Approach to Architecture*, London: Peter Lang Publishing.

Yaneva, Albena (2009b): *Made by the Office of Metropolitan Architecture: An Ethnography of Design*, Rotterdam: nai010 publishers.

Zerbi, Stefano (2011): *Construction en pierre massive en Suisse*, PhD thesis, École polytechnique fédérale de Lausanne.

Dimensions of Architectural Knowledge, 2022-03 ᔐ
https://doi.org/10.14361/dak-2022-0309

GRAPHIC NOVEL
Making *Neualtland* – Ficto-criticism in Architectural Historiography

Janina Gosseye and Meitar Tewel

Abstract: This paper offers a reflection on an educational experiment. In the spring of 2021, a group of nine architecture students at the Delft University of Technology participated in a research elective that invited them to narrate architectural and urban design history through a ficto-critical short story in graphic-novel format. This paper is based on a conversation between Janina Gosseye, the instructor of the elective, and Meitar Tewel, who made *Neualtland* as part of this course. In their conversation, Janina and Meitar consider whether the shift away from the more conventional modes of historiography, represented by the ficto-critical graphic novel short story, is merely a shift in genre and tools – from writing to drawing – or if it represents an epistemological shift that can help architecture students unlock and develop new knowledge about the history of architecture and urban design. Could it be a new »species of thesis«?

Keywords: Ficto-criticism; Graphic Novel; Short Story; Architectural Historiography; Urban Design Historiography; Architectural Pedagogy; Literary Genre and Conventions.

In the spring of 2021, Janina Gosseye, one of the authors of this paper, organized a research elective at the Architecture Department of the Delft University of Technology entitled »The Heteronomy of Urban Design: Faith in the City«. In this research elective, students were invited to examine how urban design is influenced by developments that are »heteronomous« (or external) to the discipline proper; meaning by changes and shifts in the social, political, economic, or cultural realm. The particular »heteronomous« element that students were asked to consider for the spring 2021 installment of this course was the challenge of secularization, and how in the second half of the 20th century, religious organizations responded to this challenge through urban design programs and initiatives aimed at providing leisure infrastructure for congregations and communities.

Corresponding authors: Janina Gosseye (TU Delft, Netherlands); J.Gosseye@tudelft.nl; https://orcid.org/0000-0003-2437-3090; Meitar Tewel (TU Delft, Netherlands); meitartewel@gmail.com; https://orcid.org/0000-0001-6927-9351

The research elective was composed of two parts, each spanning four weeks. In the first part of the course, the students – nine Master's students participated in total – were given lectures and readings, and worked in groups of three to identify 20 potential case-study projects (per group of three) by using databases such as the Avery Index to Architectural Periodicals and the Royal Institute of British Architects (RIBA) Library. This resulted in a long list of 60 potential projects for further research. In the second part of the course, each individual student was asked to choose one case study from this list of 60 projects and analyze the urban and historical setting of the project, its program and design, the various actors who were involved in its development, and the particular way in which it responded to the challenge of secularization. Building on Hélène Frichot and Naomi Stead's work on ficto-criticism, which holds that »fiction is a powerful means of speculatively propelling ourselves into other imagined worlds, [while] criticism offers the situated capacity to ethically cope with what confronts us on the way, and once we arrive there« (Frichot/Stead 2020: 11–12), and informed by Chris Ware's *Building Stories* (Ware 2012), the form that this analysis was to assume was that of a graphic novel short story.

The work produced by the students was astonishingly creative and very diverse, ranging from a graphic novel short story analyzing the Gladbeck-Rentfort North Community Centre in Germany (»Gemeindezentrum Gladbeck-Rentfort Nord« 1985) through a deadpan and secularized interpretation of the Stations of the Cross[1] – each station set in a different space within the community center, showing visitors performing (mostly) mundane tasks – to a graphic novel short story that blended the literary genre of airport novella with that of the fairy tale to examine how a multi-denominational religious center built in Langendorf, Switzerland (»Kirchliches Zentrum Langendorf SO« 1972) might create bonds – a romance even! – between those adhering to different religious beliefs.[2]

Meitar Tewel, the other author of this paper, was another student who participated in this research elective. For her graphic novel short story, Meitar selected the Neue Synagogue in Darmstadt, Germany, which was inaugurated in 1988 to commemorate the fiftieth anniversary of Kristallnacht (»Synagoge mit Gemeindezentrum in Darmstadt gestiftet« 1991). The Neue Synagogue in Darmstadt was designed by architect Alfred Jacoby, a Frank-

---

1 This graphic novel short story was produced by Giulia Kiernan.

2 This graphic novel short story was produced by Kimberly van Vliet.

furt-based German-Jewish architect and educator, who is still today considered one of Germany's leading synagogue architects.[3] For her graphic novel short story (included on pages 126-133), Meitar chose the title *Neualtland*, a reference to Theodor Herzl's novel *Altneuland* of 1902, which sets out a Zionist vision for a Jewish return to the land of Israel. *Neualtland*, which is German for »new old land«, proposes an alternative to Herzl's utopia. It portrays the subsistence of the Jewish community in Germany in the post-World War II era, which became the key theme of Meitar's graphic novel short story (Tewel 2021).[4]

This paper is the result of an email conversation between Meitar and Janina that took place over several days in the summer of 2021, and during which each invited the other to reflect on the pros and cons, and the felicities and failures of architectural and urban design historiography through graphic novel ficto-criticism, from the student and instructor perspective respectively.

Meitar: In the course, we were asked to study post-war secularized religious projects through graphic novels, an undeniably specific topic and tool. Why did you think that this medium in particular would suit the study of this building type?

Janina: Great question! To be honest, the combination of the object of study (post-war secularized building projects developed by religious organizations) and the medium of representation (the graphic novel) was to a certain extent incidental. Both components of the task that was set for the elective were informed by different research interests of mine: a fascination with »Faith in the City« and the influence that religious organizations have (had) on our post-war built environment (when secularization was supposed to have set in) on the one hand, and an interest in alternative modes of architectural and urban design historiography on the other hand. I don't think that the graphic novel is uniquely suited to the study of this particular building program, but I did (and do) believe that this format would remove some of

---

3 Apart from his design of the Neue Synagogue in Darmstadt, Jacoby is also known for his design of the Neue Synagogue in Aachen. With degrees from Cambridge University and ETH Zurich, Jacoby started his architectural practice in Frankfurt in 1980. In 1998, he became a professor of architecture at Anhalt University where he founded the Dessau Institute of Architecture (DIA) in 2000. For more information about Alfred Jacoby's work and background, see: Engel (2018) and »Prof. Alfred Jacoby« (n.d.).

4 For full online reading experience, please view Meitar Tewel's graphic novel short story in double-sided scrolling.

Old synagogues in Europe always seemed so **foreign** to me.

They're so much bigger and more ornamented than the ones I knew in Israel,

To be frank, my religious experiences as an Israeli Jew only went as far as cycling around the Moshav's synagogue in Yom Kippur.

some of them almost look like churches.

Twenty-something years later, I'm studying architecture in Delft.

While digging through archive materials for postwar religious buildings (who am I kidding, churches) with a secular twist,

NEUALTLAND by Meitar Tewel

You know, this Israeli embracement of Modernist traditions — it's there to cut off historic ties.

In the Holy Land, there were no Jews for a very long time, while this year we celebrate 1,700 years of Jewish tradition in Germany.

It's a **very** long history — of being a minority in a foreign land, sometimes even a hostile one.

ALFRED JACOBY

MEITAR TEWEL

The idea of diaspora Jews felt almost archaic to me.

I've always carried this childish assumption that everyone who survived **The War** immigrated to Israel, and that postwar Europe remained, well, Jew-free.

I came across this synagogue in Darmstadt (are there still enough Jews in Germany to open a synagogue for? Really?)

RIBA

Synagoge mit Gemeindezentrum in Darmstadt gestiftet

Projektverfasser: Architektenge-meinschaft Alfred Jacoby, 6000 Frankfurt
Planung und Bauleitung: Alfred Jacoby, Dipl.-Arch. ETH/BDA Martin Neugebauer, Ing.-Arch.

Im Jahre 1984 beschloß die Stadtverordnetenversammlung der Stadt Darmstadt, spätestens bis zur 50. Wiederkehr der Reichsprogromnacht, am 9. November 1988, der Jüdischen Gemeinde Darmstadt als Stiftung eine neue Synagoge mit Gemeindezentrum zu errichten. Bis ins späte 19. Jahrhundert waren Synagogen oft hinter einem Gemeinde- oder Rabbinerhaus versteckte Bauwerke, lagen außerhalb der Innenstädte oder waren an die Nachbarbebauung angeglichen, um im Stadtbild möglichst unauffällig oder unauffindbar zu sein. Für den Neubau in Darmstadt wurde bewußt gegensätzlich mit einem Solitärgebäude mit einer ausgeprägten Straßenfassade reagiert. Die Wilhelm-Glässing-Straße be-... städtebaulichen Bedeu-... zurück und faßt die Synago-ge als städtisches Monument.

Designed by Alfred Jacoby... hey, I **know** this guy!

Right. There's something so casual about being a Jew in Israel, you don't even have to think about it. But in Germany it's a **completely** different story, isn't it?

I mean, looking at your design for this synagogue, it almost screams — "look at me, I'm **Jewish**!" — with these symbolic elements, the domes, the Star of David.

Weren't you scared?

NEVER! That was **exactly** my intention!
We have **no** reason to hide.

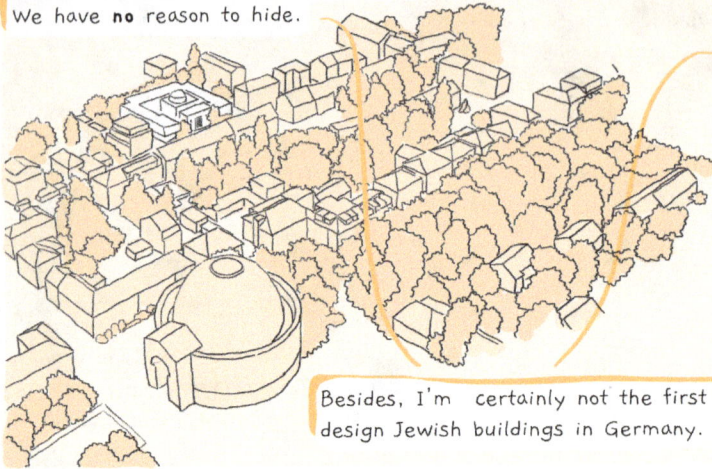

German synagogues of the 19th
century **dramatically** influenced
Jewish architecture worldwide.
Gottfried Semper introduced this
typology

Besides, I'm certainly not the first to
design Jewish buildings in Germany.

But then, Moritz Neumann — who was
the chair of the Jewish community and
a childhood friend of mine, **was** scared.

He asked me to put a fence around the
building. He fell ill just when we started
working on this synagogue, and from that
moment until he passed away a few years
ago, it seemed like he was **always** scared.

Being a Jew in post-war Germany was a very
lonely affair. We were four Jewish kids,
Moritz, myself and two other kids born after
the war, and that's it.

My experience of being a Jew in a German
school was horrid, it was **terrible**. I went to
school in 1956, 1957. Who could be the
teachers? Count the years back, and you
know who they were. I had this terrible
experience, where you had to write an essay.
One of the teachers said —

EVEN YAKOBOVITCH,
WHO IS NOT GERMAN
AT ALL

My design obviously isn't Moorish, but I did want to refer to this typology. That was my guidebook, and that's why I used these symbolic elements — the courtyard, the domes, the facades with punched stone holes.

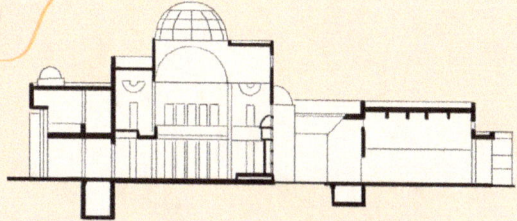

Unlike **Edwin Oppler**, who believed that synagogues — like churches — should be built in a Gothic style, **Semper** thought that due to our Oriental origins — we should follow a Spanish Moorish style.

This building was meant to inspire hope rather than fear. And this is a central question here, how do you design for a traumatized community?

My parents were deeply traumatized, all my life. I didn't want to build a holocaust memorial, this was out of the question. I **lived** in this memory of the holocaust, had it for lunch.

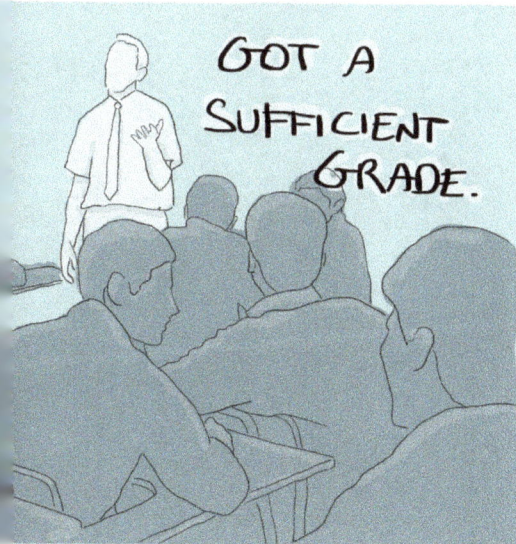

GOT A SUFFICIENT GRADE.

On another day, I found a swastika etched on my desk, and some writing —

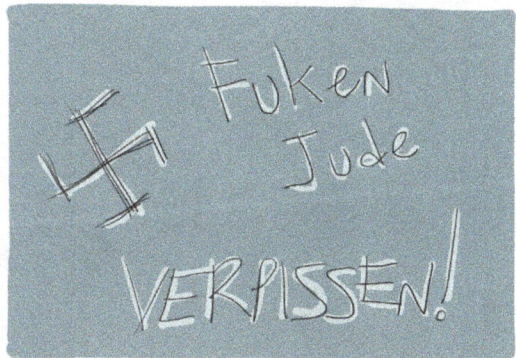

Fuken Jude VERPISSEN!

I went back home — and told my parents that's my last day in that school.

So in spite of the proud presence of this synagogue, its design couldn't ignore this collective and personal trauma.

No, it certainly couldn't. This is why we had to complete its construction by November 9th, 1988 — **exactly** 50 years after the **Kristallnacht**.

Looking back at the photographs from that night and the horrid days following it, it almost seemed to me like your scheme tries to **protect** the synagogue.

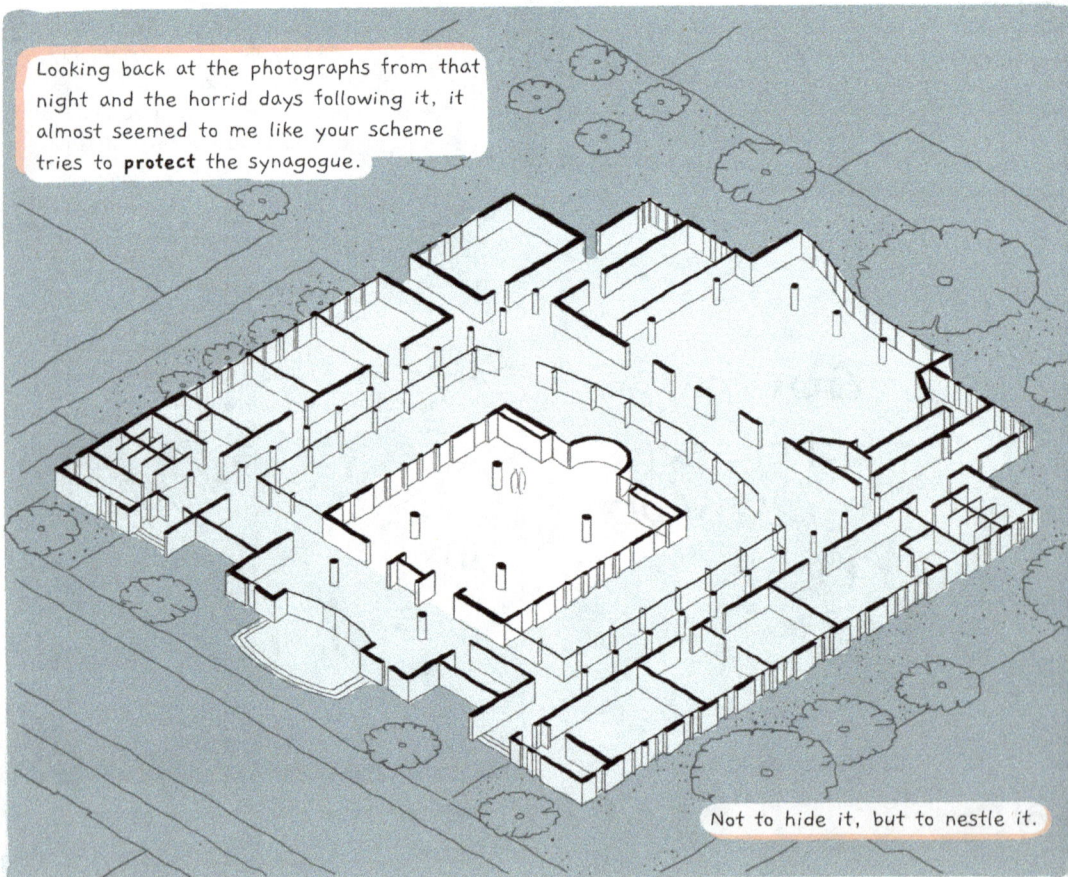

Not to hide it, but to nestle it.

I discovered Brian Clarke, a very famous constructivist stained-glass artist. I invited him to Darmstadt, where he met with Yehoshua Frenkel – a survivor of Theresienstadt, who told him his story. Clarke then agreed to design the synagogue's windows free of charge.

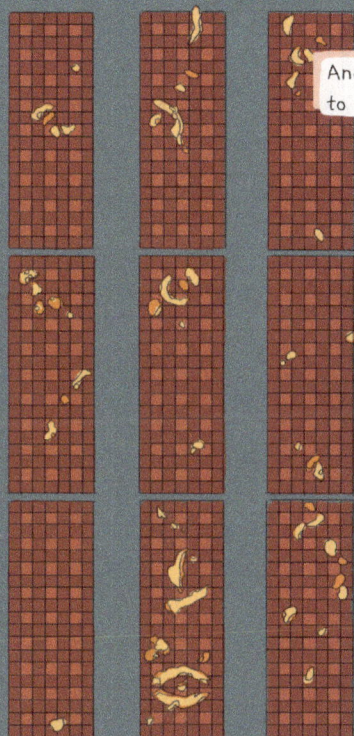

And his work throws us back to that awful night...

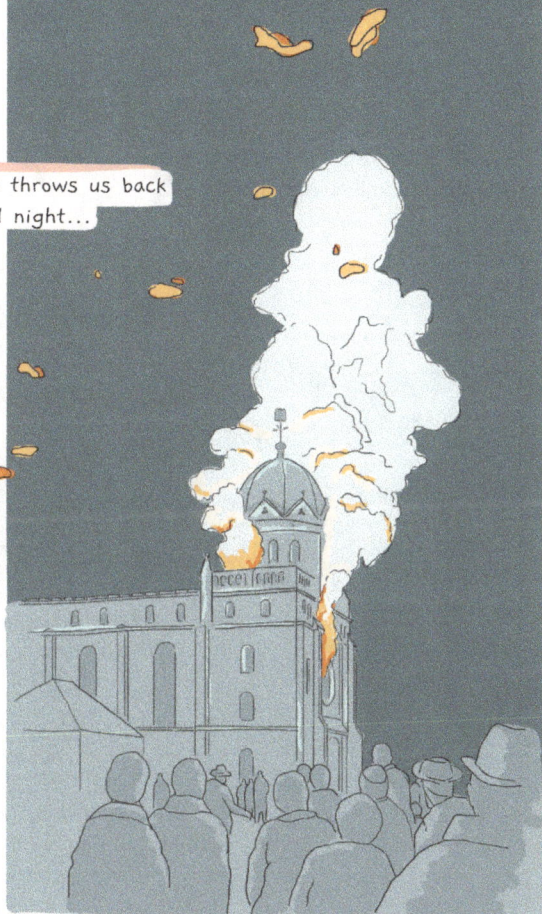

It's like a gem. It's the cherished piece.

Aldo Rossi, who was my teacher, had this idea that a city is like a fabric inlaid with "monuments" – that are not necessarily monumental, but **personal** ones.

Places that have something to do with your own identity. The synagogue, this gem, is meant to be the monument that guides the everyday.

Designing in a city where the synagogues were burnt — it can't be just a community center. It's like a **gate** for a Jewish cultural world that you can explore.

In the middle you have the synagogue, and around it there's an array of secular rooms that could exhibit our culture.

Prince Charles's aunt was the princess of Darmstadt. She had an old cupboard that the Jews gave her grandfather, the Prince of Hessen.

This is a beautiful building, but do you **really** think that we should build synagogues these days?

And on the plot where the gestapo's headquarters stood, no less!

On the opening day, one of the sons of Thomas Mann came to me with the princess and said —

You ask — how the hell can you be so forgiving? And I say — that's my **only** choice.

If you decide to stay, you have to learn how to live with your neighbor.

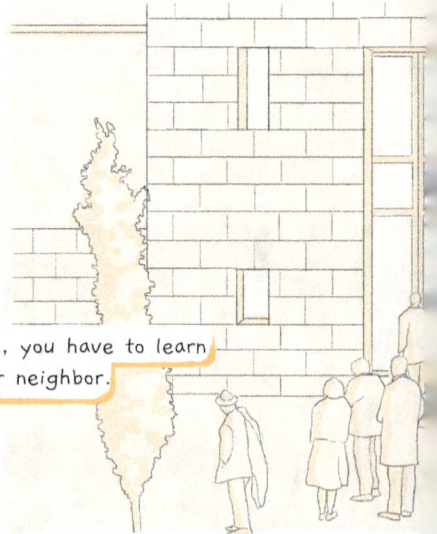

After the war, she wanted to give it back to the community.

To that were added more pieces that people brought, and together they formed the Darmstadt Jewish history museum.

I was actually not aware of that until my friend Moritz told me about it. I think it just happened to be available. This plot was owned by the municipality, and they could just procure it.

This kind of coincidence really makes you think though, right?

I was away from Germany for a long time. I only came back when I was thirty, after reading Ernst Bloch's writings about the principle of hope. It's the only force that can drive you out of such darkness.

Neualtland © Meitar Tewel 2021

the »weight« or the »seriousness« of the subject of religion. The graphic novel is often perceived, for better or worse, as a »lighter« or, to put it more positively, more accessible form of literature. So, this mode of representation, in combination with ficto-criticism, as defined by Frichot and Stead, seemed to offer a good (not all too heavy or earnest) »way in«; a way for students to focus on the everydayness of these projects, while at the same time drawing on their own »constructive, creative and critical situatedness« (Frichot/Stead 2020:12). I thoroughly enjoyed seeing the diversity of (hi)stories that resulted from the assignment that was set, and how everyone approached their graphic novel short story in a very different way.

Janina: In *Neualtland*, you opted for a somewhat autobiographical approach; embedding yourself in the narrative. Could you say a few words about what prompted this approach? Why did you choose to embed yourself in the story, and entangle your personal history with that of Alfred and the Darmstadt synagogue? Do you still see your graphic novel short story as a form of ficto-criticism? Or is it rather non-fiction?

Meitar: To be honest, becoming an illustrated figure in the graphic novel was not my original intention, but it turned out to be the natural way for me to approach the story of this particular project. In fact, I would say that my personal background set the tone for this entire creative process in a much more prominent way compared to my previous professional work. As a Jewish-Israeli granddaughter of the sole Holocaust survivor in the Dutch branch of my family, moving to The Netherlands quickly translated into a constant urge to position myself, both personally and professionally, in relation to the place and its traditions. There is a constant tension between the reality I grew up in, and some parallel version of post-war Europe, where I probably would have been born under different circumstances. Above all, the decision to study the Neue Synagogue stemmed from a personal interest: the opportunity to learn about post-war Jewish communities in Europe. I was also fortunate enough to personally know the project's architect, Professor Alfred Jacoby, who was the organizer of a workshop in the Bauhaus in which I had participated two years earlier. In our correspondence and the interview that I conducted as part of this elective, I realized that my emotional connection to the building's story cannot be denied, and that the frequent (unavoidable) gaps between Alfred, myself and the cultural baggage that each of us carries, revealed unexpected layers in the building's genesis and life. I embraced my curiosity and my approach to the unearthing of narratives as the structure

for this short graphic novel. I tend to believe that my own search for identity
and self-definition, for instance, pushed me into accentuating the expressions of such questions in the synagogue's design.

As for the second part of your question, I feel that the fact that my work is
based on an interview with Alfred did not veil the fictional nature of the
graphic novel as a medium of storytelling. Unlike more traditional forms of
historiography, the storyline illustrated in *Neualtland* constantly shifts between actors, places, moments in time, memories and speculations. These
shifts are intuitive, with no clear hierarchy between historic facts and subjective ideas, feelings or interpretations. In some segments of the graphic
novel, this can be seen in a very direct way: it is obvious that Nazis have never
actually walked in the corridor surrounding this post-modern building's
courtyard, and that Brian Clarke's stained-glass windows have never dissolved into the flames bursting out of the old synagogue during Kristallnacht. I believe that these obvious shifts from reality can be intuitively
understood by the reader, without harming the authenticity of the historic
events presented in the work. In other words, by being freed of the conventions of academic rigidity and using the opportunities afforded by this sort
of visual storytelling, I believe that my narrative, although non-fictional in
origin, can be understood as a form of ficto-criticism.

Janina: What is your evaluation (or appreciation) of the graphic novel ficto-critical short story as a mode of conducting research/narrating a history
in architecture?

Meitar: I have noticed that graphic novels are often dismissed as inferior
cultural products: they are rarely recognized as museum-worthy works of
visual art and only seldomly become Pulitzer-winning pieces of literature.
The upshot of this (perceived) dismissal is that it gives the format greater
freedom from literary conventions, allowing graphic novels to tell stories in
ways that are more accessible to the general public than high-brow art and
literature, thus gaining popularity in expanding informal cultural circles. In
architecture, in which discussion and research almost exclusively hinge on
words and drawings, the graphic novel, which is a hybrid of these exact tools,
seems to remain a surprisingly underexplored method of study. It might
seem excessively flamboyant as a mode of representation, but I believe that
the world of graphic novels (or comics) can offer architectural students an
entirely new set of tools for reading spaces. Perhaps above all, the graphic
novel is able to project a story onto a silent plan, section, and facade. When

creating architectural graphic novels with the intention of studying a building, we could expect a result that is less technical and more expressive compared to the discipline's more conventional analytical tools. By proposing an
alternative to the traditional way of reading architecture, this medium holds
the potential to reveal layers in a building's (hi)story that often remain hidden in the disciplinary discourse.

Meitar: Were we to finally take graphic novels seriously and welcome them
into the disciplinary set of tools — how do you see our influence, as architects, on the graphic novel as a medium? How could it change when going
through our professional filters? How do you evaluate the educational/peda-
gogical aspects of conducting this type of architectural exercise (opportunities and challenges)?

Janina: The first part of this question is very difficult for me to respond to.
On the one hand, I have insufficient knowledge of the history and diversity
of the graphic novel as a medium, and on the other hand, I have so far only
given this particular assignment to students once – to the group that you,
Meitar, were in – so I have not been able to observe first-hand how students/
architects-to-be might experiment with the medium and alter its codes and
conventions. That said, I do think that the graphic novel is a very accessible
medium for architecture students – particularly for courses that are more
historical/theoretical in nature. Needless to say, in most (if not all?) architecture schools, the emphasis in education lies on design, which is conveyed
through drawings: plans, sections, elevations, perspectives. Courses in history and theory are often perceived as a »necessary evil«. Of course, architects need to know their history (or histories), and need to be aware of the
social, political, cultural, environmental, etc. implications of their designs.
However, the output of these more historical and theoretical courses is often
a written paper, a medium that requires skills and tools that architecture
students are less familiar with than drawing and thus (often) dread or even
avoid. Situated in-between writing and drawing, and combining aspects of
both, the graphic novel, I believe, is more accessible to architecture students,
and allows them to draw on their strengths – be these drawing, or writing.
That said, I not only set the graphic novel as an assignment because of the
practical or technical merits of this medium. For me, more important still
was the invitation that the graphic novel short-story format extended to tell
a story about a building and to reflect on the life in and of the building; to
consider the building not just as a three-dimensional object that should be

described or drawn very drily and factually, but as something dynamic and four-dimensional, that exists through time; that leads a life and that also accommodates the lives and stories of many people. An important reference in this respect, as you know, was Ware's compendium *Building Stories*.

Janina: Could you say a bit more about the research process and the research methods that you used to develop your graphic novel short story? In the course, you were given readings, and also asked to conduct a survey of journal databases, but what other research methods did you rely on to develop the story – oral history, plan analysis, research into narrative analysis, research into graphic novels, …? How familiar were you with these methods prior to this elective, and how did these methods compare to the ones you used for your thesis, which you produced earlier this year? Did the set format (graphic novel short story) force you to venture down different research-method avenues? Or not?

Meitar: As you have suggested, this research process was profoundly different from my previous academic work. While in my history thesis I relied heavily on archival research and other forms of textual information, most of the data gathered for this graphic novel was based on oral history, i.e. my video calls with Alfred. I did have the opportunity to conduct a series of interviews for academic purposes in the past, but I would say that back then I often tried to strip the text from information that might distract from the facts. For example, any personal anecdotes that seemed unrelated to the research topic or to the field of architecture were removed. This approach could not have been more different from the process I had with Alfred. Our conversations were very open and associative, and we often seamlessly shifted between historical fact and subjective memory. As a result, the architectural discussion quickly became very emotionally charged – carrying narratives that go far beyond the building's plot and time. I think that in this case, oral history was necessary as a means to create this certain historiographic product, which gives just as much importance to emotions, memories, and thoughts as it does to archival documentation. For this elective, I also conducted research into graphic novels as a medium. I only had a few casual encounters with graphic novels before. Luckily, my partner is a fan of graphic novels, and could recommend some contemporary works and give me a private crash course on some of the graphic and narrative tools used. My most important reference was *Maus* by the American cartoonist Art Spiegelman, the only graphic novel ever to win a Pulitzer prize.[5] Aside from the similarity in theme – *Maus* focuses on the experiences of Spiegelman's father as a Polish Jew and Holocaust survivor – the method of research was also similar: Spiegelman also conducted a series of interviews with his father to form the basis for this visual story, which alternates between their dialogue as the framing narrative and his father's memories as the story within the story. A similar technique is used in the Israeli animated documentary *Waltz with Bashir*, in which the creator recollects his memories from the First Lebanon War through a series of conversations with other soldiers who served alongside him (Folman/Polonsky 2009). These two references helped me a lot in my process, both in terms of narrative structure and visual tools.

Meitar: What's next? Learning from our shared experience in the elective, how would you imagine further use of graphic novels as a fictio-critical tool in architectural education? Would you change anything in the course's structure?
Janina: Another difficult question! On the one hand, I do not like repeating myself. There are so many interesting methods and formats to experiment with to probe the bounds of architectural historiography, that I find doing the same thing twice a pity. I would, for instance, really like to run a course inspired by *Flat Out Magazine*, which asks contributors to assume a particular (predefined) character or persona when writing, such as »The Mortician«, who is asked to write a »memoir of a brush with death«, or »The Muckracker«, who »follows the money« (»Audition« n.d.) . It would be a really interesting exercise to organize an elective focused on one particular building project and have each student assume a different persona in their analysis of that building project. That said, I was tremendously pleased and impressed with the work that came out of our elective last semester. So, I will likely run it once more. Maybe even two more times! As already mentioned in response to a previous question: this format seems to suit students of architecture particularly well. So, I hope that in the future, this medium will be recognized, and the format will not be »banished« to operating only in quirky little research electives (like the one that I ran last semester), but will also be accepted for the writing of actual theses in architectural history and theory – a new species of thesis! I did come to realize during the course that I should

---

5 The graphic novel was serialized from 1980 to 1991 in the magazine *Raw*. In 1992, *Maus* won the Pulitzer Prize for literature. All issues of the graphic novel have since been gathered together in Spiegelman (1994).

probably have offered more information about the background and (style) conventions of the graphic novel as a format. This can be very practical; for instance, to show examples of different graphic ways in which you can clarify the reading »direction«. But it can also be more focused on how the format can allow the weaving together of different stories and temporalities. This is something that, I think, you did brilliantly in yours, thanks to your own research into the format of the graphic novel.

Janina: What will you »take with you« from this course? If anything?
Meitar: I think it is fair to say that my architectural education so far has been pretty old-fashioned. As a result, most of my written works rigorously follow academic conventions and my design methods tend to be rather conventional. While my love for good old technical drawing remains intact, the opportunity to create this short graphic novel, and to experiment with alternative means of examining architecture has been truly eye-opening, and was also further enhanced by reflecting on it together with you right now, in this email conversation. Above all, this experience showed me that I can become an active participant rather than a passive observer in the telling of a building's story. In light of my upcoming graduation project, I'm very excited by the possibility to further explore the graphic novel as a medium – and perhaps other media that are yet to be introduced to our discipline. I am particularly curious to see whether I can translate this exercise into a design tool and inject a first-person narrative into a building that does not yet exist. I hope to see it open more opportunities for a richer design process and architectural product, in a similar vein to the way in which the graphic novel challenged the scope of historiographic research in architecture.

Over the past two decades, under the influence of developments in critical theory and connected to revisionist trends in other fields, scholarship in architectural history has transformed. This transformation has not only affected the subjects that are addressed in architectural history – creating space for topics such as gender, race, and the environment – but has also thrown its methodological approaches into the limelight. In the introduction to *Writing Architectural History: Evidence and Narrative in the Twenty-First Century*, which appeared only a few months ago, Daniel M. Abramson, Zeynep Çelik Alexander, and Michael Osman, ask: »What kinds of evidence does architectural history use? How is this evidence organized in different narratives and towards what ends? .... And finally, how can considerations of evidence and narrative help us all to reimagine the limits and the potentials of the field?« (Abramson/Çelik Alexander/Osman 2021: 3). Books such as *Writing Architectures: Ficto-Critical Approaches*, as well as *Speaking of Buildings: Oral History in Architectural Research*, address precisely such questions (Frichot/Stead 2020; Gosseye/Stead/van der Plaat 2019).[6] In the conclusion to the last book, its editors point toward the bias toward text that exists in academic work, as they ponder the efficacy of other forms and formats to capture architectural history (Stead/van der Plaat/Gosseye 2019: 275). *Neualtland*, as well as the research elective that informed its production, and the current paper that reflects on this exercise, builds on this body of scholarship. It is an attempt to test and question the pros and cons, and the felicities and failures of architectural and urban design historiography through graphic novel ficto-criticism. The hope is that the shift away from more conventional modes of architectural historiography that it represents, is not merely a shift in tools – from writing to drawing – but an epistemological shift that can help scholars of architecture, be they Master's students, PhD candidates, senior researchers, or »do-it-yourself historians«, unlock and develop new knowledge about architecture and its history.

References

Abramson, Daniel M./Çelik Alexander, Zeynep/Osman, Michael (2021): »Introduction: Evidence, Narrative, and Writing Architectural History«, in: Aggregate Architectural History Collaborative (eds.), *Writing Architectural History: Evidence and Narrative in the Twenty-First Century*, Pittsburgh: University of Pittsburgh Press, 3–16.

»Audition« (n.d.). In: Flat Out, https://www.flatoutmag.org/audition, accessed July 27, 2021.

Engel, Matthew (2018): »Germany Reclaimed: Berlin's Jewish Revival«. In: *The New Statesman*, May 23, https://www.newstatesman.com/uncategorized/2018/05/germany-reclaimed-berlin-s-jewish-revival, accessed February 10, 2022.

Folman, Ari/Polonsky, David (2009): *Waltz with Bashir: A Lebanon War Story*, New York: Metropolitan Books.

Frichot, Hélène/Stead, Naomi, eds. (2020): *Writing Architectures: Ficto-Critical Approaches*, London: Bloomsbury.

---

6 These two examples are, of course, only the tip of the iceberg. The body of scholarship examining the modes and sources of writing architectures is, of course, much more extensive, and growing rapidly.

»Gemeindezentrum Gladbeck-Rentfort Nord« (1985), in: *Deutsche Bauzeitschrift* 33/12, 1594–1596.

Gosseye, Janina/Stead, Naomi/van der Plaat, Deborah, eds. (2019): *Speaking of Buildings: Oral History in Architectural Research*, New York: Princeton Architectural Press.

»Kirchliches Zentrum Langendorf SO« (1927), in: *Werk* 59/4, 214–217.

»Prof. Alfred Jacoby« (n.d.). In: *Dessau Institute of Architecture*, http://dia-live.com/18/people-2/prof-alfred-jacoby/, accessed February 10, 2022.

Spiegelman, Art (1994): *The Complete Maus: A Survivor's Tale*, New York: Voyager.

Stead, Naomi/van der Plaat, Deborah/ Gosseye, Janina (2019): »Ways to Listen Anew: What Next for Oral History and Architecture?«. In: Janina Gosseye/Naomi Stead/Deborah van der Plaat (eds.), *Speaking of Buildings: Oral History in Architectural Research*, New York: Princeton Architectural Press.

»Synagoge mit Gemeindezentrum in Darmstadt gestiftet« (1991), in: *Deutsche Bauzeitschrift* 39/2, 180–181.

Tewel, Meitar (2021): »Neualtland«. In: *Meitar Tewel*, https://www.meitartewel.com/neualtland, accessed February 10, 2022.

Ware, Chris (2012): *Building Stories*, New York: Pantheon Books.

Dimensions of Architectural Knowledge, 2022-03 ᚽ
https://doi.org/10.14361/dak-2022-0310

METALOGUE
Conversing across Student and Teacher,
Human and Inhuman Relations

Therese Keogh and Hélène Frichot

Abstract: This experimental piece of writing explores how a metalogue can open a space of conversation expressed across student and teacher, human and inhuman relations. Drawing on the metalogues between father and daughter in Gregory Bateson's *Steps to an Ecology of Mind*, the performance of this metalogue seeks to disrupt habitual power relations and mix conceptual with material expression. Of central concern are the ways in which both materials and concepts are extracted for use in built environment industries and industries of higher education, begging the question of how to work ethically within material and educational industries. The metalogue performs unruly interruptions and contradictions of voices, following a flow of materials both conceptual and concrete to grapple with pressing environmental imbroglios. The structure of the metalogue is necessarily open-ended, avoiding specific recommendations or answers to problems, instead fostering a glimmering understanding of how entangled we are amid environmental relations.

Keywords: Materiality; Extraction; Pedagogy; Creative Practice.

The Metalogue is a genre that apes the Platonic dialogue, challenging its implicit power relations. Where in the Platonic dialogue Socrates always wins out in the end, talking his interlocutor into a position of submission, the Metalogue addles such power relations. The Metalogue comes from the second edition of Gregory Bateson's *Steps to an Ecology of Mind* and describes an open-ended conversation between a father and his daughter (Bateson 2000). The authority of the patriarchal position is established and then undone through the deceptively simple questions raised by the daughter. The meta of metalogue suggests what is above or comes after, that which operates on another level. Here, what is at stake is the complexity of abstract concepts, especially where they have become ungrounded. The Metalogue demonstrates

Corresponding authors: Therese Keogh (University of Melbourne, Australia); keogh.t@unimelb.edu.au; https://orcid.org/0000-0003-4674-9431; Hélène Frichot (University of Melbourne, Australia); helene. frichot@unimelb.edu.au; https://orcid.org/0000-0002-1755-5075

1.
Rainbow Lorikeet Fledglings Sheltering in Elm Tree Nook, Princes Park.
Photographer: Hélène Frichot, 2021.

in its wandering, peripatetic form that concepts risk being empty unless thought through specific problems or situations.

In a serendipitous homonymic slip, »Metalogue« also sounds like »Metal-logue«, suggesting a dialogic form that transforms both thinking and matter. Here, questions concerning the extraction of ore and the burning of coal set the grounds for a conversation that reshapes itself according to agglomerations and transmutations produced in smelting metals from ore bodies. This Metalogue further takes place in the relation of doctoral education, between a supervisor and a doctoral researcher, where, we argue, knowledge is not located in one position or the other, but passed back and forth, emerging and transforming in the very act of dialoguing.

Understanding that transformation does not happen without remainder, the Metalogue enunciates its own excesses, with inhuman voices from the world of ores and slag offering interjections and disruptions to each call and response. Themes of extraction – pertaining to both geological materials and intellectual institutions – are turned over throughout this exchange. The »voice« of slag is enacted as a discontinuous alloy of citations, where the writings of others are built up through a series of disruptions to our conversation; fragments of text that reshape our writing and interrupt our thinking with each other. The »voice« of clinker undertakes the pragmatic work of contextually situating the reader and offering sometimes indecorous narrative asides.

In this conceit of offering voice to non-living matter, we are at risk of committing an anthropomorphic sleight of hand. This is part of an ongoing struggle with human exceptionalism and anthropocentrism, or how we are ever at risk of claiming points of view and positions of power amid environment-worlds. There is also humor that we hope to communicate through the material asides offered by slag and clinker in our Metalogue below. While we can never hope to adequately represent these non-human materials, nevertheless, the attempt might bring us closer to an understanding of the complex and dynamic stratifications of life and non-life (Hird/Yusoff 2020).

This Metalogue commences in Princes Park, Parkville, Melbourne, a park that by its very name points to the history of Empire and struggles toward decolonization. Histories of settler colonialism are evident in the royal allusions of this naming, obscuring place names or dreaming lines that might have been known and practiced by the original Indigenous custodians, the Wurundjeri of the Kulin nation. We sometimes take these supervisorial strolls on account of the pandemic and the rolling lockdowns imposed on the city of Melbourne. We meet where MacPherson intersects with Princes Park Drive. Appropriate

2.
Therese›s Homemade Forge. Photographer: Therese Keogh, 2020.

3.
Clinker and Slag. Photographer: Therese Keogh, 2020.

to the seams of ore we follow, Thomas MacPherson, as it turns out, was a 19th-century iron and steel merchant, as well as a Melbourne City councillor and mayor. This Metalogue thus sets itself in motion by wandering in a local park.

Slag: »Dialogue begins where one is, and thus is always situated ... Dialogue is open, and thus ... The outcome is not known in advance.« (Rose 2015: 129).

TK: I've brought along some clinker for you to handle. This comes from the forge I built on my Mum's farm in Central Victoria during the first Melbourne lockdown in 2020. I had been living in London prior to Covid and found myself suddenly back in Australia and trying to imagine what fieldwork and spatial practice might look like from the position of being still. Do you want to hold it?

Clinker: composite|rock-like|handle it|care|crumbles|she|meant to receive|in hands|-looking up|distracted|lorikeet|disappeared|nest-nook|tree branch|she turns|back|paying attention now|takes possession|of it|turning it|carefully|her hands|it feels|crumbs of itself|pulling apart|falling to pieces|

HF: I'm worried it will break, it's so fragile. It looks like it has metal on one side and gravel on the other.

TK: I have an overabundance of clinker, so it's not an issue if it breaks (it's fragmented anyway). I thought you could take it home if you'd like. In lieu of us meeting in my studio. Perhaps taking a bit of studio home is the next best thing. A way that we can relate materially to one another through writing.

Slag: »The ›we‹ being invoked here *includes* both the human and drastically inhuman. It includes the communities of people on the surface of the earth *and* the earth itself, riven with fractures.« (Bosworth 2016: 24).

HF: Really? What happens if it breaks?

Clinker: [...] and|the time|she home|broken|three parts|caught in carpet|lie lacklustre|shelf|sighing|sloughing off crumbs|of itself|now and again|

4.
Clinker Rests on a Steel Picnic Table, Princes Park.
Photographer: Hélène Frichot, 2021.

HF: I'm still trying to get my head around some of the terminology that is relevant to your project on writing on or to material excess. Can you explain to me the difference between slag and clinker? I understand that both are waste products that result from mining, or from processes of extraction. It has been astonishing to see the proliferation of discourse and close material attention being paid to the devastations of extractivism in recent years, and I'm especially excited by your project.

> Slag: »Waste is simultaneously civilization's *other* - a threat to the bonds that keep the obscene and the unspeakable repressed from the social sphere - as well as the trace or *remainder* of civilization: The pollution, discards, and unwanted productions of the past that haunt our present.« (Schmidt 2014: 16).

TK: I guess I have a couple of answers to this. On a material level, »slag« is a term used to describe the leftover from the process of smelting metals from ore (steel, silver, aluminium etc.), where the ore – extracted from the ore body – is heated at a high enough temperature that it separates out the metal from the rock. What's left is steel –to be used in manufacturing – and slag – an agglomeration of all the stuff that isn't steel. It's part mutated alloy, part strange geology.

»Clinker« is the name for a type of slag that comes from the process of burning coal – more often than not, bituminous coal – where all the non-combustible matter stored within the coal is left to particulate-congeal-melt-fuse into new geological configurations. The presence of clinker makes coal burning less efficient. It builds up – in the furnace/boiler/forge – to create a blockage that cools, and eventually smothers the fire. It's a loose end in a linear material process.

> Slag: »This too is how we might see the role of fire in crafting social worlds. Not only do flames transform the very stuff of the world, but fire has a special role in simmering, fusing, melding, alloying, and annealing the heterogeneous elements of social life into workable unity. To which must be added fire's omnipresent capacity to unravel and obliterate the very order it has helped bring into being.« (Clark 2018: 6).

TK: The second part of your question though, entirely depends on what definitions of »waste« we're happy to subscribe to, doesn't it? What if slag is something else? Its own creative matter that rearranges narratives/histories/

desires of extraction and burning into something other than the dominant/ normative? That fragments these narratives and re-fuses[1] them into new formations that offer alternative possibilities for understanding the structures of power/history/economy that they are produced by?

> Slag: »To illuminate the contested character of history, narrative, event, and fact, to topple the hierarchy of discourse, and to engulf authorized speech in the clash of voices ... [in a] ›recombinant narrative‹, which ›loops the strands‹ of incommensurate accounts and which weaves present, past, and future.« (Hartman 2008: 12).

TK: »Slag« is a by-product of melting rock. It's a word kids in Australia use instead of »spit«. It derogatively describes the sexuality of a person who doesn't conform to cultural standards of normativity. It's the expression of an insult. Have you read *How Reading is Written* by Astrid Lorange? In her chapter »Queering« she adopts Lee Edelman's concept of »homographesis« as a framework to analyse extensions of queerness in and of the writings of Gertrude Stein (Lorange 2014). Homographesis assumes the position of the »homograph« – a word with multiple meanings, but a single spelling (e.g. »slag«, »forge«, »mine«, »gob«, »fault«, »flux« etc.) – as an example of a double signifier, an inscription of textual multiplicity. Operating against fixed etymological origins, homographesis explores the capacity for queerness to simultaneously signify incongruous meanings. I've been thinking about these textual slippages for a while now and wonder how our »metalogue«/ »metal-logue« might be playing out a kind of textual/material multiplicity. And what this might open up for both our thinking around these material conditions and our relating to each other through dialogue?

> Slag: »And language is material in a radical sense: not the medium through which thought communicates, but a multiplicity of relations and traces that enables what comes to experience itself as thought.« (Cohen & Colebrook 2016: 13).

HF: Your projects engage in following the materials of iron and coal by acknowledging their purported waste materials and now I'm beginning to understand a bit better how this assumption about what constitutes waste

---

1   »Re-fuse« as in fuse in new form. Also, »refuse«, as in »residue/remainder/waste«, and »refuse«, as in »resist/decline/reject«.

might be placed under interrogation. Both coal and iron are connected in being dug out of the ground, and in the process of the dig producing unwanted by-products. Australia is renowned for extracting these primary resources, taken with little or no serious consideration of original Indigenous custodians. I've heard Tess Lea talk about how even where long campaigns to claim Indigenous land rights have achieved Native title, the policy is written in such a way as to establish mechanisms for securing exploitation and mining rights (Lea 2020). These rights then entangle Indigenous communities with the profits gleaned from mining. In the devastating case of Juukan Gorge in 2020, where Indigenous sacred sites exhibiting ritual use extending over 46,000 years were dynamited to make way for the expansion of the Brockman 4 mine, the agreement between Rio Tinto and the Puutu Kinti Kurrama and Pinikura was effectively and all too easily abused. There was talk in the media of a gag that had been placed on the Indigenous custodians, restraining them from speaking out against the mining company.

Slag: »Patriarchal white possession disavows aboriginal sovereignty by using racist techniques premised on western conventions, laws and knowledges. The Australian government in fact circumscribes native title rights by privileging the interest of pastoralists and mining companies.« (Moreton-Robinson 2015: 66–67).

Clinker: looping stroll|carried along|wandering southwards|heading back|north on|western side|crossing|white lines|demarcate quiet soccer|fields|emptied of play|pausing|now|beside grove|iron|bark|trees|

TK: Coal and steel go hand in hand; their industries developing in symbiotic exchange, their matter repurposed in the creation of Australia as a nation-state under British rule, their positions as this nation's first and second largest exports (followed by LNG in third place, and education in fourth), their twinned discharge of slag and clinker (Brett 2020: 9).

Here is the stand of ironbarks I mentioned, shall we have a look at them?

HF: Look at how red the bark is! Why are they called ironbark? It looks like they have sucked iron, or even blood from the earth.

TK: I've been walking around a couple of clumps of ironbark trees (Eucalyptus sideroxylon) in Royal Park for the past couple of months and have slowly

5.
Ironbark Trunk, Princes Park.
Photographer: Hélène Frichot, 2021.

become obsessed with them. For a while I assumed they were named »iron-bark« because they kind of look metallic. One day, I saw red sap oozing down the side of one of the trees. It looked like blood, and it made me think that perhaps the »iron« in »ironbark« came from the fact that the tree itself contained iron – that it was partly metallic. I once heard about some trees in Germany that were growing in iron-rich soil. The roots of the trees drew water from the ground up and into the fibers of timber, carrying particles of iron so that the trees grew hard and heavy. They're a hardwood, and their hardness and strength made them useful in building: ships, bridges, foundations. I read that the name »ironbark« comes from their resemblance to iron slag, that they're a kind of partial representation of the material remainder of smelting steel from iron ore.

Clinker: it repeats itself|it repeats itself|it repeats itself|regurgitation of thinking|back and forth|endlessly additive|seen all before|pass through|those|material processes|- fire|and air|and molten stuff|now coagulated|

TK: I wonder how we grapple with this proximity? The proximity of a tree – endemic to the east coast of this island – to a geology formed by burning iron ore on a large enough scale and a high enough heat to result in slag. The proximity of a tree to an industry of conquest and export, of nation building, of extraction, of fire. Its colonial namesake being a material produced by its own excessive production and reproduction of itself.

> Slag: »Disorientation involves contact with things, but a contact in which ›things‹ slip as a proximity that does not hold things in place, thereby creating a feeling of distance.« (Ahmed 2006: 166)

HF: When we last went for a walk, we circled Royal Park. Remember how we talked about scar trees then? I'm still struggling to complete my essay on scar trees, but I've read in the meantime that there is a scar tree somewhere in Royal Park. I'm thinking of them now because they might be understood as another kind of resource.

TK: Can you talk a little more about your interest in scar trees? I'm keen to hear. I'm especially interested in your description of them as resources. What do you mean by ›resource‹?

HF: I think it has been something to do with the shock of returning to Australia after being away for nearly a decade. There appears to have been a distinct and positive shift of consciousness in relation to Indigenous knowledge practices. I've found this really fascinating, as well as humbling. It seems that scholarship is not possible while standing on these unceded lands without somehow, at some point, addressing the ancient legacy of Indigenous knowledges. I was writing an article on witnessing and wanted to make it about an encounter with Country, and what might be learned through such an encounter. I'm interested in what we don't or can't see, and what we refuse to see. The scar tree emerged as a distinct figure to help me frame my questioning, a thing that gathers so much lore, and so many stories. A good place to have a yarn. Serendipitously, the Tree School event was on at MADA (Monash Art Design Architecture), composing part of the *Tree Stories* exhibition at MUMA (Monash University Museum of Art).[2] An old, gray, dismembered scar tree was the centerpiece, laid out with reverence on large pillows, procuring a place around which to gather to share stories.

> Slag: »This ordinary word *ding* or thing, one we use on a daily basis to stand in for things we have forgotten the names for, or, a word for just about anything, is also one of the oldest words we have to designate the oldest of sites in which our ancestors did their deals and attempted to settle their disputes. The humble thing around which we gather to share our concerns.« (Latour 2004: 233).

HF: I spent a remarkable morning there listening to N'arweet Carolyn Briggs talking about Indigenous knowledge practices and care for Country (the »Arweet« in her title indicates her important tribal position in the Indigenous Kulin nation). I'm especially interested in how the scar tree is harvested for its resources, but rather than being felled, it remains alive. With care, an oblong wedge is cut from the trunk to shape a canoe, or a coolamon, or another similar container technology. Scar trees are associated with both Indigenous resources and rituals, and the concepts of wound and scar suggest both violence and healing.

---

2   The Tree School is one of a series of such schools organized by architects Sandi Hilal and Alessandro Petti. This iteration of the Tree School was coordinated by Yorta Yorta and Woiwurrung artist, organizer, and educator, Moorina Bonini. See https://www.monash.edu/mada/events/2021/The-Tree-School.

This makes me think that different registers of resource need to be conceptualized. Coal and iron are resources extracted for profit. The scar tree is also called a resource tree, but the way the resource is taken here indexes an entirely different kind of practice of land use. Resources are also intellectual resources. When articles are peer reviewed, a reviewer can be asked to remark on whether the article is adequately resourced, that is, whether the literature review is appropriate in scope and depth. I've been wondering what are the implications of discussing our literature and our methods in terms of so many resources for future production of yet more research outcomes?

TK: What's the etymology of resource?

HF: I don't know. I wonder whether it comes from source, and thereby from a notion of origins. If it leads to a notion of source and we think this in relation to how disciplinary knowledge is legitimized, we can see how certain approaches to Knowledge, capital K, as distinct from knowledge practices or know-how come to be privileged. The difference between primary and secondary sources in the scholar's literature review, for instance.

> Slag: »A different kind of knowledge is thus invoked, a knowledge that is neither transparent nor rational, but secret and subterranean, ambivalent and contingent. A kind of knowledge where questions of provenance and origin - what time, when, who? - are redistributed to encompass lateral sensations of proximity and distance, intensity or indifference.« (Barikin 2017: 270).

HF: Returning to the right source promises to legitimize our research, heading in the wrong direction, or toward a source that is less well known or more marginal, may mean receiving a negative review. But when we think of sources, and our knowledge as a resource, then we can begin to reflect on how it is extracted, which is something that is discussed in Laura Junka-Aikio and Catalina Cortes-Severino's work on the cultural studies of extraction (Junka-Aikio/ Cortes-Severino 2017). What about the material excesses of a literature review...

Clinker: graphematic pause|marked|three small dots|already started|become dust|particulating|conversation|transcribed in hindsight|bits of it eavesdrop|sighing at|mention of margins|

TK: I love the idea that a literature review might have material excesses (I mean, of course!), and now I'm thinking about what they might be, what shape they might take. My first instinct is to look at the notes I've scrawled in my book, the fragments of thinking that help me to sit with texts, to understand or inhabit them more deeply, but which will never be made public. I imagine them as the loose ends of my reading and the transformative remainders of my own processing of another's writing. I imagine the conversations I have with friends about texts that confront or trouble me, or inspire me to think and work differently to my habits. Could the material excesses of a literature review be the fragments of textual thinking that radiate outward from our movements between reading and writing? From the transformative motion that turns one (reading) into another (writing), in an ongoing process? I'm really enjoying thinking with this idea and wondering how this might be practiced throughout our metalogue/metal-logue, (which itself is a collection of fragments).

> Slag: »If we concede that we do not yet have a language with which to speak the radical intimacies of the inhuman, nor know what it means to receive its solar gifts without recourse to mastery, it is only through entering the processes that those loves and desires spark that such language might be forged ... If we employ a mode of attention or experimentation that is not an interpretation, but attempts to follow the geography of the underground, its holes, passages, and burrows, its dead ends, seams, and collapsed shafts, then this is to affirm an alternative that is uninterpretable, an experiment that is an alternative to interpretation. To affirm fragments.« (Yusoff 2015: 214–215).

TK: I want to ask you a question about disciplinarity. It feels a little obvious, or a little blunt, but I wondered to what extent you choose to maintain a commitment to disciplinarity? I suppose this is in the context of architecture for you, but it's something I've been thinking about a lot in relation to art too. This comes back to the Maria Fusco quote I sent you a few weeks ago, where she writes that »to be the amateur is vastly preferable to being the professional, for the amateur proceeds with alacrity and resourcefulness. By its nature, interdisciplinary research renders each of us precarious, each of us the amateur— by necessitating as it does adaptation across discipline boundary.« I'm curious about the precarity of moving from one discipline to another – as researcher, artist, writer etc. – but also wonder if what could be added to this is the ways that interdisciplinarity also renders disciplines themselves – disciplinary structures, silos, institutions – precarious in a way too. What do you think?

Clinker: *pausing|south side| stadium|machines scrapping|and pulling|slowly demolishing|part|stadium seating|watching| fixated|hose sprays|water|scene|of destruction|dust caught|particles|water|mechanical hand|pulls|crunches concrete|detaching concrete|embedded|reinforcement bars|crumbling and tearing|of concrete|strange kind|fascinated pleasure.*

HF: I began with architecture and drifted into philosophy seeking a line of escape from a discipline that felt so restrictive. Some of my most interesting encounters in architecture involved being introduced to feminist theories and continental philosophies. But holding a PhD in philosophy is not much use as a resource these days. Philosophy departments are shrinking and disappearing, philosophy is going extinct.

> Slag: »No one needs philosophers to think for them anymore. It›s no use asking philosophers to offer their reflection on things, for anyone is capable of reflecting. Their job is different, they need to form, foster, create concepts, and only concepts that are pertinent to problems. Philosophy does not contemplate, reflect or communicate, they attend to the grounds of immanence. The ground shelters the seeds of concepts, and the philosopher cultivates the field so the concept-seeds grow. Sometimes, uncultivated fields of weeds can be the result, for better and for worse.« (Deleuze/Guattari 1994: 6–7).

HF: The result for me, finally, is that I am at home in neither discipline, and even worry about being a figure of suspicion when standing in one field or the other, never quite right, either too architectural, or too conceptual. Honestly, I still feel like an amateur in both. Being cross-disciplinary is not something that is easy to achieve, you must know how this feels yourself, working across art, landscape architecture, and geography.

I have a dear friend and former colleague in Sweden, Cecilia Åsberg, who works in the feminist post-humanities, and she speaks of post-disciplinarity. I guess this is a position that argues against situating ourselves as what Isabelle Stengers calls the »guardians of knowledge«, protecting our domains, challenging trespassers. Where does being possessive lead us if not into closed-minded enclosures!

Slag: »Slag! Slag! Slag! Slag!« (More 2021).

TK: Yes, this is something I've been thinking and working with for a while now (with varying levels of success!). My interest in art and art practice is around what art can do beyond itself; how art contributes to the material-social conditions of the world and its possibilities for transforming these conditions in some way. For me, I approach everything I do from the position of being an artist and coming from a grounding in art practice. But from that position, I'm interested in what can be offered and learned from thinking and working through other frames. In this way I feel like I'm constantly moving into the outskirts of art. What's perhaps different about art – compared to »disciplines« like history or geography or philosophy – is that it doesn't share quite the same lineage in terms of a post-Enlightenment academy of disciplines. Most art schools in Australia have a history of being technical colleges, which have then become spaces for contemporary art education, and have then been subsumed into universities. Is this the same for architecture? I'm not quite sure. This shift in art education has come with a lot of tensions (which I won't go into here), and the disciplinary structuring of art is definitely not an easy one. From that uneasy relationship though, I think there's a lot of potential for art to seep in and rearrange some of the disciplinary structures of the larger academy, and art practice offers a lot of strategies for challenging disciplinarity outside of itself. Perhaps this is a little optimistic! But this is how I'm thinking about my own work at the moment. As a kind of seepage. This leakage definitely makes me feel less stable on the grounds of art though, and like you, I don't feel particularly »at home« in any of these spaces. Maybe leaking is something that needs to happen peripherally (if I can push that metaphor a little more), and also resituates my relationships to disciplines within a slightly peripheral space.

Slag: What are your seams? ... Can we look at each other and say this is the distance between us? Or here, this is our edge?« (Singh 2017: 336).

TK: To your second point! Have you read *Unthinking Mastery: Dehumanism and Decolonial Entanglements* by Julietta Singh? I think you'd like it a lot. In the book Singh explores modes of unthinking mastery through an investigation of relations that intersect matter and narrative to »reach for different ways of inhabiting our scholarly domains« (Singh 2018: 8). »Unthinking« is used as a way of reimagining possibilities for relating – between human, nonhuman, inhuman – where Singh proposes dehumanist practice (drawing on anti-co-lonial politics and queer inhumanisms) to understand mastery as a materi-al-narrative entanglement. What I love about this book is the ways that Singh works at the threshold of matter and narrative to propose alternative modes of inhabiting spaces of knowledge production and material practice through an undoing rather than disavowal. I find this thinking really helpful in figuring out how one might move between social/structural/material spaces of the university, adopting a practice of undoing.

> Slag: »Mastery is a concept that is situated at the threshold of matter and narrative. As a fundamentally narrative problematic, mastery assigns partic-ular roles (the master, the slave) and holds those roles in place (it ›character-izes‹ them) in a temporal, narrative structure... Once mastery is understood as an entanglement between narrative and matter, or ›matter and meaning‹ (BARAD 2007), it becomes crucial to recognize how the narratives of mastery are always fragile, threatened, and impossible.« (Singh 2018: 17–18).

TK: Can this material-narrative fragility accompany Fusco's precarity of in-terdisciplinary practice in a way? If we can align disciplinarity with mastery, with – as you say – a type of possession, can interdisciplinary/postdisci-plinary/undisciplined practice offer a way of undoing some of these struc-tures of mastery, toward a kind of leaky amateurism?

HF: This makes me think of Sepideh Karami who once alerted me to the con-nection between the amateur and the lover (Karami 2018). That's where the word amateur comes from: to love, to be a lover. To love, to be loved. So, now we are imagining researchers and their materials as leaky lovers getting all entangled. The leakage is also a line of escape from what is most oppressive, a new path that can be forged, a means of rethinking our material-semiotic relations. And again, we have this relation to extraction. The undergrowth is cleared or extracted all the better to forge a path, when we make our way, sometimes fumbling, often blindly, hoping for the best.

> Slag: »For, I too sucked satiny coals. Once I burned my tongue... Ever since I have no longer dared to suck real fire; for a long time I lived off electricity. But I have never forgotten the fiery taste of eternity.« (Cixous 1983: 24).

Clinker: *interlocutors part ways|compressed in darkness|shedding parts of itself in a transfer between hands|in a dialogic exchange of pieces|a re-situating of matter|fragments|rearranges as dust|concepts turnover|change shape|calls and responses|authority and knowledge|and sigh.*

References

Ahmed, Sara (2006): *Queer Phenomenology: Orientations, Objects, Others*, Durham, NC and London: Duke University Press.

Barikin, Amelia (2017): »Sound Fossils and Speaking Stones: Towards a Mineral Ontology of Contemporary Art«, in: Christopher Braddock (ed), *Animism in Art and Performance*, London: Palgrave Macmillan.

Bateson, Gregory (2000): *Steps to an Ecology of Mind*, Chicago: University of Chicago Press.

Bosworth, Kai (2016): »Thinking Permeable Matter through Feminist Geophilosophy: Environmental Knowledge Controversy and the Materiality of Hydrogeologic Processes«, in: *Environment and Planning D: Society and Space*, 35/1 .

Brett, Judith (2020): *The Coal Curse: Resources, Climate and Australia's Future*, Quarterly Essay, Melbourne: Black Inc Books.

Cixous, Hélène (1983): *The Book of Promethea*, transl. Betsy Wing, Lincoln, NE: University of Nebraska Press.

Clark, Nigel (2018): »Earth, Fire, Art: Pyrotechnology and the Crafting of the Social«,in: N. Marres/M.Guggenheim/A. Wilkie (eds), *Inventing the Social*, London: Mattering Press.

Cohen, Tim/ Colebrook, Claire (2016): *Twilight of Anthropocene Idols*, London: Open Humanities Press.

Deleuze, Gilles/Guattari, Félix (1994): *What is Philosophy?*, New York: Columbia University Press.

Fusco, Maria (2019): »No Assignment for Cowards: What Is to Be Gained through Interdisciplinary Research«, in: C. Caduff/T. Wälchli (eds), *Artistic Research and Literature*, T. Paderborn: Wilhelm Fink, 82–83.

Hartman, Saidiya (2008): »Venus in Two Acts«, in: *Small Axe* 12, 2.

Junka-Aikio,Laura/ Cortes-Severino, Catalina (2017): »Cultural Studies of Extraction« , in: *Cultural Studies* 31/ 2–3, 175–184.

Karami, Sepideh (2018): *Interruption: Writing a Dissident Architecture*, PhD, Critical Studies in Architecture, School of Architecture and the Built Environment, KTH Stockholm, Sweden. http://kth.diva-portal.org/smash/record.jsf?pid=diva2%3A1191313&dswid=-8326 [Accessed: September 3, 2021].

Latour, Bruno (2004): »Why Has Critique Run Out of Steam«, in: *Critical Inquiry* 30 (Winter), 225 –248.

Lea, Tess (2020): *Wild Policy: Indigeneity and the Unruly*, Stanford: Stanford University Press.

Lorange, Astrid (2014): *How Reading is Written: A Brief Index to Gertrude Stein*, Middletown,CT: Wesleyan University Press.

More, Rebecca, (2020): *Slag Wars: The Next Destroyer.* | Trailer available from: https://www.youtube.com/watch?v=XgAoFFQBcMA [Accessed: September 12, 2021].

Moreton-Robinson, Aileen (2015): *The White Possessive: Property, Power, and Indigenous Sovereignty*, Minneapolis: University of Minnesota Press.

Rose, Deborah Bird (2015): »Dialogue«, in: K.Gibson/D.B.Rose/R.Fincher (eds), *Manifesto for Living in the Anthropocene*, Brooklyn: Punctum Books.

Schmidt, Christopher (2014): *Poetics of Waste: Queer Excess in Stein*, Ashbery, Schuyler, and Goldsmith, New York: Palgrave Macmillan.

Singh, Julietta (2017): »Interview for Another World«, in: *Women & Performance: A Journal of Feminist Theory* 27/3.

Singh, Julietta (2018): *Unthinking Mastery: Dehumanism and Decolonial Entanglements*, Durham, NC and London: Duke University Press.

Stengers, Isabelle (2015): *In Catastrophic Times: The Coming Barbarism*, Ann Arbor, MI: Open Humanities Press and Meson Press.

Yusoff, Kathryn (2015): »Queer Coal: Genealogies in/of the Blood«, in: *philoSOPHIA*, 5, 214–215.

Yusoff, Kathryn/Hird, Myra (2020): »Lines of Shite: Microbial-Mineral Chatter in the Anthropocene«, in: Rosi Braidotti/Simone Bignall (eds), *Posthuman Ecologies: Complexity and Process After Deleuze*, Lanham: Rowman and Littlefield, 265-282.

Dimensions of Architectural Knowledge, 2022-03 ⁂
https://doi.org/10.14361/dak-2022-0311

MINIATURE
Ugly Buildings – Reflections on the Reconstructivist Trend in Central and Eastern Europe

Rachel Győrffy

Abstract: The late modernist architectural heritage of Central and Eastern Europe has undergone a peculiar transformation in the last couple of years. I consider this transformation from the perspective of the taming of ugly late modernist buildings into harmless miniatures as embedded in the grander phenomenon of architectural reconstructivism, concomitant with the demolition of late modernist building stock. This article aims to explore the current trend for reconstructivism in architecture by applying a two-fold conceptual framework, projection as a discursive method and Mark Cousins's theory of ugliness to inspect the interwovenness of diverse socio-cultural factors by unraveling the manifold ways in which late modernist architectures are perceived with unease and discomfort in post-socialist contexts. These hyoptheses are tested in the case of the Electrical Power Distribution Station by architect Csaba Virág in Budapest.

Keywords: Late Modernist; Socialist-modernist Architecture; Architectural Heritage; Aesthetics in Architecture; Ugliness

Introduction

The uncanny miniaturization of late modernist or socialist-modernist architectures in Central and Eastern Europe ranges from souvenirs such as keychains depicting the demolished German Democratic Republic (GDR)-era Palace of the Republic, sold in the museum shop of the newly rebuilt Humboldt Forum in Berlin, to artworks such as graphic prints and small scale models of socialist-modernist buildings in Hungary or gamified versions of socialist housing blocks, which one can build out of cardboard. What makes this objectification so puzzling is that they reveal a paradoxical attitude toward late modernist architectural heritage in post-socialist societies, whereby certain iconic buildings are aesthetically appreciated en miniature,

Corresponding author: Rachel Győrffy (Moholy-Nagy University of Art and Design, Budapest, Hungary; Technische Universität Graz, Austria); r.gyoerffy@tugraz.at; http://orcid.org/0000-0002-7913-9376

reimagined as marketable commodities, while being demolished in the process of neo-historical reconstruction.

The erasure of late modernist architectural remnants of the socialist past, rendered as symbols of a failed collective utopia, often takes programmatic character, as it is enacted on specific sites that play an important role in the urban and cultural topography. It is typically historicist architectural ensembles referring to a pre-socialist past that replace these buildings. Such ensembles can be regarded as the materialization of highly politicized historical narratives shaped by political and economic actors (Győrffy 2022, Rampley 2012). At the same time, the widespread denigration of socialist-modernist architecture by the general public leaves many heritage, built environment, and cultural professionals bewildered and confused.

One way of understanding the multiple layers and interlinked aspects of contemporary reconstructivism in Central and Eastern Europe is by approaching this complex matter through an investigation of late modernist built heritage as a form of projected ugliness. »Ugly« is the term most frequently applied to these edifices. This seemingly inadequate intrusion into professional jargon should not be dismissed as irrelevant, amateurish debate on aesthetics, but rather regarded as an opportunity to analyze the proclaimed unpopularity of late modernist architectures and the sweeping neoliberal, market-driven reconstructivism. Dismissed in their built reality as monuments, yet appreciated as souvenirs from the past, late modernist architecture evidently has to lose its immanent sublime, or more so, ugly element, to be accepted.

The »last refuge« of rejected or demolished ugly modernism appears to be cuteness, as defined by feminist cultural theorist and critic Sianne Ngai as being one of the three most characteristic aesthetic categories of the »performance-driven [...], hypercommodified world of late capitalism« (Ngai 2010: 948). Widely rejected, abandoned, out-of-function, or already demolished architectures are experiencing a revival as pleasant or tame cute small-scale objects or objects of decoration. The only option for ugly architecture being socially appreciated is apparently a condition in which it is eternally bereft of its character of the sublime or the ugly, the condition in which architecture is architecture no more, but commodified to decorum. The shift of aesthetic categories or discursive judgements can be regarded as a process analogous to the replacement of collective utopias with individual longing or, as architectural theorist and researcher Ana Jeinić phrases it, »neoliberal po-

litical pragmatism [...]vacating the utopian content of architectural design«
(Jeinić 2013: 69).

The Electric Power Distribution Station by architect Csaba Virág in Budapest, which was completed in 1979, serves as a case to investigate the underlying causes, performativity, and effects of current reconstructivism, for
it represents an excellent example of the many possible interpretations of
»ugliness«.

Individual Utopias and Collective Longing

This article argues that late modernist buildings are displays of disturbing
individuality. As most of this built substance was erected in Eastern Europe,
still under Socialism, and in Western Europe, still within the ambitions of
the welfare state, there lies an undeniable tension between their material individuality (as architecture) and their represented collectivism. These late
modernist buildings make different generations experience different kinds
of discomfort; however, this unease often results from the disappointment,
trauma or feelings of failure that is projected onto these buildings.

A combination of »shameless ugliness« and disturbing individuality are
the traits by which the Electric Power Distribution Building in Budapest
could best be described. The articulation – form and shape – and materiality
of the building, its site, the date of its erection, as well as its function and
common perception, and its final partial demolition and conversion bear
traits of all the factors intertwined in the rise of reconstructivism. However,
the former enthusiasm for unchallenged technical development cannot be
held solely responsible for the disappointment, but even more frustration
with, and deep resentment toward, late modernist built heritage. This built
heritage is partly rejected by society and sometimes not even regarded as an
architectural heritage worthy of protection because the architecture is la-
beled as ugly.

I argue that the aesthetic judgment above is actually a psychological projection of society's feelings of their own undisputed, unprocessed, and
therefore unresolved past onto architecture. The resentment toward late
modernist architecture in particular shows the frustration with, and bit-
terness about, the unaccomplished modernist »mass utopia« in both the East
and West, which » once considered the logical correlate of personal utopia, is
now a rusty idea« (Buck-Morss 2000: ix-x.). The collective utopia was replaced by a diffuse collective nostalgia for a non-existent past that is coupled

with a rejection of the present and possibly enhanced by the anxiety surrounding an environmentally, economically, and politically uncertain future. Although the retrograde movement of reconstructivism would appear to contradict late consumer capitalism, the two actually do enhance each other: diffuse restorative nostalgia (Cf.: Boym 2001), that is unable to help process and rehabilitate the very traumas that evoke projection, is coupled with the tendencies of neoliberal economies, thus manifesting itself in scenery-like facadist architecture, a reconstruction of a subsequently transfigured past.

Case Study: The Electric Power Distribution Station in Budapest

The semi-industrial building (fig. 1) was supposed to control all the electricity that was coming into or generated in the country and distribute it according to customer loads. This function, which was formerly located sub-terrain in a cavesystem running beneath the Castle Hill, had to be brought »up« and placed in a building. As all the cabling already existed, the building had to be located in the historic surroundings of Buda Castle, which despite experiencing heavy damage during World War II, displayed an intact scenic image of late medieval architecture uncommon in the city of Budapest, where the art nouveau and historicist architecture of the fin-de-siècle is dominant. The architect, Csaba Virág (1933–2015), who worked at the state owned design-firm IPARTERV (appointed for industrial establishments) and LAKÓTERV (designated for state-owned and state-run housing projects) designed the building and co-operated with Judit Simon on the interior design. The planning took from 1972 until 1974, with construction work starting in the latter year and finishing in 1979.

The Electric Power Distribution Station was used in its original function until 2007. After the premises had been emptied and the building closed off, it was left unmaintained, although some kind of sun protection has been mounted to the apparently wrong side of the glass surfaces of the curtain-wall system, which, because of the heat, burned into the glass and created a matte and opaque layer radically different from the facade's original intention and effect, which was supposed to be more translucent and reflect its surroundings (figs. 5, 8). From then on, the building's existence has been constantly questioned. There has been a direct commission for converting the »Distributor« into an office building, for which the plans were completed (Győrfi 2020). Moving the functions of the neighboring National Archives as well as offices of the state departments into the building was also considered.

1. – 2.

Facade of the Electric Power Distributor Station from Nándor Street, Budapest (left),
from the Anjou Bastion Promenade, Budapest (right).
Photographer: Gyuláné Penner, 1979.

rʒ ꝟcjőn nⱦꝭcꝺ ?

3.

»Do you fancy this?«. Image: Petra Csizik,
Boglárka Pető, Karina Szűcs-Tassy.

4.

Modernist Open-Air Museum (Modernista Skanzen).
Image: Katalin Huszár-Berényi, Tamás Huszár.

However, the relocation was never implemented. In 2016, the government decided to pull down the Distributor which attracted professional criticism. The demolition began in July 2020.

Upon its completion, the building was presented and regarded as an exceptional work of intervention in a heritage site (Cf. Virág et al. 1979) and belonged to the somewhat small circle of internationally known and appreciated buildings in Budapest, at the time. Nonetheless, its dismissal by society was equally persistent. How can we begin to understand this rejection, which emerged almost as a gut feeling? One way to disassemble the case of the Distributor as reconstructivism is to interpret it as an example of ugly architecture, whereby ugliness, as an aesthetic category, is not a property of the object, the building, but the subject, the beholder´s projection onto the object. Hereby, the three-way understanding of »The Ugly« by architectural theorist and cultural critic Mark Cousins might be enlightening. In his view, the perception of ugliness arises because of the individuality (it disassembling or resisting completeness) and incongruity of the ugly object, its character as an obstacle in the way of desire, and because of the inner matter leaking through the surface or the representational shell of the ugly object. All of these momentums can be traced back to the Distributor.

Individuality of the Ugly

If the individuality of the object or a building is the result of its power to resist completion or deform it, then late modernist architectures are undoing or disturbing the texture of a Central or Eastern European town on two levels simultaneously: They are unsettling the image of the city because of the unusual repertoire of formal language and the display of unusual materials, as well as disturbing the morphology of the city, as many late modernist buildings integrate with their volumetric mass differently into the urban fabric than their predecessors. Their individuality is disturbing and dismantles the feeling of wholeness, hence their being perceived as ugly.

Though, morphologically, the building blended in commendably with the remnant late-medieval and baroque building structure of the Castle, it did not fully integrate into its historic surroundings in terms of the applied materiality and architectural imagery or stylistic vocabulary. Virág implemented formal and stylistic citations precisely, not with a restorative but with a reflective attitude: This manifested itself in the fragmentation of the volume, whereby the reinforced concrete towers (accommodating radar antennas) seem to cite a church tower, the shed-roofs integrate in height and placement through careful dimensioning into the neighbourhood and even quotations of sitting booths were established in the entry area, which appear as abstract versions of the typical gothic buildings in the Castle District. Yet, the references are abstract and the materiality is unapologetically modern, as Virág himself states:

> »I have concluded that for me the essence of such tasks is to try to envision a completely modern (up-to-date) building or building part, which, if it were taken out of its environment and suspended in a neutral space, would still meet the requirements [to be modern]. If I took it out of its environment and put it on a glass plate, I want it to be an up-to-date house, but when putting it back, it should fit exactly into its place.«[1]

The building should be read as a semi-industrial building and the function should be apparent, hence opting for a – then – high-tech curtain wall facade system.

There was an undeniable tension between the materiality and the morphology of the building, almost as if a large-scale industrial plant had been shrunk to fit the plot (fig. 2).; what could have been an industrial furnace on a larger scale appears as a modernist paraphrase of a medieval campanile.

It follows that the Distributor, as an object, despite the applied playful gestures, was unable to establish the desired coulisse in order to maintain an image of completeness in the eyes of the subject, suggesting historic continuity. The building made its function – despite the aforementioned ambiguities – obvious in materiality and the architectural formal language. By displaying individuality or resistance it was perceived as ugly.

Denouncing individuality by reproducing architectures in their imagery is however the main characteristic of reconstructivist edifices, such as the intended successor building[2] with the facade of a burgess-house typical of the Castle-district, but with the function of offices for the Home Office (figs. 6, 7).

---

1 This is one of Virág's most quoted statements. In: Szabó 2019: 196. (Virág et al. 1979. Translation: Levente Szabó).

2 According to current information this plan will not be implemented. A never constructed wing of the neighboring National Archives will be realized, partly on the plot of the former Distributor.

Obsessive Neurosis

Cousins's central hypotheses concerning ugliness, according to which ugliness is not only an aesthetic category and can under no circumstances be reduced to being the opposite or the lack of beauty (Cf.: Cousins 1994: 62), in so far as ugliness, disclosing itself to the subject, is in fact an object not in the right place (Cf.: Ibid. 63). Furthermore, it follows that there is no right place for the ugly object from the perspective of the subject. This means that the incorrect or mistaken situatedness of the object is immanent to the ugly: »the ›wrong place‹ is an absolute« (Ibid. 63). If the wrong place constitutes an absolute and if, as Cousins cites the famous phrase attributed to Mary Douglas (Cf.: Campkin 2013), dirt is matter out of place, an indifferent entity or being placed not where it belongs, then it follows that the ugly has to be relocated or re-placed. The removal of the ugly can thus be seen as a kind of necessity, or more so, a compulsion that largely resembles, according to Cousins, obsessive neurosis. The out-of-placeness of the ugly, coupled with its capacity to radiate into and onto its surroundings and also contaminate them could even motivate its iconoclastic removal. Thereby, can reconstructivism be seen as a form of collective obsessive neurosis?

Due to its individuality (late modernist architectural formal style and materiality) and its out-of-placeness as a semi-industrial building and a building being designed and constructed in the post-war socialist era, the Distributor was regarded as unsuitable for the idealized context of the Castle district with its inherent diffuse and indeed, somewhat dusty atmosphere of historicity. The building was accurately perceived as an interloper who is out of place. Yet could there have been a fitting place for this »unfitting« building? Could a new function have convinced the public that demolishing the building is in fact not the »only alternative«, as stated by the Home Office in a written reply to an inquiry by Krisztina Somogyi, Editor-in-Chief of the online architecture journal Építészfórum (Somogyi 2020)?

The same question was asked in May 2020 in a call for contributions to the ad-hoc competition entitled »Alternative to the Decision« by the Hungarian architecture student zine The Frozen Musician, when the demolition of the Electric Power Distributor had already been decided upon. Conditioned by the competition's three-day duration, many of the submissions preferred to caricature the future possibilities rather than suggest realistic proposals. As the decision to demolish was made against the declaration of the Hungarian committee of the International Council on Monuments and Sites (ICO-

MOS) and the petition of the Association of Hungarian Architects against any disassembling intervention, the attitude of the contenders was hardly surprising. Whereas in some submissions reconstructivism presented itself as reflecting on or with the help of other mediums, neo-historicist facades were suggested as a parody (»Which dress should I put on?« or »Am I good enough like this?« asks the anthropomorph Distributor with an ornamental plaster facade, fig. 3), other contestants argued that the structural and functional layout was in fact flexible enough to host a broad range of new functions (an office building of any kind, a design museum or a museum of architecture).

One competition entry however approached the brief differently. The submission entitled »Modernist Open-Air Museum« shows the building out of context, on a green field or hill (fig. 4), somewhat reminiscent of the screensaver of the Windows XP operating system series. In one image, this suggestive montage seems to convey Cousins's notion of the displacement or out-of-placeness of the ugly building being eternal, a fitting place not existing, as a museal, artifact-like piece of architecture is hardly architecture anymore: we see the Distributor out of context, in the midst of a green field, creating an almost surreal place.

Just as the post-socialist societies of Central and Eastern Europe struggle to process and rehabilitate their post-war history, there seems to be no place for late modernist architectures in the urban fabric.

Representational Overcoat

The obsessive neurosis-like compulsion of cleaning away late modernist ugly architectures in order to prevent them contaminating their surroundings is not solely triggered by their out-of-placeness. According to Cousins, an object exists twice, once as its inner matter or substance and once as its outer representation. Ugliness can be interpreted as something arising, as the inner matter, »leaking or bursting out of a representational shell« (Cousins 1995:3).

The inner substance of the ugly object exceeds its outer, representational coat. With this, the inner existence of the ugly object or building also permeates the subject's fantasy of the inside (Cf.: Ibid. 3). Expanding upon that thought, architecture can be understood as a projection surface – from the perspective of the subject. Ugly buildings are unable to fulfil the expectation to function as a surface for multiple projections. Thus, the aesthetic desires

5.
Facade of the Electric Power Distributor. Nándor (Petermann bíró) utca 5.-7. in 1984.
Photographer: Viktor Gábor.

6.
Rendering of proposed new building (after partial demolition of the Distributor).
Courtesy: Szécsi and Partners Építész Stúdió Kft.

7.
Rendering of proposed new building (after partial demolition of the Distributor).
Courtesy: Szécsi and Partners Építész Stúdió Kft.

8.
The Electric Power Distributor Station seen from Anjou Bastion Promenade.
Photographer: Attila Gulyás.

of individualist late capitalist societies, either personal micro-utopias or collective nostalgias, cannot be projected into and onto these buildings, constituting them as ugly.

The Distributor was unable to establish this representational overcoat or shell; not when being a pristine new edifice with translucent rasterized facades, which did not hide its function, nor in its desolate condition when the premises were vacated. The building being out of function was immediately traceable on the decay of the exterior and was therefore unsuitable as a projection surface for desires. Reconstructivist architectures however, carefully shield off the inner matter of the building, not letting it leak or permeate through the facade, fortified by illusory conceptions. Disguising itself as reclaiming apparently forgotten conceptions of atmosphere, when in fact it is a re-enactment of an arbitrarily chosen timeframe from the past, reconstructivism is able to provide contemporary societies with what they are apparently mostly in need of: in the Castle district, projection surfaces for touristic fantasies of a historical Budapest, revisionist desires of historical continuity, or all in all, surfaces that can be efficiently charged by the images of consumer capitalism.

Ugliness reveals itself not only in the object being in the wrong place, without the relative option of a right place, but also in its character as an obstacle. Cousins argues that deriving from Freud's theory, existence itself is an obstacle to the accomplishment and fulfilment of our desires; it is existence that manifests in an ugly object. This quite literally wakes the subject up to the truth, to reality through its out-of-placeness, its imperfection or deformity. Hence, it defies as an obstacle to the desired reality: »Its character as an obstacle is what makes it ugly« (Cousins 1994: 64). In the exalted socio-economic system of late capitalism which is based on representation and the establishment of unfulfillable desires, Cousins's feeling of »permanent lack« (Cousins 1994:64), corresponds to similar sentiments such as the philosopher and cultural critic Slavoj Žižek´s condition of »Hysteria« (Žižek 1994:145) and the philosopher Gernot Böhme´s »aesthetic capitalism« (Böhme 2016:18) that interfere with and determine both reality and phantasy. Every ugly object can be regarded as an obstacle and its radical and immediate removal be called for, such as with the case of the Distributor.

9.

The Death of a Building by A-A Collective,
Exhibition at the Hungarian Pavillion,
17th Biennale di Venezia.
Photographer: Dániel Dömölky.

10.

The Distributor (Teherelosztó).
Print: Boróka Felső.

11.

»Panelki - Construct Your Socialist Prefab Panel Block«. Courtesy: Zupagrafika.

Burying and Taming the Ugly

In his paper »Modernism and Changing Historical Context. Case Study of the Former Electric Power Distributor Station of the Hungarian Electrical Grid«, Hungarian architect and academic Levente Szabó identifies the possible reasons for the rejections of the edifice as nostalgic (longing for the prewar period), obsolete (of the spatial structure, the materiality, and the details) and connoting the establishing oppressive regimes (Szabó 2019: 203), whereby the above mentioned factors are put into a wider scope of »the interference of parallel motivations« (Ibid.: 190), the changing value of the local context, of the Castle Hill, and the changing judgment of the building (Ibid.: 190).

Elaborating upon the aforementioned factor of »rejection of the partly abandoned heritage of the 1960s and 1970s« (Ibid.: 203) it can be argued that the denial of adaptive re-use of these buildings by national planning departments and the building industry is also a central factor for their dismantling not being opposed by wider parts of society. When a building is without a function, fenced off, and slowly decaying, there must be a reason: it was surely aesthetically unfitting in the context (individuality of the ugly), functionally unfitting (wrong placement), or it was even seen as literally or phenomenologically contaminating.

The cultural anthropologist Melanie van der Hoorn provides further details on the marginalized status of ugly architecture and its potential as a threat and where the spatially and socially marginalized, quarantined, hidden or closed-off, and therefore inaccessible edifices potentially forecast their future removal. However, she also stresses that marginalized architectures, in an inaccessible state, are almost determined to be objects of speculation, rumors, or even myths because the edifice has not been experienced in function or from the inside for many years. These rumors and myths can on the one hand contaminate a building through suppositions and presumptions but, on the other hand, they can also generate public discourse about the building and why it is thought to be contaminated and public discourse could help the processing of a dark past or a collective traumatic experience. (Cf.: Van der Hoorn 2009: 1, 8-9). Corrupt or contaminated (Van der Hoorn) or ugly (Cousins) architectures without a current function can be kept »alive« through collective storytelling practices (Van der Hoorn 2009: 8) that can be understood as being part of reflective nostalgia.

12.
Hotel Budapest
(Szrogh György, 1966-1967)
Photographer: Lilla Liszkay.

13.
Semmelweis University Budapest
(Gerlóczy Gedeon, Südi Ernő,
Wágner László, 1971-1978).
Photographer: Lilla Liszkay.

14.
Spa Hotel Thermal Karlovy Vary
(Věra és Vladimír Machonin, 1968-
1977), concrete cast small
dimensional models, Hype&Hyper,
Soc/Mod Series. Photographer: Lilla
Liszkay.

The European architects' collective, A-A Collective's, proposal for the 17th Architectural Biennale in Venice in 2021 (fig. 9) in the scope of the »Othernity« exhibition of the Hungarian Pavilion tries to provide much needed public access to the Distributor by opening up the building on many levels: the contribution suggests tearing down all facades, hence eliminating all potential projection surfaces. Through the removal of all walls and facades, the collective proposes to establish a green spot full of plants, an urban oasis, and to give the building back to nature, which is supported by the proposal's title »The Death of Building«. The project is seen as part of a well-deserved and emblematic burial of the Distributor: » [...]we think that such a building deserves a funeral. Demolition would obliterate a part of history in a manner unbefitting Castle Hill, a place where history is celebrated« (Kovács et al 2021: L63). This rather poetically phrased passage of how burying edifices and enabling grief, just as with humans, allows loss to be processed resonates with Van der Hoorn's concept (Cf. Hoorn 2009).

Interestingly, there also appears to be another way in which ugly (late) modernist buildings can linger on in collective discourse – though only in their imageability. Levente Szabó remarks in his paper that the current condition of the Distributor »does not provide the untrained public with a pleasant sight« (Szabó 2019: 201). Only if the immanent sublime or ugly element is taken from such buildings are they rendered harmless and pleasant, as, for example, in their miniaturized condition. When the sublime is tamed into cuteness, a previously rejected architecture is stripped of its ugliness. This occurs when a building becomes architecture no more, only a reminiscence of it: In this way, the Distributor inspires a graphic print (fig. 10), that can be framed and hung on walls, late modernist buildings become tiny concrete paperweights, (figs. 12–14) and socialist housing blocks become paper cutouts and small-scale models (fig. 11).

Conclusion

The Electric Power Distribution Station in Budapest by architect Csaba Virág can be analyzed as an exemplary case study of the perception of ugly post-modern architectures by post-socialist societies in Central and Eastern Europe. In a speculative approach the aesthetic genre of ugliness is introduced not as an architecturally irrelevant term but rather as an opportunity to better understand the reconstructivist claim of this late modern built heritage being unfitting. The terminology is analyzed in the context of late capitalist consumer culture. Mark Cousins's interpretations of ugliness prove to be especially relevant in the context of aesthetic capitalism and the possibility of understanding reconstructivism as a kind of obsessive neurosis, the compulsion of cleaning away difficult, unwanted architectures. The history, reception, and treatment of Virág's Distributor can be seen as paradigmatic for this reconstructivist attitude. By looking at the proposal to re-use the building in the recent »Othernity« project and stripping it of its external walls, it seems unequivocal that late modernist architecture can only (re)gain pleasantness, or find its place as an ugly object eternally out-of-place, as architecture no more. Ugly architecture can live on either as a kind of built sculpture or, tamed into miniatures, as ornament or staffage, reduced to abstract imagery without built reality.

References

Böhme, Gernot (2016): *Aesthetic Capitalism / Ästhetischer Kapitalismus*, Berlin: Suhrkamp.

Boym, Svetlana (2001): *The Future of Nostalgia*, New York: Basic Books.

Buck-Morss, Susan (2000): *Dreamworld and Catastrophe: The Passing of Mass Utopia in East and West*, Cambridge, MA: MIT Press.

Campkin, Ben (2013): »Placing ›Matter Out of Place‹: ›Purity and Danger‹ as Evidence for Architecture and Urbanism«, in: *Architectural Theory Review* 18/1, 46–61. doi: 10.1080/13264826.2013.785579.

Cousins, Mark (1994): »The Ugly [part 1] «, in: *AA Files* 28, 61–64.

Cousins, Mark (1995): »The Ugly [part 2] «, in: *AA Files* 29, 3–6.

Csizik, Petra/Pető, Boglárka/Szűcs-Tassy, Katarina (2020) »Do you fancy this?«, *Behance*, https://www.behance.net/gallery/96532593/Mirt-nem-vagyok-elg-Neked (Accessed 23 June 2021).

Dömölky, Dániel (2020): »The Death of a Building by A-A Collective, Exhibition at the Hungarian Pavillion, 17th International Architecture Exhibition, La Biennale di Venezia«, *Instagram*, https://www.instagram.com/a.a.collective/ (Accessed 23 June 2021).

Felső, Boróka (2020): »The Electrical Power Distributor, Budapest, demolished in 2020«, *Facebook*, https://www.facebook.com/Fels%C5%91-Bor%C3%B3ka-Design-439204579551911/photos/pcb.19112 33245682363/1911225512349803 (Accessed 23 June 2021).

Gábor, Viktor (1984): »Facade of the Electric Power Distributor from Nándor (Petermann bíró) street 5.-7.«, *FORTEPAN*, https://fortepan.hu/en/photos/?id=193629 (Accessed 23 June 2021).

Gulyás, Attila (2016): »The Ex-Electric Power Distributor Station, Csaba Virág, 1972-1979«, *Építészfórum*, https://epiteszforum.hu/az-icomos-magyar-nemzeti-bizottsag-allasfoglalasa-a-budavari-orszagos-villamos-tehereloszto-epuletenek-lebontasaval-kapcsolatban (Accessed 23 June 2021).

Győrffy, Rachel (2022): »Ikonoklasmus, Musealisierung und Hyperrealität. Eine Annäherung an den architektonischen Rekonstruktivismus in Mittel- und Osteuropa« (Iconoclasm, Musealisation and Hyperreality. Approaching Architectural Reconstructivism in Central and Eastern Europe), in: *Censored? Conflicted Concepts of Cultural Heritage*, Weimar: Bauhaus Universitätsverlag.

Győrfi, Dániel (2020): »Szabó Tibor, a felújítás tervezője a Teherelosztóról (Tibor Szabó, the architect of the refurbishment proposal, on the Distributor)« (Megfagyott Muzsikus). Available at: https://open.spotify.com/episode/7rp5A5a6lQn89JPTWMrOwk?si=BWEmQLp3TGSKgyptJe3PwQ&nd=1 (Accessed: May 2, 2020).

Huszár-Berényi, Katalin/Huszár, Tamás (2020): »Modernist Open-Air Museum«, *Behance*, https://www.behance.net/gallery/96526267/Modernista-Skanzen (Accessed 23 June 2021).

Jeinić, Ana (2013) : »Neoliberalism and the Crisis of the Project … In Architecture and Beyond«, in: Anselm Wagner/Ana Jeinić (eds.), *Is There (Anti-)Neoliberal Architecture*, Berlin: Jovis, 64–77.

Kovács, Dániel et al. (eds.) (2021): »Othernity. Reconditioning Our Modern Heritage, 17th International Architecture Exhibition La Biennale di Venezia, Hungarian Pavilion«, Budapest: Ludwig Museum/ Museum of Contemporary Art.

Liszkay, Lilla (2020): »Hotel Budapest«, »Semmelweis University Budapest«, »Spa Hotel Thermal Karlovy Vary«. *Hyper&Hyper*, https://store.hypeandhyper.com/hu/collections/socmod (Accessed 23 June 2021).

Ngai, Sianne (2010): »Our Aesthetic Categories«, in: PMLA: *Publication of the Modern Language Association of America* 125/4, 948—958.

Penner, Gyuláné (1979) »Országos villamos teherelosztó, (OVT) Budapest I (Electric Power Distribution Station, Budapest I)«, in: *Magyar Építőművészet* 1979/6, 22—27.

Rampley, Matthew (2012): »Contested Histories: Heritage and/as the Construction of the Past: An Introduction«, in: Matthew Rampley (ed.): *Heritage, Ideology, and Identity in Central and Eastern Europe: Contested Pasts, Contested Presents* (Vol. 6). Boydell & Brewer, pp. 1-20., http://www.jstor.org/stable/10.7722/j.ctt3fgm0r, (Accessed June 15, 2021).

Somogyi, Krisztina (2020): »Mégis lebontják? - Végveszélyben Virág Csaba vári épülete (To be demolished after all? Csaba Virág´s Castle Hill building at ultimate risk)«, *Építészfórum*, https://epiteszforum.hu/megis-lebontjak--vegveszelyben-virag-csaba-vari-epulete- (Accessed: March 14, 2022).

Szabó, Levente (2019): »Modernism and Changing Historical Context: Case Study of the Former Electric Power Distributor Station of the Hungarian Electrical Grid«, in: *Seasoned Modernism. Prudent Perspectives on an Unwary Pasts* 7, 189–204.

Szécsi and Partners Építész Stúdió Kft (2020): »Zsolt Szécsi´s (Szécsi and Partner) plan for the conversion of Csaba Virágs´s Distributor«, *Építészfórum*, https://epiteszforum.hu/uj-homlokzatot-kap-es-tornyat-veszti-a-tehereloszto (Accessed 23 June 2021).

Van der Hoorn, Melanie (2009): *Indispensable Eyesores: An Anthropology of Undesired Buildings*, New York: Berghahn Books.

Virág, Csaba/ Mendele, Ferenc (1979): »Országos villamos teherelosztó, (OVT) Budapest I (Electric Power Distribution Station, Budapest I)«, in: *Magyar Építőművészet* 6, 22–27.

Žižek, Slavoj (1994): »Genieße Deine Nation wie Dich selbst! Der Andere und das Böse – Vom Begehren des ethnischen ›Dings‹«, in: Joseph Vogl (ed.) ,*Gemeinschaften: Positionen zu einer Philosophie des Politischen*, Frankfurt a. M.: Suhrkamp Verlag, 133–164 (»Enjoy Your Nation as Yourself«, in: *Tarrying with the Negative: Kant, Hegel and the Critique of Ideology*, Durham: Duke Press: 1993, 200-238).

Zupagrafika (2020): »Panelki - Construct Your Socialist Prefab Panel Block«, *Zupagrafika*, https://www.zupagrafika.com/shop/panelki (Accessed 23 June 2021).

Dimensions of Architectural Knowledge, 2022-03 ͻ
https://doi.org/10.14361/dak-2022-0312

PERFORMANCE
Migrant Imaginaries through Soft Spatialities

Amina Kaskar

Abstract: This research documents the encounters of the built fabric with migrant imaginaries. It observes the articulation of social narratives, cultural practices, and everyday rituals within diasporic communities ordered around textiles. Migrant spaces often include »soft« architectures in both the literal construction of their spaces and through the »soft« spatial systems tied to certain micro-transactions and community organizations. The work explores ways of engaging with participatory research methods through the dynamic and performative nature of people, objects, rituals, symbols, and knowledge. The performative practices layered onto this work activate inclusive and ethical forms of enquiring and representing information. The work further develops a repertoire of rituals and events ordered around textiles.

Keywords: Migrant Spaces; Soft Architecture; De-Colonized Knowledge; Inclusive Ethnography; Performative Methods.

Introduction

The soft spatialities of migrant communities are highlighted in this article through the narratives described in italics.

> An old family album of photographs shared with me over a dining table highlights intimate moments and small re-enactments of rituals brought by grandparents and great grandparents as they created their home (fig. 1). Traversing the streets, yards, balconies, and home, one notices the adaptations and re-creations of tactile and ephemeral memorabilia and the values of migrant agendas. This is seen in the manner in which they furnished the house, their pictures, and music (»qawwali«), the games that they played (»five stones«, »dayakatti« or »gulli danda«), and the textiles draped, worn, and stored (»misars« and beautifully embroidered »dupattas«). The yards are adorned with fabrics, with clothes hanging from washing lines, huge pots (»dekhs«) on open

Corresponding author: Amina Kaskar (KU Leuven, Belgium); amina.kaskar@kuleuven.be; https://orcid.
org/0000-0003-3003-4669

1.
Visual representation of the interview process with the Amijee family in the home.
Collage: Amina Kaskar, 2021.

fires and tables laid with foods and spices. Family-owned shops that sell fruit, vegetables, and flowers and shops lined with blankets, textiles, and clothing adjoin the homes and spill onto the street. The shop re-creates the domestic space, lined with curtains and styled pointedly to display the aspirations of the home. The streets with their splendor of colors, textures, and smells are shrouded by ethnic blankets, fabrics, and paraphernalia that reveal migrant imaginaries and the multiplicity of cultures and practices that exist in the city. [15 October, 2020, Amijee House, Mayfair West, Johannesburg, South Africa]

Migrants often shape spaces through various forms of temporal space-making. They appropriate space by interacting with movable objects, such as textiles, arranging them in imaginative and creative ways. There is a bridging of past and future infrastructure as they import material cultures from a distant »homeland«. Re-creating these traditions in new and blended forms to adapt to a new local context, making a new home within the city. This is done by re-using material constructions and by reforming and resituating connections with others (Johung 2012). Butler (1988: 519) defines this notion of performativity through a repeated set of propelling acts that become customary over time. This is evident within the city as specific rituals become common practice within ethnic communities. These rituals are performances that constitute or become representative of identity. There are a myriad of cultural forms and approaches within grounded architecture as well as within transitory, mobile, and ritual experiences. These practices form a legitimate and valuable architecture of the city by both impeding and supporting solid architectural forms tied to the built fabric (Ingold 2010: 138–147).

This work explores ways of engaging with the dynamic and performative nature of people, objects, rituals, symbols and knowledge. The methodology used in this research aims to investigate »soft« architectural methods and material practices created by textiles in migrant spheres. As described by Kaskar (2021: 108) »amongst the diverse materials that migrants have carried with them, textiles play an important role in the material practices of migrant identities«. Not only do textiles provide insight into the performances of everyday ritual practices within the built environment, they are also historical markers, design agents, and political instruments that highlight the performative nature of cultural spaces. This material artefact is intrinsically tied to »social and labour networks, micro-transactions and community organizations« (Kaskar 2021: 108). Textiles are further linked to the cultural,

social, religious and political agency of people who have experienced disloca-
tion. This is particularly evident in their daily customs, such as eating, cooking, and praying (Altman/Low 1992). These everyday rituals, gestures, and
habits seep into the hard-built fabric, bringing with them a spatial language
with new codes and agendas.

A performance lens focuses on cultural activities, recognizing embodied experiences and how certain bodies and sites overlap in order for meaningful experiences to be initialized and reinstated (Diamond 1996).
»Performance« is more than the tectonic and practical functions of a building. It entails the unfolding of human activity in space and the »impact of
these social forces on architectural and urban patterns« (Heynen 2013: 349).
The theatrical aspect of performance includes space-making and the »theatre of practice« where materials and people are inter-woven and »act«
upon each other to conceive spatial arrangements (Ingold 2010). Textiles are
part of a durational performance with their own trajectories and tendencies.
The social nature of textiles allow them to be continuously assembled and
re-assembled in a myriad of ways over time to produce new spatial configurations (Latour 2005: 63–68). Textiles exist in both the public realm, as well
as within nuanced moments of household practices and communal appro-
priations. These are observed by »the hanging of tablecloths on washing
lines, the shops draped in textile merchandise, blankets laid out onto the
floor for social gathering and the fabrics that adorn homes« (Kaskar 2021:
109). Textiles are embedded with the »needs, desires, aspirations, behaviour
and actions« of migrants (Kaskar 2021: 109). The social and cultural reproduction continues as migrants make, sell, use and celebrate different forms
of fabric. Although soft architecture loses its newness, degrades, and is often either recycled or discarded, it still remains an important dynamic of
something continuous and more enduring. It speaks to the speculative nature of textiles as it is able to create improvised temporal events that change
and weather over time. Textiles have an ongoing narrative as they are continuously re-located and changing, opening up to contemporary culture
and future speculation.

This article investigates how these soft spatial practices are defined
through methods. It is important for the methods used to address the challenges of working with diasporic space and the material entanglements of
migrant lives. They are often located within contested or vulnerable sites,
and the nature of their spaces are transient as people are on the move. This
research includes searching for a method as part of the process of what Law

2.
Visual representation of the interview process with the Bulbulia sisters in their curtain shop. Collage: Amina Kaskar, 2021.

(2004: 390–410) calls the »messiness of the social world of the city«. The aim is to capture »fleeting, ephemeral and often embodied and sensory aspects of the movement of people and objects« (Spinney 2011: 161–182). This includes the integration of soft performative spatial systems with soft performative methods.

It challenges conventional forms of architecture and explains the »erasure of the unseen due to its non-normative materiality and tight disciplinary boundary« (Kaskar 2021:105). It is important to visualize the things that migrants use or carry, as this makes visible the expertise and agency employed by individuals in creating their own spaces. The mapping of long histories, exchanges, and networks of people and textiles address the global situation of the migrant identity. How does the migrant navigate the space between diverse contexts and identities? Are there specific objects and processes that assist in navigating the »here and there« and the multiple roles that migrants need to enact in order to prosper?

The approach to the fieldwork is inclusive and ethical in the manner of enquiring and representing information. This is done through the involvement of new and varied architectural references and narrators. It values the various lived experiences and environments built by migrants. It is important that these voices are not veiled or expunged in the work, and rather considered as »productive and interpretive lenses« (Kaskar 2021:107). As suggested by Siddiqi (2011) the concept of »togethering differences« entails a way of living and philosophizing communally, which challenges forms of »othering«. It is further argued that »migratory objects and methods can bring about new perspectives through collaborative processes that enrich the writing of architectural histories« (Kaskar 2021: 107). The ethics of collaboration are defined by the intimacies and distances between agents that come across two-fold in this method:

1. the relationship of human bodies and the positionality of the researcher relating to intimate versus distant relationships with participants and the imposed effect on the knowledge outputs.

2. the relationship of textiles and human bodies and the value of embodied ephemeral knowledge in the way textiles interact with human and built forms.

Intimate/personal

> A day spent with the Bulbulia sisters in their shop at the Oriental Plaza seated on plastic chairs surrounded by organza and lace curtains eating »chevro«, a spiced nut and cornflake mix, out of an ice-cream container and sharing a 2 liter Coca Cola (fig. 2). The time is shared with stories of their family life and memories of assisting their father in the shop and playing in the streets with the neighbors' kids. There is a short pause to perform the daily midday prayer, Dhohr Salaah, in a corner of the store. Their brother listens in from behind the counter. Later, women from neighboring shops join the dialogue. [06 October, 2020, Curtain Centre, Oriental Plaza, Fordsburg, Johannesburg, South Africa] (Kaskar 2021:106)

The interview process depicts societal and physical behaviors that are common to the spatial practices evident in migrant communities. The interactions between the participants are similar to those of a social gathering or being hosted at someone's home. The discussion transcends that of academic investigation and becomes a shared space for dialogue. Furniture is strategically positioned and moved around the room to best serve the conversation. The immediate setting of the interview reveals the mechanics of how people choreograph their environments to support different types of purposes and agendas. By representing the spatial arrangements of the enquiry process through drawing and collage, the manners and rituals of the interview can be illustrated. The intimacy of the interactions are translated in the way that the furniture is arranged; plastic stools huddled together, blanket mounds crowding the room, a delineated cashier counter or the comfort of a ceremonial dining-room table. These arrangements dictate the duration spent with the participants within their homes and shops. The entire day can be spent engaged in conversation and observing everyday activities. Situating the interview within the natural setting of the participants allows for impromptu collaborations with passers-by and other »guests«. They either pull up a seat and eagerly add to the conversation with personal anecdotes and lived experiences, or they casually engage with the people around them through their usual familial exchanges.

Textiles are immersed in the scenario through customary habits and practices. Textiles play an important role in ordering the space of the interview – »there is an emotional closeness with the material as it is purposefully prepared and choreographed by its user« (Kaskar 2021: 109). The flexibility of the fabric allows it to occupy space in various ways, either hung from the ceiling, stretched out on the floor, draped loosely over one's body or stretched to conform to multiple shapes (Thomas 2001). The material micro-scenarios of the interviews allude to the role textiles play in other forms of diasporic space-making. This can be seen in the spatial ordering of many defining moments in life, such as the birth of a child, initiations, weddings and funerals. In addition, it plays a significant role in gendered activities, especially in relation to domestic crafts. The embodied historical and emotional knowledge of the fabric adds an ethereality to the seemingly conventional nature of the material (Kaskar 2021:109).

The intimacy demonstrated by the material aspects of this space is further reinforced by the closeness between, and similar background of, the researcher to the participants. This allows the interviewer to take on multiple roles in the interaction as a granddaughter, neighbor or confidante. This association establishes trust and initiates an expanded network of potential participants within the community. The familiarity with some of the customs and colloquial language reinforces the emotional and subjective nature of the interviews and its outputs. This is often not considered by established frames of knowledge. The interviews reveal a »temporally layered unfolding of space that is influenced by intangible factors such as rumour, emotion, smell, sound, memory and perceived atmosphere« (Kaskar 2021:106). The participants collectively shape and re-formulate the perception of existing sites by providing diverse perspectives and accounts. This enriches the complexity of existing historic sites by layering onto them a range of subjectivities (Stein/Rowden 2019: 29–35). These personal oral histories add crucial value to how people understand and experience space beyond permanent markers of occupation (Kaskar 2021: 106).

The intimacy of the encounters creates a subconscious bias in the filtering and selection of information from the audio recording of interview sessions. It is thus difficult to enlist a third party to transcribe interviews. The jargon used, the pauses in conversation, and unexpected interruptions contribute to this. A hands-on approach is a useful way of working with qualitative data. The use of automated or digital over manual processing distances the researcher from the process. This may yield a different set of results if the interviews are processed through a data software program.

3.
Visual representation of the interview process with the owners of »D. I. Dadabhay
Fabrics« in their textile warehouse. Collage: Amina Kaskar, 2021.

Detached/distant

> Streets lined with men on chairs. There is an awkwardness and uneasiness in a male-dominated space with many foreign-national traders. There is a distrust that is extended toward the researcher as an outsider. The smaller shop-owners are more hesitant, conversing for brief moments on the street between draped facades, or in their shops over colorful blankets stacked from floor to ceiling. The larger shop owners often extend an invitation into their offices or a quieter section of the store among a landscape of paraphernalia – stacked fabrics, adorned mannequins, and baskets full of haberdashery, bags, and clothing. [22 October, 2020, Newtown, Johannesburg, South Africa]

There is a continuous movement of new migrants entering established ethnic spaces lured by the profitability of trade in textiles. These unfamiliar spaces are intimidating, closed-off, and defensive toward the researcher as an outsider in the space. The streets and shops are bustling and people are not always keen to slow down and engage with research agendas. It is not always safe to walk around with cameras and people are hesitant to be photographed. However, once trust is gained, the researcher is invited in and there is comfort in the hospitality of the people, sharing stories over tea or a hot meal.

Being hosted translates the role of the researcher into that of a guest. This ensuing caring environment contributes to an ambiguous power structure. This highlights the agency, awareness, and the value of migrant communities refuting their marginal and vulnerable status. In this way, the usual model of »us« helping »them« is subverted (Kaskar 2021: 107). This raises the questions: What can the researcher give back to the community in lieu of the knowledge gained? What is the incentive for people to participate, and how valuable is it for them?

Legacies

> Sitting in the office of D. I. Dadabhay's fabrics, I am handed a bound memoir of the Dadabhay family and their business. They share old photographs of the building and refer me to the family tree and collected histories on the family website. It is intriguing how this information is exhibited in their homes and shops – a map of Gujarat, original trading licenses, title deeds and watercol-

or paintings hanging in thin gold frames (fig. 3). [20 October, 2020, D. I. Dada-bhay's Fabrics, Newtown, Johannesburg, South Africa]

It is becoming popular among 3rd and 4th generation migrants to document their family histories and biographies. They are proud to share this knowledge as it speaks to their family legacies and achievements in overcoming the struggles commonly faced by migrants. A lot of these histories are lost with no material evidence of their existence. However, many families proudly display watercolor paintings of their homes and businesses that have been gifted by architects and artists who have worked in the area. In recognition of this tradition and as a gesture of gratitude, drawings of their personal spaces are gifted to the participants as a testament to their family history (Kaskar 2021:107).

The encounters generated by interviews and participant observation produce a discursive space that doubles the architectural or spatial outputs. The intricacies of dialogue have value beyond factual accuracy. The character of the interaction is invariably tidied-up when translated into text or visuals and is at risk of being lost when presented in public. Drawing is important in capturing the spatial aspects of dialogue. In addition to distinguishing the tectonic and practical »performance« of a building, they provide atmospheric qualities of space. The drawings capture the »soft« systems layered onto space and serve as a powerful physical gesture in revealing parts of migrant histories that have been lost or rendered invisible (Kaskar 2021: 107). The legacy of these families and communities are solidified through the longevity of the drawings that can be passed down through generations.

Conclusion

Migrants have prescribed an alternative spatial language that allows for improvisation and disrupts rationalized and oppressive built forms. This research shifts away from conventional methods and representation and explores new ways of capturing the performative nature of buildings, sites, and design processes through the layering of »soft« spatial systems. It creates a new language of architectural practice that is textured and dynamic in representation. The visual language evokes sentimental feelings in the viewer so that they can place themselves in the environment with its familiar smells, textures, and colors. In a world of re-location, practices of migrant spatiality constitute alternative spatial languages and agency that transcend architectural limits and encompass non-normative materialities.

I would like to thank my supervisors Professor Hilde Heynen (KU Leuven)and Professor Hannah Le Roux (University of the Witwatersrand) for their generous feedback and notes on this article.

References

Altman, Irwin/Low, M. Setha (1992): »Place Attachment«, in: Irwin Altman/M. Setha Low (eds), *Place Attachment: Human Behavior and Environment (Advances in Theory and Research)*, 12, Boston, MA: Springer. doi: https://doi.org/10.1007/978-1-4684-8753-4_1

Butler, Judith (1998): »Performative Acts and Gender Constitution: An Essay in Phenomenology and Feminist Theory«, in: *Theatre Journal*, 40, 519. https://doi.org/10.2307/3207893

Diamond, Elin (1996): *Performance and Cultural Politics*, London: Routledge

Heynen, Hilde (2013): »Space as Receptor, Instrument or Stage: Notes on the Interaction between Spatial and Social Constellations«, in: *International Planning Studies*, 40 (3-4), 349. doi: 10.1080/13563475.2013.833729,

Ingold, Tim (2010): »The Textility of Making«, in: *Cambridge Journal of Economics*, 34, 91–102. doi: 10.1093/cje/bep042

Johung, Jennifer (2012): *Replacing Home: From Primordial Hut to Digital Network in Contemporary Art*, Minneapolis: University of Minnesota Press

Kaskar, Amina (2021): »Insider Ethnography: Research Methods for Engaging with Soft Spatial Practices«, in: *The Observer Observed: Architectural Uses of Ethnography*, Jaap Bakema Eighth Annual Conference Proceedings, 105

Latour, Bruno (2005): »Third Source of Uncertainty: Objects Too Have Agency«, in: *Reassembling the Social: An Introduction to Actor-Network Theory*, Oxford: Oxford University Press, 63–68

Law, John/ Urry, John (2004): »Enacting the Social«, in: *Economy and Society* 33/3, 390–410

Siddiqi, Anooradha Iyer (2018): »Writing with: Togethering, Difference, and the Feminist Architectural Histories of Migration«, in: *Structural Instability E-Flux Architecture*. doi: https://www.e-flux.com/architecture/structural-instability/208707/writing-with/

Spinney, Justin (2011): »A Chance to Catch a Breath: Using Mobile Video Ethnography in Cycling Research«, in: *Mobilities* 6/2, 161–182 . doi: 10.1080/17450101.2011.552771

Stein, Jesse Adams/Rowden, Emma (2019): »Speaking from Inside: Challenging the Myths of Architectural History through the Oral Histories of Maitland Gaol«, in: Janina Gosseye/ Naomi Stead/Deborah Van Der Plaat (eds.), *Speaking of Buildings: Oral History in Architectural Research*, New York: Princeton Architectural Press, 29–35

Thomas, Thelma K. (2001): »The Fabric of Everyday Life: Historic Textiles from Karanis, Egypt«, Kelsey Museum of Archaeology, University of Michigan

Dimensions of Architectural Knowledge, 2022-03 ᑫ
https://doi.org/10.14361/dak-2022-0313

POLYPHONIC MORPHOLOGY
Unseen Acts – The City as Reflection

Yara Al Heswani

Abstract: What if we imagined a mirror that reflects the city's reality to itself? What if the city's components identified themselves and defined meaning in their own reflections? This article aims to explore the critical dimensions of the contemporary reality of a place from multiple and unexpected points of view. It explains the theoretical framework of a project which is being conducted as part of wider research that focuses on the informal behaviors and interventions in the urban morphology that is made by the inhabitants of the urban cluster around Damascus.

Keywords: Informality; Urban Morphology; Reflexivity; Post-conflict; Dialogue; Theater of the Absurd.

The Spotlight

Today, Jaramana, a city district south-east of central Damascus, holds the largest concentration of refugees in Syria. Several waves of immigrants – from Palestine in 1948 and from Iraq in 2003 – have caused significant population growth. Since the war in Syria, the large number of internally displaced people living and working here has further fueled urban expansion and development. (ETH Studio Basel 2009). Jaramana's current population density[1] is greater than 15,000 inhabitants per square kilometer (UN-OCHA 2017). In this context, informality has become the default condition.

However, while there are existing studies charting the city's history, its expansion and migrant influx, as well as its social fabric and population, a detailed investigation of Jaramana's informal architectural and urban development in this current phase of rapid change is still missing. In addressing

---

1   The metro area population of Damascus in 2021 was 2,440,000, according to United Nations population projections. This is nearly 20,000 inhabitants per km².

Corresponding author: Yara Al Heswani (Damascus University); yara.al.heswani@outlook.com; http://orcid.org/0000-0001-8804-4646.

this lack, my work builds on, and expands, Jaramana Council's own historical analysis of the city (2000), ETH Studio Basel's study on Iraqi refugees and urban planning (Fahmi/Jaeger 2009), and anthropologist A. Maria A. Kastrinou's detailed ethnographic account of historical changes in modern Syria that sheds light on the diversity and stratification of the close-knit social fabric of the Druze neighborhoods during wartime (2014).

A large proportion of Syria's population lives in informal housing. According to estimates, informal housing represented 30 to 40 percent of the total number of dwellings before 2011. A recently published analytical report on informal settlements in Syria (Sukkar/Abou Zainedin/Fakhani 2021) maps and analyzes the government's approach toward informality. It provides a critical reading of the legal framework that underpins government policies on land management and argues that informality is an outcome of the government's chronic and systematic failure in coping with the increased need for housing.

The phenomenon of informal housing began to spread in Syria around the middle of the twentieth century. Unplanned housing areas and settlements sprang up in places not originally destined for construction, violating construction laws and encroaching on state property and agricultural land. Since then, they have spread and become an unavoidable feature of the city; in other words, in most cases, they NORMALIZE the INFORMAL by adding these features to the city.

Jaramana's growth over the last 20 years may at first seem like any normal city expansion. However, the speed of informal growth by far exceeds the planned one. New neighborhoods are built outside the formal city boundary before the drawings can be adjusted accordingly. In addition, new building permit legislation in 2003 made the construction of informal housing easier than the normal process. Informal building modifications, now commonplace, are frequently tolerated by the city. For instance, adding an extra floor to a building can be agreed upon with the council after it is inhabited, even if this exceeds the maximum number of storys permitted according to the construction laws.

Mirrors in the field

My project seeks to make visible this normalization of the informal. It encourages reflection on building details and overlooked aspects of the city through the act of mirroring, exposing the various components that actually face each other in the urban space. I argue that it is worth observing and learning from these practices, especially in a city full of contradictions like Jaramana. Depending on the scale of construction and its effect on the city's morphology, the informal vocabulary can be classified into three types: an intervention, for example an additional unauthorized floor; a modification that turns a balcony into an enclosed space; or an expansion, which means building a new block in an unplanned area or in a spot that is not zoned for residential buildings. Those »absurd« physical additions are part of the city's reality today. They cannot be ignored when thinking of the urban future. Yet, beyond buildings, they also include the internally displaced people who came from other regional districts during the war, and who will leave large empty informal neighborhoods if they decide to return to their hometowns.

Here, the word »absurd« denotes elements of informal urban development, including people, and refers to their invisibility and how they are un-considered in official documentation and future planning. From this governmental perspective, they are considered negative and undesirable additions to the city. However, those actors affect the urban environment as much as they are affected by it. They are part of the uncertainty of life that the city is experiencing today.

What if we held up a mirror to reflect Jaramana's reality to itself? What if, in these mirror images, the city's building components became identifiable and gained meaning in this act of self-reflection? Those are the questions this project poses.

The idea of reflection leads to the concept of the mirror stage in the psychoanalytical theory of Jacques Lacan. Lacan argues that the literal external-ity and otherness of the reflected image with which the child becomes totally identified creates a defensive »illusion of autonomy« (Lacan 1949: 80). The mirror stage thus describes the first felt sense of identity: »the image of one's own body is sustained by the image of the other, in fact introduces a tension: the other in his image both attracts and rejects me« (Julien 1995: 34).

Lacan's early theory, including the mirror stage, centers on the imagi-nary register.

»Lacan associated the Imaginary with the restricted spheres of consciousness and self-awareness. It is the register with the closest links to what people experience as reality. Who and what one ›imagines‹ other persons to be, what one thereby ›imagines‹ they mean when communicatively interacting, who and

1.
Visual representation of the interview process with the owners of »D. I. Dadabhay Fabrics«

what one ›imagines‹ oneself to be, including from the imagined perspectives of others« (Johnston 2018).

Interestingly, the mirror plays an ambiguous role. It is crucial for our sense of self, but at the same time it is the origin of our imaginary order, as it is based on an image reflected back at ourselves, rather than our actual selves which are always threatened with fragmentation. We might say that the mirror stands between us and an unattainable »real« in the Lacanian sense. It stands between understanding ourselves and the others around us. How might Lacan's theory assist our understanding of the city's potential for self-identification based on its living consciousness, memories, and emotions?

The project is an imaginary experiment to mirror the stage of city life. The city is a separate but simultaneous entity, because of its ability to self-reflect. The project observes some specific »absurd« scenes around the city, by using photography and collages as tools to represent the fictional mirror images of those invisible components of the informal city that have been metaphorically placed in front of it. Doing so, it considers the city as a living consciousness and invites its entities to identify their »real« selves in front of a mirror to collectively form a full understanding of the city itself. The reflections of this reality, which the project proposes as the city's fictional conscious, will be in the form of written theater acts –a dialogical mode of storytelling that insists on the existence of those entities that are obvious features in the city, but which are rendered invisible.

Unseen Acts

The second part of my project explores urban activities and snapshots from the reality of the city, outside time frames. The goal is to shed light on these phenomena and tell their story through the voice of inanimate components in the form of dialogue, theater, and storytelling. The result is reflections that record the city's life in a new voice that is coupled with human emotion. Instead of being the silent background for the personal stories of their occupants, this project places the buildings, their elements, and spaces center stage as those who speak and confront their reality.

2.
Seen and unseen buildings – can you hear the conversation?.
Collage: Yara Al Heswani.

Act 1:

A Crowded Neighborhood in Jaramana City.
Afternoon.
Two buildings stand in the middle of an urban crowd. The first is a high, multi-story building with shops on the ground level. The other is a two-story residential concrete block.

Building 1: Will you take your walls off my balcony? It isn't fun anymore.
Building 2: Are you talking to me? I still exist, you can see me!
Building 1: Yes, of course I see you, annoying block. *(Talking to oneself)*
Here we go, a non-stop talker. I wonder when they will remove this noisy neighbor from here? It has been ages!
Building 2: I am not crazy! Someone just talked to me! This entire neighborhood acts as if there is an empty spot here. I almost believed that I'm dead ... No, wait a minute, I still feel kids and cats playing on my stairs ... I am here, my friend!
Building 1: Great! Enough with the sleepy cat story, let's solve our problem. You are stepping on my foot! So, how about you take a step back?
(Silence)
What? Don't you like the solution?
Building 2: SHHHHH ... you will wake her up ...
Building 1: Who?
Building 2: The cat!

(Days of silence ... months of silence ...)

Building 2: Hey, my friend! I think I'm getting old, I can't remember who stood here first, me? Or you?
Building 1: Not sure who was the first, but we can check the new picture of the city to see who will stay here.

Building 2: I knew you would say that. I heard the gossip, the city council drew your face in their new picture and they skipped mine. They didn't see me, it's all your fault. Your height blocked the sun and blocked the sight.
Building 1: It's nobody's fault, they only have new plans for the future. We all turn into dust eventually.

3.
Residential buildings with informal additions in Jaramana.
Collage: Yara Al Heswani.

Building 2: If they only saw the families, the kids, the cats. I am sure they would turn you into dust first.

Building 1: Will this ever end?! We both sit here side by side, neither of us remembers who came first nor knows who will last longest. And all our arguments end up with cats!

This city is going crazy...

Act 2:

The same neighborhood.
A summer day.
The two buildings are still in the same spot. A running window enters the alley.

The Window: Run ... run ... save your life! RUN!

Building 2: *(Coughing)* Stop ... stop! What is all this chaos about? Aren't you a window?!

The Window: Oh, hello building, I beg your pardon. I got a little excited.
(Stops to take a breath)
Yes, I am a window and I ran from the north part of the city. I am looking for a proper wall to settle down on. Do you know any suitable walls?

Building 2: Oh dear Lord! Are we in Doomsday?
You are not supposed to run in the first place! You are born to be fixed in a wall, aren't you?

Building 1: I heard that they cut all the trees in the north and they are building new neighborhoods there. It is the perfect place to find a wall, so why did you escape from there?

The Window: Well... Allow me to tell you my story from the beginning.
(Takes a deep breath)
I am not from this city, I came here with my family five years ago. They assumed that it wouldn't be long before we returned home, so they didn't manage to settle down. My family rented an unfinished apartment, that's what they could afford, then they fixed me in the wall opening. It did not match my dimensions, but my father knew how to solve the problem using some sheets and wood beams. It was not the perfect life, but I felt good doing my job and making that unfinished apartment more suitable for them to live in.

Building 1: That is touching ... But what made you want to leave them?

The Window: HOWEVER ... In that kind of place, usually the owner will need to finish the building or sell it, sooner or later, the families will move to another block structure. From then on, my family kept adding to, or taking something from, my frame to fit me in.

Building 2: Wow my friend! You are the most adaptive window I've ever met!

The Window: You think it is cool! Well, it is not!

I don't feel like a window anymore, even though I look like one.

I used to be that magical connector between in and out. I owned that border line! I had full control over light and ventilation. Now, I am just some useless decoration that they avoid touching so that I don't fall apart and I can be easily replaced with any plastic sheet.

I am tired, so I decided to look for a normal life ... Good bye!

(The window runs away)

Building 2: But wait ... *(Shouting)* What about your family?

The Window: *(Voice from outside)* They will leave this city eventually, after a year...or two... or ten ... who knows?!

Building 1: That doesn't sound good...

Building 2: *(Crying)* Poor window!

Building 1: I was talking about the north part of the city.

Building 2: What about it?

Building 1: It was mainly built for those new arrival families. They call them »displaced«. I was not sure what that meant, but I realize now from talking to the window, they will be »placed« again in their original homes, elsewhere.

Building 2: So?

Building 1: So, we will end up surrounded with empty concrete walls instead of trees! *(Silence)*

You don't get it, do you?

Building 2: No, I do not. It is just too sad! *(Wiping tears)*

Building 1: By the way, you are getting too emotional lately. I bet it is all coming from your little cats. Thank God they don't play on my stairs!

Jaramana, Dialectic or Dialogic?

Life is dialogic and a shared event; living is participating in dialogue. Meaning comes through dialogue at whatever level that dialogue takes place. We are always in dialogue, not only with other people, but also with everything in the world. Everything »addresses« us in a certain sense.

The city of Jaramana carries many controversial issues in its story: The transformation from a rural village to an urban city with some rural aspects; then the refugees flowing in and out of it, ending up with the current situation of expansion and being crowded with the internally displaced people. The urban morphology here has various components that mostly live in a parallel situation, in other words, they live side by side in the city without any interaction as if they don't see each other. Different components refer to different kinds of people, settlements, and lifestyles. In order to understand the reality of this city or make any positive changes to it, these components should see and hear each other. A dialogue should be made to understand the dialectical relations in this urban cluster, taking into consideration those relations in time and space. What if the mirrors of this project reflect imagined dialogues between things around the city? What could these observers tell us, or what could they gossip about?

If we want to take this idea to a philosophical level, we can refer to Mikhail Bakhtin's linguistic theory about polyphonic voices in the novel. It is an idea inspired by music, and Bakhtin transferred it to linguistics. Polyphony literally means multiple voices. Things don't exist »in themselves«, but only in their relations. Bakhtin sees being as a »unique and unified event«. Being is always »event« or »co-being«, simultaneous with other beings.

For Bakhtin, human life is an open dialogue. The world thus merges into an open-ended, multi-voiced, dialogical whole. Its separation (as in Marxist alienation) or splitting (as in Lacanian master-signification) is overcome through awareness of its dialogical character – in effect, as one big borderland. The reader does not see a single reality presented by the author, but rather, how reality appears to each character. In a fully dialogical world-view, the structure of the text should itself be subordinate to the right of all characters to be treated as subjects rather than objects.

In my project, the mirrors idea will be analyzed by fictional dialogues and characters. Those polyphonic voices in this particular city's story will present their reflections on the transformation that have been made in Jaramana, especially when the argument is about informality, which is the construction logic in most cases. Absurd reality will need an absurd representation as a new perspective to reflect and analyze the place.

The Theatre of the Absurd, from Martin Esslin's point of view, shows the world as an incomprehensible place. The audience's confrontation with characters and happenings that they are not quite able to comprehend makes it impossible for them to share the aspirations and emotions depicted in the play.

Emotional identification with the characters is replaced by a puzzled, critical attention. For, while the written dialogues are absurd, they still remain recognizable as somehow related to real life with its absurdity, so that eventually the readers are brought face to face with the irrational side of their existence. Thus, the absurd and fantastic goings-on of the Theatre of the Absurd will, in the end, be found to reveal the irrationality of the human condition and the illusion of what we thought was its apparently logical structure. This form of theatrical expression represents the after-war reality that this city is living in by giving voices to the »things« that make the physical body of the city; its eternal silent observers.

Back to reality

People tend to change their surroundings in order to make their habitat the most suitable to live. However war, with all its consequences, mostly led to an absurd reality in most of the affected cities and compelled their citizens to dream of imagined realities that might (»not«) become true.

This project is an attempt to fully understand the city of Jaramana, which is part of the wider Damascus municipal area. Even though it has not been exposed to war destruction, it currently plays an important role as it contains people from many scattered cities. If we look at the case of Syria from a wider perspective, ten years of conflict has produced some kind of governmental deficiency regarding urban settlements and this increased informal construction. These kinds of actions and productions expand the sense of uncertainty about land and the distribution of resources.

The mirror insists on showing the city its actual reality, as it currently is, not as it was planned. This poses the question: When placed in front of a mirror, is the city aware of its own reality, or is it determined to overlook the truth?

References

Bakhtin, Mikhail Mikhailovich (1981): *The Dialogic Imagination: Four Essays*, Michael Holquist (ed.) and transl. by Caryl Emerson and Michael Holquist, Austin/ London: The University of Texas Press.

Bakhtin, Mikhail Mikhailovich (1986): *Speech Genres and Other Late Essays*, Caryl Emerson and Michael Holquist (eds.), transl. by Vern W. McGee, Austin: The University of Texas Press.

Esslin, Martin (1960): »The Theatre of the Absurd«, in: *The Tulane Drama Review* 4/4, 6–15.

Fahmi, Fujan/ Jaeger, Patrick (2009): »Jaramana: Refugee City. Zurich: ETH, Studio Basel, Contemporary City Institute«. URL: https://archive.arch. ethz.ch/studio-basel/projects/beirut/ damascus/student-work/jaramana-refugee-city.httml. (Accessed: July 20, 2021).

Jaramana Council (mijlis balad jaramana) (2000): *Jaramana... jara al-fayha': bayna al-turath wa al-hadatha*. Jaramana, Syria: Jaramana Council.

Johnston, Adrian (2018): »Jacques Lacan«, *The Stanford Encyclopedia of Philosophy*, Edward N. Zalta (ed.), URL: https://plato. stanford.edu/archives/fall2018/entries/ lacan. (Accessed: July 20, 2021).

Julien, Philippe (1995): *Jacques Lacan's Return to Freud: The Real, the Symbolic, and the Imaginary*, New York: New York University Press.

Kastrinou, A. Maria A. (2014): »Sect and House in Syria: History, Architecture and Bayt amongst the Druze in Jaramana«, in: *History and Anthropology* 25/3, 313–335.

Lacan, Jacques (1949): »The mirror stage as formative of the I function as revealed in psychoanalytic experience«. In: *Écrits*, trans. B. Fink. New York: W. W. Norton & Company, 2006, pp. 75–81.

Lacan, Jacques (1988): *The Seminar of Jacques Lacan, Book I: Freud's Papers on Technique 1953–1954*, New York: W.W.Norton & Company.

Sukkar, Ahmad/ Abou Zainedin, Sawsan/ Fakhani, Hani (2021): »Informal Housing in Syria: What Approach after the Conflict? Whose Rights Will be Protected?«, Arab Reform Initiative, https://www.arab-reform.net/publication/informal-housing-in-syria-what-approach-after-the-conflict-whose-rights-will-be-protected/. (Accessed: January 24, 2022).

Sukkar, Ahmad/, Abou Zainedin, Sawsan,/ and Fakhani, Hani (2021): »Informal Settlement in Syria: An Interactive Timeline«, Arab Reform Initiative, https://www.tiki-toki.com/timeline/ entry/1680805/Informal-Settlement-in-Syria/. (Accessed: January 24, 2022).

UN-OCHA, »Whole of Syria. 2017 Protection Needs Overview«, June 19, 2022, https://www.humanitarianresponse. info/sites/www.humanitarianresponse. info/files/documents/files/wos_ protection_needs_overview_2017_ oct_2016_2.pdf. (Accessed: July 20, 2021).

Dimensions of Architectural Knowledge, 2022-03 ∂
https://doi.org/10.14361/dak-2022-0314

PROTOTYPE
Cast Concrete Strategies and Fabric Formwork for Construction Waste Reduction

Rasha Sukkarieh

Abstract: This article addresses explorations of the digital world through the physical world by conducting experiments to reach prototypes that test the aspect of waste reduction and material technology within the design process. Choosing concrete as a material of investigation, and molding techniques as the starting point for explorations of the construction process, it introduces the concepts of prototypes and demonstrators in this practice-based research. The article presents a series of experiments testing material performance and construction techniques, and their impact on a digital model. The last section demonstrates the logic extracted from these experimental investigations to propose a 1:1 scale demonstrator that results from the prototypes and aims at reducing construction waste through investigating techniques to create architectural elements. This novel method promotes possibilities for design research and fabrication techniques beyond producing a product according to predetermined specifications.

Keywords: Prototype; Cast Concrete; Fabric Formwork; Construction Waste Reduction; Demonstrators; Experiments

Introduction

Throughout the past two decades, a research field has emerged exploring the impact of digital technology on how architects think, design, and build. In this practice, the experimental investigations, in particular the prototype, has become a shared research tool. Exploring the physical prototype as an integrated tool that tests and informs the digital has shifted the focus to material performance and subsequently, to fabrication techniques.

Meanwhile, over the past 50 years researchers have started to view Earth as a finite world with limited resources that could be depleted. With that, a new approach toward nature was framed by the preservation of its material and energy resources, paving the way for sustainable development and its

Corresponding author: Rasha Sukkarieh (Beirut Arab University, Lebanon); rashasukkarieh@gmail.com;
https://orcid.org/0000-0002-2216-989X

introduction to architecture's imagery. According to John Dernbach, a leading scholar in the area of environmental law and sustainability, sustainability means »freedom, opportunity, and quality of life; more efficiency; more effective and responsive governance; a desire to make a better world for those who follow us; a willingness to find and exploit opportunities; a quest for a safer world« (Dernbach 2000). This leads us to question the resources employed in the built environment.

With the development of digital technologies and the awareness of the scarcity of material resources, a new sensitivity toward the intangible properties of matter and the complex organizational processes of nature arose in architecture. In other words, there has been a new interest in the behavior of matter, not in its appearance, as it started to be comprehended as a process and not as a product. With that in mind and considering the prototype as a tool to explore research fields – in construction – this research addresses the relationship between the physical and digital prototyping as a particular means of informing design decisions. The article demonstrates conducted experiments to reach prototypes that test the aspect of waste production and material technology within the design process.

Which Material and Fabrication Techniques?

Being the most dominant building material in the construction industry, concrete is the material under investigation in this research. While concrete alone has a relatively low embodied energy, its extraordinary rate of consumption means that cement manufacture alone is estimated to account for around 5 percent of global CO_2 emissions (Orr et al. 2011). Concrete is essential to the construction of many of the world's most avant-garde buildings, but is criticized for leaving them all looking alike, so it remains controversial and yet is worth improving to match our growing movement toward ecological sustainability.

Inspired by Martin Pawley's investigation into transforming consumer waste into building materials, this research chooses to address the reduction of construction waste by introducing waste materials into the concrete mixture itself. Pawley wrote » the secondary use, instead, involves a re-usage of the materials as they are, optimizing its resources needed for the job; old products are given life without being murdered first« (Pawley 1982). The focus therefore is on replacing some of concrete's natural aggregates with waste products from the construction process. Accordingly, the experimental investigations into concrete's materiality focus on replacing sand and (partially) gravel with plastic shreds, Styrofoam, wood shreds and stone waste (a by-product of the construction process considered difficult to dispose of).

The research focused on choosing construction waste materials that were largely abundant at the Digital Fabrication Lab (where the experiments had been conducted), that are typically generated in large quantities, and are of a greater threat to environmental sustainability. Plastic waste, although not usually associated with the construction industry, is still a major material in vast productions like the automotive industry and manufacturing, and is a major contributor to landfills and marine pollution. Therefore, finding effective alternatives to recycling this plastic waste will go a long way toward ensuring a sustainable environment. Accordingly, this research chooses to include plastic particles within its experimental investigations.

With regard to the fabrication technique, this research addresses formwork systems, which are the most applied construction technique worldwide. It also explores measures to improve their performance and reduce their environmental impact. As a noun, the word »mold« implies fixity; as a verb it implies action and change. Flexible molds remain unfixed until the very end of their action. That action is not one of strictly commanded matter and events, but rather consists of finding an accommodation within rigidly set limits. Boundaries are set and openings are sought, through which the material world is invited to offer solutions on its own terms.

Fabric forms are permeable synthetic textile structures that have the ability to contain concrete mixtures, rendering their final form. Knowing that the synthetic fabrics industry is responsible for 8 percent of annual global carbon emissions (World Bank 2019), reusing discarded textiles in casting concrete structures has a positive environmental and economic impact. In her research on developing KnitCandela, Mariana Popescu addresses economic and ecological concerns and proposes custom-fabricated formwork for non-standard and doubly-curved structures to decrease the structure's cost, reduce its manufacturing time (when compared to conventional CNC milling), and generate a lighter and effortlessly transported structure (Popescu et al. 2020). This fabrication technique facilitates variety in form generation according to natural forces (Veenedaal et al. 2012).

From Digital to Physical Prototyping

>Prototypes are loaded with content, meaning, potential and mystique« (Sheil, quoted in Burry/Burry 2016).

Designers prototype their work to test it but whether the prototype works or not is not the real issue. Instead, prototyping is a process through which a designer gains insight into how their experiment is proceeding. Failure offers important information, which, when fed back into the creative process, increases the chances of a more successful outcome. Unlike physical prototyping, virtual prototyping as a design tool is when the prototype exists as a digital simulation only. The latter is a means of visually communicating concepts, whereas the former is for communicating performance and to envisage and test new ideas, while engaging with real materials and real techniques (Burry/Burry 2016). This article chooses to address the exploration of the digital world via the physical by conducting experiments to reach prototypes that test the aspect of waste reduction and material technology within the design process. The intention is to test this methodology on a concrete element that serves the function of urban furniture. The selection of urban furniture was made based on the purpose of exploring small scale non-structural elements that require an acceptable durable performance.

In his book Concrete and Culture, architectural historian Adrian Forty suggests that concrete is more of a process than a material. He writes, »prior to the arrival of the constituent ingredients, cement, sand, aggregate, steel, at one place —a building site, or a casting factory—and it is only at the moment when human labor combines them together that they become concrete« (Forty 2012: 43 –44). With that, Forty insists that concrete demands process-based description by its very nature. This aligns with the intention of this research to address the exploration of the digital world through the physical by conducting experiments to reach prototypes that test the aspect of waste reduction and material technology within the design process.

Inevitably, understanding, formalizing, and designing material properties and employing them in the design process, while considering the material's environmental value and fabrication process, has become a major focus. The prototype, in the digital design practice, has become the major means of evaluation as well as the central conductor for a new digital approach, serving as both an internal validation tool and a digital design model.

Accordingly, based on the work of architects and researchers Mark and Jane Burry and their classification of the attributes represented by prototypes as an approach to research and production (Burry/Burry 2016), this analysis investigated these approaches by studying the material performance and construction technique based on the following:

a) A tool of thinking: Design is a process, a conversation between the design and its tectonic characteristics (materiality and construction). Prototypes can be used to refine the proposal and sometimes generate a new design.

b) Testing performance: Prototypes can be used to test the functionality of the aspects of design such as texture, surface quality, or aesthetic representation.

c) Workflow processes: The system of production needs to be designed in order to reach a point where it is possible to produce a first physical prototype. These operations may be influenced by material behavior, fabrication constraints, formal objectives, and choices of technology in the production techniques. The process is based on trial and error.

d) Manifestation of data: Digital design is data-related. Prototypes give form to data as a physical outcome and as a fundamental route to decision-making.

e) A tool for experimental verification and/or falsification: Prototypes are used to fail earlier and faster. These operations investigate the precise mechanisms and modes of failure or the aspects of a design that do not meet.

Prototyping

>I would even go so far as to say that built forms should not be designed at all – the architect can only provide assistance at the point when the forms start to take shape« (Otto 1958).

In his article »The Architecture and Operative Aesthetics in the Work of Frei Otto«, architectural theorist Georg Vrachliotis highlights the originality of

Otto's process, whereby Otto had »radically extended the interaction of model and materiality when one considers the spectrum of materials, substances, and fabrics that he worked with« (Vrachliotis 2017: 22). He explains how Otto's prototyping forms the platform of experimental culture that constantly includes

> »scientific observations, technical skills, a self-adjustment of manual and intellectual facets in which the act of design may not only entail the production of individual insights but also serve as the striating point for collective discourse on the future of the discipline« (Vrachliotis 2017).

Additionally, Anne Beim, who researches industrial architecture, and Mette Ramsgaard Thomsen, whose research centers on the intersection between architecture and computer science wrote »to understand the broad field of prototypes, we differentiate between different types of prototyping activity generating material evidence as testable design artefacts« (Beim/ Ramsgaard Thomsen 2011). They differentiate models from prototypes whereby the former are understood as speculative and scaled while the latter are fully scaled examining the realization of an idea. Similarly, Mark Burry (2012) in his paper »Models, Prototypes and Archetypes«, suggests a differentiation between the model that occupies a representational realm »generally in miniature, to show the construction or the appearance of something« and the prototype that is far closer to the realized.

In this research, prototypes – considered as an intermediate practice scoping ideas and testing concepts and techniques – exist as partial objects tested in isolation on their own terms. Accordingly, elements, details or assembly systems aim to explore the partial performances in prototypes, while demonstrators »conversely aim to set all these divergent investigations into a common and concluding text« (Ramsgaard Thomsen/Tamke 2009). Demonstrators will be explored further in the third section of this article.

While Otto's models are described as a narrative of an »operative aesthetic« that involves scientific precision, a creative mindset, and artifact skills, this article will try to explore these schemes. This section is therefore divided into two parts, one exploring the attributes of physical prototypes and their impact on design decisions, and the other explaining the methodology that these experimentations employed in order to pave the way for the 1:1 demonstrator.

Prototyping Attributes

Based on Burry and Burry's classification of prototype attributes, the article will demonstrate the digital and physical prototypes used to inform the design of urban furniture, which will be discussed in greater detail in the last section of this text. Primary prototype testing and verifications of the material performance and characteristics, coupled with fabrication techniques, explorations, and assessment were demonstrated later. This section is therefore divided into five parts, each exploring the impact of the experimental investigations on design decisions and considering the aim of reducing construction waste.

a) A tool of Thinking

Prototypes assisted the research in thinking within various parameters by enabling the exploration of options for the choice of the waste material, the texture, the workability of the mixture, and the aesthetics (fig. 1). The outcome was a catalog of 24 mixtures that included different percentages of waste materials. Fig.2 highlights the eight selected mixtures that included a variety of waste materials and acceptable workability. The waste materials chosen were based on their ability to be reused, such as plastic (shredded at the fabrication lab or processed at the recycling factory and transformed into pebbles), wood shreds (waste from the wood boards milled at the lab on the CNC milling machine), Styrofoam balls (a waste product of milled Styrofoam boards or blocks produced at the lab), and stone waste (a waste product of stone factories near the lab). These materials were replacing the natural and manufactured aggregates in concrete such as sand, gravel, and cement.

b) Testing Performance

Prototypes are an effective platform to test the performance of the concrete mixture. After exploring several mixtures, cylinders of a 10 centimeter diameter and 20 centimeter height, moist cured for 28 days were prepared to test the mixture's response to the load distribution. The cylinders were measured, and Compressive Strength ASTM C-39 stress tests were performed at the engineering lab (fig. 3). Based on our observations, the mixtures that contained wood shreds (9, 10, 13, and 18)

1.

Early explorations in the density and appearance of the concrete mixtures using several types of waste materials (plastics, Styrofoam particles, wood shreds, and stone waste). Photographer: Rasha Sukkarieh.

03 | 16.67% Plastic Waste
16.67% Foam Waste

04 | 33.33% Plastic Waste
33.33% Foam Waste

09 | 33.33% Plastic Waste
16.67% Wood Waste

10 | 16.67% Plastic Waste
16.67% Foam Waste
16.67% Wood Waste

12 | 0% Plastic Waste
0% Foam Waste

13 | 25% Plastic Waste
8.33% Foam Waste
16.67% Wood Waste

17 | 33.33% Plastic Waste
16.67% Foam Waste

18 | 33.33% Plastic Waste
20% Foam Waste
16.67% Wood Waste

2.

Experiments resulting in concrete mixtures each including a range of waste materials, rendering diverse aesthetic and structural performances. Photographer: Rasha Sukkarieh.

weighed less than those that included plastic and stone waste, however, given the nature of the material and its ability to retain water particles in the mix, it was rendered hazardous and non-compliant with fire safety measures. It was also observed that a small portion of foam particles occupied a large volume in the mixture which produced lighter prototypes.

The short-term properties of concrete, such as elastic modulus, shear strength, tensile, compressive strength, and the stress-strain characteristics are expressed in terms of the uniaxial compressive strength (fig. 4). This compressive strength is used as the design basis.

Table 1 demonstrates the outcome of these compressive tests. Considering the previous parameters, and as indicated in the table, prototype 17 was the most suitable in terms of performance (enduring the second highest level of loads).

After experimenting with wood shreds, the tests indicated high compressive strengths (mixture 9 in Table 1), however, wood shreds were eventually discarded from the mixture given their high level of water absorption and their weak resistance to fire in comparison to other mixtures.

c) Workflow Processes

This section demonstrates experiments and investigations that were performed on different construction techniques to explore the mechanical characteristics of the textile and the mold. Accordingly, workflow processes are divided into two parts that evaluate the options of the textile and fabric-formworks and their possible outcomes.

Textile
The structure associated with the textile is a parameter that controls the elasticity of the mold depending on the axis of its weave. These experiments were performed on the two most common materials in fabric formwork; Lycra and cotton.
In these experiments, textile mechanical properties were studied (fig. 5). Taking into consideration the relevant engineering properties in play (strength, stiffness, and failure mode) (West 2017), the deductions made are below:

3.
After curing the cylinders for 28 days at the engineering lab, they were tested for their compressive strength. The sampled tests were weighted and their dimensions measured. Photographer: Rasha Sukkarieh.

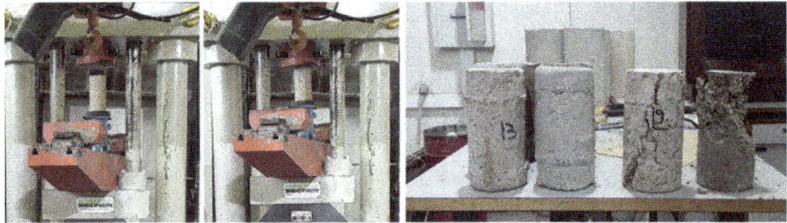

4.
Compressive test before applying the load (KN) and during the crushing point. Photographer: Rasha Sukkarieh.

Sample nb.	Diameter (cm)	Height (cm)	Area (cm²)	Load (KN)	Pressure (KN/cm²)	Pressure (MPA)	Kg-Force/m²
3	10	20	78.54	34	0.432	4.4329	432901
4	10	20	78.54	8	0.101	1.0185	101859
9	10	20	78.54	30	0.381	3.8197	381971
10	10	18	78.54	12	0.152	1.5278	152788
12	10	20	78.54	46	0.585	5.8569	585691
13	10	19	78.54	6,5	0.082	0.8276	82760
17	10	20	78.54	26,5	0.337	3.3741	337408
18	10	20	78.54	18	0.229	2.2918	229183

Table 1
Test samples results. Samples were chosen based on the variety of the included waste materials.

Lycra. Lycra is a highly expandable fabric and facilitates the process of generating complex structures. Fig. 6 identifies the prototypes performed on the Lycra-based fabric formwork:

- The fabric texture was printed on the concrete.
- During the oozing process, the mixture reserved water for a long
  period of time (three days) which rendered a relatively heavy prototype.
- The overall quality of the fabric (Lycra-Spandex) affected the form
  finding of the exterior surface.
- The concrete mixture remained in the mold for 24 hours. The textile was in good enough shape to be reused for another experiment.

Cotton (cheesecloth). Given the abundance of this material and its use in several industries in the Middle East region (such as cheese and yogurt), this research chose to explore this material as it is stiffer than Lycra, yet more permeable (fig. 7):

- The fabric texture was printed on the concrete.
- During the oozing process, the mixture reserved water for approximately 30 hours.
- The overall quality of the fabric affected the form finding, however, given the stiffness of the material, the shape was less deformed than the previous prototype.
- The concrete mixture remained in the mold for 24 hours. The textile was in good enough shape to be reused for another experiment.

Formwork Techniques

This research chose the two most common fabric-formwork pinning techniques: stay-in-place knitted formwork and draped mold.

Draped textile within a rigid mold enclosure. The molds are made from single flat sheets of fabric suspended from a basic wooden structure (made of three layers of wooden cross sections connected together with steel rods with connecting bolts). The

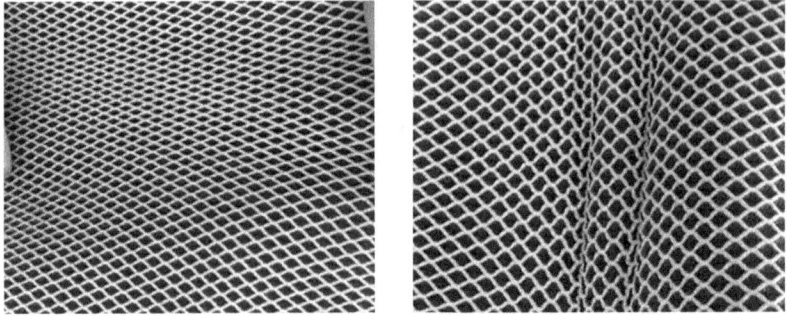

5.
The result of the tension forces applied to a woven fabric (left) along the axis of its weave (right), on the bias of 45 degrees. Photographer: Rasha Sukkarieh.

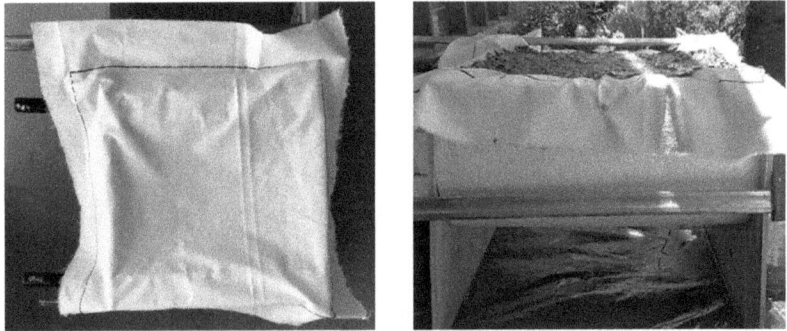

6.
Response of Lycra and gradual water dripping within the fabric mold. Photographer: Rasha Sukkarieh.

7.
Response of Cotton and gradual water dripping. Photographer: Rasha Sukkarieh.

prototypes are cast upside-down at the lab. The plywood sheets that pressed up against the bottom of the mold, flattened its bottom (later, when flipped, became the seating part of the urban furniture) while the middle sheet manipulated the form (fig. 8).

Stay-in-place knitted formworks. Using knitted technical textiles as stay-in-place molds for concrete structures are discovered by these experiments to be cost-effective, produce less waste, and less time consuming than conventional molds. According to Mariana Popescu, »the knitted materials can be tailored to doubly curved and spatially complex 3D shapes, allowing the integration of features and the design of very specific properties without the need for gluing, welding or stitching several parts together« (Popescu et al. 2020). Fig. 9 illustrates the prototype generated from this experiment.

d) Manifestation of Data

The data-driven computational design has introduced the possibility of addressing parameters that can be manipulated and that ultimately point to the relationship between data and design. Design can lead to the production of data that is highly relevant to the whole process, while data can be used to steer the design. This section manifests this relationship by demonstrating the digital model designed and modeled using Rhinoceros 6 + Grasshopper software, while the simulation of the forces and the manipulation of the fabric sheet is demonstrated using the Kangaroo Plugin (Solver) (fig. 10). The link between the data, the algorithm, and production is explored in the experimental investigations and »prototypical improvisations‹ – ways of making things that mirror the shift from descriptive geometry to a more computationally based process« (Menges 2020).

e) A tool of experimental verification/falsification

Failure is an inherent part of prototyping (Burry/ Burry 2016). While prototypes are designed to learn from their failures and accordingly, discover the causes of failure (or the aspects of the design that do not comply with the aims of the research, eventually verifying/falsifying the hypoth-

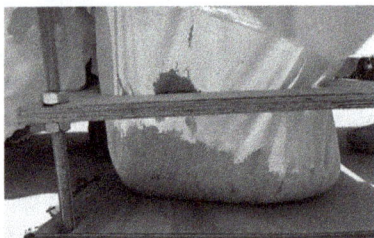

8.
Draped textile technique and the resulting model. Photographer: Rasha Sukkarieh.

9.
Stay-in-place formwork technique and the resulting model.
Photographer: Rasha Sukkarieh.

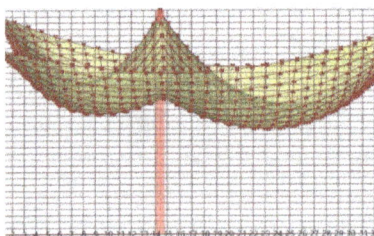

10.
Digital prototype (Rhinoceros 6 + Grasshopper) and physical prototype.
Model and photographer: Rasha Sukkarieh.

esis), figs. 11 and 12 demonstrate the failures observed in two prototypes: the former showing an uneven finish as a result of trapped air bubbles in the mold (vibrations in the mold needed more attention), while the latter demonstrates failure in producing refined edges, since the pinning of the fabric sheet was uneven, as was the distribution of the poured concrete mix.

Methods of Experimental Investigations

While the experiments have been carried out, questions relating to their impact in reaching prototypes that test the aspect of waste production in the design process have arisen. How can fabric formwork, coupled with a novel cast-concrete mixture be reimagined to create an environmentally sustainable design process? How can this process – from physical to digital – be establishing a computational model that articulates new methods of fabricating architectural elements?

In developing these questions, it is critical to refer to »Ways of Drifting: 5 Methods of Experimentation in Research through Design« by the design scholars Peter Gall Krogh et al. (2015). In their paper they identify five research methodologies that can be applied to evaluate experiments that are carried out to test hypotheses. Along the course of experimentations and based on the work development, this research has adopted the comparative and series typologies (Table 2).

The comparative experimentation method is found in the work of the interaction design researcher Maiken Hillerup Fogtmann (2012) and design researcher Philip Roland Ross (2008) who explore their subjects using a number of design cases. The method may comprise a main design case that is tested in a selection of parameters or contexts, or a set of different design cases tried in both identical and different parameters. Revealing undocumented qualities of the concept of introducing recyclable waste in concrete mixture is the main approach followed in the material experimentations and accordingly, this will adopt the comparative typology.

The serial experimentation method represents the logical order of the experiments and indicates a sequence that the experiments follow to influence one another. Complementing the comparative method, the stages of knowledge production generate insights and raise questions that lead the work onward. In this research, the serial typology will be useful in evaluating the value of the conducted experiments which then impacts the decisions taken

11. – 12.
Uneven finishing due to air bubbles trapped in the mold during the curing process (left). Failure to produce straight edges due to a misplaced pinning system. Photographer: Rasha Sukkarieh.

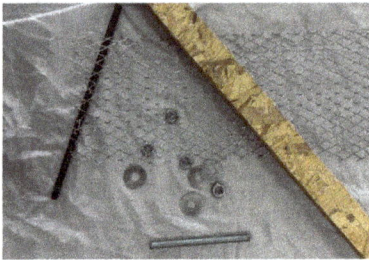

13.
The elements used to create the proposed flexible formwork (left), final sampling for the concrete mixtures (right). Photographer: Rasha Sukkarieh.

14.
After selecting the mixture with an acceptable structural performance, a demonstrator on an outdoor bench was produced using the proposed fabrication technique. Photographer: Rasha Sukkarieh.

to produce prototypes. As this is ongoing research, in-depth experimentation that compares the environmental performance of conventional concrete casting strategies to the proposed strategy will be conducted.

Demonstrators: Learning at 1:1

As discussed in the previous section, while prototypes have been a useful internal tool to experiment with novel materials and fabrication techniques, and eventually validate the digital design model, demonstrators define the scope of these proposed design methods. According to Ramsgaard Thomsen and Tamke, the emphasis on the design and implementation of material design experiments allowed the research to engage directly with the investigated techniques, moving from design to analysis (and eventually to fabrication).

Presently, the rising appreciation of the sustainable built environment (from design to process to production) has emphasized the need for new methods in construction and materiality. This research has explored the possibility of developing an ecological building strategy to reduce raw material consumption and construction waste through experimental investigations performed on the concrete mixture and the molding technique to produce a 1:1 scale urban furniture. It has developed a new concrete mixture that replaces natural aggregates with construction waste materials. Moreover, the fabric formwork strategy used to design and mold the component has adopted the same line of thought. Prototyping and testing, design, fabrication, and construction were carried out over a period of two months in the digital fabrication lab with the assistance of a team of researchers.

The proposed mold was based on the draped textile system, as it was observed that this system was able to generate durable prototypes. Using a salvaged cotton textile sheet, the mold incorporated wooden bars that included an adjustable steel channel which allowed the possibility of altering the pinning position of the textile, allowing the possibility of generating numerous forms. Once designed and generated, the demonstrator weighed 36 kilograms and required 30 hours for the oozing process to finish before the mold was removed (figs. 13 and 14).

This research has identified comparisons between the conventional casting technique and the designed fabric formwork technique. Fig. 15 demonstrates the elements of both molds and highlights how waste reduction was

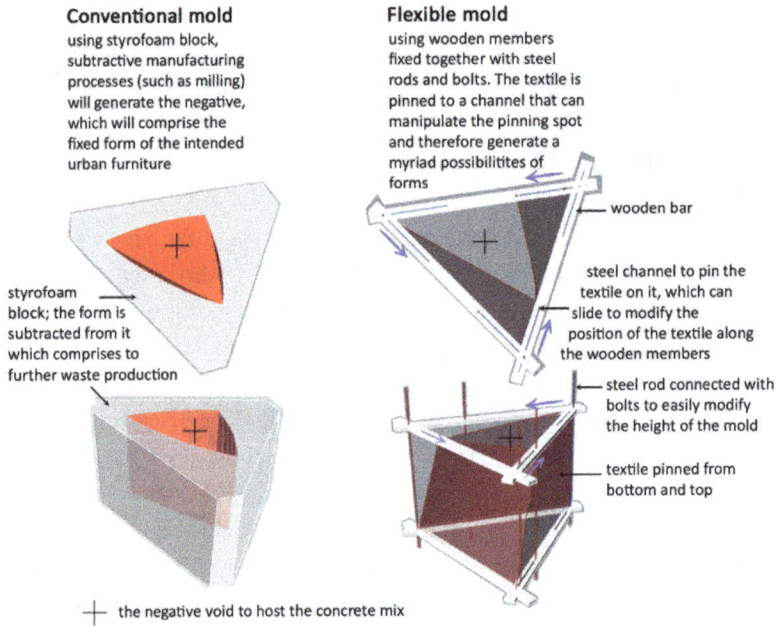

Conventional mold
using styrofoam block,
subtractive manufacturing
processes (such as milling)
will generate the negative,
which will comprise the
fixed form of the intended
urban furniture

Flexible mold
using wooden members
fixed together with steel
rods and bolts. The textile is
pinned to a channel that can
manipulate the pinning spot
and therefore generate a
myriad possibilitites of
forms

wooden bar

styrofoam
block; the form is
subtracted from it
which comprises to
further waste production

steel channel to pin the
textile on it, which can
slide to modify the
position of the textile along
the wooden members

steel rod connected with
bolts to easily modify
the height of the mold

textile pinned from
bottom and top

✛ the negative void to host the concrete mix

15.
After selecting the mixture with an acceptable structural performance, a
demonstrator on an outdoor bench was produced using the proposed fabrication
technique.

Method	Graphic Model	Keywords
Comparative		Acknowledging complexity
Serial		Systematising local knowledge

Table 2
Methodologies implemented: comparative and serial.
Note: Adapted from Peter Gall Krog et al., »Ways of Drifting«, 2015.

achieved by generating a variety of possible outcomes from the proposed mold, in contrast to the rigid conventional system.

Conclusion

As this research is an ongoing investigation, learning from failures and challenges is necessary to develop a more efficient and environmentally conscious system. Further investigation into scaling up the proposed casting system is necessary, keeping waste management as the foremost aim. Through the design explorations, the research seeks to evaluate existing casting techniques and concrete mixtures, and recontextualize them within the realm of environmental sustainability in construction. The research explored various techniques through carefully designed physical prototypes that eventually fed in the computational model the necessary parameters to produce a demonstrator. These decisions, which explore a novel method of flexible formworks using the concrete mixture, aim to reduce construction waste. The ability of a flexible formwork to express the materiality of concrete and predict the design outcome, while keeping construction waste to a minimum, is largely unexplored in the architectural research. This research also explores opportunities for fabricators to take an interactive role in the design of the form, rather than producing a product according to exact, predetermined specifications. As such, the transition from design to industry is facilitated through prototypes and demonstrators coupled with digital models and simulations.

This work was supported by participants in, and collaborators at, the IAAC Global Summer School Beirut, 2019. I wish to thank our network of colleagues and advisors at Beirut Arab University.

References

Beim, Anne/Ramsgaard Thomsen, Mette, eds. (2011): *The Role of Material Evidence in Architectural Research: Drawings, Models, Experiments*, Copenhagen: School of Architecture Publishers.

Burry, Mark(2012): »Models, Prototypes and Archetypes: Fresh Dilemmas Emerging from ›File to Factory‹ Era«, in Bob Sheil, (ed.), *Manufacturing the Bespoke: Making and Prototyping Architecture*, AD Reader Series, London: Wiley and Sons, 42 – 57.

Burry, Mark/Burry, Jane (2016): *Prototyping for Architects*, London: Thames & Hudson.

Dernbach, John (2002): » Synthesis«, in: John C. Dernbach (ed.), *Stumbling Toward Sustainability*, 3. Washington, DC: Environmental Law Institute.

Fogtmann, Maiken Hillerup (2012): *Designing with the Body in Mind*, PhD thesis, Aarhus School of Architecture.

Forty, Adrian (2012): *Concrete and Culture: A Material History*, London: Reaktion Books.

Krogh, Peter Gall/Markussen, Thomas/ Bang, Anne Louise (2015): »Ways of Drifting: 5 Methods of Experimentation in Research through Design«, in: *Proceedings of ICoRD Research into Design Across Boundaries. Volume 1: Theory, Research Methodology, Aesthetics, Human Factors and Education*, London: Springer.

Menges, Achim (2020): »Prototyping the Process: Algorithmic and /Making«, in: *Prototyping for Architects*, London: Thames & Hudson, 218–221.

Orr, John J/Darby, Antony P./Tim, Ibell/ Mark, Evernden (2011): »Concrete Structures Using Fabric Formwork«, in: *The Structural Engineer*, 89(8), 20–26.

Otto, Frei (1958): »Die Kritik«, in: *Baukunst und Werkform*, 19.

Pawley, Martin (1982): *Building for Tomorrow: Putting Waste to Work*, San Francisco: Sierra Club Books.

Popescu, Mariana/Rippmann, Matthias/ Van Mele, Tom/Block, Philippe (2020): »Knit Candela Challenging the Construction, Logistics, Waste and Economy of Concrete-shell Formworks«, in: Jane Burry/Jenny E. Sabin/ Bob Sheil/ Marilena Skavara (eds.), *Fabricate 2020*, London: UCL Press, 194–201.

Ramsgaard Thomsen, Mette/Tamke, Martin (2016): »Prototyping Practice: Merging Digital and Physical Enquiries«, in: Christoph Gengnagel/ Emilia Nagy/ / Rainer Stark, (eds.), *Rethink! Prototyping: Transdisciplinary Concepts of Prototyping*, 49–62. DOI: 10.1007/978-3-319-24439-6_5

Ross, Philip Roland (2008): *Ethics and Aesthetics in Intelligent Product and System Design*, PhD thesis, Eindhoven University of Technology.

Veenedaal, Diederik/Block, Philippe (2012): »Computational Form-finding of Fabricworks: An Overview and Discussion«, in: *Proceedings of the Second International Conference on Flexible Formwork*, 368 – 378.

Vrachliotis, Georg/Kleinmanns, Joachim/ Kunz, Martin/Kunz, Philipp, eds. (2017): *Frei Otto: Thinking by Models*, Leipzig: Spector Books.

West, Mark (2017): *The Fabric Formwork Book*, New York: Routledge.

World Bank (2019): »How Much Do Our Wardrobes Cost the Environment?«, September 23,2019, https://www.worldbank.org/en/news/ feature/2019/09/23/costo-moda-medio-ambiente, accessed July 25, 2021.

Dimensions of Architectural Knowledge, 2022-03 ∂
https://doi.org/10.14361/dak-2022-03015

REFLECTIVE ANIMATION
Navigating the *What-What*

Jhono Bennett

Abstract: Critically engaging with one's positionality in contemporary architectural research in a post-Apartheid South African context requires an approach that blends concerns about identity, location, and voice in responsibly creative means, while not reinforcing the existing power dynamics inherent in such work. This essay employs Jane Rendell's Site-Writing modality to develop a means of navigating these inter-demographic and inter-locational dilemmas – the *What-What* – that emerge when working from a »northerly« located institution and speaking from a »Southern« position through multiple audiences. A reflective-animation method has been developed that provides a proto-methodology for both documenting and speculating with the tacit nature of spatial design practice in post-Apartheid South African cities.

Keywords: Site-writing; Reflective Animation; Practice-oriented Research; *What-What*

Situating an Inquiry

Situated approaches to research call for critical, transparent, and vulnerable acknowledgments of self, location, and other dimensions, of both the re-searcher, as well as the research topic. Such scholarship understands knowl-edge as limited, specific, and partial (Rose 1997). The recognition of inter-positional dynamics within contemporary doctoral research continues to increase in use around critical and urban scholarly concerns about voice, identity, and knowledge-paradigms across academic disciplines and global locations. While design fields – architecture in particular – still often tacitly carry their traditional practice approaches.

This contribution seeks to offer a partial and situated reflection on a journey through a series of positional and locational concerns that were re-vealed while creating the initial visual and design artifacts during the first stages of the author's doctoral study. These creative-research products were developed through a site-writing modality as a means of navigating these

Corresponding author: Jhono Bennett (Bartlett School of Architecture, UCL, UK); jhono.bennett@ucl.
ac.uk; https://orcid.org/0000-0002-3901-7040

difficulties – framed here as the *What-What*.[1] Articulating the dynamics within the *What-What* as a locally understood South African term, and operationalizing it for knowledge production in a cross-global platform play an important role in making local nuance visible and »thicker«. This is a key aspect of Southern practice as it asks the reader to re-situate their understanding of this term based on its locational roots. In addition, this article will discuss the early methodological findings and journey, while acknowledging important »incommensurable« limits encountered and acknowledged by the author.

Situating Myself

Growing up in the coastal city of Durban, learning to ride my bicycle on the (then) predominantly white beachfront, having a black nanny who cared for my two brothers and myself, and even attending school in classes that inversely represented the country's demographics were all (in hindsight) unquestionably »normal« to me and those around me. I grew up with a common language and imagery of party politics and shallow readings of »race or identity«: with »the new« South Africa as a backdrop to my memories of early life. While I started school in a period (1992) that allowed students from different racial backgrounds to attend, and was the first school year to undergo the »new curriculum«, as a class we had little critical exposure to the nature of my country's recent relationship to the Apartheid regime.

More than a decade later, during my master's year in architecture, a handful of fellow students and I stumbled into the Slovo Park project (located in an »informal settlement«) and began a process of fundamentally questioning many of the assumptions that we had held as unquestionably true. My introspection into this realization, alongside my thesis work, led me along a path of deeper personal criticality and learning how spatial design, policy, and law play all play a significant role in shaping cities and the people who inhabit them: people like me.

---

1 The concept borrows from a South Africanism that is used in conversation when describing a group of dissimilarly connected items/things/ideas/conditions that one recognizes tacitly and is implied through the context of a conversation. It is effectively a blank placeholder term for something that is very difficult to describe – but is known tacitly between discussants. The term was used by South African novelist Ivan Vladislavic in his 2006 publication entitled Portrait with Keys: Joburg & What-What (Vladislavic 2006).

The #FeesMustFall protests that coincided with my early career development
as a researcher, practitioner, and educator at the University of Johannesburg
gave power to the critique that had been boiling under the surface of most
South African universities for decades and allowed many students and staff a
space to challenge and shape the university systems (within limits) toward a
»decolonial« future of tertiary education.

The *#FeesMustFall* protests in South Africa brought important and systemi-
cally critical questions around identity, positionality, and privilege in universities across South Africa to the fore (Mpofu-Walsh et al. 2016).[2] While
there is much critique of the efficacy of the response from the various institutions (Chikane 2018), the multi-year demonstrations allowed for difficult
and important discussions and institutional shifts within the academic and
scholarly sector in South Africa, particularly around the built environment
disciplines. There has been much reflection, theorization, and speculation
on and about this period of time (Mpofu-Walsh et al. 2016; Habib 2019; Morrell 2019), but for this contribution, the discourse within architecture and
around design, as well as urban studies, is more acutely considered.[3] Traditional design research from this context, in particular around questions on
whose »voice« guides research topics, or what frames »contemporary knowledge contribution« lacks much depth or nuance when conducting both spatial research or design work – a point made clearly by South African urban
researcher Tanja Winkler (2018) when describing the nature of such challenges. In regard to such challenges more globally, urban studies scholar Ai-
sha Giwa (2015) discusses similar dynamics while referencing a host of
contemporary scholars who further expand on these points.[4]

    This article intends to frame the challenges and the initial methodologi-
cal findings from the author's early journey situating a research approach
through various positional »dilemmas« – collectively framed as the *What-*

2 The protest's message centred around access to the resources of South Africa through
    education as well as the inclusion for those beyond the university's reach.

3 The framing of the author's contribution to these topics is not unique to South Africa, but
    this work focuses on the positional challenges facing researchers who occupy counter-po-
    sitions within the academy and practice as outlined by Tariq Toffa (2020: 8) in their work
    Class Conversations.

4 These include urban scholars Tariq Jazeel and Colin McFarlane's (2010) interrogation of the
    nature of »responsible« academic research between Northern and Southern scholars, to
    which they suggest methodological detours and a revaluing of research frameworks.

1.
Developmental Gestures Series. Images: Jhono Bennett, 2021.

What. The work is structured through descriptive findings from an iterative creative exercise that facilitated the development of a proto-research method employing animation, architectural drawing, and an experimental form of reflective writing. This contribution to the discourse on situated forms of research practice will share the emerging issues around concerns about location, audience, voice, and incommensurability in South African cities.

Situating an Approach

I spent a decade of my professional career working in a part of the built environment that is considered by my architectural peers to be described as »the developmental sector«. I have done this through the cross-disciplinary platform of my co-founded social enterprise and research practice, 1to1, Agency of Engagement, as well as my role as an educator in Johannesburg.

This experience took me into the field of developmental practice, where I began working with the South African arm of Shack Dwellers International as socio-technical support. My work was largely to assist the various forms of grassroots leadership the organization worked with. This journey has now taken me abroad where I am currently encountering more complex positioning and layering of these experiences as a »Southern« doctoral scholar in a »Northern« institution – especially when the discourse is so firmly based in normatively »Northern« ideas about the city, equality, and practice.

The author's positionality in relation to research practice relates to the writings of Donna Haraway (1988), which provide a solid theoretical starting point. Haraway notes the vulnerability of knowledge production and offers a means to ground research practice in a critical recognition of one's own position toward »a more adequate, richer, better account of a world, in order to live in it well and in critical, reflexive relation to our own as well as others' practices of domination and the unequal parts of privilege and oppression that make up all positions« (Haraway 1988: 579). This acknowledgment of the importance of a critical embodiment is echoed by Sandra Harding (1991) who highlights the pitfalls of not acknowledging such dynamics, nor building systems of accountability in one's own research practice (Norber/ Harding 2005). Both Harding and Haraway, according to Gillian Rose: »argue that all knowledge is marked by its origins, and to insist that to deny this marking is to make false claims to universally applicable knowledge which subjugate other knowledges and their producers« (Rose 1997: 307).

As a means of critically acknowledging the »incommensurable limits« of the author's own positionalities around applying decolonial ideals to their academic work (Yang and Tuck 2012: 4) – while carefully internalizing Walter Mignolo and Catherine Walsh's (2018) articulated distinction[5] between decoloniality and decolonization – this study[6] has adopted a »Southern« approach to knowledge production. Such an approach is described by urbanist Gautam Bhan as »a mode of theory building that focuses on locationally specific aspects of practice in Southern cities« (Bhan 2019 : 4). Bhan describes the »South« not as a set of geographical places, but as a relational project: a set of moving peripheries, and refers to the anthropologists Jean and John L. Comaroff's concept of »ex-loci« on this point (Comaroff/Comaroff 2012; Bhan 2019).

Situating the Methodology

Reflecting on more than a decade of work in »the development sector«, I feel confident in saying that the urban built environment aspects of South Africa's spatial challenges are often disproportionately discussed through a polarized lens of »housing and infrastructural services« with an unhelpful focus on a »better design« for a home for one of the most tangible symbols of the country's unequal development: the »informal settlement«.

My experience showed me and my colleagues that at the core of many of the challenges that face »informal settlements«'lies a 400+ year system of socio-spatial inequality that was the foundation of the Apartheid project and is now the framework that continues to shape South Africa and South African cities. It was important to recognize when thinking through contemporary »global» developmental frameworks and when reading »post-Apartheid« city dynamics. What was even harder to disentangle was our »Northern« influenced framings of »informality«, »urbanity«, and »development« as these principles

---

5 Decolonization refers to the undoing of colonization (in regard to the nation state) while decoloniality focuses on untangling the production of knowledge from what is claimed to be a primarily Eurocentric »episteme« (Mignolo 2018).

6 This has been done using a critical engagement with Linda Tuhiwai Smith's code of conduct for »decolonial« research practice (Smith 1999: 120). For this reason, the study acknowledges but refrains from citing texts by more seminal decolonial scholars whose work is directed toward and in support of voices other than the demographic position of the author.

2.

Slovo Park, an Informal Settlement on the outskirts of Johannesburg.
Photographer: Jhono Bennett, 2013.

3.

An earlier Inquiry into Writing-from-Site with Marlboro South.
Image: Jhono Bennett, 2021.

4.

An Extract from the First Series of Exploring the Marlboro South Experience through
Site-Writing. Image: Jhono Bennett, 2021.

5. – 6.
Extracts from the First Series of Exploring the Marlboro South Experience through
Site-Writing. Images: Jhono Bennett, 2021.

(taught to us through university and literature) did not typically allow for more localized readings of what form practice might take.

Designer and design-learning researcher Jolanda Morkel and media studies scholar and educator Franci Cronje (2019) offer an insight into the history of spatial design in South Africa through the role that design education played in the legal segregation of the population through the built environment during the Apartheid era. Her work, alongside several other architectural scholars (Le Roux, 1999; Watson, 2009; Low, 2019; Osman et al., 2020), reveals more details about the socio-political nature of work carried out since 1994[7] to make space for the humanities and »design« in higher education during the country's infrastructural redevelopment, and points out (among many other concerns) how the societally consequential dynamics of the relatively »precarious« resources available to higher education infrastructure place an inordinate amount of pressure on institutions, scholars, and students. These tensions continue to manifest themselves in post-Apartheid South Africa, where African Futures Institutes founder, Lesley Lokko, explains that »the inequalities are far more deeply entrenched in southern Africa than they are in the rest of the continent, and are inextricably bound up in race, language and identity – issues that are at the very core, the very root of who people are« (Lokko 2017: 2). In recognition of this need for epistemic reconsideration, the critical, iterative, and visually driven modalities of Jane Rendell's Site-Writing (2010; 2020) provided a relevant methodological starting point for the author's project. The following section will unpack the work produced from these methodological framings.

Situating the Research

Due to both the physical and emotional distances that have been created between myself and South Africa, the site-writing work began t in my own practice photo archive as a way to »re-visit« Marlboro South in Johannesburg: this was the site of my first project in the developmental sector and where I spent many months supporting grass-roots leadership groups during an eviction of over 500 homes. Here, I worked between the non-governmental organization (NGO) Shack Dwellers International, the City of Joburg, the Johannesburg Metropolitan

---

7 The year that South Africa was seen to be »politically free« and the new post-Apartheid regime began.

7.

The first Series of Animative Reflections in the Spirit of the Order Series Developed from the initial Site-Writing Exercises that Emerged through Reflective Drawing. Drawings: Jhono Bennett, 2021.

8.

The Later Series of Animative Reflections Developed from the Initial Site-Writing Exercises that Emerged through Reflective Drawing. Image: Jhono Bennett, 2021.

Police Department, and the University of Johannesburg, and was often placed in very emotionally and technically difficult positions.

Initially, I struggled with what felt like »extracting« from this situation; this positional paralysis felt crippling and had me trapped in cyclical patterns of guilt, anger, and shame but, through the support of the Site-Writing cohort, I pushed myself »to make it« through these feelings, and began working more closely with the archival photos.

I started with simple tracings, creative writings, and role-playing exercises. I then worked through physical prints and used illustration alongside handwriting as a means of re-telling the stories of my time »on-site«. As I wrote, traced, and re-drew the events of that time, the emotions of those moments were made tangible, while other actions and events began to make more sense alongside deeper understanding of South Africa's socio-spatial landscape.

These exercises were highly cathartic and almost meditative as I worked freely and intuitively through the tacit act of writing, drawing, and »re-visiting« the site through the imagery of the project. This iterative and repetitive act of writing and drawing worked as a form of reflection as well as documentation of both the experience and the method, and is assisting in the further development of the broader study's ethical framework.

During an iteration of this process that focused specifically on the images that captured aspects of materiality, and individuals through digital illustration software that employed a layering structure, I noticed how the drawings, when overlaid, imitated a series of movements. I leaned into the animative quality of the image and the drawing that allowed a rapid production of content through intentional and slower means of image making. This rhythm of reflection and making opened a line of experimental inquiry into animation as both a form of reflection-on-practice, as well as situational analysis.

I then re-visited my practice photo archive and searched for more accidental stop-frame sequences that engaged people, material, and action. From these, I developed the final series of explorations that captured the »spirit« of the actions around the Marlboro South project. This story and the work itself is captured in more detail in the digital exhibition of the work.[8]

There is a dynamic relationship between the image, the movement, and the practice of producing an animation that resonated strongly with the reflective nature of the study's work through Site-Writing. Such a relationship led

---

8 https://spiritoftheorder.cargo.site/ The website password is: stayingwithmytrouble

to the exploration of animation as a means of documenting not only a spatial act of making, but the embedded tacit layers of place. This comes from a decade of exploring architectural drawing beyond functional duty or aesthetic abstraction, and a disciplinary interest to show that other forms of spatial instruction can exist outside of the traditional two-dimensional or static drawing format. The architectural scholars Linda Groat and David Wang (2013) discuss the elements of rigor and repeatability that are required to produce design-drawings in detail, and don't distinguish between work produced for a built product or a process. They stand by the distinction that design is a particular activity within research that carries its own »distinct knowledge« and embedded practices.

Situating the Trouble

This initial series of design inquiries has been intuitively guided by my own feelings around critical questions on positionality, ethics (personal, contextual, and institutional), and the »right« to conduct or be involved in research on this, and related topics. While I believe that one can practice through their own individually considered »positional power-moves« without there being a »correct« means of responsibly engaging with such dynamics, the developmental sector still seems to be missing a set of recognizable (and shareable) »ethics-in-action« protocols that work toward building accountability and better practice values in spatial design. I point this out to name the aspect of the What-What dilemma – that I am also a part of, – as a means of strengthening the collective discourse and preparing the ground for further layers of inquiry about what form positional power-moves may take and entail.

This recognition of one's own position within their immediate and larger socio-political context is discussed at length in the critical qualitative field of knowledge production (Jacobson/Mustafa 2019) and is generally framed through broader concerns on roles (Herr 2015), accountability (Butler 2001), and power-dynamics (Norber/Harding 2005) toward knowledge production. However, positionality remains more ethically troublesome when called upon to »act« – in this case, spatially design or make within the built environment. While positionality is considered to be a multi-dimensional and evolving concept (Simandan 2019), the concerns discussed in this article are drawn from those framed by Gillian Rose (1997: 305–322), who in their own work, guides us to feminist scholar Linda McDowell's statement that we must recognize and take account of our own position, as well as that of our research participants, and write this into our research practice (McDowell 1992: 409). These entangled positionalities intersect with local practices and critiques, as well as global readings of South Africa, and intermingle with the author's own concerns about accountability, guilt, and audience direction.[9]

This study is placed at the intersection of architecture, urban studies, and arts practice and seeks to develop methods and approaches that support the navigation of seemingly paradoxical and counter-positional situations, and that acknowledge the inherent contradictions of attempting to »de-center« perspectives (Orelus 2013; Mbembe 2017; Patel 2020). While this could be interpreted as an act of »re-centering« and avoiding other more immediate scales of action, the author trusts in the emerging design-research modalities that have already begun to support the development of their own ethics-in-action approach to knowledge production. This comes with the intent of contributing an additional partial perspective toward shifting, disrupting, and hopefully (at some level) challenging some of the larger issues of power, as well as Northern normativity and the centrality (Yang/ Tuck 2012) of knowledge production from the author's own current »centre«.

Situating an Opportunity

This body of reflective writing and drawing have not been offered here as an external critique toward the new communities that I am becoming a part of here in »the North«, but possibly as an opportunity to add additional perspective from a cross-locational »outsider/insider« to the concerns about place, drawing production, and research practice discussed above. This could be considered an opportunity to lay the groundwork for developing additional ways to responsibly and critically practice such ethics-in-action –but I would like to clearly acknowledge the troubles, limits, and contradictions inherent in such actions. This acknowledgment does not seek to absolve me of any accountability, rather I frame here a means of emphasizing what such positional power-moves mean for me as a South African versus those of others here in the »North« and abroad.

---

9 Toward which I have interpreted the concept of the *What-What* as a means of simultaneously acknowledging and working through these concerns via my own Southern-located practices.

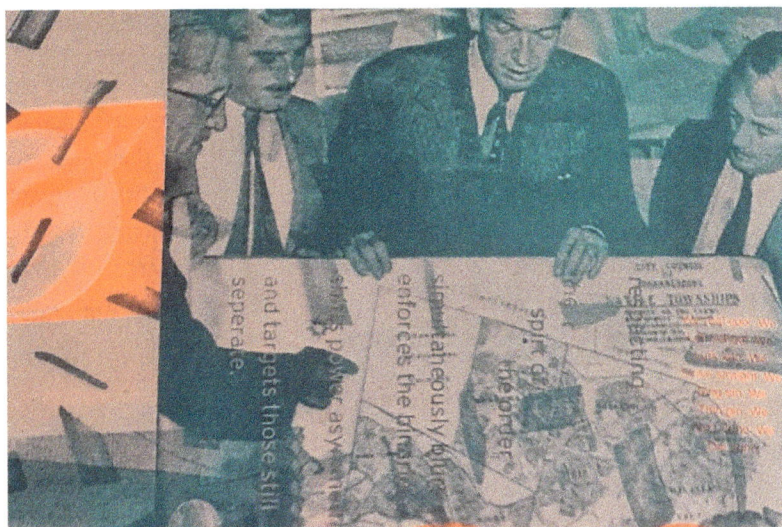

9.
An extract from a co-produced Risograph print exercise produced by Hato Press with the 2021 Site-Writing cohort that depicts a group of Apartheid Era City officials planning the layout of a Black African »Township« layered with creative writing from other Situated Practice peers. Image: Jhono Bennett with 2021 Site-Writing Cohort: https:// echoesandintersections.cargo.site, https://site-writing.co.uk/

Donna Haraway (2016) suggests »making-with« rather than »self-making« as a means of learning how to »stay with the trouble« and build more livable futures. While Haraway's introductory text does not specifically speak to the topics held within the *What-What*, their work offers a compelling reference point for a more actionable set of possible »ethics-in-action«. The study draws on Haraway's call to stay, embrace, and situate oneself within the systems of complication and complicity that they describe as the »thick present« (Haraway 2016: 9): a call that encourages one to stay with, sit within, and work carefully and slowly through the *What-What* – not around it.

The author suggests that there are other means of staying with one's *What-What* and offers this journey in reflective-animation as an example of dwelling in »the trouble« by working through such complex dynamics using iterative, deliberate, and careful means. In this case, the author has attempted to introduce more context-specific nuance, situated detail, and multi-voiced subjectivities to the imagery of Southern African spatial practices through animation as a means of architectural instruction. As animation sits between the mediums of image and film, it has not been deeply explored as an architectural means of instruction or documentation and – in this case – when combined with text, has allowed for a means of synthesizing the trouble inherent in the *What-What* and offers more than a singular frame or comment on a complex site condition such as Marlboro South. This methodology of using animation to deepen and situate the research in place is still in the early phases of development. It will be developed further and methodologically speak to the larger aims of the doctoral project: which seeks to contribute an additional perspective to the growing discourse on Southern Urbanism through a focus on the designerly aspects of an approach that works from place, recognizes concepts of periphery, and engages with Brazilian Southern urbanist Teresa Caldeira's request to »take seriously the idea of thinking with an accent« (Caldeira 2000).

References

Bennett, J. (2021): *Spirit of the Order: Navigating the What-What*. Available at: https://spiritoftheorder.cargo.site/ (Accessed: 22 February 2022).

Bhan, G. (2019): »Notes on a Southern Urban Practice«, in: *Environment and Urbanization* 31/2, 639–654. doi: 10.1177/0956247818815792.

Butler, J. (2001): »Giving Account of Oneself«, in: *Diacritics* 31/4, 22–40.

Caldeira, T. P. do R. (2000): *City of Walls: Crime, Segregation, and Citizenship in São Paulo*, Berkeley: University of California Press.

Chikane, R. (2018): *Breaking a Rainbow, Building a Nation: The Politics behind #MustFall Movements*, Johannesburg: Pan MacMillan.

Comaroff, J/Comaroff, J. L. (2012): »Theory from the South: or, how Euro-America is Evolving toward Africa', in: *Anthropological Forum* 22/2, 113–131. doi: 10.1080/00664677.2012.694169.

Giwa, A. (2015): 'Insider/Outsider Issues for Development Researchers from the Global South', in: *Geography Compass*, 9/6, 316–326. doi: 10.1111/gec3.12219.

Groat, L. N./ Wang, D./ Groat, Linda N. (2013): *Architectural Research Methods*. 2. Aufl, Somerset: Wiley.

Habib, A. (2019): Rebels and Rage: Reflecting on #FeesMustFall, Johannesburg: Jonathan Ball Publishers.

Haraway, D. (1988): »Situated Knowledges: The Science Question in Feminism and the Privilege of Partial Perspective«, in: *Feminist Studies* 14/3, 575–599. doi: 10.4324/9780203427415-40.

Haraway, D. (2016) *Staying with the Trouble: Making Kin in the Chthulucene*, Durham, NC: Duke University Press.

Harding, S. G. (1991): *Whose Science? Whose Knowledge?: Thinking from Women's Lives*, Ithaca, N.Y.: Cornell University Press.

Herr, K./Anderson, G.L. (2015): *The Action Research Dissertation: A Guide for Students and Faculty* 2nd ed, Thousand Oaks: SAGE Publishing.

Jacobson, D/Mustafa, N. (2019): »Social Identity Map: A Reflexivity Tool for Practicing Explicit Positionality in Critical Qualitative Research«, in: *International Journal of Qualitative Methods* 18, 160940691987007. doi: 10.1177/1609406919870075.

Jazeel, T./McFarlane, C. (2010): »The Limits of Responsibility: A Postcolonial Politics of Academic Knowledge Production«, in: *Transactions of the Institute of British Geographers* 35/1, 109–124. doi: 10.1111/j.1475-5661.2009.00367.x.

Le Roux, H. (1999): '»Undisciplined Practice: Architecture in the Ccontext of Freedom«, in: Blank: Architecture Apartheid and After. 1st ed, Rotterdam: NAi D.A.P./Distributed Art Publishers, pp. 351–358.

Lokko, L. (2017): *Hope, Platform: Architecture & Design*. Available at: https://www.platformarchitecture.it/lesley-lokko-hope/ (Accessed: July 6, 2018).

Low, I. (2019): »Space and Transformation: The Struggle for Architecture in Post-Apartheid South Africa«, in: *Afrika Focus* 31/2, 69–86. doi: 10.21825/af.v31i2.9919.

Mbembe, A. (2017): *Critique of Black Reason*, L. Dubois (ed), Durham, NC: Duke University Press.

McDowell, L. (1992): »Doing Gender: Feminism, Feminists and Research Methods in Human Geography«, in: *Transactions : Institute of British Geographers* (1965) 17/4, 399–416. doi: 10.2307/622707.

Mignolo, W. (2018): On *Decoloniality :
Concepts, Analytics, and Praxis*, C. Walsh
(ed), Durham, NC: Duke University Press.

Mignolo, W./Walsh, C. E. (2018):
»Decoloniality in /As Praxis Part One«, in:
On Decoloniality: Concepts, Analytics, Praxis,
304.

Morkel, J./ Cronjé, J. (2019): »Flexible
Learning Provision for Architecture in
South Africa«, in: *Faculty Perspectives on
Vocational Training in South Africa*, 19–33.
doi: 10.4324/9781351014311-3.

Morrell, R. (2019): »Review: Adam
Habib Rebels and Rage : Reflecting«,
in: *Transformation: Critical Perspectives on
Southern Africa* 100, 209–219. doi: https://
doi.org/10.1353/trn.2019.0029.

Mpofu-Walsh, S. et al. (2016): *Fees Must
Fall*, S. Booysen (ed), Johannesburg:
Wits University Press. doi:
10.18772/22016109858.

Norber, K./ Harding, S. (2005): »New
Feminist Approaches to Social Science
Methodologies: An Introduction«, in: *Signs:
Journal of Women in Culture and Society* 30/4,
2009–2015. doi: 10.1086/428420.

Orelus, P. (2013): »Whitecentricism and
Linguoracism Exposed«, in: *Reference &
Research Book News*, 28/4, 10805.

Osman, A. et al. (2020): *Cities, Space and
Power*, Cape Town: AOSIS Publishing.

Patel, K. (2020): »Race and a Decolonial
Turn in Development Studies«, in:
Third World Quarterly 0(0), pp. 1–13. doi:
10.1080/01436597.2020.1784001.

Rendell, J. (2010): *Site-Writing: The
Architecture of Art Criticism* 1st ed, London/
New York: I.B.Tauris & Co. Ltd.

Rose, G. (1997): »Situating Knowledges:
Positionality, Reflexivities and
Other Tactics«, in: *Progress in Human
Geography* 21/3, 305–320. doi:
10.1191/030913297673302122.

Simandan, D. (2019): »Revisiting
Positionality and the Thesis of
Situated Knowledge«, in: *Dialogues
in Human Geography* 9/2, 129–149. doi:
10.1177/2043820619850013.

Smith, L. T. (1999): *Decolonizing
Methodologies: Research and Indigenous
Peoples*, London/ New York: Zed Books.

Toffa, T. (2020): »Learning to Speak? Of
Architecture and the Colonialities of
Transformation, Race«, in: A. Osman (ed.),
Cities, Space and Power 1st ed, Cape Town:
AOSIS Publishing.

Vladislavic, I. (2006): *Portrait with Keys:
Joburg & what-what* 1st ed,. Johannesburg:
Umuzi.

Watson, V. (2009): »Seeing from the
South: Refocusing Urban Planning on
the Globe's Central Urban Issues« in:
Urban Studies 46/11, 2259–2275. doi:
10.1177/0042098009342598.

Winkler, T. (2018): »Black Texts on White
Paper: Learning to See Resistant Texts
as an Approach towards Decolonising
Planning«, in: *Planning Theory* 17/4,
588–604. doi: 10.1177/1473095217739335.

Yang, W./Tuck. E (2012): »Decolonization
is Not a Metaphor«, in: *Decolonization:
Indigeneity, Education, & Society* 1/1, 1–40.

Dimensions of Architectural Knowledge, 2022-03 ᗡ
https://doi.org/10.14361/dak-2022-0316

RESEARCH BY DESIGN
Architecture is a Time Machine

Jonathan Hill

Abstract: Expanding ideas that I previously explored in »Design Research: The Next 500 Years« (Hill 2022), this article considers the contributions to temporal understanding of three analogies: architecture as a time machine, as a history, and as a fiction. Assembled from materials of all ages: from the newly formed, to those centuries or millions of years old, and incorporating varied rates of transformation and decay, a building is a time machine, transporting us to many times separately or simultaneously. Like a history, a design is a reinterpretation of the past in the present. Equally, a design is equivalent to a fiction, freely moving backward and forward in time and between types of time. In conclusion, I emphasize temporal understanding as a means by which to learn from the past, reassess the present, and speculate on future models of practice and discourse.

Keywords: Design Research; Architectural History; Fiction; Types of tTme; Future Models of Practice and Discourse.

Time Travel

Contemporary physicists dismiss anyone who believes in time – the past, present, and future – as equivalent to people who still think the earth is flat or the sun revolves around us. Carlo Rovelli acknowledges a few «dissenting voices«, including Lee Smolin, who he describes as a »great« scientist (Rovelli 2017: 191), However, Smolin traces contemporary physics back to the metaphysics of Ancient Greece. In *Timaeus*, c. 360 BCE, Plato claims that all the things we experience in the material world are modelled on ideal forms defined by geometrical proportions (Plato 1929: 121). Consequently, there are two distinct realms. One consists of timeless originals, which only the intellect can comprehend, the other of imperfect copies subject to decay. According to Smolin:

Corresponding author: Jonathan Hill (Bartlett School of Architecture, UK); jonathan.hill@ucl.ac.uk;
http://orcid.org/0000-0001-8595-1857.

»Those burdened by the metaphysical presupposition that the purpose of science is to discover timeless truths represented by timeless mathematical objects might think that eliminating time, and so making the universe akin to a mathematical object, is a route to a scientific cosmology. But it turns out to be the opposite [...] The research program based on the timeless universe that embraces quantum mechanics and the multiverse as the final theory has been around for more than two decades. It has not yet produced a single falsifiable prediction for a currently doable experiment.« (Smolin 2013: 238–239, 249).

Since the 18th century, knowledge has been subdivided into specialisms with limited understanding of each other's debates. Consequently, the temporal understanding of a geologist, a historian, a medical practitioner, or an architect is quite distinct. Instead, Smolin argues that temporal understanding should be disciplinary and transdisciplinary, concluding that: »a civilization whose scientists and philosophers teach that time is an illusion and the future is fixed is unlikely to summon the imaginative power to invent the communion of political organizations, technology, and natural processes – a communion essential if we are to thrive sustainably beyond this century« (Smolin 2013: 258). Distinctions between the artificial and natural are rooted in the metaphysical hierarchy of the timeless and (supposedly) mindless:

»To learn to live with our planet, we have to rid ourselves of the vestiges of this old yearning for elevation from it [...] We need to see everything in nature, including ourselves and our technologies, as time-bound and part of a larger, ever evolving system« (Smolin 2013: 257).

Time is relative. Affected by speed and mass, time is slower in the far north than at the equator, slower in the plains than in the mountains, and slower at your feet than at your head (Rovelli 2017: 12; Sorenson 2008: 79). Light weaves through spacetime. Given the speed of light and thus the time that light takes to reach us, the stars we see in a night sky are in the past not the present. Equally, the sun we observe on a summer's day is the past sun not the present sun.

Rovelli quips: »Time travel is just what we do every day, isn't it? Every single day we travel one day ahead in time« (Rovelli 2019). According to Dean Buonomano, »the brain is a time machine« collecting the past and assessing the present to anticipate the future (Buonomano 2017: 15). Some people are better time travellers than others. An exceptional footballer can project themselves forward in time and predict the movement of the ball and opponents. The building is also a time machine. Assembled from materials of various ages, from the newly formed, to those centuries or millions of years old, and incorporating varied rates of transformation and decay, a building can curate the past, inform the present and imagine the future, transporting us to many different times simultaneously. The stones of a building belong to the geological time they were wrought, the time they were quarried, the time they were integrated into a construction site, the ever-progressing time of subsequent environmental change, and the varied times they are experienced. We may seem to travel back in time, while architectural materials and components have literally traveled forward to us. Just as much as any collection of papers or drawings, a building is an archive. Rather than static, it is an evolving collection of ideas, values, materials, and lives, with the capacity to acknowledge the histories and timeframes of related disciplines, whether thousands of archaeological years or millions of geological ones. Gazing at a marble wall, we can appreciate the geological »Abyss« of deep time (Gould 1987: 61–65). Our thoughts may be cast back to a pre-human era when ancient creatures inhabited the earth or forward to a post-human era when humans are extinct. If we contemplate a sedimentary stone, we see time's arrow and the possibility of ruin. If we gaze at an igneous or metamorphic stone, we see time's cycle and the possibility of repair.

In many time travel tales, the protagonists wish to change the past not just observe it. But since H.G. Wells coined the term in 1895, the time machine is notably unreliable (Wells 1895). The unpredictability of time travel is exploited for narrative tension. Architecture is also an erratic rather than a reliable time machine. It cannot change the past but may alter our understanding, while it can potentially change the future. A building does not just exist in time; it creates time, traveling forward as a message to the future. However, there is nothing as old-fashioned as a past vision of the future. We have all experienced the sense that time has reversed. An era that seemed to be in the past becomes the future. In the early 21st century, the environmental catastrophe of agricultural overproduction sees hedgerows replanted, industrial pesticides discarded, and farms rewilded. The low tolerance and high susceptibility to failure of complex building systems sees thermal comfort reassessed and traditional technologies revived.

Architects of History and Fiction

Architecture's time travel tools and techniques are varied and interdependent: buildings, books, models, and drawings, histories, fictions, memories and designs. Architects use history in differing ways. Either to indicate thoughtful continuity with the past or cathartic divergence from it. From the Renaissance to the early 20th century, the architect was a historian in the sense that a treatise combined design and history, and a building was expected to manifest the character of the time and knowingly refer to earlier eras. Sometimes continuity and catharsis combined, as in the 19th-century critique of classicism and revival of gothic.

Modernism ruptured this system in principle if not always in practice. Walter Gropius excluded the history of architecture from the Bauhaus syllabus, breaking from previous educational models and advocating designs specific only to the present. In the »Manifesto of Futurist Architecture« (1914 CE), Antonio Sant'Elia and Filippo Tomasso Marinetti proclaimed: »This architecture cannot be subject to any law of historical continuity« (Sant'Elia and Marinetti 1914: 34–38). However, even early modernists who denied the relevance of the past relied on histories to validate and articulate modernism. Books such as Nikolaus Pevsner's *Pioneers of the Modern Movement* (1936)[1] and Sigfried Giedion's *Space, Time and Architecture* (1941), identify a modernist pre-history to justify modernism's historical inevitability, rupture from the past, and systematic evolution. These authors present modernism as homogenous and primarily Western, which implies that other regions should be judged against this model. For example, in China and Japan, the idea of the architect as a designer, and architecture as an art, arrived with modernism. Consequently, Arata Isozaki concludes that a pre-modern Japanese building could retrospectively become architecture and the architect could »be interpolated, however anachronistically, between patron and master carpenter« (Isozaki 2006: 293).

By the mid-20th century, modernism was no longer new and was ripe for reassessment. World War II was more scientific than World War I, undermining confidence in technological progress as a means of social transformation. Notably, for the generation of architects who were old enough to see military service, modernism's previously dismissive reaction to social norms,

---

1 *Pioneers of the Modern Movement* was reprinted as *Pioneers of Modern Design* in 1949 and revised in 1960.

cultural memories, and historical references became anachronistic. Modernism developed into a polycentric, worldwide network of distinct, varied, and interdependent regional and local modernisms.

In a radio broadcast in 1966, a decade before Charles Jencks familiarized the term, Pevsner characterized the post-war designs of Le Corbusier and Denys Lasdun as »postmodern«, which he associated with the anxious aftermath of war. (Pevsner 1966: 299, 307; Hudnut 1945: 70–75). But it is more accurate to categorize their designs as simultaneously pre-modern, modern and post-modern. Associating history writing with storytelling, Lasdun remarked that each architect must devise their »own creative myth«, a collection of ideas, values, forms, and techniques that stimulate design. He concluded: »My own myth [...] engages with history«, emphasizing that »I don't mean myth in the sense that it is untrue« (Lasdun 1984: 137,139; Lasdun 1979: 9). In a similar vein, in 1969, Vincent Scully stated that the architect will »always be dealing with historical problems –with the past and, a function of the past, with the future. So the architect should be regarded as a kind of physical historian [...] the architect builds visible history« (Scully 1969: 257). Thus, the architect is a historian twice over: as a designer of buildings and an author of books.

A history is an interpretation of the past in the present. It is also a reflection on earlier histories. One history may need to be categorically rejected so that another can be formulated. Instead, selective appraisal may be fruitful. Alternatively, past ideas, forms, practices, and histories can be acknowledged as incomplete, and thus ready to be revived, enriched, and expanded in the present.

As a design is equivalent to a history, we may expect the architect »to have a certain quality of *subjectivity*« that is »suited to the objectivity proper to history«, as Paul Ricoeur concludes (Ricoeur 1965: 22). Historical writing requires imagination as well as analysis, but the architect does not usually construct a history with the rigor expected of a contemporary historian and may combine varied qualities and genres instead.

Histories and novels need to be convincing in different ways. Although no history is unbiased, to have any validity it must appear truthful to the past. However, a novel may be believable but not true. In »The Fiction of Function« (1987), Stanford Anderson emphasizes that there was no coherent theorization of functionalism in the early 20th century and little indication that it was rigorously applied to design. Instead, he argues: »modern architecture, more than that of any other time, emphasized stories about function« (Anderson 1987: 21). This encourages us to consider the stories about history that architects fabricate.

The architect is a »physical novelist« as well as a »physical historian« (Hill 2021: viii–xix). Like a history, a design is a reinterpretation of the past in the present. Equally, a design is equivalent to a fiction, convincing users to suspend disbelief. We expect a history or a novel to be written in words, but they can also be delineated in drawing, cast in concrete, or seeded in soil.

Exceptional architects are exceptional storytellers. Such tales have special significance when they resonate back-and-forth between private inspiration and public narrative. A building tells stories through its forms, spaces and uses, means of construction, combination of materials, and relations with physical, social, and environmental contexts. Architectural stories can address the most important, stimulating issues of the day. For example, ideas about climate express wider values, including attitudes to nature, ethics, and governance. Conceiving the architect as a storyteller places architecture at the center of cultural and social production, stimulating ideas, values, strategies, and emotions that inform and influence individuals and societies.

Technologies of the Self

The earliest known histories originated over 4,000 years ago through record-keeping in Mesopotamia and Egypt, while the term »history« derives from Ancient Greece. Emphasizing Enlightenment reason, objectivity, and progress, the Western idea of history spread around the world with the colonial powers. Rather than necessarily enlightening, it was a means to perpetuate Western ideology, establishing a benchmark against which alternative histories were deemed deficient. In the second half of the 20th century especially, suspicion of meta-narratives developed in many regions of the world, including the West. A historical method embedded in skepticism became subject to skepticism. Although the Western idea of history remains influential and widely disseminated it has been informed and transformed by its travels. Other models are also evident. For example, there is a strong oral history tradition in Africa, where historical writing initially developed through contact with Christianity and especially Islam in North Africa. History today does not offer a singular model but a multiplicity of hybrid approaches.

Concepts of fiction today are equally varied. The history of long prose fiction is around 2,000 years old, but the novel is a more recent innovation. The date and location of the first novel is disputed, depending on the literary tradition that is selected. Admired for its convincing depiction of court life in early 11th-century Japan, Murasaki Shikibu's *Tale of Genji* is a candidate for the first novel. Often characterized as the first European novel, Miguel de Cervantes' *Don Quixote*, (1605–1615), claims to be an accurate account of an actual person. The Catholic Counter Reformation ensured that Cervantes' skeptical, secular relativism was comparatively rare in 17th-century Spain (McKeon 1987: 293). The novel's development into a distinctive, popular literary form is often identified with early 18th-century England. In valuing direct experience, precise description, and a skeptical, questioning approach to »facts«, empiricism created a fruitful climate for »factual fiction« (Davis 1983: 213). In contrast to the epic or romance, which incorporated classical myths and archetypes, the novel concentrated on everyday lives in enterprising, expansionist, and increasingly secular societies, emphasizing individualism as well as imperialism, unfortunately.

The dilemmas of personal identity and fortune were ripe for narrative account. Frequently described as the first English novel, Daniel Defoe's *Robinson Crusoe* (1719), is a fictional autobiography. Defoe describes his other famous novel *Moll Flanders* (1722) as »a private History«, and *Roxana* (1724), as »laid in Truth of Fact« and thus »not a Story, but a History« (Defoe 1722: 3; Defoe 1724: 21). Supporting authors' claims that their novels were histories, the transition to a methodical, comparative method was slow and most 18th-century histories inherited some of the rhetorical approach of earlier histories.

The early novels – fictional autobiographies – developed in parallel with early diaries – autobiographical fictions. People have written about themselves for millennia but the formation of modern identity in the 18th century is associated with a type of diary writing that Michel Foucault describes as a »technology of the self«, the process of self-examination by which moral character and behaviur are constructed and reimagined (Foucault 1984: 369; Foucault 1988: 18–19). Objectivity may be an aspiration, but no diary is entirely truthful, and the diarist cannot fail to edit and reinvent their life while reflecting upon it, altering the past and influencing the future.

In 1714, William Kent began a visual and textual diary, »Remarks by Way of Painting & Archit.« which records his journeys around Italy. Written in English and Italian, the diary analyzes buildings, gardens, and paintings, and includes small drawings and diagrams in the margins and the text. The most impressive section is the final one, which contains delicate illustrations of complex perspectival techniques in line and wash (Kent 1714–1717: 25–36).

Equivalent to a visual, textual, and spatial diary, the process of design –from one drawing to the next iteration and from one project to another – is itself an autobiographical »technology of the self«, formulating a design ethos for an individual or a studio.

Emphasis on individualism and self-reflection triggered fractured narratives, alternative scenarios, and myriad digressions in the garden as well as the novel and diary. Equally, the early 18th-century landscape is equivalent to a history, reimagining the past in classical reconstructions and imported trees. Kent's Rousham, Oxfordshire, 1737–1741, is a fiction and a history, as well as an allegory of the life and declining health of Kent's patron, General James Dormer, who died just as the garden was completed.

In 17th and 18th–century societies, the emergence of a secular understanding of time focused more on life and less on the afterlife, giving greater emphasis to distinctions between the past, present, and future, and stimulating abundant temporal metaphors such as the setting sun, weathered and ruined buildings, and decaying vegetation. The pleasures of life were especially poignant because they were fleeting and perishable. Reference to the seasons of the year and the seasons of a life suggest both a cyclical concept of time from one spring to the next, in which death renews life, and time becomes a linear concept from one year to another.

Architectures of Remembering and Forgetting

Rousham is an early and influential example of the picturesque landscape. For an 18th-century architect or patron, classical buildings in an Arcadian setting would have conjured associations with the architecture and landscape of Ancient Rome – including those depicted by 17th-century painters such as Claude Lorrain and Salvador Rosa – translated and improved for a new time and site. But for many visitors a picturesque estate that now seems quintessentially English would have also seemed shockingly new.

A prospect of the future is implicit in many histories, novels, and diaries, but it is explicit in many designs. An architect does not necessarily design for today and may have a different time in mind. Some architects plan for the present, some imagine a mythical past, while others conceive for a future time and place. Alternatively, an architect can envisage the past, the present, and the future in a single architecture. In many eras, the most fruitful architectural innovations have occurred when ideas and forms have migrated from one time and place to another by a translation process that is as inventive as the initial conception. Thus, a design can be specific to a time and place and a compound of other times and places.

In *The Seven Lamps of Architecture* (1849), John Ruskin remarks that »we cannot remember without« architecture (Ruskin 1849: 169), yet each building is an attempt to forget some things and remember others (Forty 1999: 16). Written during the troubled aftermath of war and foreseeing a dystopian near-future, George Orwell refers to the Party slogan in 1984: »Who controls the past controls the future. Who controls the present controls the past« (Orwell 1949: 44). A building is commissioned, designed, and constructed with specific agendas in mind, promoting some values and ignoring others, but it is rarely so didactic and dogmatic, and may be open to numerous interpretations. Original meanings are soon obscured or transformed unless they are continuously reaffirmed through everyday behavior and careful maintenance, which are as necessary to perpetuating collective memory as any material object. Whether collective or personal, memory varies according to who is remembering and when. Our perceptions and memories are fallible and creative. For example, the eyes receive inexact information and the brain extrapolates from previous knowledge and experience to create a plausible, seemingly comprehensive image. Rather than just living in the moment, we filter the present through memories of the past, and speculations on the future that are permeated by personal and collective values woven many times into one. As we move from place to place, we may seem to move backward or forward in time or oscillate between them.

Future Practices

Twenty-first-century architects can appreciate the shock of the old as well as the shock of the new (Edgerton 2008). To ask what is new involves other questions: why is it new, how is it new, and where is it new? In William Gibson's memorable statement: »The future is already here – it's just not very evenly distributed« (Gibson 1992). To understand what is new, we need to consider the present, the past, and maybe even the future: we need to think historically. Defining something as new is an inherently historical act because it requires an awareness of what is old.

The first such program in the United Kingdom, the PhD in Architectural Design at The Bartlett School of Architecture, UCL, was established in the mid-1990s. The first student completed the doctorate in 2000, and over 80 students have graduated since. The architectural design doctorate is a comparatively new architectural qualification but its methods and means are not. Indeed, they have been invaluable to architects for centuries.

The Renaissance's concern for history was inseparable from its own history. Erwin Panofsky identifies a creative and critical nostalgia for classical antiquity »that distinguishes the real Renaissance from all those pseudo- or proto-Renaissances that had taken place during the Middle Ages« (Panofsky 1955: 302–303). In *Anachronic Renaissance*, Alexander Nagel and Christopher S. Wood write: »The ability of the work of art to hold incompatible models in suspension without deciding is the key to art's anachronic quality, its ability really to ›fetch‹ a past, create a past, perhaps even to fetch the future« (Nagel and Wood 2010: 18).

The Renaissance reasserted classical antiquity's appreciation of the timeless, immaterial geometries of ideal forms but introduced a fundamental change in perception to proclaim that drawing mediates seamlessly between the mind and the world, allowing the three visual arts – architecture, painting, and sculpture – to be acknowledged as arts concerned with ideas, acquiring advanced status that they had not received before the 15th century. The term »design« derives from the Italian *disegno*, which means drawing, and associates drawing a line with drawing forth an idea. The status of painters, sculptors, and architects is founded on the myth that artistic creation is solitary and private, even though it is more often collaborative. The painting and sculpture are unique, thus appearing closer to the world of the individual intellect in contrast to the architectural drawing, which is seen in relation to other drawings and a building. A painting or sculpture may require more physical labor than an architectural drawing, but fabrication is less public than on the construction site. The architectural drawing depends on two related but distinct concepts. One indicates that drawing is an intellectual, artistic activity distant from building labor. The other emphasizes the architect's mastery of the collaborative construction process. Creativity as well as confusion has arisen from this contradiction.

In the new division of labor, architects acquired complementary means to practice architecture: drawing, writing, and building. To affirm their advanced status, architects began to theorize architecture both for themselves and for their patrons, ensuring that the authored book became more valuable to architects than to painters and sculptors, whose artistic status was more secure and means to acquire and complete commissions less demanding. A multi-directional web of influences – drawing, writing, and building – have all stimulated architects' creative development for over 500 years.

Celebrating the creative interdependence of drawing, writing, and building, The Bartlett's architectural design doctoral thesis is founded on the tradition of the architectural book and stimulated by the many forms it has taken globally in the past 500 years. Emphasizing the value of historical understanding, critical analysis, and »factual fiction« to design, the thesis consists of a project and a text that share a theme and express a mutually productive dialogue. The project can be filmed, sculpted, drawn, or built and employ any methods and media that are interesting and appropriate to the subject. When establishing the PhD, we retained the existing 100,000-word limit for UCL doctorates because we appreciated that design can be written as well as drawn and speculated that a student might want to produce a purely written design PhD. That happened just a few years later, with a thesis that included lyrical texts, analytical texts, and writings that combined the two.

Architectural design PhD students often create a thesis that integrates various research methods and distinct narrative voices. If you produce a singular piece of work with one type of output, you may tend to have a singular idea of authorship but if you work between media, as you do with an architectural design doctorate, you need to conceptualize your place within that creative process (Hill 2022).

Architectural books tend to adhere to a Western, linear conception of time but other models are possible when time is understood as cyclical or non-progressive. Architecture changes but it does not necessarily get better. We can learn from novels that freely move backward and forward in time and between types of time. We can also conceive of alternative architectural trajectories if we study the practices of other disciplines.

UCL is a large multi-disciplinary university. The principal doctoral supervisor is within The Bartlett School of Architecture, while the subsidiary supervisor can be from any department in UCL, whether anthropology, computer science, medicine or fine art, for example. Our intention is for doctoral subjects and supervisions to be as broad as the discipline of architecture and to connect research to related disciplines in order to foster productive and rewarding collaborations. Looking at a subject through another discipline's eyes enables a doctoral student to reassess architectural research and to critically expand their research methods and authorship.

Studying the history of practice, as well as the history of architecture, allows us to appreciate that architecture is not only made by architects. The architectural design doctorate is not accredited by the profession and can look beyond it. The contemporary relevance of interdisciplinary research, which occurs within and between disciplines, indicates that the profession is but one model of practice and implies that a combination of past and future models may be more rewarding. In many current disciplines, numerous practices and procedures of differing ages remain relevant and stimulating. The result is an interdependent network of diverse – new and old – models of architectural authorship that exist alongside each other, or in conjunction, not simply because they are useful but because they have social and cultural value. The architectural design doctorate is a means to learn from the past, reassess the present, and speculate on future models of practice and discourse.

References

Anderson, Stanford (1987): »The Fiction of Function«, in: *Assemblage* 2, 18-31.

Buonomano, Dean (2017): *Your Brain is a Time Machine: The Neuroscience and Physics of Time*, New York and London: W. W. Norton & Company.

Cervantes, Miguel (1605–1615): *Don Quixote.* English Translation: Don Quixote, transl. by John Ormsby, https://www.gutenberg.org/files/996/996-h/996-h.htm, 2004 (accessed March 24, 2020).

Davis, Lennard J. (1983): *Factual Fictions: The Origins of the English Novel*, Philadelphia: University of Pennsylvania Press.

Defoe, Daniel (2007) [1719]: *Robinson Crusoe*, Oxford: Oxford University Press.

Defoe, Daniel (2004) [1722]: *Moll Flanders*, New York: Norton.

Defoe, Daniel (2009) [1724]: *Roxana, or the Fortunate Mistress*, P.N. Furbank (ed), London: Pickering and Chatto.

Edgerton, David (2008): *The Shock of the Old: Technology and Global History Since 1900*, London: Profile Books.

Forty, Adrian (1999): »Introduction«, in: Adrian Forty/ Susanne Küchler (eds.), *The Art of Forgetting*, Oxford/New York: Berg, 1–18.

Foucault, Michel (1984): »On the Genealogy of Ethics: An Overview of Work in Progress«, in: Paul Rabinow (ed.), *The Foucault Reader*, London: Penguin, 340–372.

Foucault, Michel (1988): »Technologies of the Self«, in: Luther H. Martin/Hugh Gutman/ Patrick H. Hutton (eds.), *Technologies of the Self: A Seminar with Michel Foucault*, London: Tavistock Publications: 16–49.

Gibson, William (1992): https://quoteinvestigator.com/2012/01/24/future-has-arrived, (accessed 24 March, 2020).

Giedion, Sigfried (1967) [1941]: *Space, Time and Architecture: The Growth of a New Tradition*, Cambridge, MA: Harvard University Press.

Gould, Stephen Jay (1990) [1987]: *Time's Arrow, Time's Cycle: Myth and Metaphor in the Discovery of Geological Time*, London: Penguin.

Isozaki, Arata (2006): »Authorship of Katsura: The Diagonal Line«, in: David B. Stewart (ed.), transl. by Sabu Kohso, *Japan-ness in Architecture*, Cambridge, MA/London: The MIT Press, 291–305.

Hill, Jonathan (2021): »Introduction«, in: Jonathan Hill (ed.), *Designs on History: The Architect as Physical Historian*, London: RIBA Publishing, viii–xix.

Hill, Jonathan (2022): »Design Research: The Next 500 Years«, in: *ARENA Journal of Architectural Research* (AJAR), 7/1,1, http://doi.org/10.5334/ajar.287.

Hudnut, Joseph (1945): »The Post-Modern House«, in: *Architectural Record* 97, 70–75.

Kent, William (1714–1717): »Remarks by Way of Painting & Archit.«, Oxford: Bodleian Library, University of Oxford.

Lasdun, Denys (1979): »Interview with Denys Lasdun, revised draft, 13 June, 1979«, in: Lasdun Archive, RIBA Library Drawings and Archives Collections, Victoria and Albert Museum, London.

Lasdun, Denys (1984): »The Architecture of Urban Landscape«, in: Denys Lasdun (ed.), *Architecture in an Age of Scepticism: A Practitioner's Anthology Compiled by Denys Lasdun*, London: Heinemann, 134–159.

McKeon, Michael (1987): *The Origins of the English Novel 1600–1740*, Baltimore: The John Hopkins University Press.

Nagel, Alexander/Wood, Christopher S. (2010): *Anachronic Renaissance*, New York: Zone Books.

Orwell, George (1949): *1984*, https://www.planetebook.com/free-ebooks/1984.pdf (accessed 7 March, 2022).

Panofsky, Erwin (1982) [1955]: »Et in Arcadia Ego: Poussin and the Elegiac Tradition«, in: *Meaning in the Visual Arts*, Chicago: University of Chicago Press, 302–333.

Pevsner, Nikolaus (1936): *Pioneers of the Modern Movement: From William Morris to Walter Gropius*, London: Faber & Faber.

Pevsner, Nikolaus (2002) [1966]: »The Anti-Pioneers«, in: Stephen Games (ed.), *Pevsner on Art and Architecture: The Radio Talks*, London: Methuen, 293–307.

Plato (1929): *Timaeus, Critias, Cleitophon, Menexenus, Epistles*, transl. by R.G. Bury, Cambridge, MA: Harvard University Press.

Ricoeur, Paul (1965): »Objectivity and Subjectivity in History«, in: *History and Truth*, transl. by Charles A. Kelbley, Evanston, IL: Northwestern University Press.

Rovelli, Carlo (2019) [2017]: *The Order of Time*, transl. by Erica Segre and Simon Carnell, London: Penguin. First published as L'ordine del tempo.

Rovelli, Carlo (2019): »Time travel is just what we do every day …«, *The Guardian*, 31 March 2019, https://www.theguardian.com/science/2019/mar/31/carlo-rovelli-you-ask-the-questions-time-travel-is-just-what-we-do-every-day-theoretical-physics (accessed 6 January 2022).

Ruskin, John (1981) [1849]: *The Seven Lamps of Architecture*, New York: Farrar, Straus and Giroux.

Sant'Elia, Antonio/Marinetti, Filippo Tomasso (1970) [1914]: »Manifesto of Futurist Architecture«, in: Ulrich Conrads (ed.), *Programs and Manifestoes on 20th-Century Architecture*, Cambridge, MA: The MIT Press, 34–38.

Scully, Vincent (1969): *American Architecture and Urbanism*, London: Thames & Hudson.

Smolin, Lee (2013): *Time Reborn: From the Crisis in Physics to the Future of the Universe*, London: Penguin.

Sorenson, Roy (2008): *Seeing Dark Things: The Philosophy of Shadows*, Oxford: Oxford University Press.

Wells, H.G. (1895) *The Time Machine*, https://www.gutenberg.org/files/35/35-h/35-h.htm (accessed 4 October, 2021).

Dimensions of Architectural Knowledge, 2022-03 ႒
https://doi.org/10.14361/dak-2022-0317

SCORE
Practices of Listening and Collision

Nicholas Drofiak

Abstract: A score is a research tool that approaches knowledge as a series of relations. A consciously authored, creative work, a score precipitates and establishes the initial terms of an encounter between stories or actors; performed (translated) into a context it can never fully anticipate, a score simultaneously declines certainty or control over the knowledge that results from its performance, while binding that knowledge (and by extension, all learning) to the peculiar circumstances of its construction. This paper is both an exploration of scoremaking's possibilities and an enaction of a collision of its own: of sonic materialities and epistemologies on the Enisej river.

Keywords: Knowledge Generation; Practice-Based and Performative Research; Relations as Heritage; Sound and Material Culture; Memory; Media and Translation; Transdisciplinarity; Kamas and Tuvan Sonic Cultures.

I think there is a method here, though I do not know that score is its name.

There's score,
but then there is also *research by happening*,
or by *provoked* or *engineered event*;
by the *constellation* of a set of actors
(so as to trace the fallout of their relation) —
Or, we might think through a framework of the *interposition of a tool*, through
or by which to grasp or crystallize or articulate a set of circumstances;
of an agentive *thing* by whose presence the encounter (and thus the knowledge that that is created by it) is changed.
A song sung into the mountain to ascertain its resonance.

There are different ways to frame this practice, whatever, this attitude by which to generate practices; none are mutually exclusive. That the swarm

Corresponding author: Nicholas Drofiak (unaffiliated researcher, UK); n.drofiak@gmail.com; http://orcid.org/0000-0002-0788-0333.

cloud is here filed under *score* ascribes specificities to the encounter, determines our approach – but the filing is not definitive or conclusive. *Score* is not all that is going on. (Sometimes we describe ourselves as employing a certain *lens* in our approach to a research situation, but alongside the suggestion of a hierarchy in agency between detached, observing researcher and discrete, circumscribed topic, this ascribes to research laws of optics that it does not follow. More than one plane may be in focus at any one time.)

Still: Of all terms, *score* is useful. It places us near to *reconstruction* (an interrogable *re*) and to *sketches* (a series of essays, attempts to narrow down the salient facets of an emerging and unstable story): an interesting meeting. Furthermore, the determination to interpose a *thing* or *tool* (or *sculpture*) into a scenario already constitutes, itself, *scored* activity. Most important: To take *score* as our interlocutor brings particular possibilities. *I know a story about a score.*

Abalakovo, I, Rumblings

Here's what I think happened.
(*Here's how I think it goes.*)

In 1965, the *Finno–Ugric Society of Helsinki* published a slim volume of transcriptions of Indigenous Siberian sonic art – scores, in the sense that each notates a vocal line presented as the notional sum of a musical performance – prepared by ethnomusicologist A.O. Väisänen from recordings made on wax cylinders by ethnographers Kai Donner and Toivo Lehtisalo in 1914 (Väisänen 1965). Of these 80 transcriptions, 4 notate melodies recorded by Donner in Abalakovo, a village sited where the Sayan foothills give rise to the river Il'bin, that runs into the Kirel', that runs into the Kan, that runs into the Enisej some way upstream of its confluence with the Angara and the waters of Lake Bajkal. (This river system is at present North Asia's largest, by volume.)

Abalakovo was the final settlement inhabited by speakers of Kamas, itself the last Uralic language to survive in the Sayan Mountains. Donner's wax cylinders comprise the only record of Kamas at a time when it was spoken as a first language, and the only recording from any period of Kamas acoustic aesthetic culture (Klumpp 2013: 45; on the non-universality of the concept of »music«, see Polli 2012: 260). By 1914 the youngest fluent speaker of Kamas was 45 years old and the principal languages of Abalakovo had shifted to Khakas and Russian; the last person with any substantial knowledge of Kamas, Klavdiâ Plotnikova–Andžigatova, passed in 1989 (Donner 1926: 188–189; Künnap 1999: 8). As Kamas has receded as a lingual bodily practice, a sonic presence, and finally, as a memory in the landscape, so too has its associated ethnic self-identification (Matveev 1965: 33). Two persons identified as Kamas in the 2010 census.

At some point between 1965 and 1994, the wax cylinders from which Väisänen's scores were prepared were either lost in or disappeared from the archives of the Institute for the Languages of Finland; linguists report Donner's travel diaries as seemingly mislaid in the same interval (Arkhipov/Lasse Däbritz/Gusev 2019; Klumpp 2013: 45–46, 48; Klumpp 2016: 23). Eight minutes of the phonographic recordings were, at some unknown time, copied onto magnetic tape and hence preserved at the University of Tartu; these eight minutes include no singing (Klumpp 2016: 23). *We can say*: The acoustic aesthetic heritage of the Abalakovo Kamas community is represented, today, in its entirety, by four single-stave transcriptions of the melody lines of songs.

(This is not true but it is a starting point.
There is something interesting in this story.)

Thin

It's little to go on. Whatever Donner heard in 1914 – whatever was sung, wherever, in whatever reverberant company – this (fig. 1) is a poor record. Five-eight / two-four / three-eight? It's barely contained. What arrives to us as this score is a sketch of a sound; the product of a triple mutation, predicated upon needle and wax, Väisänen's ears, and a system of notation both alien to and reductive of the human listening and sonification cultures of the northern Sayan Mountains: A system that attends to and records a different culture's selection of what might be the salient facets of aesthetic sound. As means of acoustic transcription or recording in the Sayan Mountains, both the phonograph and the form of stave notation that evolved to permit the (supposed) repetition and migration of European art musical performances are deficient: The former in dynamic range, frequency spectrum, directionality (indifference to the environment in relation or active dialogue with which a performance took place) and susceptibility to degradation; the latter in the tortuous manner by which it must include details of timbre, phrasings unreconciled to expectations of durational regularity or repeated rhythmic measure, and variations in pitch that exceed standardized tonalities. Stave

1.

Score No. 59: »Phon. 19. Kamassisches Lied. Šamanka. Abalakovo 7/8/1914.«
Published in A.O. Väisänen's Samojedische Melodien (Väisänen 1965).

notation records pitch in absolute terms, neglecting the interrelation of a performance's relative frequencies with contextual, environmental noises and the resonant frequencies of its spaces of performance. The sonic art of one dynamic tradition, at a specific and hybrid moment in place and time, is squashed unceremoniously into the representational categories of another. The joints strain.

Thick

And fracture. The very thinness of Score No. 59 makes it potent. So little is encoded that there may be no single way by which to sonify these marks, and they become instead a leaping point: A space of possibility, a prompt to kaleidoscopic augmentation, adaptation, extrapolation, improvisation, creolization and appropriation.

We can say: A score is a set of instructions for a performance. Does that scan? Engagement with a score is certainly instructive – we learn by it – and yet a score is incapable of the dogmatism or pedantry associated with instruction as a pedagogy. A score does not dictate. It cannot hold its performers to account. It cannot prevent its being performed partially – or *badly*. Furthermore, as a set of instructions, a score is thin: deficient. Its media (whether they be written words; a map; the name of a rock; a sequence of sounds and smells; the approach to, and interior of, a bird hide) being necessarily other than those of the actions that will be generated from it, an act of translation is required, and this involves subjectivity, creativity, decision-making and additive intervention. A score is like — a folk tale, held distributed in the minds of its community, whose latent existence is as a cloud of individual constructions of events and encounters bound up in attitudes concerning delivery, prosody, and the appropriate demarcation of the space of telling. The bones of the tale exist – shifting, but relatively consistently agreed through semi-regular re-statement (exposure) and negotiation (contestation) – and establish its communal role: set out the significative parameters that underpin any community member's determination to reach for that tale, at any particular moment (Basso 1984: 39–41). But each telling constitutes, itself, a unique and creative encounter between tale, teller, and setting, informed by the agencies of each (Hymes 1979: 391–392; Hindman 1996: 64). A tale is told into the world, and since the world is always changed, what emerges is creolized: the teller and context adding something of themselves.

»Each telling makes use of common ingredients, but it is precisely in the difference in the way they are deployed and shaped that the meaning of each is disclosed.« (Hymes 1979: 392).

A score is played into the world and the results are prismatic. Its instructions cannot foresee or comprehend every facet of the conditions with which it will be confronted: against the friction of a concrete network of intersecting human and nonhuman past lives, subjectivities, preoccupations and agencies (whether anticipated by the score or otherwise) the events that arise are inflected by chance and reaction, contingency and circumstance. A score is not re-enacted; each performance is a new event, taking place in an uncontrolled and uncontrollable context. It is in the score's ellipses and silences that new knowledge is produced (cf. Becker 1995: 391). And so the happenings must always exceed the score.

»Dans la Relation, ce qui relie est d'abord cette suite des rapports entre les différences, à la rencontre les unes des autres. Les racines parcourantes (les rhizomes) des idées, des identités, des intuitions, relaient: s'y révèlent les lieux-communs dont nous devinons entre nous le partage.« (Glissant 2009: 72).

»He promises that he will find ways through and around and will ›slip through cracks‹ and re-crack the cracks if they fill up.« (Halberstam 2013: 6–7).

Cultivating the Crowd, Pointillating the Cloud (Scoremaking as a Tool in Research)

Scoremaking responds to intuition rather than a clear, guiding question. It does not solve a known, well-formulated problem: It makes problems. Or, its repercussions assist in their delineation and verbalization (or nonverbal articulation) – a non-resolving process. Scoremaking is a response to the nebulous presentiment of a connection, or a suspected resonance, between apparently independent phenomena: *There is something about this assemblage of actors and agencies.* To design a score is to seek a performative means to understand that connection: To tease out a question, to sonify the mountain, to precipitate a situation, and let it speak.

»One of the most dramatic examples of resonant reverberation is the vocal genre called in Tuvan *uzun yr* or in Mongolian *urtyn duu*, literally 'long-song'. [...] In using his voice to excite the [distinctive] reverberant qualities of the cliff, Kaigal-ool [Xovalyg]'s aim was not simply to hear his own voice amplified, but rather to feel an interaction with the [...] scenario in which he emplaced himself through singing. ›I love to hear the voice of the cliff speaking back to me‹« (Levin/Süzükei 2019: 37–38).

Abalakovo, II, Cursory Palpation and Wild Array of Actors (First Postulation of the Presence of a Project)

1)   Four scores contained in A.O. Väisänen (1965): *Samojedische Melodien*, Helsinki: Suomalais–Ugrilainen Seura.

1.1)   Score No. 59: »Kamassisches Lied. Šamanka. Abalakovo 7/8/1914.«

1.1.1) The Kamas language/s. *(The settlement of the entire Kamas language community in a single village, within a single generation, meant that every family spoke their own dialect; as reported by Donner, every speech act seems a kind of scat phonological improvisation [Klumpp 2013: 56; Klumpp 2016: 40; Joki 1944: 122]. In the absence of Donner's travel diaries no other name can be attributed to Šamanka, although photographs of her exist in Donner's archive at the Finnish Heritage Agency [Joki 1944: xxxiv; Donner 1926: 192]).*

1.2)   Score No. 61: »Tatarisches Lied. Abalakovo. 6/8/1914.«

1.2.1) »Tatar« as a language of Abalakovo / of the northern Sayan Mountains. *(In this context, »Tatar« likely means the Kačin or Haas dialect of Khakas. Performer and context of performance unknown).*

1.3)   Score No. 62: »Kamassisches Lied. Abalakovo. 7/8/1914.« *(The name of the performer whose song became score No. 62 can be deduced from Donner's published grammatical materials: Avdakēja Anďžigātova, Abalakovo's eldest resident in 1914 (Joki 1944: 87, 103–104). Photographs of Anďžigātova – not reproduced here – are held at the Finnish Heritage Agency).*

1.3.1) Lyrics attributed to melody No. 62.

1.4)   Score No. 76: »Türkisches Lied aus Konstantinopel. Gesungen von einem alten Griechen in Abalakovo.« *(The name of the performer is not recorded. Photographs of the man – not reproduced here – are held in Donner's archive at the Finnish Heritage Agency).*

2.
Kai Donner, »Solförmörkelsen den 21 augusti [Sunrise on 21st August]«. Glass plate negative, color inverted, cropped. View from Abalakovo (looking away), 1914. Ethnographic Collection, The Picture Collections of the Finnish Heritage Agency (VKK532:3645).

1.4.1) Conjecture: Greek/Urum/Pontic Greek/Turkish as languages of Abalakovo?

1.4.2) Conjecture: The imaginary of late Ottoman Istanbul/the pre-Soviet Black Sea (?) as a palimpsest upon Abalakovo; the landscape of the Bosporus (?) as a referent geography in Abalakovo.

2)   The village of Abalakovo;

2.1)   Its present inhabitants (human/nonhuman communities, landforms, &c.);

2.1.1) their (repertoires of) embodied knowledge,

2.1.2) collective memories,

2.1.3) and cultural (oral/performed) histories;

2.2)   the attitudes they hold toward the above (at any given moment and as unfolding through time).

3)   The researcher;

3.1)   Its present inhabitants;

3.1.1) their (repertoires of) embodied knowledge,

3.1.2) collective memories,

3.1.3) and cultural (oral) histories;

3.2)   the attitudes they hold toward the above (at any given moment and as unfolding through time).

We can say: A score is a set of guidelines for an encounter. A means by which *to set into relation* things, the productivity of whose meeting is suspected, in an attempt to understand why this may be so.

Scoremaking's first act is the determination (demarcation of the limits of, within the phenomenal mass) and array of the actors that its actions will convoke: a process we might call their *constellation*. This first stage already constitutes design activity. The act is not a survey (which may profess, at least, objectivity or omniscience) but a sketch: creative, selective, authored, and dependent upon the subjectivity of the scoremaker (researcher) – who is, furthermore, implicated among the actors from the outset; one agency among a mutually informing many. (»Scoremaker« is a shorthand; the agencies of the researcher may be individually incorporated or distributed among many bodies.) Scoremade research (all research) is autobiographical in that this constellation is, from the outset, a product of the unique and specific meeting of the researcher and the multiple other agencies of a terrain: The encounter determines what is (perceived to be) encountered. The act is also not a survey in that its ends are not utilitarian. It is not concerned with the efficient or comprehensive itemization, categorization, and potential deployment of all present parties. The opening encounter is curated. The score does *not* include everyone.

(In this way, scoremaking is about access and thus inherently political. This gives the scoremaker responsibilities. Research scores are particularly suited to address themselves toward relations and encounters that have been restricted or are disadvantaged; that are unlikely to occur under prevailing political, economic, or environmental conditions. Scoremaking may be prompted by alterations in the ability of a community, human or nonhuman, to access knowledgemaking processes that take place through enduring relations with territories, materially or mentally invested spaces, non/human neighbors, languages – although in such cases it must be borne in mind that scores never restore or enact a return to former conditions; the relations that are enabled are new. Scoremaking may involve the introduction of marginalized, counterhegemonic tools or epistemologies to settings in which they are otherwise absent or unattended; in such cases, questions must be asked as to whose attention is being sought, and if after all, it is their attention that is relevant. Scoremaking may address itself toward encounters that are speculative or [that seem at first to be] absurd; in these cases it also tries to unpick *why* the encounter impresses itself so. Insofar as architecture is a practice of assembling conditions in which new encounters may occur, scoremaking is an inherently architectural research tool.)

>>A companion text is a text whose company enabled you to proceed on a path less trodden. Such texts might spark a moment of revelation in the midst of an overwhelming proximity; they might share a feeling or give you resources to make sense of something that had been beyond your grasp; companion texts can prompt you to hesitate or to question the direction you are going, or they might give you a sense that in going the way you are going, you are not alone.<< (Ahmed 2017: 16).

Kamas may (seem to) have disappeared as a cultural identity in the Sayan foothills, but the village of Abalakovo remains, inhabited by 51 people (2010): 51 creative sites of the construction, creolization, assembly and exchange of stories, memories, embodied repertoires of knowledge and intimate acoustic, haptic, navigational and territorial familiarities. Väisänen's scores are not the heritage of *nobody* — but they find no setting, at present, in which to act as agents, constellators of meaning-making relations; or as loci for the exchange and evolution of acoustic and territorial knowledge, notions of identity, or shared memories. They do not presently interact with, resound within, or make resonate the topographies (human and nonhuman) in which their previous forms once had (and made) relevance and significance.

Abalakovo, III, Orchestra of Orphaned Ghosts

That reminds me of a story. In a storage unit in the yard of the Centre for the Development of Tuvan Culture and Crafts in Kyzyl – across the Sayan Mountains from Abalakovo; there, where the blue of the Kaa-Hem and clouded brown of the Bii-Hem merge to form the Enisej – lies an orchestra, abandoned. A complete collection of musical instruments whose motivating logic has been swept away. These are the nonhuman material components of one iteration of the Soviet-era Orchestra of National Tuvan Instruments, and belong to a period in which instrumental traditions from the Caucasus to the Arctic were standardized and made compatible with western modalities and intonation: able as well to produce locally colored renderings of Grieg as sanitized arrangements of »national« folk tunes (Levin/Süzükei 2019: 45–46; cf. Gudaev 2014; Tomskaâ 2019). Stringed instruments were elaborated and hybridized into multiple sizes, frets chromaticized and tunings homogenized so as to fulfill the modal expectations of the European classical tradition: made able, collectively, to produce 12 even-tempered pitches across a wide spectrum of octaves (cf. D'âkonova 2014). Sounds were cleansed and purified – in a way that echoed the early USSR's codification and standardization of minority languages (had Kamas been sufficiently widely spoken to arouse administrative interest, its dialectal polyvalence would surely have been deemed an uncontrollable threat to the correct dissemination of socialism [cf. Drofiak 2020: 49–50 & 124–128]).

The instruments of the Kyzyl lock-up are made inanimate by circumstance: shorn of the ideology, embodied knowledges and practices that made them whole. Tuvan acoustic aesthetic culture has moved on. Beginning in the 1980s, fieldwork by ethnomusicologist Valentina Süzükei and renewed intergenerational collaborations resulted in a reassessment of the particular characteristics of Tuvan sonic art and a new appreciation of what had been lost in its and its instruments' formalization. Listening practices and acoustic aesthetic appreciation were rebuilt upon the exploration and valorization of timbre – the overtonal layering and thick internal complexity of sounds – as much as upon melodic variation; the strings of newly built igils were made, like those of pre-orchestral instruments, of parallel rather than wound strands of horsehair or fishing line, stopped in the air rather than upon frets, and bowed with hair that can be slackened and tightened between the fingers to produce a more or less breathy sound (Levin/Süzükei 2019: 46–55). Timbral listening is not unique to the wind-blown valleys of the west of Tuva, Mongolia, and Xinjiang, but among the headwaters of the Enisej it has acquired particular organologies and sonic epistemologies as a result of long-term, mutually informing relations (imitation, sound as offering, deliberate reverberation of landforms) with the acoustic shapes of topographical features and the sonic images associated with life in and movement through them (ibid.: 28–39, 56–61 & 71; cf. Lockwood 2009: 45; Pezanoski-Browne 2015: 11; Polli 2012: 259–261; Talianni 2020: 73–74). A dialogic practice of attunement to alterations in the timbral thickness of an environment, it has particular significance on the Enisej, where the clouding of the Bii-Hem is attributable to upstream mining and environmental degradation; where hydroelectric installations both hinder piscine communities' movements and require terrestrial communities' resettlements; where cultural and linguistic policies render environmental sounds and heritage sonic epistemologies alienable forms of material culture.

>Towards the end of his life, Marconi became somewhat mystical and was convinced that sounds, once generated, never die; they simply become fainter and fainter until we no longer hear them. For him, to enable us to hear these past, faint sounds, we only (sic) need to develop equipment of a sensitivity sufficient to pick up these old sounds and to avoid subsequent, stronger sounds from the present and immediate past. Ultimately, for Marconi, it would be possible to hear Christ delivering the Sermon on the Mount.« (Bryars 1975: liner notes).

4)   The abandoned, material remains of the Soviet-era Orchestra of National Tuvan Instruments;

4.1)   musicians from the present-day Centre for the Development of Tuvan Culture and Crafts;

4.1.1)   their (repertoires of) embodied knowledge pertaining to timbral listening and acoustic ecology.

The constellation distends, and implications extend. Relations continue to accrete. How to sonify a village? As if by timbral listening and ministration of the correct resonating impulse, we –

Cracks

A score is not a means of establishing control over the terms of an encounter, but of surrendering it – and living with what occurs. A means of putting oneself, deliberately, in a position of uncertainty. The score establishes a starting premise – an initial constellation of agencies of interest, an ex- or implicit process (a set of opening moves) by which to effect their collision, and a means of tracing the spiraling engendered relations – and does so knowing that none of these things is fixed. What are set out as the key actors are never only a proxy, a thinking partner, a straw presence through which to approach other things – the investigation of the stave transcriptions and the instruments and the river is committed to, utterly, it remains always in the belly – and yet also, at some point, the constellation cracks. A score is performed into a setting, and the world grates against its assumptions and proposals. Unforeseen agencies intrude and their intrusions are embraced. Scoremaking is a means of generating knowledge at odds, askance, by parable, *par hasard*, of the context into which the performance is pitched (of environmental actors not encompassed by the score). The skill is in creating conditions in which to listen: in letting edges become ragged; in allowing events to run away with themselves; in attending to the agency of the river; in watching, with the corner of the eye, as the wind lifts the page and something else is glimpsed. The performance ungrounds the certainties of the score itself. Having convened the meeting (and being thus in a privileged position), the scoremaker must ask— how will I make myself aware of who is present? How will I recognize their wishes? By what means will I listen? How will I work to undermine and dismantle the authority of the score (impossible, but constantly attempted), once its actions and conditions are set in motion? Who should be told about what has been done? How to distill the emerging stories, and introduce them, blinking, as further loci of negotiation to their constitutive communities? (You can write the first score, but you'd better co-write the next one.)

»They were never sure if I was talking to them or the town.«
(Femi 2016: audio recording).

»The work of theory is to unravel the very ground on which it stands. To introduce questions and uncertainties in those places where formerly there was
some seeming consensus about what one did and how one went about it.«
(Rogoff 2008: n.p.).

»Displacement involves the invention of new forms of subjectivities, of pleasures, of intensities, of relationships, which also implies the continuous renewal of a critical work that looks carefully and intensively at the very system of
values to which one refers in fabricating the tools of resistance. [...] Displacing
is a way of surviving. It is an impossible, truthful story of living in-between reg-
imens of truth. The responsibility involved in this motley in-between living is
a highly creative one: the displacer proceeds by unceasingly introducing difference into repetition. By questioning over and over again what is taken for
granted as self-evident, by reminding oneself and the others of the unchange-
ability of change itself.« (Trinh 1991: 19, 21).

We can say: There are things that fall between ideologies. Futures interrupted
and left behind, materialities of sound dissolved in the vibrant air. Material
remnants abandoned as embodied practices and epistemologies inflect.
There is a story here about the dynamic nature of cultural heritage; about its
media, transmission and transmutation; about acoustic phenomena as heritage; about relations with such phenomena as heritage; about the role played
by such relations in a community's negotiation, evolution and transmission
of knowledge and identities, as they accompany experiences of political re-
pression and anthropogenic ecological change. There is a story here about
the alienability of such relations; about the implications of their restriction,
rupture, or disjuncture. A story about listening and territory and fragility;
about hybridity and haunting and creative survival; about the ownership of
narratives; about extrinsic projections of loss and inauthenticity in relation
to Indigenous cultural heritage. About the pathologization of cultural
change. Abalakovo is not what it was but it is still what it is, at least until tomorrow. *We can say*: There are introductions to be made. Meetings that might
help us talk through some stories. Processes to mediate, communities to assemble, relations that have meaning but that require attention and assistance to occur. A score might imagine an encounter between Väisänen's
scores, the community and territory of Abalakovo today, Kyzyl's hybrid or-
phans and its experts in dialogic sonification. And maybe that's enough for a
beginning. You work out what the song's about by singing it.

We could say: Two lost futures; two timelines interrupted. But scoremaking is not interested in Kamas acoustic aesthetic culture as a repository of endangered, »authentic« knowledge to be recorded and documented prior to its loss. Scoremaking is not interested in the idea of authenticity at all.

Artifice

>»Je crois que nous sommes arrivés à un moment de la vie des humanités où l'être humain commence d'accepter l'idée que lui-même est en perpétuel processus, qu'il n'est pas de l'être, mais de l'étant, et que comme tout étant, il change [...] l'être n'est pas un absolu [...] l'être est relation à l'autre, relation au monde, relation au cosmos.« (Glissant 1996: 27–30).

The score sets up an altered world. A play world – demarcated, but with porous edges. A constructed scenario; a world in which the imaginary holds sway. It happens for, and to, and with the community of its presentation, as an explicitly authored and selective event that precipitates discussion and contestation, and exchanges of attitudes; it represents nothing outside of that community. Scoremaking is not interested in whether the relations it fosters would arise without the score's interposition. Or in the encounters that would take place between its actors in the absence of the scoremaker, or how these might take place differently. What is investigated is precisely what happens *in these particular circumstances, given this particular constellation*; how the score's implicated actors relate under *these* specific conditions. Nothing further is claimed. Other configurations would produce other stories. Knowledge identified through scoremaking is not extracted from a situation but constructed emically within it, with, and as part of, and inseparable from its gathered agencies. Issue may be taken with the constellation that has been made, but *that is* the world under investigation. The actions and relations that emerge in a score's performance emerge within a space of conscious artifice— and the knowledge that those actions and relations constitute is entirely specific to that space. This does not invalidate scoremaking as a research tool.

Resting upon such intervention and specificity, knowledge that derives from scoremaking is wild and declines to settle (claim certainty or finality). It resists extrapolation, generalization, and appropriation; it will not conform to a narrative or support attempts to assemble broader definitions. It

offers no insight into its participant actors outside of the relations it con-
vokes. There are only the relations. The relations are what is learnt.

> »Delinquent narrative is a concept that cultural critic Michel de Certeau uses
> to refer to stories, or fragments of stories, that cannot be recuperated for city
> branding or politics, or for the critical discourses of activists or researchers.«
> (Pint, in Havik et al. 2020: 61).

> »Our aim is to move beyond essentialist or generalizing metanarratives […] and
> to instead look for multiple, minor narratives that are specific to sites and com-
> munities, therefore allowing for a diversity of situated perspectives. […] That
> which is minor may creep in from behind the scenes, in places where we least
> expect it.« (Havik/Pint/Riesto/Steiner, in Havik et al. 2020: 8,13).

Scored encounters emphasize the particularity of the circumstances of *all*
knowledgemaking; emphasize that learning cannot be divorced from the
circumstances of its arrival, which always constitute a unique confluence
of agencies and identities and self-presentations, however curated the in-
stigating circumstances. A scored performance no more takes place within
a model than does any other encounter. The relations that result are no
more artificial (and by the same token, no more authentic) than those that
result from any event that goes unrecorded. All encounters involve the performance of attitudes and reactions based upon past relations and encounters. The integrity of scoremaking as a research tool rests upon the claims
it does not make: upon its awareness and clear delineation of the concrete
– perceived – conditions of its relations' arising, the community among
which its knowledge is generated, the actions undertaken, and the means
of listening engaged.

> »Sie ist ein Tanz um einen gegebenen Gegenstand, sie greift ihn von verschie-
> denen Seiten aus an, sie entfernt sich von ihm in verschiedene Richtungen, um
> sich ihm wieder zu nähern und dort mit anderen Reflexionen zusammenzus-
> tossen […] Ein Horizont, gegen den immer wieder vorgestossen wird, ohne dass
> er je durchgestossen würde.« (Flusser 1995: 141).

> »One possible approach to this lack of wholeness is to collect individual ele-
> ments; such elements, however, are not fragments, as this would mean they
> originally formed part of a whole. Rather they have a reality and significance

of their own that is worth looking at. [...] What is required [...] is an attentive observer who collects the various phenomena as individual elements, relates them to each other, and rearranges them – not in the single universal order of nature, but in an individual cosmos of diversity. The cabinet of curiosities is a personal collection that others can look at.« (Bornhauser/Kissling, in Vogt/ Bornhauser/Kissling 2015: 211–212).

Well met, friends? No theory agglomerates in scoremaking. Scoremade tales are too irregular, too singular in their construction to permit the synthesis; there's nothing to lay out and let us say, definitively and defensibly, this is the arc that runs through and explains all these occurrences. I can find a spirit in the mass, and we can talk about that, but that's as far as it goes and I don't stake any claims. You can make your own arrangements. All there is to do is to set each score's relations into yet further, equally concrete encounters; tell further specific stories in response to what emerges, and from further positions; let each tale become an actor in another, future swirling score, implicated in another set of branching relations. Perhaps, by the accumulation—? Perhaps, in the circulation—? But I don't know, after all. Five strangers meet as friends, a not-quite-chance encounter on a distant shore. A crowd assembles. It's not much to go on. It's almost dawn.

References

Ahmed, Sara (2017): *Living a Feminist Life*, Durham, NC: Duke University Press.

Arkhipov, Alexandre/Lasse Däbritz, Chris/ Gusev, Valentin (2019): »INEL Kamas Corpus: User Documentation«, in: Valentin Gusev/Tiina Klooster/Beáta Wagner-Nagy (eds.), *INEL Kamas Corpus, Version 1.0, INEL Corpora of Indigenous Northern Eurasian Languages*, Hamburg: Hamburger Zentrum für Sprachkorpora, http://hdl.handle. net/11022/0000-0007-DA6E-9, accessed February 8, 2022.

Basso, Keith H. (1984): »Stalking with Stories«: Names, Places, and Moral Narratives among the Western Apache«, in: Edward M. Bruner (ed.), *Text, Play, and Story: The Construction and Reconstruction of Self and Society*, Washington: American Ethnological Society, 19–55.

Becker, A.L. (1995): *Beyond Translation: Essays Toward a Modern Philology*, Ann Arbor: University of Michigan Press.

Bryars, Gavin (1975): *The Sinking of the Titanic*, Vinyl Album, Obscure Records, United Kingdom.

D'âkonova, Varvara Egorovna (2014): »Stanovlenie i razvitie âkutskogo koncertnogo instrumentariâ i problemy orkestra narodnyh instrumentov v Âkutii«, in: *Gramota* 5 (43/2), 73–76.

Donner, Kai (1926): *Bei den Samojeden in Sibirien*, Stuttgart: Strecker und Schröder.

Drofiak, Nicholas (2020): *Irúsan or, Canting for Architects*, Zurich: gta Verlag.

Femi, Caleb (2016): »Coconut Oil«, on *Coconut Oil – Single*, Digital Album, Caleb Femi/iTunes, United Kingdom.

Flusser, Vilém (1995): *Jude Sein: Essays, Briefe, Fiktionen*, Mannheim: Bollman.

Glissant, Édouard (1996): *Introduction à une Poétique du Divers*, Paris: Éditions Gallimard.

Glissant, Édouard (2009): *Philosophie de la Relation: Poésie en étendue*, Paris: Éditions Gallimard.

Gudaev, L. (2014), »Čečenskie hroniki. 1936 g. 1-yj čečenskij orkestr narodnyh instrumentov«, in: *Čečen Info*, January 8, 2014, http://www.checheninfo.ru/19047-chechenskie-hroniki-1936-g-1-yy-chechenskiy-orkestr-narodnyh-instrumentov.html, accessed February 8, 2022.

Halberstam, Jack (2013): »The Wild Beyond: With and for the Undercommons«, in: Stefano Harney/Fred Moten, *The Undercommons: Fugitive Planning & Black Study*, Wivenhoe: Minor Compositions, 2–12.

Havik, Klaske/Pint, Kris/Riesto, Svava/Steiner, Henriette, eds. (2020): *Vademecum: 77 Minor Terms for Writing Urban Places*, Rotterdam: naio10 publishers/COST.

Hindman, Jane E. (1996): »I Think of That Mountain as My Maternal Grandmother‹: Constructing Self and Other through Landscape«, in: *Interdisciplinary Studies in Literature and Environment*, Fall 1996, 3/2, 63–72.

Hymes, Dell (1979): »How to Talk Like a Bear in Takelma«, in: *International Journal of American Linguistics*, April 1979, 45/2, 101–106.

Joki, A. J., ed. (1944): *Kai Donners Kamassisches Wörterbuch, nebst Sprachproben und Hauptzügen der Grammatik*, Helsinki: Suomalais–Ugrilainen Seura.

Klumpp, Gerson (2016): »Kamas«, in: *Erasmus+ Strategic Partnership Project InFUSE (Integration of Finno–Ugric Studies in Europe) e-learning materials*, Munich: Institute for Finno–Ugric Studies/Ludwig–Maximilian University, https://www.infuse.finnougristik.uni-muenchen.de/e-learning/kamas/01_kamas.pdf, accessed February 8, 2022.

Künnap, Ago (1999): *Kamass*, Munich: Lincom Europa.

Levin, Theodore/Süzükei, Valentina (2019): *Where Rivers and Mountains Sing: Sound, Music, and Nomadism in Tuva and Beyond*, new edition, Bloomington: Indiana University Press.

Lockwood, Annea (2009): »Sound Explorations: Windows into the Physicality of Sound«, in: *Leonardo* 19, 44–45.

Matveev, A.K. (1965): »Novye dannye o kam. âzyke i kam. toponimike«, in: *Voprosy toponomastiki* 2, 32–37.

Pezanoski-Browne, Alison (2015): »The Tragic Art of Eco-Sound«, in: *Leonardo* 25/1, 9–13.

Polli, Andrea (2012): »Soundscape, Sonification and Sound Activism«, in: *AI & Society* 27/2, 257–268.

Rogoff, Irit (2008): »What is a Theorist?«, in: James Elkins/Michael Newman (eds.), *The State of Art Criticism*, London: Routledge, 97–109.

Talianni, Katerina (2020): »The Soundscape of Anthropocene: Exploring the Instrumentality of Collaboration and Agency in Environmental Field Recordings«, in: *Airea: Arts and Interdisciplinary Research* 2, 63–76.

Tomskaâ, Anna Ivanovna (2019): »Âkutskie muzykal'nye instrumenty: tradicii i sovremennost'«, in: *Ajar Kut*, https:// ayarkyt.ru/yakutskie-muzykalnye-instrumenty-tradicii-i-sovremennost/, accessed August 9, 2020.

Trinh T. Minh–ha (1991): *When the Moon Waxes Red: Representation, Gender and Cultural Politics*, London: Routledge.

Väisänen, A.O. (1965): *Samojedische Melodien*, Helsinki: Suomalais–Ugrilainen Seura.

Vogt, Günther/Bornhauser, Rebecca/ Thomas Kissling, eds. (2015): *Landscape as a Cabinet of Curiosities*, Zürich: Lars Müller.

Dimensions of Architectural Knowledge, 2022-03 ʚ
https://doi.org/10.14361/dak-2022-0318

SCULPTURAL ARTIFACT
A Gestural Reading of the Atmospheres
of Sacral Space

Dirk Bahmann

Abstract: This article explores a pedagogical approach of using sculptural artifacts as a practical tool to explore the ineffable but powerfully evocative atmospheres found within sacral architectures. However affective these spatial experiences may seem; in architectural pedagogy we struggle to speak of their nature and nuance, since they resist the mediums through which architectural discourse typically circulates. The making of sculptural forms allows undergraduate students to gesture to aspects of the atmosphere. An extended body schema established by the making process facilitates an embodied understanding of the atmospheric qualities. Object Oriented Ontology (OOO) provides a useful theoretical underpinning as a way to understand the students' interactions, relationships between the sculptural artifacts, the processes of making and the atmospheres created. Through these processes, students become aware of, feel, engage, articulate and express the nuances and qualities of sacral architectural atmospheres.

Keywords: Making; Sacral Atmospheres; Sculptural Artifacts; Object Oriented Ontology; Embodiment

Architecture has the capacity to create highly evocative and emotionally charged spatial atmospheres that are frequently sensed to be existential and meaningful. Typically, these are found in sacral spaces throughout history. The experience of these sacral atmospheres is often of an ineffable nature. Discourses of this experience in architectural practice and pedagogy, as a consequence, tend to be of a nebulous nature.

To explore the nature and qualities of these atmospheres, I propose that a tacit and embodied way of knowing can serve as a valuable format of investigation. To engage with this inquiry, this research turns to a speculative creative praxis that is framed by a theoretical underpinning of Object Oriented Ontology and by the processes embedded in the making of sculptural artifacts, which serve as a probe to explore and articulate the ineffability of at-

Corresponding author: Dirk Bahmann (University of the Witwatersrand, Johannesburg, South Africa);
dirk.bahmann@wits.ac.za; http://orcid.org/0000-0001-9404-9080

mospheres and their effects. The artifacts are useful dynamic representations, since they utilize material, light and spatial qualities, and include and exploit the bodies' sense perceptions and spatial relationships to the artifact. The intention with these sculptures is to try and translate, express and gesture the atmosphere and the qualities of the space under study into another form.

This article discusses a project that was run as an initial trial, during the pandemic, with second-year architectural students at the School of Architecture and Planning, University of the Witwatersrand, Johannesburg, South Africa. Here, students attempted to make a reading and express aspects of the atmospheres of Le Corbusier's Notre Dame du Haut at Ronchamp (1954). The chapel was selected as a case study as it is extensively documented online and since it comfortably and simultaneously operates in the sacred and secular domains, something that is uncommon in the South African context.

Atmospheres

A widespread trait of sacral architecture is a predisposition to use the qualities of architectural space, with its impressions on the senses, to create evocative spatial atmospheres. These are inclined to have an affective quality that elicits a profound embodied, emotive response on both its secular and religious audiences. Characteristically, the evoked atmospheric charge could be described as one of awe or of the sublime: The experience of which is non rational, ineffable and something »wholly other« (Otto 1958).

The architectural elements of light, acoustics, volume, form, rhythm, materials, touch and smell function collectively to form a curated scenography that articulates the particular atmospheric charges (Barrie 2013). Frequently, the energy and resources expended on the articulation of the atmosphere far exceeds the liturgical and ritual spatial requirements. For instance, the uplifting and rhythmic qualities of the soaring vaults of a French gothic cathedral, while not functionally necessary for the assembly of the congregation, renders the space with certain emotive tones. While the atmosphere has its origins in the architectural qualities of space, it is not reducible to its individual architectural elements but is something that emanates from an overriding sense of the composition's totality (Griffero 2014).

So then, what is an atmosphere? Perceiving an atmosphere means becoming aware of a characteristic feeling that is present within a space (Griffero 2014). Atmospheres are sensuous embodied feelings (Griffero 2016) through which space is understood (Böhme 2001), perceived and experienced. This happens on the retina of the »lived and felt body« and more »importantly – are not projected by us onto the external world« (Griffero 2016: 6). Griffero (2014) describes an atmosphere as »something more«. It is more than the physical space itself and its qualities. Something inherent in the combined effect lends itself to the affective. When the atmospheric registers on the body, the experience is direct and since it is sensed and felt, rather than intellectualized, it appears acutely intimate and personal with a resounding psychological charge. But because it resides in the realm of feeling it becomes difficult to articulate with any precision. Feelings colour the way that we, from moment to moment, perceive and relate to the world, since as Griffero (2014) claims, this relationship is determined atmospherically rather than objectively, and as neuroscience has demonstrated, these feelings not only affect us emotionally but also facilitate an intellectual understanding (Perez-Gomez 2016).

Atmospheres are distinctly felt when they are experienced, however, they resist translation into precise linear or linguistic formulations. »And just like emotions, atmospheres too are curious situations that lose meaning when one tries to describe them: one has to be in them to understand them« (Galati 2002: 84). I claim that, since it is notoriously difficult to communicate the experience, the qualities and effects of the atmospheres through traditional architectural means – drawings, text and photos – other ways of knowing, experience and communication need to be sought out to engage with atmospheres more effectively in architectural pedagogy. The question then arises: What are other ways in which one can possibly »be« in atmospheres?

The Formation of the Architect

In his article »Hunting the Shadow«, the architectural historian of research by design, Jonathan Hill, describes how since the Renaissance architects have sought to elevate the profession to an intellectual elite (2003). This aimed to separate architectural practice from the embodied relationship to craft, the messiness of making, materiality and the chaos of the construction site that had previously been embedded in the role of the master mason (Starkey 2006). In doing so, drawing became central to the practice as it allowed architects to accurately describe a building's geometry. Accordingly, architects could direct the construction site from the comfort of the drawing office. Drawings, with their abstracted representational codes and their lim-

1.
Second-year student project by Ndivhuo Mabuda, artifact articulating exterior form.
Photographer: Ndivhuo Mabuda, 2021.

2.
Ronchamp. Photographer: Hugh Fraser, 2008. Unpublished.

ited material presence could therefore be associated with intellectual and artistic labor, as a means of signaling the distinction of the architect over the craftsperson (Hill 2003). Consequently, drawing became the locus of architectural thinking, production, discussion, communication and theorization (Starkey 2006; Hill 2003).

While the experiences of atmospheres are potentially rousing; within architectural practice and pedagogy we struggle to communicate their characteristics and nuances. Wittgenstein points out that »the limits of my language mean the limits of my world« (2001: 68). But is it possible, as architects to work beyond these limits and immerse ourselves within the realm of the ineffable qualities of the atmosphere, both for readings of the historical registers and within the design process? Are there potentially other ways of working, thinking, teaching and communicating that allow one to work more closely and directly within the atmospheric qualities of space, so as to maintain the fidelity of the spatial experience and its effects? Are there other ways of knowing that make these experiences more explicit ?

This study seeks to explore an embodied way of knowing as a potentially suitable mode of thinking, working with and teaching architecture. The unspeakable nature of the atmosphere presents a challenge and an opportunity for architectural pedagogy.

An Alternative Pedagogical Model

An experimental investigation with a second-year elective was conducted to explore possible practical, embodied modes of investigating atmospheres and ways to »be« in them. The project turned to the making of sculptural artifacts as tools to read, think and enter into a dialogue with atmospheric experiences and spaces. The aim was to seek out an embodied understanding, thinking and articulation of architecture. This elective explored the qualities and characteristics of the architectural experience of the atmosphere of the chapel of Notre Dame du Haut at Ronchamp.

Due to the pandemic and limited access to spaces, this process was undertaken using the online resources available to explore the building. In addition, the privilege of extensive travel to physically »be« in what are considered to be iconic examples of architectural history is a rare opportunity afforded to students of the south. This project experimented with approaches to overcome the disembodied digital experience and allow students to develop an understanding of atmospheric qualities so that they can be effectively conveyed, analyzed and discussed.

For this project, a case study was sought that contained a powerfully evocative sacral architectural experience, but that equally and comfortably functioned in both the sacred and secular domains. Ronchamp was thought to be appropriate as this site operates simultaneously as a Roman Catholic pilgrimage chapel, a convent, a cultural, historical, heritage and architectural tourist site, with spaces allocated for serving one or both of those domains. It annually receives 70,000 visitors, with the majority coming from various nationalities outside of France (Virot 2021).

Due to the lockdown and the inability to visit a local site, Ronchamp was chosen as an extensively documented online example, which could be interpreted through a variety of mediums: text; drawings; videos; audio soundtracks; photographs and singular and interconnected photospheres. The online documentation came from a variety of gazes: the professional; amateur; the secular and the religious.

While the research recognizes that the sacred is entangled with socio-cultural, ritualistic, mythological and symbolic contexts, the project's focus was on exploring readings of sacral atmospheres beyond an art historical interpretation.

Although students cannot experience the nuanced qualities of the atmosphere on site, it was thought that through the making of artifacts they could simulate the bodily experiences which could animate the chapel for them. Students cast iterative sculptural artifacts in plaster (plaster of Paris). These attempted to articulate the qualities of specific architectural aspects. Then, sculptural form was used as an expressive means to describe qualities of the exterior form, interior form, qualities of light, the materiality of the chapel and finally, these elements were amalgamated into a closing representation as a gestural approximation of the atmospheric qualities. The artifacts then became points of focused and tangible discussions around which the students could explore differences and similarities in the groups' reading of the atmospheres. Due to the cultural diversity of the class, students were encouraged to explore and articulate their own responses and readings of the space, rather than being informed by the existing Eurocentric perspective in the literature of architectural history.

Below is an account of the outcomes of the course. The sculptural artifact of fig. 1 seeks to express a reading of the tension between a sense of grounded mass and a sense of weightless mass in relationship to the external form of

Ronchamp as expressed in the chapel walls and roof which can be seen in the view of the chapel in fig. 2. Later, this was further expanded upon through the additional articulation of texture that accentuated these tensions. While this focuses on a single quality; one of many, through this process of translating the qualities into form, students gained an ability to »be« in this particular quality and found that they, through the means of the artifact, could describe it to others. Through the class's collective submission of their readings, they formed an extensive interpretation of Ronchamp's atmospheric qualities that was generated from multiple viewpoints. There were frequently similarities in the studies, but their articulation always contained further nuances and differences that allowed for an interesting and delicate reading.

Fig. 3 explored the dynamic and complex gradations of light and shadow, and its gentleness as the light falls onto curved forms. It attempted to express the changing light qualities on, and in, Ronchamp's three light towers (fig. 4).

The artifact of fig. 5 attempts to articulate the manner in which small but intense shards of light penetrate the space. Here, light qualities are represented as a solid form.

The artifact in fig. 6 explored how indirect light is exploited in the chapel by hiding its source and bouncing light off multiple surfaces to achieve a light that has mysterious qualities.

Fig. 7 sought to evoke the dynamic nature of the building's outer skin as one moves around it describing the manner in which entrances are made and how the skin changes its qualities from heavy and taut to uplifting, and the fluidity with which these changes are articulated.

The urban and architectural researcher, Niels Albertsen, points out that »from a phenomenological [...] point of [...] view, only someone who is exposed directly to an atmosphere can characterize it« (2012: 69). This is because of the intimate relationship between lived experience, sensuousness and emotion. However, he suggests that one would be able to re-presence the atmosphere in another place and time through the notion of gestural communication. This can be further enhanced by pointing to similarities of the atmosphere within other media, such as a feeling evoked through a piece of music. An atmosphere's sensuous experience could then be communicated to others through the form of gestural means. In the case of this project, the sculptural artifact serves a medium of gestural communication that evokes and conveys sense experiences. This occurs twice: firstly, during the process

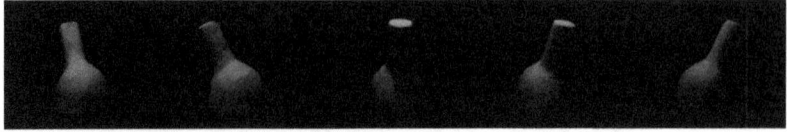

3.
Second-year student project by Duncan Powell, artifact articulating light of Ronchamp. Photographer: Duncan Powell, 2021.

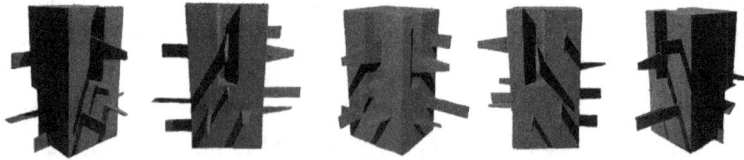

5.
Second-year student project by Joshua Kumersamy, artifact articulating how small, but bright shards of light enter the space. Photographer: Joshua Kumersamy, 2021.

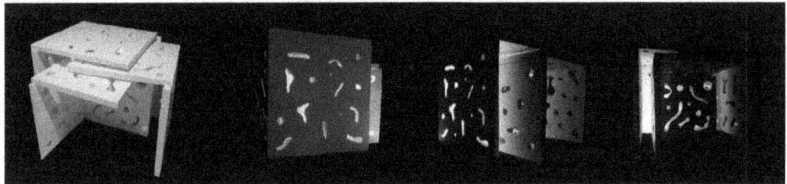

6.
Second-year student project by Maeve Human, artifact describing how bounced light enters a space. Photographer: Maeve Human, 2021.

7.
Second-year student project by Asnath Nkohla, artifact articulating exterior form. Photographer: Asnath Nkohla, 2022.

of fabrication where the artifact communicates to the student making the artifact. Then, for a second time when it is "read" and evaluated by the rest of the class.

Gestures seem then, to be an appropriate medium to convey »atmospheres atmospherically« (Albertsen 2012: 69). The sculptural artifact serves as a pointing tool to gesture and convey certain similarities in feeling (Albertsen 2012), as evoked by the study of the chapel. Sensing atmospheres is a competence that can be developed, trained, and learned (Böhme 2006), and I believe that through the process described above, it is a potential method to develop a sensitivity to architectural atmospheres.

Object Oriented Ontology

Object Oriented Ontology (OOO) provides an insightful framework and strategy for thinking about the nature of atmospheres, the sculptural artifacts' role and their relationship. Central to OOO thinking is that objects of all scales are the fundamental elements that make up the universe (Harman 2013). Any »thing« can be an object, and that includes human and non-human worlds, living and non-living things, as well as artificial objects and conceptual and imaginary ideas. (Harman 2013). This all-encompassing framework gives one an ability to think about the ineffable experiences of atmospheres and sculptural artifacts as »things«, and that these »things« can exist within a flat ontology. In other words, the experience of an atmosphere, the making process, the sculptural artifact and the students' experience of it all, are things on an »equal ontological footing« and that none of them, » whether artificial or natural, symbolic or physical, possesses greater ontological dignity than other objects« (Bryant 2011), and that any of these »things« has the ability to be affective.

OOO proposes that a »thing« can have a vast number of qualities, relations and realities; some of which are knowable and some which are hidden. It speculates that it is not possible to know the true nature of the object as this nature is inexhaustible. We can know aspects of it – its role or what it is made of – but this is not its complete reality. With this framing, one acknowledges that while one can perceive certain qualities in the atmosphere and in the sculptural artifact, that they form part of an unknowable complex reality. This contributes to an understanding that the reading of the chapel and its atmospheres is inexhaustible and that one cannot arrive at a definitive conclusion. The experience and articulation thereof is only ever a revela-

4.
Chapelle Notre-Dame-du- Haut de Ronchamp
Nebenkapelle. Photography: Peter Pielmeier, 2018.
Public domain.

tion of certain qualities, while others will continue to remain hidden. Due to this complexity, one cannot create an understanding in a direct way. Like the atmospheres, one has to arrive at it through allusion, by coming at it obliquely. Through the sculptural artifacts we can hint at deeper more complex realities that lie below the perceivable surface (Gage 2015). More often than not, the artifact will reveal qualities of its own accord because it exists in reality on its own terms, irrespective of the intention or conceptualization of the maker. Through understanding the sculptural artifacts as tools of evocation, there is an appreciation that readings remain open to highlight partial aspects and that the »something more« nature of the atmosphere continues to remain intact.

Architecture in the Making

OOO postulates that there are not only human-human and human-object interactions, but that objects also interact with each other. In these scenarios, the interacting objects never exhaust each other's qualities, but in the process they transform and deform each other. This can relate to the processes of making, thinking through and with materials and their agency, as well as their effects on us. Materials tend to assert their own identity during the making, and working with them needs to take this into account. This process exposes the dialogue with the material. The artifact routinely comes out differently than originally expected. This deformation of expectations causes one to constantly re-evaluate the process of making and look closely at the artifact with its own material qualities. It sets up a dialogue between the artifact and the chapel to enable a refinement of the articulation of the visual and spatial language.

One can think with and through the sculptural artifact (Starkey 2006) to make the atmospheric experience and its nuances explicit. The dialogue with the medium allowed students to make readings of the atmospheres. Based on their bodily experiences and their ability to sense the qualities, they were more articulate about the architectural experiences in comparison to when spatial analysis had been done through the more abstract and analytical medium of drawing. While making, students were in contact with the materials and forms in a range of body-artifact relationships that started from the conceptualization stage, mold making, casting, and finishing to conclude in the presentation phases.

Towards an Embodied Practice

Merleau-Ponty's concept of body schema describes the awareness of the body, of itself, in space (Merleau-Ponty 2002). It obtains this information from several bodily sensory feedback loops (Kreutzer et al. 2018a). Since it operates on a subconscious level, one is normally unaware of it (Kreutzer, DeLuca and Caplan, 2018b) until such a point that something goes wrong, if you stub your toe for instance. However, the body schema is not only fixed to the body, it also allows for bodily awareness to extend beyond itself into the environment, as well as incorporate external objects into it (Gallagher 2021). The use of tools describes this process well, such as when a hammer becomes the extension of an artisan's hand (Gallagher 2021). In this way the body can project itself onto, and extend itself into, the qualities of the sculptural artifact, aided through the processes of making. Students then experience the qualities of the atmospheres through their own bodies (Maravita and Iriki 2004). So even though the artifacts are not spatially immersive, I argue that through this projection, students are able to be »in« the artifact. In this way, the sculptural artifact and its atmospheric quality has a visceral quality and the ability to be affective.

The extended body schema and the ability to be projected into real and virtual environments (Maravita and Iriki 2004) co-creates atmospheres. I claim that a different relationship to, and understanding of, space emerges through this process of material making as compared to design drawings. While it may not be the actual atmosphere experienced on site, those created by students in the artifacts gave them concrete architectural experiences that they could reflect on, discuss and analyze. The artifacts could be read by each member of the class and the spectrum of readings allowed them to experience a variety of qualities. This process opens the possibility of thinking about and articulating atmospheres with, and through, the material engagement which is not enabled in the same way through drawing (Starkey 2006). The body-artifact relationship develops over time with continuous and varied multi-sensory inputs and feedback loops that allow for the multi-level reflection on, and articulation of, experiences.

While this project is still in its early stages, it explores the potential for a practical embodied mode of investigating the tacit atmospheres of sacral architecture. The process of making sculptural artifacts offers a means to access bodily and emotive sensations. The artifact can assist in articulating and communicating non-verbal and non-linear readings that are beneficial for learning about sacral atmospheres in design and to gain an understanding of the historical registers of sacral spaces.

References

Albertsen, Niels (2012): »Gesturing Atmospheres«, in: Thibaud et al. (eds.), *Ambiances in Action : Proceedings of the 2nd International Congress on Ambiances*, Canadian Centre for Architecture, Montreal 2012. Mayenne: International Ambiances Network, 69–74.

Barrie, Thomas (2013): *The Sacred In-Between: The Mediating Roles of Architecture*, London: Routledge.

Böhme, Gernot (2001): *Aisthetik. Vorlesungen über Ästhetik als allgemeine Wahrnehmungslehre*, Munich: Wilhelm Fink Verlag.

Böhme, Gernot (2006): *Architektur und Atmosphäre*, Munich: Wilhelm Fink Verlag.

Bryant, Levi R. (2011): *The Democracy of Objects*, London: Open Humanities Press.

Gage, Mark Foster (2015): »Killing Simplicity: Object-Oriented Philosophy in Architecture«, in: *Log* 33, 95–106.

Galati, Dario (2002): Prospettive sulle emozioni e teorie del soggetto, Torino: Bollati Boringhieri.

Gallagher, Shaun (2021): »Body Image and Body Schema: A Conceptual Clarification«, in: *The Journal of Mind and Behavior* Autumn 1986, Vol. 7(No. 4 (Autumn 1986)), pp. 541–554.

Griffero, Tonio (2014): *Atmospheres: Aesthetics of Emotional Spaces*, Farnham: Ashgate Publishing, Ltd.

Griffero, Tonio (2016): »Atmospheres and Felt-bodily Resonances«, in: *Italian Journal of Aesthetics* Anno XLIV(1/2016 IV serie)

Harman, Graham (2013): *Bells and Whistles: More Speculative Realism*, Winchester: Zero Books.

Hill, Jonathan (2003): »Hunting the Shadow: Immaterial Architecture«, in: *The Journal of Architecture* 8/2, 165–179. doi: 10.1080/13602360309588.

Kreutzer, Jeffrey/DeLuca, John/Caplan, Bruce (2018a): *Encyclopedia of Clinical Neuropsychology*, Cham: Springer International Publishing.

Kreutzer, Jeffrey/DeLuca, John/Caplan, Bruce (2018b): *Encyclopedia of Clinical Neuropsychology*. 2nd ed, Cham: Springer International Publishing.

Maravita, Angelo/Iriki, Atsushi (2004): »Tools for the Body (schema)«, in: *Trends in Cognitive Sciences* 8/2, 79–86.

Merleau-Ponty, Maurice (2002): *Phenomenology of Perception*, London: Routledge Classics.

Otto, Rudolf (1958): *The Idea of the Holy: An Inquiry into the Non-rational Factor in the Idea of the Divine and its Relation to the Rational*, New York: Oxford University Press.

Perez-Gomez, Alberto (2016): *Attunement: Architectural Meaning after the Crisis of Modern Science*, Cambridge, MA: The MIT Press.

Starkey, Bradley (2006): »Models, Architecture, Levitation: Design-based Research into Post-secular Architecture«, in: *The Journal of Architecture* 11/3, 323–328. doi: 10.1080/13602360600931508.

Virot, Jean-Jacques (2021): Renovation of the Chapel, Le Corbusier, Ronchamp. Press Kit. Available at: https://www.collinenotredameduhaut.com/wp-content/uploads/2021/10/DP-Chantier-_-ANGLAIS.pdf [Accessed: April 23, 2022].

Wittgenstein, Ludwig (2001): *Tractatus Logico-Philosophicus*, London/New York: Routledge.

Dimensions of Architectural Knowledge, 2022-03 ⑥
https://doi.org/10.14361/dak-2022-0319

SPECULATIVE DESIGN WORKSHOPS
Building Bridges for Flooding Cities

Santosh Kumar Ketham

Abstract: The impact of climate change on cities is multifold and critical; one of them is flooding. The aim and objective of this article is to speculate how the needs of flooded cities are addressed using the method of speculative design. This technique involves various actors, disciplines, local, and international participation in brainstorming and generating scenarios, discussion, and reflection. It is practiced through workshops, competitions, and exhibitions. This article showcases the speculative design practice of the non-governmental organization (NGO), Thinking Hand, and Ketham's Atelier Architects; which takes a bottom-up and collective approach in Hyderabad, in India. Their work attempts to bring different concerned groups into a conversation about climate change and flooding, some of which are not often included in urban decision-making processes. Owing to their greater responsibilities and participation, involving all stakeholders is significant in order to rethink policies for climate responsive architecture and urbanism.

Keywords: Flooding Cities; Speculative Design; Collective Workshops

Introduction

Climate change is no longer a future scenario that is going to happen in forthcoming years: It has already happened. Climate change in the form of flooding affects millions of people and urban infrastructures across the world, especially in densely populated coastal, riverside, and low-lying areas. It is affecting the environment, economy, and social and political relations. And the worst affected are the urban poor and neglected communities.

Countering climate change is imperative for flooding cities. In order to instigate positive change, cities have to be developed more coherently by including all inhabitants in a shared conversation where all stakeholders participate. I put forth that one way to achieve this is through a design practice with speculative means. In this article, I will present parts of my own work

Corresponding author: Santosh Kumar Ketham (University of Innsbruck, Austria); kethamsatelier@
gmail.com; https://orcid.org/0000-0002-9192-4676

conducted in my studio, 'Ketham's Atelier Architects' with the NGO 'Thinking Hand' that I co-founded in 2015 in Hyderabad, India.

Currently, I am also pursuing a doctoral thesis project that is concerned with reflecting upon and theorizing the speculative design method we have developed in our work in the atelier, as well as in the NGO. In my thesis, I am redefining my ongoing practice with various community groups, together with multiple actors, to further emerging common narratives, with a larger impact to combat climate change. I claim that our method can act as a catalyst for collectively reviewing our relationship to the reality of rising sea levels. It is based on the assumption that a collective method in practice can make a difference and open up new ways of thinking together through scenarios concerning climate change, and especially the flooding of urban areas. It aims to create formats that collectively speculate, negotiate, and finally, reconstruct cities prone to flooding for more hopeful futures.

The work I pursue with the NGO Thinking Hand is based on spatial learning by collectively drawing, modeling, presenting, discussing and assessing »what-if« scenarios in workshops and design competitions, and disseminating the work to a wider public through exhibitions and in my doctoral thesis. I use a number of cities, such as Mumbai and Hyderabad, as case studies. In this article, I will reflect on the mediating formats of our practice: namely collective workshops.

Speculative Design

»Speculative design«, a concept which is often attributed to the British designers, Fiona Raby and Anthony Dunne, encourages designers to think further ahead and widen the possibility of design by going beyond merely finding solutions to problems and asking different questions (Dunne/Raby 2013). In Dunne and Raby's terms, speculative design combines design-thinking methods with storytelling and future-world-building techniques from speculative fiction to produce prototypes and experiences. These may take the form of a physical or digital product, video, documentary, book, manual, website, sculptures or other form of art. Their purpose is to generate discussion, debate, and awareness beyond projected or plausible futures so that designers, companies, and the public are not only aware of how their actions contribute to manifesting certain futures, but that they can also begin to imagine and articulate preferable futures (Lutz 2020).

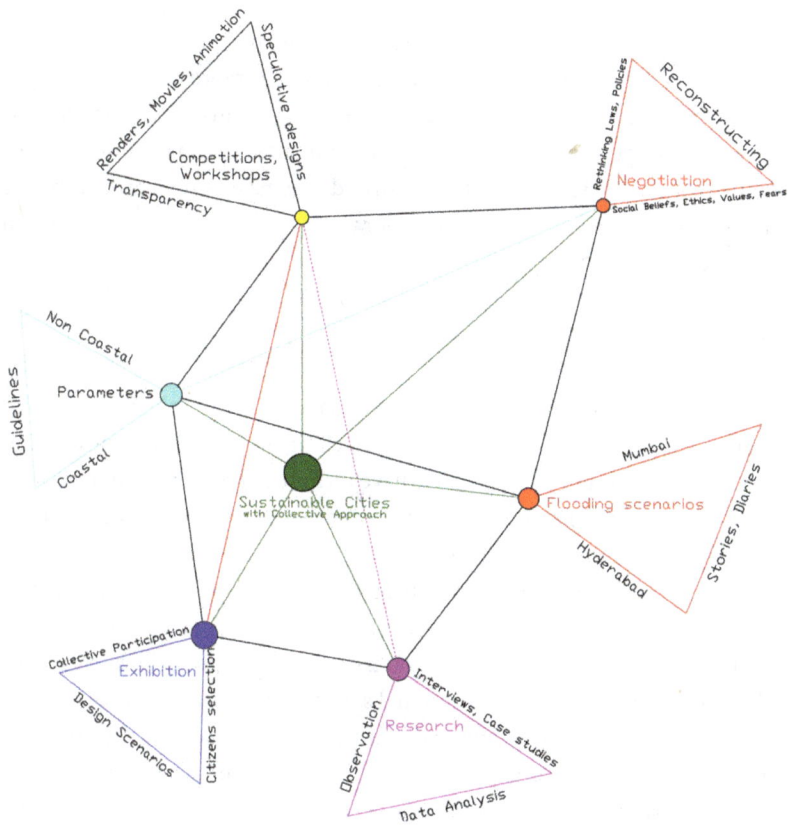

1.

Research diagram: Santosh Kumar Ketham.

»Futures are stories we create to analyze, plan and build consensus«, according to design researcher Elliott P. Montgomery. His »narrative futures cones« represent the subjective limits of our capacity to envision probable stories; they are often just one alternative to earlier representations that suggest a singular present, linear past, and infinitely expanding futures (Montgomery 2020). In speculative design thinking, however, ideas of possible futures can be used as tools to better understand the present and discuss the kind of futures we need to create for our survival.

The communications scholar and participatory designer, Sasha Costanza Chock, also reminds us that design is something far more pervasive and profound than is typically recognized by designers, cultural theorists, philosophers, or lay persons; »designing is fundamental to being human – we design, that is to say, we deliberate, plan and scheme in ways which prefigure our actions and makings ... we design our world, while our world acts back on us and designs us« (Chock 2020:13).

»Wet« Design Approaches in India

Architect and landscape architect, Anuradha Mathur, and the architect and planner Dilip da Cunha, both currently teaching in the USA, pursue an activist and critical design practice. They have introduced pedagogical initiatives to explore the problem of flooding, along with other concerned actors in numerous cities, mainly in India and the USA.

In the largely normative milieu of professional practice, the work of Mathur and da Cunha has been recognized as notable for concentrating less on client-driven commissions than on issue-centered public investigations; »they work to identify not conventional solutions but rather a range of possibilities, points of departure for transformative projects« (Ward 2010). They see a need for architectural practices to change in order to address flooding, and they describe the difference between a concerned design practice and a mainstream professional approach by stating: »An activist practice means first that we are initiators. Rather than waiting for a commissioned project, we ask the first question, frame the issue and propose possibilities. Our purpose is to affect change, from policy to pedagogy right down to how people image and imagine environments, both built and natural« (Mathur/da Cunha 2010). Their design practice includes writing, imaging, teaching, and the use of a variety of artistic media »to produce works and pedagogical processes that strive to draw out the material complexity and inherent dynamism of places«. Their collaborative work imagines new possibilities for designing the built environment and explores the lines separating land and water, and urban and rural environments (Mathur/da Cunha 2017).

The work of the Thinking Hand NGO has largely been inspired by Mathur and da Cunha's imaginative speculative design practice, as a way forward in counteracting climate change and dealing with flooding cities. In six years, the organization, which consists of NGO members and volunteers, and the author, all of whom have experience in both architectural practice and architectural education, have developed a bottom-up approach which we call a collective speculative design approach. The name »Thinking Hand« is associated with the idea of thinking and building simultaneously, and emphasizes a hands-on and careful approach to the built environment. It is an effort to create awareness about environmental issues through design and its processes by collaborating with local communities and organizations, and building in the scale 1:1. We claim that doing such collective speculative design workshops and exchanging experiences and launching competitions to encourage original thinking, while creating exhibitions to share ideas with a wider public, can advance a new way of thinking about, and building, cities as an innovative way of dealing with crises and challenges (Thinking Hand/Ketham's Atelier 2015).[1]

Our collective participatory format aims to bring actors from various sectors, disciplines, and communities together, including students, professionals, and experts, who are rarely able to meet to discuss the issues and problems neighborhoods and cities are facing. It addresses these through speculating, thinking, constructing, narrating, and ideating future possibilities and probable solutions which contemplate and adapt to the local culture, material, climate, context, community needs, and socio-economic realities, together. We use the term »collective« as metaphor – directly and

1 Thinking Hand is a non-profit organization I established in 2015 with colleagues and students of the Planning and Architecture Institution in Hyderabad, India. The Thinking Hand NGO is registered under the Telangana Societies Act, 2001, and has seven members: Santosh Kumar Ketham (President); Varalakshmi (Vice President);Mamatha Vani (General Secretary); Vijay Prakash (Treasurer); Padmaja Rudroj (Executive Member); Mohamed Sulaiman (Executive Member); Prudvi Raj Reddy (Executive Member) and 20 volunteers: Praveen Kumar Ketham; Ravi Kumar Rudroj; Ali Hashmi; Rasha Fathima; Kubra Anjum; Deepak Thapa; Rasha Fathima; Zebunisa, Ameen Siddiqui; Mohamed Anwar Mirza; Yoganand Naidu; Tejaswini; Mohamed Asim Shareef; Mohamed Irfan Khan; Ifthikhar Ahmed and Rakshaan Fathima.

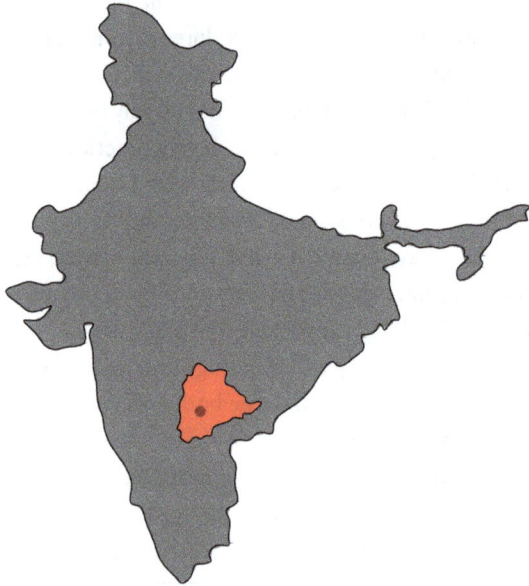

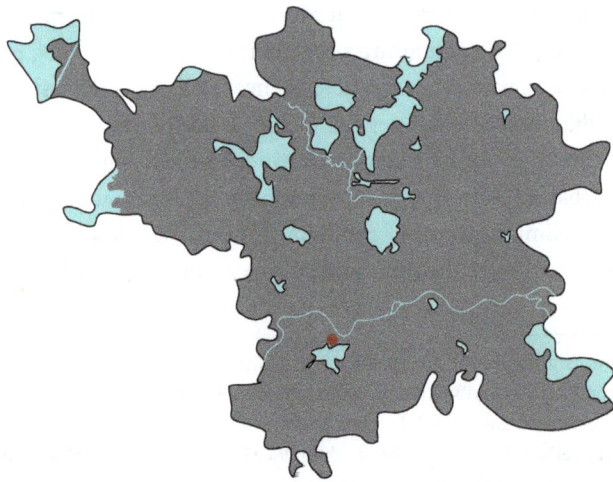

2.

Maps of India, with the city of Hyderabad and the region Telangana, and the city with the neighborhood, Kishan Bagh. Drawings: Santosh Kumar Ketham.

indirectly inspired by speculative design, as a method and tool to collectively document (case studies), to collectively speculate on futures (in workshops and competitions), to collectively evaluate (in exhibitions and discussions), and to collectively reform cities (through building with community participation).

Case Study: Kishan Bagh – Collective Speculative Design Workshops by the Thinking Hand NGO

Kishan Bagh is a neglected community in Hyderabad, India, with a population of around 7,000 inhabitants; of which 3,000 are children from the ages of five to fifteen. Most of the women there are widows or single mothers. On average, a family consists of five to six members. There are some who stay in a single room tenement, and in the whole community, less than 100 children have completed their schooling. Of those children, only three girls in the whole community have graduated. Surveys show that the main reason for children not attending school is poverty, and the lack of awareness shown by their illiterate adult guardians. A frequent problem in the area is flooding from Musi River, which runs through the city.

The neighborhood's built environment is provisional and of poor quality. There are few toilets in the community. One toilet is shared among ten families, while in some cases; a household of ten people has a single toilet (figs. 3–4). Earlier on, water from the nearby artificial lake, Mir-alam-tank, was used for drinking, but after the construction of a zoo adjacent to it, access has been denied. Now, the drainage water goes to Mir-alam-tank and contaminates it, while spreading diseases in the vicinity. Piped drinking water is only available for two hours once every two days through a community tap.

During rains, the community gets heavily flooded as there are no drains and roads in the neighborhood. Floodwater from Musi River enters most of the houses and remains for many days until rescue teams arrive. People lose their belongings, their work, and remain starving if help does not arrive in time. Even small rains cause pools in the area that can cause damage to the houses and belongings. Floods also raise frequent concerns about contagious diseases such as malaria and dengue fever.

With the Thinking Hand NGO we made an effort to raise the local residents' awareness of design and its processes through a series of speculative design workshops, an exhibition, open public talks by experts such as local and international architects, urban designers, and conservationists. The

3. – 4.
Interior of a dwelling. Photography: Ketham's Atelier Architects.

workshops involved building on-site, in collaboration with international and local student groups, and their teachers from several schools of architecture and planning[2], professionals, companies, and members and volunteers of other NGOs in Hyderabad.[3] The activities resulted in a site documentation that included interviews with community members, observation studies, photos, drawings, sketches, and maps. These were featured in Indian media such as Hindu, Eenadu, and Siasat Urdu newspapers.

From the January 12 to January 15, 2017, during the Sankranthi holidays (the kites festival), we conducted the first workshop called »Shelter in Need« for the flooded community Kishan Bagh on the National Institute of Tourism and Hospitality Management (NITHM) campus, in Gachibowli, Hyderabad.[4]

Over forty local students participated in the first workshop led by two tutors, Ravi Kumar Rudroj and the author.

The brief for the workshop »Shelter in Need«, asked attendees to design a portable shelter, which could be erected quickly, disassembled easily, and would be transferable to both cities and villages. The structure should also act as a pavilion to host different activities all year round. It may also be envisioned as a meeting point for different cultural and leisure circuits. The idea was to use the same space for a broad range of daytime and nocturnal activities that would cater to its surroundings. In four days, the local students drew simple structures that could be constructed quickly from found material. The proposals ranged from pop-up lightweight structures to floating platforms as infrastructures that would stay intact during the flooding season and help everyday life maintain some normalcy. An evaluation was conducted with local community experts such as architects, urban designers, graphic and product designers, and the faculty of the local schools of architecture, who acted as a jury to critique the students' speculative designs.[5]

In the same year, from September 25 to September 27, 2017, the NGO Thinking Hand joined forces with the University of Innsbruck to continue

---

2 Involving JNIAS, JBR, JNTUA, Vaishnavi, SPAV, and CSIIT.

3 These included charity organizations such as Cherish Orphanage and Safa Baitulmal. Safa-Baitulmal has started a welfare scheme in which they aim to support single mothers. They work alongside the organization, Dear. The latter includes doctors, who campaign for free medical services.

4 The workshops were supported by Ketham's Atelier Architects.

5 The local community experts were Jothirmayi Mitta, Neelima Gudavalli, Shashidhar Reddy, Masood Shaik, Padmaja Rudroj, Avinash Raipally, and Santosh Sarkar.

5.

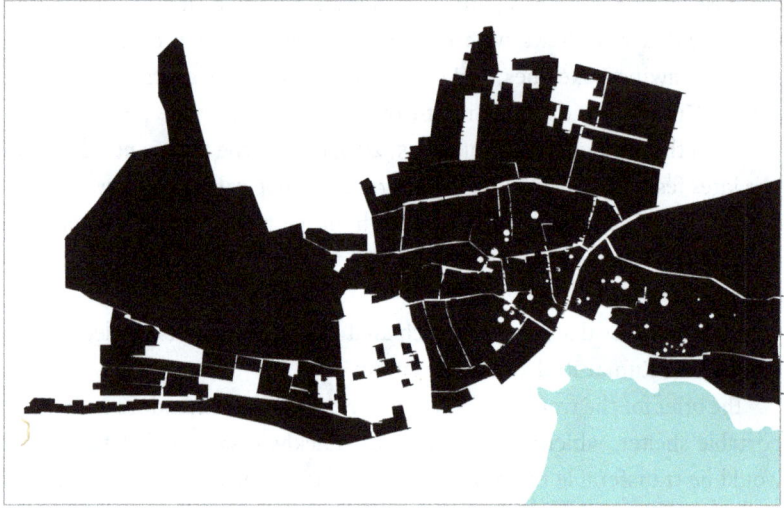

Site drawings of the hardscape (dwellings) and softscape (made of pools after flooding) of Kishan Bagh. Drawing: Ketham's Atelier Architects.

the work on speculative design proposals with the Kishan Bagh community in a second workshop, again at the NITHM Campus. The idea was to learn from others and through self-exploration. The workshop theme was »Climate Responsive Architecture« for Kishan Bagh. Over 40 students participated in the workshop; 20 students from architecture schools in Hyderabad and 20 students from Innsbruck University. As part of the workshop, students got a chance to visit the settlement of Kishan Bagh soon after the monsoons, the rainy season in India. The workshop was divided into lectures and tutoring by local tutors and international guest professors from various disciplines.[6]

In three days, workshop participants created speculative design proposals that ranged from roof solutions that collected rainwater to be channeled to Musi River, drainages, percolation pits and water storages for future use; dwellings adapted to the topography and with roof designs that protected houses from heavy rains; cross-ventilated dwellings that used local brick and construction techniques, and most importantly, maintained community spaces for interaction and social activities.

These ideas were presented to invited guests and the general public for them to discuss what the options and strategies developed for this particular community could be. The workshops speculated on and showcased potential ideas which could then be reflected upon and developed. The common activities raised awareness and provided a sense of responsibility, not only for the students and the experts, but also for the representatives of institutions and organizations, and the general public.

This workshops collaboration inspired us to make two calls for international competitions for innovative furniture for neglected communities (2018; 2020), which would be built 1:1 by Ketham's Atelier in collaboration with the Thinking Hand NGO. The competition call got an overwhelming response and received hundreds of design entries from the USA, Europe, Africa, and Asia. The winning projects were exhibited online and two were built 1:1 and shared with the community of Kishan Bagh.

---

6 The workshop tutors were Stefan Holst of Transsolar, Volker Flamm of the University of Innsbruck, Rames Najjar, Oliver von Malm, and the author; and guest jury members included Ravindran K.T, Ateeq Mirza, Ravi Kumar Rudroj, the convenor of the Indian National Trust for Art and Cultural Heritage Anuradha Reddy, Shanker Narayan, Nitin Bansal, the Indian Administrative Service officer Nitin Singhania, and Praveen Kumar.

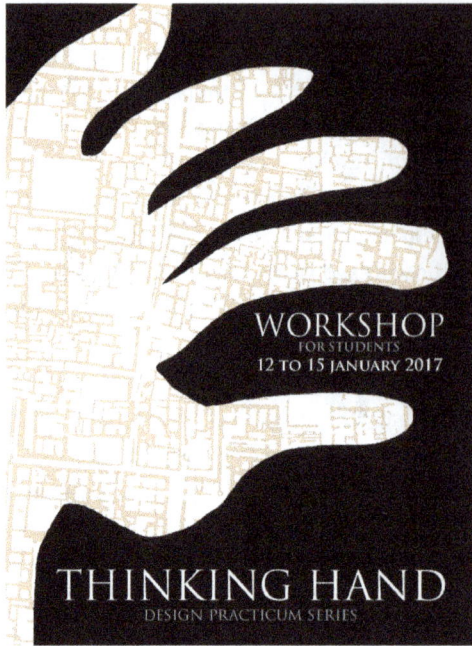

6.
Workshop poster: Thinking Hand NGO, January 2017.

7.
Site visit to Kishan Bagh with architecture and urban design students from the Universities of Hyderabad and Innsbruck, September 2017.
Photography: Ketham›s Atelier Architects, 2017.

Conclusion

This article suggests that communities and institutions need to collectively reflect on flooding scenarios to counter climate change in the long run. It presents the work of the Thinking Hand NGO, which conducts workshops together with vulnerable communities most affected by flooding and involves local organizations, international professionals, researchers, and students. Our collective method follows a bottom-up approach to study, think, build, evaluate, and negotiate the communicative formats of speculative design workshops, competitions, and exhibitions; starting small and thinking long-term through building social cohesion.

Speculative design workshops hereby give a chance to experiment with new concepts in design; they are a way to build future narratives and involve many. Workshops and competitions can bring creative and non-conformist ideas to the table, and provide an opportunity to test the possibilities and limits of what architecture can do for society; they challenge the profession, and politics, to create more dialogue with the parties most affected by climate change (Guida/Crossley/Gismondi 2017).

Through our collective workshops with local and international guests, creative ideas from various disciplines and backgrounds and from around the world could be tapped. They provided an avenue to evaluate different conditions and then experiment, play, and explore. I argue that they are an excellent arena for studying the multiple challenges of, and obstacles to, integrating diverse sources of knowledge on flooding cities. They are an attempt to make sense of deeply interconnected and interdependent problems through developing probable and possible scenarios; both theoretical and practical that envision change. I argue that speculative design workshops can bring transparency to issues and act as catalysts in negotiations. Furthermore, the workshops can bring a sense of responsibility to various communities and building professions.

In our activities, we offer a collective approach to design. We argue that such collective efforts can put pressure on governments and politicians to rethink climate issues and force them to take serious action on policy change, while integrating stakeholders and local actors in decision-making. These processes are complex, messy, difficult, and time-consuming. But we believe that, in the long run, only collective action from the bottom-up can have a strong impact on rethinking current laws, political and economic systems, social beliefs, and behaviors and that we need to develop communicative for-

8.
*Site visit to Kishan Bagh with architecture and urban design students from the
Universities of Hyderabad and Innsbruck, September 2017.*
Photography: Ketham's Atelier Architects, 2017.

9.
*Site visit to Kishan Bagh with architecture and urban design students from the
Universities of Hyderabad and Innsbruck, September 2017.*
Photography: Ketham's Atelier Architects, 2017.

mats like speculative design workshops to bridge the gap between, rich and poor, educated and neglected communities to help them grow together and bring about change.

I would like thank my doctoral research supervisor Prof. Marjan Colletti (Head of the Institute of Experimental Architecture, Hochbau) for his guidance and support. Special thanks to Prof. Dr. Ulrike Tanzer (vice rector of University of Innsbruck) for a doctoral scholarship (2020–2022). Additional thanks goes to the University of Innsbruck for the 1669 Committee International Conference Grant. Special thanks to the Thinking Hand NGO and Ketham's Atelier team in Hyderabad, India, for supporting my research studies. Thanks also to my friend Ravi Kumar Rudroj and Praveen Kumar Ketham for corrections.

References

Chock, Sasha Costanza (2020): *Design Justice: Community-Led Practices to Build the Worlds We Need*, Cambridge, MA: The MIT Press

Dunne,Anthony/Raby,Fiona (2013): *Speculative Everything: Design, Fiction and Social Dreaming*, Cambridge, MA : The MIT Press.

Guida,George/Crossley,Tatjana/ Gismondi, Carolina (2017): »Interview, United Kingdom«, June 7, 2021, https:// architecturecompetitions.com/ mclc-hon-2-interview/

Lutz, Damien (2020): »Future Thieving #1: Stealing from the Future with Speculative Design«, April 3, 2021, https://uxdesign. cc/stealing-from-the-future-with-speculative-design-e769059b6689

Mathur, Anuradha/Cunha, Dilip da (2017): »Pew Fellows of the Week: An Interview with Landscape Architects Anuradha Mathur and Dilip da Cunha«, in: *Pew Center for Arts & Heritage, May 2018*, https://www. pewcenterarts.org/post/pew-fellows-week-interview-landscape-architects anuradhamathur-dilip-da-cunha (Accessed: November 4, 2021.

Montgomery, Elliott (n.d.): »Mapping Speculative Design, Future Cone«, March 4, 2021, https://www.epmid.com/projects/ Mapping-Speculative-Design

Pevzner, Nicholas/Sen, Sanjukta (2010): »Preparing Ground: In Conversation with Anuradha Mathus and Dilip da Cunha«, in: *Places Journal*, June, https://placesjournal. org/article/preparing-ground-interview/?cn-reloaded=1&cn-reloaded=1 (Accessed: November 4, 2021).

Thinking Hand NGO (2015): »NGO Mission«, June 6, 2021, https:// thinkinghandngo.com/mission/https:// kethamsatelier.com/thinking-hand-ngo/

Thinking Hand NGO (2017a): »Workshop Shelter In Need«, June 6, 2021, https://kethamsatelier.com/thinking-hand-workshop-01/

Thinking Hand NGO (2017b): »INDO-EURO Workshop«, June 6, 2021, https://kethamsatelier.com/indo-euro-workshop-02/

Ward, Maitiú (2012): »Design Activism: Dilip da Cunha and Anuradha Mathur«, in: *Australian Design Review*, August, https://www.australiandesignreview.com/architecture/design-activism-dilip-da-cunha-anuradha-mathur/ (Accessed: November 5, 2021).

Dimensions of Architectural Knowledge, 2022-03 ∂
https://doi.org/10.14361/dak-2022-0320

STORYBOARD
Character-Led Architecture in Architectural Pedagogy

Anita Szentesi

Abstract: This article draws from ongoing research situated between architecture and film. It focuses on introducing film and its narrative formats into architectural design pedagogy at the Wits School of Architecture in Johannesburg, South Africa, with the aim of establishing a more inclusive and collaborative design studio environment. Techniques such as screenwriting and storyboards are discussed as part of a methodology for designing and representing buildings through characters' lived experiences, something I call »character-led architecture«. In this article, which is accompanied by a script that explores my own affective experience as I grappled with creating and introducing this methodology during a moment of social transformation in South Africa, character-led architecture becomes a tool for self-reflection. My research is situated in the field of narratives in the design process to contribute new knowledge to architectural pedagogy and design theory.

Keywords: Architecture and Film; Narrative in the Design Process; Screenwriting; Character-Led Architecture; Architectural Pedagogy.

Introduction

I developed the concept of »character-led architecture« after learning about the importance of a character's journey within screenwriting. A character-driven story is one in which the audience invests and believes. As Syd Field states, »Character is the essential foundation of your screenplay. It is the heart and soul and nervous system of your story. Before you put a word on paper, you must know your character« (Field 1982: 22). My question was how this notion of a character-led story might be translated into a character-led architecture, where narratives grounded in characters become an important layer to be considered in the design process.

Corresponding author: Anita Szentesi (University of the Witwatersrand, Johannesburg, South Africa);
Anita.Szentesi@wits.ac.za; https://orcid.org/0000-0002-7807-1293

Within my ongoing research, I have explored character-led architecture in three contexts. First, the architectural design studio, where students are encouraged to create characters and narratives in imagined worlds to develop inclusive and emotionally charged projects. In this context, I am the facilitator, while the students are the participants. Second, in community-based design practice, where stories from community members enable an empathic analysis of past and present social, political, and cultural environments to inform future collaborative place-making. In this context, I am the facilitator, while different local communities are the participants. Although I have defined clear roles for the facilitator and participants, the boundaries between these roles frequently blur, especially as I found myself participating to some extent, as well. Both of these described contexts resonate strongly with the work of the non-profit organization *Action Archive*,[1] created by Meike Schalk, Sara Brolund, and Helena Mattsson, which seeks to enable participative modes of history writing to construct an active archive (Mattson 2018). Emma Cheatle's *Part-Architecture* (2013),[2] which expands historiographic methods through material, site-specific, performative, and speculative practices to highlight previously unrecorded marginal voices in history, is another key reference. The third context for character-led architecture, which will be explored in the remainder of this article, is self-reflection; here, character-led architecture forms a reflexive layer that accompanies the text to expose the affective dimension of the experiences I write about. In this context, I am the participant.

The article is structured into three scenes, which provide a frame for developing an emotive narrative that allows me to reflect on my own position as an architect, filmmaker, lecturer, and researcher in the process of changing the curriculum to introduce an alternative design pedagogy. I situate

---

1 1 »Action Archive« (Mattson 2018) situates architects and historians as active participants within a network facilitating the collection of often unrecorded stories within history, chiefly the invisible voices of the other, through social inquiries and participatory methods. In a similar vein, I ask how my position as an architect, filmmaker, lecturer, and researcher facilitating character-led architecture in the design studio might enable an inclusive participatory environment, as well as record more ephemeral and affective aspects not typically expressed in more static architectural representations.

2 In her work, Cheatle combines fiction with archival information about Pierre Chareau's Maison de Verre, which housed a gynaecological clinic in 1930s Paris, by creating the characters of women she imagined occupying the building to speculate on their unrecorded experiences.

myself as a character across all scenes, represented through a simplified line drawing in the storyboard and scripts below (fig. 1). The narrative unfolds from this character's point of view. The first scene, titled »Character-Led Architecture« depicts my realization of this concept. The second scene called »#FeesMustFall« highlights my first personal encounter with the #FeesMust-Fall protests, a significant socio-political event that created an openness for change among colleagues in the School of Architecture, and which leads into the third scene titled »Decolonizing the Curriculum«, which shows my personal experience of grappling with the call for a decolonized curriculum in the architecture school. In the final part of this article, called »What Does Character-Led Architecture Look Like?«, I return to the first of the above-mentioned contexts, the design studio and discuss the implementation of a first-year course titled »The Utopias Project«.

Centering on narratives in the design process, my work seeks to contribute new knowledge to architectural pedagogy and design theory. While the use of narratives in design varies, with different types including minimal, sequenced, logically sequenced, value-laden, and entertainment narratives (Grimaldi/Fokkinga/Ocnarescu 2013), I work with the last, and least explored, of these types — entertainment narrative. The main function of this type of narrative, for the designer, is to explore empathy, identification, and memory through the process of personal narratives, with the aim being to understand and include a person's attachment to history, identity, and connection to a place in the design process. These character narratives support the design process by including multiple voices, those of the users as well as that of the designer. Within the different types of narrative its use can be clustered according to whether the audience is a designer and/or user, the timing of the narrative in the design process, whether the design recalls a narrative, is accompanied by a narrative, creates a narrative, or creates a narrative-experience. These clusters of narrative use usually overlap which is true for how character-led architecture informed The Utopias Project showcased in this article.

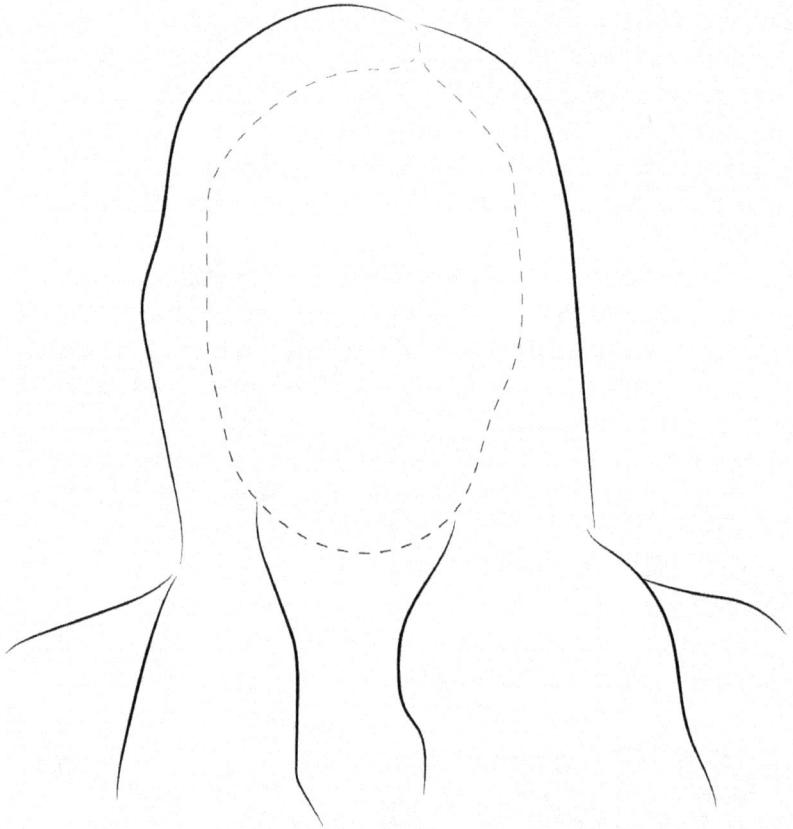

1.
My Character Line Drawing. Drawing: Anita Szentesi.

INT. WITS FILM AND TV SCREENING ROOM, DAY

Anita stands alone in the Wits Film and TV Screening Room. The LARGE
FILM SCREEN behind her. POPCORN on a TABLE next to her. She leans
forward to adjust one of the CHAIRS facing the screen. She waits,
staring at the DOUBLE DOORS at the back of the room. She takes in
several DEEP BREATHS.

The double doors open. TWO LECTURERS walk into the room. One of them
is Anita's MASTERS' SUPERVISOR.

Anita ushers them to their seats, and hands them popcorn. The room
fills up.

Anita dims the lights to black and presses PLAY on the SCREENING
DEVICE.

On the film screen, visuals of a CHARACTER in the city of
JOHANNESBURG. IMAGES OF ARTWORK dissolve through the scenes.

                                                        CUT TO:

INT. WITS SCHOOL OF ARCHITECTURE, DAY

Anita approaches the COMMUNAL MEETING TABLE in the STAFF OFFICE AREA.
The new first year STUDIO CONVENER sits at the table drinking COFFEE.

                        ANITA

        Hi, how is the new project design coming along?

                    STUDIO CONVENER

        Good so far. Remember last year's history
        project? The one where student's formed tribes
        and created tribal artefacts? I'm introducing
        that project into design. The students will need
        to design the place that their tribe inhabits.

                        ANITA

        That sounds amazing. What if we added a narrative
        to the project, like a film script that has
        a beginning, a middle and an end, where the
        students become the tribal figures in the story
        and the story is about how their tribe was formed…

                    STUDIO CONVENER

        …a mythological story about a tribal cosmogenesis,
        an alternative imagined world that they design.

2.

(A) Scene 01 – Character-Led-Architecture. Script: Anita Szentesi.

ANITA

Yes exactly, they inhabit and experience the
space as characters in the story that they
create. The acts from the script could translate
into spatial emotional experiences that are
represented in a diorama with the figures that
are acting out their tribal cosmogenesis. I
could teach them how to make a film or stop
frame animation as part of their presentation.

STUDIO CONVENER

I think that your ideas about combining these
techniques from film are very powerful… I'm
excited about this.

3.

(B) Scene 01 – Character-Led-Architecture. Script: Anita Szentesi.

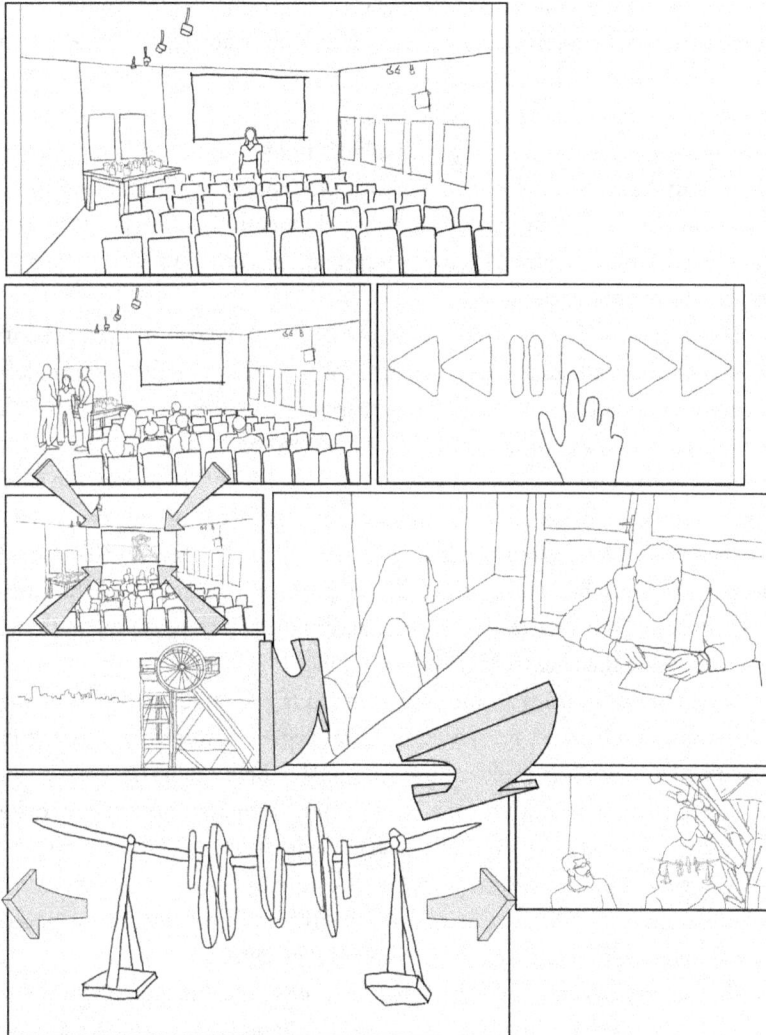

4.
Scene 01 – Character-Led-Architecture. Storyboard: Anita Szentesi.

Scene 01

The scene in (fig. 2) is written to show my realization of character-led architecture. It is written in a typical screenplay format which follows the premise of a »story told with pictures« (Field 1982: 7). The capital letters indicate the introduction of a new prop, an extra(s), or an important aspect in the scene. The script is written in such a way as to describe how the narrative will be shown as a film, in contrast to telling it like it is written in a novel (Field 1982). Each scene is a miniature story with a beginning, middle, and end that describes »an action through conflict in a unity or continuity of time and space that turns the value-charged condition of a character's life« (Mckee 1997: 233). There is no limit to a scene's length, but its objective is to reveal an aspect within the journey of the whole story.

The storyboard in (fig. 3) is a visual translation of the scene. The frames in a storyboard usually follow a structured linear temporal sequence from left to right, top to bottom. Each frame captures a major event in a story which keeps a flow in the overall narrative, while also being able to summarize events. The drawing for every frame needs to consider the setting, the characters and their postures and positions, the angle of the shot, the foreground, middle-ground, background, the time of day or atmosphere, and objects and elements that might be relevant to, and important in, that part of the story. The storyboard sets up the *mise-en-scène* within the frame, revealing both the main story and the backstory at the same time.

My narrative journey in the first scene in (fig. 2) and (fig. 3) shows the screening room where I presented my final degree film for my Master's in Film and TV in 2018. It explored the relationship between narrative (screenwriting) and the construction of *mise-en-scène* (that which appears inside the film frame), as well as the architectural considerations of place-making. Already at this stage, I was intrigued that the human-place connection exists in both disciplines, filmmaking and architecture, and considered the potential of exploring these aspects in architectural pedagogy.

That same year, 2018, I was assigned to teach in the First Year Design Studio at the University of the Witwatersrand. A change in the studio teaching team meant that one of my colleagues became the new course convener for the first- year design course, which resulted in a greater openness to change and collaboration in order to transform the existing architecture curriculum. The new first-year project sought to explore a different world view – of architecture as part of a larger cosmos – to offer an alternative to the current situation. Encouraging collaborative teaching, taking everyone's opinions and ideas in the first-year design teaching team seriously, was part of this shift. I proposed to contribute to these efforts by introducing techniques from my own practice, filmmaking. This provided an opportunity to continue my research into the relationship between architecture and film in architectural pedagogy. We discussed the potential of film; that it could be a powerful method to imagine a parallel universe, as well as represent it. Filmic narrative could be a method of designing a building through fiction rather than inherited conventional methods. The idea of designing characters, including indigenous characters, could make the process relatable to all students. Film can reach a wider audience and be understood without the use of spoken language. With the prospect of creating imagined worlds, we began to develop our studio briefs.

Scene 02

The second scene in (fig. 4) and (fig. 5) depicts my experience of the #FeesMust-Fall student protests, which started on October 14, 2015, at The University of the Witwatersrand in Johannesburg, South Africa. Students started protesting when the university administration announced an increase in university fees from 2016. That morning, I was on my way to the university for a job interview for the position of Associate Lecturer. I had applied, hoping this might allow me to transition from my tutoring job to a more permanent academic career that included teaching and research. Close to campus, I hit a wall of traffic. I understood what was happening only when the department contacted me to let me know that protesting students had blocked access to the site. I was directed to another entrance and so managed to attend the interview, albeit slightly delayed. After the interview, I was advised to leave because student protesters were gaining in number and moving to block all access points. I left campus, uncertain of what was to come.

The protest spread to Rhodes University, – joined by the #RhodesMust-Fall movement– the University of Cape Town and soon after, all the universities nationwide. University operations were suspended while protest action and negotiations took place and staff were advised to stay at home. Although our constitution protects the right to protest peacefully, violent outbursts between police and students occurred on all campuses and surrounding streets resulting in injuries and arrests. Many buildings on campuses were vandalized and damaged. Some staff who had remained on campus at the

EXT. EMPIRE ROAD, JOHANNESBURG – DAY

Early in the morning, driving in her car on her way to campus, Anita feels calm that she is on time for her interview. As she turns onto EMPIRE ROAD, she hits a wall of TRAFFIC. Not moving. She is very near the entry gate but cannot move forward. Panic sets in. She will be late. CELL PHONE DINGS. Anita looks over at the cell phone on the car seat. She reads the message.

SCHOOL SECRETARY (TEXT)

Hi, are you on your way to campus?

ANITA (TEXT)

Yes, I am, but I am stuck in a traffic jam, and I don't know what's going on, it's not moving.

SCHOOL SECRETARY (TEXT)

There is a student protest, and they are blocking the gates to the campus, you won't be able to get in.

5.

Scene 02 – #FeesMustFall. Scipt: Anita Szentesi.

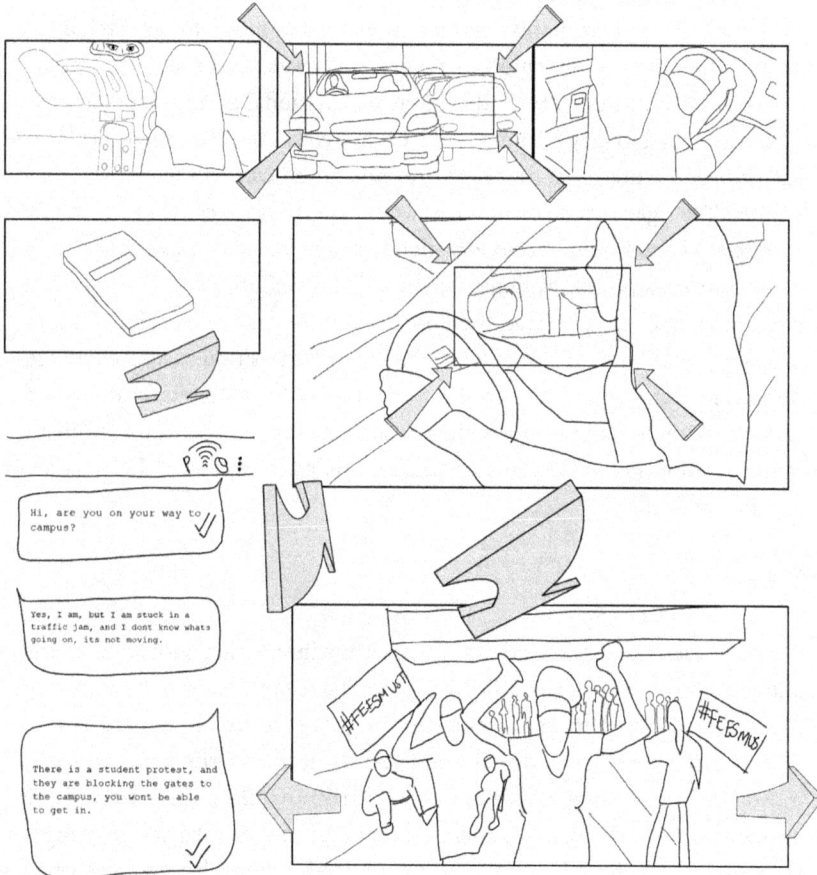

6.

Scene 02 – #FeesMustFall. Storyboard: Anita Szentesi.

beginning of the protest were intimidated by student protestors and their vehicles were vandalized and damaged. After reopening on November 2, 2015, following a two-week closure during negotiations with student representatives, the University of the Witwatersrand asked staff and students to catch up to conclude the academic year, delaying the end of year program.

At the time, I was both a staff member and a student at the university and was highly affected by the experience. As a staff member, I was affected by the call for transformation and made aware that most students felt alienated by the existing curriculum. As a student, I was concerned that I would not be able to conclude my studies. Since the national government gave the guarantee of a bursary for poor and working-class students, the #FeesMust-Fall protest did not recur during this period, and I was able to conclude my studies. The legacy of the protests, however, was that the country's youth demanded fair and equal access to higher education and universities were made aware that black students felt excluded by inherited curricula. When our new course convener was appointed to run the first-year design studio a couple of years later, he not only responded to his position as a black indigenous male lecturer, but also to the students' call for a decolonized curriculum. Working collaboratively with my colleague in this context meant that I, in my position as a white female lecturer, needed to engage with decolonizing the curriculum.

Scene 03

The third scene in (fig. 6) and (fig. 7) shows my interaction with some of the students during a design-studio workshop. The scene highlights how a group of students wanted to use indigenous language in the filmic narrative of their project. During apartheid, the South African government only recognized two official languages, English and Afrikaans. The post-apartheid government, under Nelson Mandela, recognized eleven official languages which are still in the democratic constitution today. English, however, seems to be most widely used in the spheres of government, business, education, and the media, as it is globally. As a lecturer in this context, I became aware that, unless these students chose to translate their story into English, I would not be able to understand it. I realized that I needed to be open to learn and listen: »Instead, vulnerability can foster a self-reflexive, safe, and inclusive learning environment, where class members' interactions are based on mutual respect« (Sendra 2020: 69). Linda Tuhiwai Smith states that indigenous languages are »in various states of crisis« (Tuhiwai Smith 2012: 148). The revitalization and regeneration of these languages is currently being pursued by indigenous communities as one of 25 indigenous projects that constitute a complex decolonizing research program (Tuhiwai Smith 2012). Could the character-led architecture methods in the design process of this project have created a space for this kind of engagement to happen?

As we set out to imagine alternative worlds through character and fiction, I connected the creation of these alternative paradigms to Walter Mignolo's concept of the pluriverse. »Pluriversality as a universal project is aimed not at changing the world (ontology) but at changing the beliefs and the understanding of the world (gnoseology), which would lead to changing our (all) praxis of living in the world« (Mignolo 2018: x). Pluriversality renounces that the world must be perceived as a unified totality but views the world as an interconnected diversity — a world in which many worlds coexist. Western universalism would have the right to coexist in the pluriverse as one of many cosmologies, but it would no longer be the one that subsumes and regulates all the others. Pluriversality is the entanglement of several cosmologies (Mignolo 2018). Could character-led architecture contribute to creating alternative paradigms or worlds, a pluriverse? Could a screenplay as the starting point in the design process enable a design from the point of view of characters? Could character-led architecture enable the reading of a place from multiple characters' points of view, including previously unrecorded indigenous voices, and oppose a singular hegemonic view?

Could the filmic narrative methods of screenwriting and storytelling be connected to the decolonizing methodologies of storytelling? Linda Tuhiwai Smith makes reference to storytelling as one of the indigenous research projects (Tuhiwai Smith 2012). »Story telling, oral histories, the perspectives of elders and of women have become an integral part of all indigenous research. Each individual story is powerful. But the point about the stories is not that they simply tell a story, or tell a story simply. These new stories contribute to a collective story in which every indigenous person has a place« (Tuhiwai Smith 2012: 146).

The following section will briefly showcase The Utopias Project, which was the first project where character-led architecture was introduced according to context one described above.

INT. WITS SCHOOL OF ARCHITECTURE - DAY

Anita and her COLLEAGUES are in the FIRST YEAR DESIGN STUDIO.
STUDENTS are seated at WORK BENCHES. Teaching staff meander around the
work benches. Students stop them to ask questions as they walk past.

                              STUDENT

        Ma'am, please can we discuss our narrative
        with you?

                               ANITA

        Yes, please go ahead.

                              STUDENT

        So, our story begins with a poem that one
        of us wrote, which then translates into the
        synopsis of our tribe's cosmogenesis. In both
        the poem and the synopsis, we've used the
        vernac. Is that fine?

                               ANITA

        Yes, off course, that sounds amazing.

                              STUDENT

        We'll also put in an English translation so
        that you can understand it.

                               ANITA

        Thank you, I would greatly appreciate that.

*vernac - the vernacular language

7.

Scene 03 – Decolonizing the Curriculum. Scipt: Anita Szentesi.

It gave a her a message, ga a batla go tshela botshelo bo bo iketlileng, a sa tshelele mo letshogong, go tlhokega gore a tlise lewelana la gagwe mo legageng le mo bosigong bona **(if she wants to live a life of peace, and not live in fear, she needs to bring her twin to the cave tonight).**

Group 03. (2021). Project Kgoro Ya Kuruman. *Tales of a Two Faced Snake*. Wits School of Architecture and Planning.

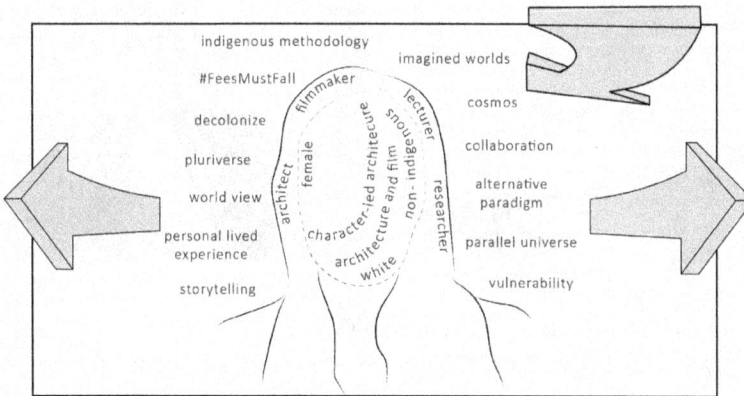

8.

Scene 03 – Decolonizing the Curriculum. Storyboard: Anita Szentesi.

9.
Storyboard: Group Selenites First Year Design Studio, Wits School of Architecture and Planning, 2019.

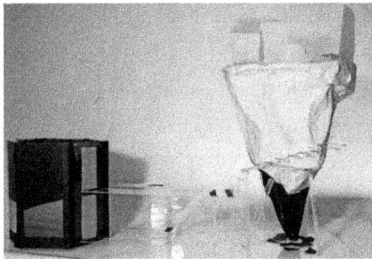

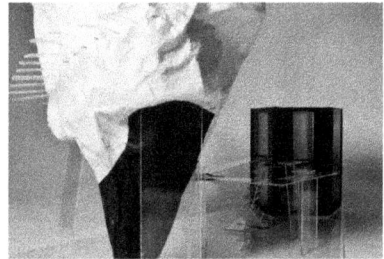

10. – 11.
Cosmos Model: Group Sitaga First Year Design Studio,
Wits School of Architecture and Planning, 2018. Photography: Anita Szentesi.

What Does Character-led Architecture Look Like?

The Utopias Project was designed to include a large group-work component and an individual design component. In groups, the students wrote a script about the genesis of a cosmos and an imagined community through invented characters. This was visualized into a storyboard (fig. 8). The fictional world from the storyboard was then translated into a cosmos model, (fig. 9) and (fig. 10), which was conceived and built, including scale-model figures of a protagonist and antagonist, who experienced the spatial journey. The cosmos model included three regions, representing the cosmogenesis narrative, following the three acts of a storytelling structure. These regions needed to relate to each other visually, conceptually, and spatially. The students were required to translate the emotional transformation of the character in each region into a spatial experience. With the narrative, cosmos model and characters in place, the students made stop-frame animations to capture the story unfolding from the point of view of the characters (fig. 11). In the next step of the project, students rewrote their group scripts to become the characters in a re-enactment of their cosmogenesis on stage. Thereafter, they created individual designs translating the cosmos model into a stage set for the three acts of performance (fig. 12). The final stage of the project was a public exhibition (fig. 13) of the drawings, models, and stage sets accompanied by a film screening of the stop-frame animations and stage performances. To include this student work in my research, I needed to address ethical obligations on numerous levels.[3]

    The filmic narrative approach in The Utopias Project was uniquely visible in terms of how it deepened the process and the method, as well as the outcomes of the inquiry. It was felt that the bar was raised regarding a rethink of

---

3 The work produced as part of my employment within the university partly belongs to this institution, so my research requires approval by an ethics committee. Second, my position as a lecturer leads to a power imbalance between me and my students. My ethical responsibility was to ensure that students did not feel forced to agree to the sharing of their work, so I created an informed consent letter, telling students how their work would be used in our research and how it might be disseminated in exhibitions and on media platforms such as YouTube. It also gave them the opportunity to withdraw their consent. Finally, it was important for students to understand where they would remain anonymous and where they would not. Creating films meant becoming aware of how visual images may cause their audience to be moved (Butler 2012), therefore image-producers also have ethical obligations toward the audience (Roberts 2021).

12.

Stop Frame Animation: Group Sitaga First Year Design Studio,
Wits School of Architecture and Planning, 2018.

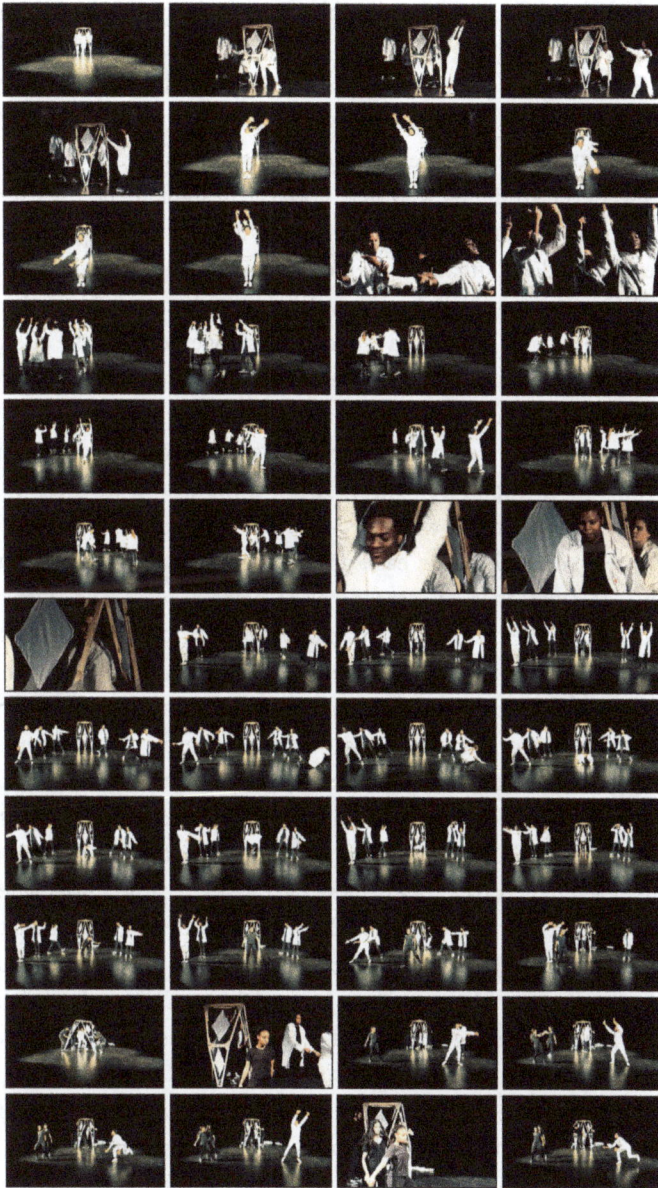

13.
Performance at Wits Amphitheatre, Group Selenites First Year Design Studio. Wits School of Architecture and Planning, 2019.
Film and stills: Anita Szentesi.

architecture, teaching, and learning for the 21st century in an African context, particularly with regard to the re-engagement of the body as a crucial media for the learning and practice of architecture. In The Utopias Project, overlapping clusters of narrative use occurred (Grimaldi/Fokkinga/ Ocnarescu, 2013). Initially, the audience of this filmic narrative in the design process were the students, who were both the designers and the users. The students created their own character-led narratives in imagined settings and then realized and inhabited their creations. Narrative occurred throughout the design process, including in the final presentations. The final designs, including the cosmos model and the stage sets, together with the interaction of the scaled figures and students, created an emotional journey in a setting that supported this emotion, thus establishing not only a narrative through the design, but also an emotional narrative-spatial experience. The Utopias Project aimed to explore empathy, identification, and memory through imagined character stories which drew from the personal stories of students from diverse backgrounds in each group. The aim was to enable an understanding, as a designer, of someone else's point of view, and their attachment to culture, history, identity, and connection to place. Character-led architecture in this scenario was intended to support the group in their design process and to achieve a design that was inclusive and collaborative.

Five lecturers worked with twelve groups of seven to eight students each. In this studio context, the facilitators were the lecturers, and the participants were the students; however, these roles blurred and the atmosphere became collaborative. From the beginning, we worked together with our students to develop their narratives. These narratives became a brief which the students created for themselves and that we responded to, instead of telling them how things ought to be. In both the project's group- and individual-work components, the narratives evolved into collaborative briefs that drove the project. The large amount of group work, despite enabling a collaborative environment, also caused issues in the marking process, as some weaker students benefited from their stronger peers, which made it difficult to assess individual students' capabilities fairly. In a second iteration of the project in 2019, we placed more emphasis on the individual set design marks to counteract this. Frictions among group members, caused by varying investments of time and effort, were addressed by a project team schedule developed in a workshop where each student discussed their role and tasks within the team, and a project manager was appointed.

14.
Utopias Project Exhibition at Wits School of Architecture and Planning, 2018.
Photography: Anita Szentesi.

The challenges of introducing this kind of filmic narrative into the architectural design studio occurred first within the teaching team who were largely unfamiliar with this working method and required guidance from myself to assist the students. The students were required to undertake an unusual amount of writing for this project and their writing skills were not strong. Additional writing assistance was required from the university to develop the students' critical writing skills in this regard.

For their narratives, the students were introduced to Western mythological stories and African myths to grasp the modern narrative structure known as »The Hero's Journey« (Campbell 1990) which translates into the three-act linear script structure used in most Hollywood films. We created a logline that we gave to the students, which is approximately a 25 word description of an entire narrative. The stories were centered around tribal members celebrating the journey of their origins within a place that they have built for celebration. The students created stories within these guidelines. Each group's story was unique in terms of the characters they created and the places that they imagined. However, there was an underlying theme of dystopia/utopia in all of the stories, due to the overall theme of the project that we gave them. Perhaps, for future explorations, we could loosen these guidelines so that students' narratives are a truer reflection of the diversity of the class, which is what we were aiming to include.

The narrative in the design process also created new opportunities to present the architectural project. First, through film, in the student's stop-frame animations, and second, through theatre and performance, which was introduced to the project by one of our colleagues in the first-year design teaching team collaboration, and third, the performances were filmed by myself to be screened at the exhibition and uploaded onto our YouTube channel. In the stop-frame animations, the students created and experienced the journey of the world they created through the scaled characters inside the cosmos model, however, the translated performance on the stage enabled them to experience this journey for themselves; creating spatial experiences on a stage between their bodies, the stage sets, and the way in which they moved the sets around. The narrative of the students' designs was expressed in different forms of presentation. The architecture became a product of the narrative, as well as a background for the narrative, but it also became one of the characters, as the students moved their stage sets around to show how the origins of their tribe progressed. Film and theater also added another layer of audience, the viewers, who were not involved in the design process, but experienced the narrative in its presentation.

Overall, The Utopias Project was a success for pedagogic transformation, as well as new and innovative ways of teaching design. This context of the project enabled students to role play, practically build their designs, experience the space and scale of their different models, gain a technical understanding of materiality, and literally inhabit the worlds that they created, personally experiencing the success or failure of their design decisions. They formed their own social codes as groups and went on to develop practices embodying their values, designing not only physical structures, but also social and perhaps even spiritual ones that could guide them into a desired future. This interdisciplinary pedagogical approach not only enhanced the students' ability to communicate their ideas but enabled them to embody their spatial experiences and contexts, as well as to self-evaluate by distancing themselves and watching their own work on film. The Utopias Project was also successful in that it enabled the inclusion of all students from different backgrounds to participate and learn from the point of view of characters who were embodied in places, rather than try and grasp context from an abstract and formal approach.

References

Butler, Judith (2012): »Precarious Life, Vulnerability, and the Ethics of Cohabitation«, in: The Journal of Speculative Philosophy26/2. Special Issue with The Society for Phenomenology and Existential Philosophy, 134–151.

Campbell, J. (1990): The Hero's Journey: The World of Joseph Campbell, New York: HarperCollins Publishers.

Candy, Linda (2002): Practice Based Research: A Guide, Sydney: Creativity and Cognition Studios.

Cheatle, Emma (2013): »Part-Architecture: the Maison de Verre through the Large Glass«. Unpublished PhD thesis, The Bartlett School of Architecture, University College London.

Cross, Nigel (2006): Designerly Ways of Knowing, London: Springer.

Escobar, Arturo (2018): Designs for the Pluriverse: Radical Interdependence, Autonomy, and the Making of Worlds, Durham, NC/ London: Duke University Press.

Field, Syd (1982): The Foundations of Screenwriting, New York: Delta.

Grimaldi, S/Fokkinga, S./Ocnarescu, I. (2013): »Narratives in Design: A Study of the Types, Applications and Functions of Narratives in Design Practice« ,Designing Pleasurable Products and Interfaces, DPPI'13 Praxis and Poetics, Northumbria University, Newcastle upon Tyne, September, 3 –5, 2013. New York: Association for Computing Machinery, 201 –210. https://dl.acm.org/doi/10.1145/2513506.2513528 (accessed: January 28, 2022).

Haseman, Brad (2006): »A Manifesto for Performative Research«, in: *Media International Australia* 118, 98–106

Mattsson, Helena (2018) »A Critical Historiography, Again: Sounds from a Mute History«, in: Frichot, Hélène/ Sandi, Gunnar/Schwalm, Bettina, *After Effects: Theories and Methodologies in Architectural Research*, Barcelona: Actar Publishers.

Mckee, Robert (1997). *Story: Substance, Structure, Style and the Principles of Screenwriting*. New York: Regan Books.

Mignolo, Walter (2018): *Constructing the Pluriverse: The Geopolitics of Knowledge*, Durham, NC/London: Duke University Press.

Roberts, David (2021): »Reflect Critically, Act Fearlessly«. Lecture on Approaching Research Practice in Architecture: Module 5, Speculative Ethics, March 19, 2021.

Sendra, Estrella (2020): »Video Essays: Curating and Transforming Film Education through Artistic Research«, in: *International Journal of Film and Media Arts* 2, 65–81.

Tuhiwai Smith, Linda (2012): *Decolonizing Methodologies: Research and Indigenous Peoples*, London: Zed Books Ltd.

YouTube Link to (fig.12) Group Selenites Performance at Wits Amphitheatre: »The Utopias Project 2019 Video 09 Group 09 Performance«, YouTube. Uploaded by Anita Szentesi, November 23, 2020, https://youtu.be/ygUndjpqU3k

Dimensions of Architectural Knowledge, 2022-03 ಶ
https://doi.org/10.14361/dak-2022-0321

TEXTBOOK
A Guide to the Teaching of Construction

Gabriel Bernard Guelle

Abstract: Between the 1920s and the 1970s in France, the teaching of construction in architecture schools has undergone major modifications in relation to its social, intellectual, and
professional context. The present article aims to understand the role played by the teaching of
construction in the architects' relationship to building techniques and to engineers. The study of
a set of textbooks, considered as pedagogical devices and professional guides, and used in 1921
by Edouard Arnaud to teach construction at the Ecole Centrale des Arts et Manufactures, and
at the Ecole Nationale Supérieure des Beaux-Arts, tackles the role of teaching construction in
architecture and engineering curricula and its influence on the profession. This study relies on
a comprehensive analysis of the set of textbooks, considering its materiality and its written and
visual content, combined with relevant elements from its author's biography, publications, and
pedagogical production.

Keywords: Teaching, Construction, Textbook, Architect, Engineer.

On the Teaching of Construction in Architecture Schools in the 20th century in France

In France, the teaching of construction in architecture schools has been debated among both teachers and professionals since the second half of the
19th century (Epron 1997: 120–121). From 1819 to 1968, construction was one of
the three main disciplines of the training provided in the architecture section of the Ecole Nationale Supérieure des Beaux-Arts in Paris, one of the
dominant models regarding architectural education in Europe (Pfammatter
2000). Yet, the teaching of construction in architecture schools in the 20th
century in France has barely been studied, even if research on architectural
and engineering education and those professions often hints at its importance
(Epron 1997; Saint 2007). Moreover, the unifying aspect of the teaching of

Corresponding author: Gabriel Bernard Guelle (Laboratoire Architecture, territoire, environnement
(EA7464), Ecole doctorale Homme, Sociétés, Risques, Territoire (ED556 HSRT), Ensa Normandie, France);
gabriel.bernard-guelle@rouen.archi.fr; http://orcid.org/0000-0003-3300-1926

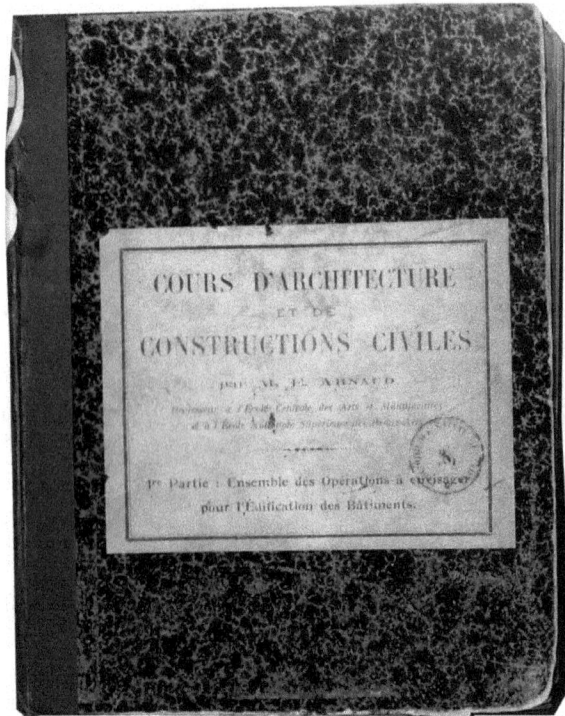

1.
Cover of the first volume (out of five) of the 1921 edition of Edouard Arnaud's textbook. Source: Bibliothèque Sainte-Geneviève, Paris, France.
Photographer: Gabriel Bernard Guelle.

construction for architects and engineers is seldom considered in the French research (Nègre 2011; Nègre 2012; Thibault 2017), while research from the German cultural space often underlines it (Lichtenstein 2012; Hassler et al. 2019).

To fill out the gaps in the existing research, my PhD thesis offers a historical study on the teaching of construction in France between the 1920s and the 1970s in relation to its pedagogical, social, and professional context. This historical study is complemented by a comparative approach between France and the German cultural space to debunk the myth of a »French cultural exception« regarding architectural education and the profession. This combined approach aims at understanding the importance of teaching construction in the definition of the architects' relationship to building techniques and to engineers, so that these aspects can be included in the design of current construction lessons.

In the first half of the 20th century, the architecture section of the Ecole des Beaux-Arts was the most influential architectural school in France as it organized the only competition that granted access to public procurement. This article offers an insight into the teaching of Edouard Arnaud in this architecture school through the study of an early version of his textbook, published in 1921, (fig. 1) which was found at the public library of Sainte-Geneviève in Paris, at a time when all archive centres in France had closed due to the Covid-19 pandemic.[1]

The existing research on Edouard Arnaud's professorial work barely analyzes the textbook itself. In his Master's thesis, Jean Thevenot (1994) studies Arnaud's teaching in both schools in relation to the teacher's career as an architect and an engineer, and to the schools' curriculum and pedagogical policy regarding construction at the time. Thevenot relies on the textbook to document Arnaud's pedagogy and focuses on the role played by reinforced concrete in its content. In his book, Jean-Pierre Epron (1997) uses Arnaud's textbook as a means to understand his pedagogy in relation to the contemporary »technical debate«. He only mentions the structure of the textbook and focuses on the chapter on »composition« to demonstrate the broader thesis of his research, the »eclecticism« theory in architecture. In her article on the use of photography in teaching construction, Amandine Diener (2016)

---

1 The teaching of construction provided at the architecture section of the Ecole Nationale Supérieure des Beaux-Arts by Edouard Arnaud (1864–1943) from 1920 to 1934, and then by François Vitale (1898–1962) from 1935 to 1962, is a focal point of my PhD research.

studies a collection of glass plates used by François Vitale, including a set designed by his predecessor Edouard Arnaud for his own teaching. In her introduction, she mentions the textbook in relation to the glass plates as part of the pedagogical devices designed by Edouard Arnaud for his teaching without cross-analyzing them. Finally, Antonio Brucculeri studies Arnaud's teaching in both schools to measure its impact on architectural and engineering training (Brucculeri 2006). He uses the textbook, presented as an »illustrated guide« complementing the glass plates to analyze Arnaud's pedagogy while focusing on the iconography, and mentions the evolution of the content between the 1920 and 1931 edition. To complement the existing research, a comprehensive study of the textbook that demonstrates its purpose as a pedagogical device, but also as a professional guide, would illuminate the role played by the teaching of construction in architectural education.

Edouard Arnaud's Textbook:
From Pedagogical Device to Professional Guide

After his nomination to the position of Dean of Construction at the Ecole Nationale Supérieure des Beaux-Arts in 1921, Edouard Arnaud proceeded to reform the teaching of construction there, as he also did in 1920 at the Ecole Centrale des Arts et Manufactures where he had already been giving lectures for approximately ten years (Arnaud 1921g: 2). His conjoint reform is meant to rectify the shortcomings of the contemporary teaching of construction in both schools and is based on the professor's first-hand knowledge as their former student and his professional experience as an architect and engineer.

To achieve his goal, Arnaud relied on two pedagogical tools: a collection of glass plates and a set of textbooks entitled »Cours d'architecture et de constructions civiles« (Arnaud 1921a,b,c,d,e,f). While the glass plates represented a technical innovation, as their use was made accessible to the public in the 1890s (Diener 2016), textbooks had belonged to French architectural and engineering teaching since the modern era, with treatises such as *Nouvelles inventions pour bien bastir a petits frais*, published by Philibert de l'Orme in 1561. But, while the use of textbooks was instituted at the Ecole centrale, who owned a printing works to publish them, their use at the Ecole des Beaux-Arts relied on the teachers' initiative. Textbooks used there were therefore more diverse in their form and content, depending on the purpose their author gave them.

In 1921, Arnaud introduced his reform of the construction curriculum at the Ecole Nationale Supérieure des Beaux-Arts with the following statement:

> »[E]n France nous avons le plus pressant besoin pour rebâtir nos régions dévastées d'une pépinière d'excellents constructeurs qu'il faut pouvoir former rapidement et sûrement, qui soient utiles sur les chantiers dès leur sortie de l'école et qui puissent se perfectionner, où qu'ils se trouvent, par leurs propres moyens.«

> »In France, we have the most urgent need for a body of skilled constructors, who can be trained properly and efficiently, who will be proficient on the construction site immediately after their graduation, and who will be able to complete their education, wherever they are, on their own, to rebuild our devastated regions.« (Arnaud, 1921g: 2).2

This statement indicates the orientation of the whole reform, including the textbook. To ensure the training of this body of skilled constructors before and after their graduation, Arnaud designed his textbook not only as a tool to improve the teaching of construction, but also as a professional guide responding to the needs of the French architecture trade after the First World War.

Textbook as a Pedagogical Device: Improving the Teaching of Construction
As he himself explained when presenting his reform of the teaching of construction, Arnaud designed his handbook to offer three major pedagogical improvements (Arnaud 1921g). First, he claimed that his textbook was meant to free students from notetaking, an error-strewn and time-consuming practice observed in »traditional« dictated lessons. As the textbook provided exact, complete, and up-to-date content, the students could concentrate on the lecture without making notes, thus sparing time for the teacher to include more information in the session. Second, the pictures projected in the amphitheater using glass plates were also reproduced in the textbook to help students memorize the lesson and to develop a visual culture as part of their training as architects or engineers (fig. 2). At home, the handbook offers a reliable study support, free of mistakes, and richly illustrated so that students can use it to prepare for exams or as material for other classes.

---

2 All translations from French to English were made by the author.

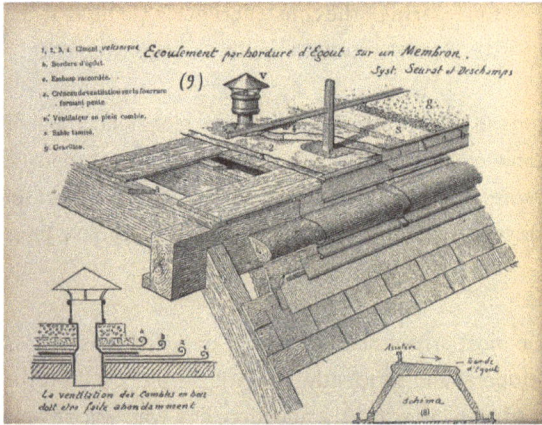

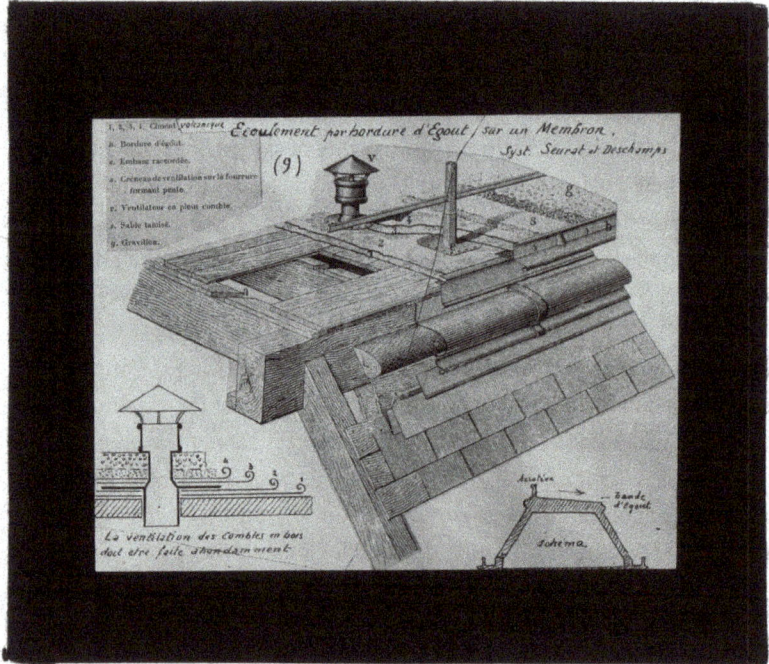

2.

Illustration of a gutter technique from the second part of the lesson (Arnaud, 1921c:380) and matching glass plate (Vitale n.d.). The glass plate shows how Arnaud composed this illustration. First he clipped the central picture and its key out of a printed source, then added a title and diagrams to clarify the constructive system depicted in the original picture. Source: 1. Bibliothèque Nationale de France, Paris, France 2. Cité de l'Architecture et du Patrimoine/Centre d'Archives de l'Architecture contemporaine, Paris, France.

This use of the textbook was probably enforced at the Ecole Centrale des Arts et Manufactures, as indicated by the yearly editions from 1919 to 1929 that were found in the school's archives gathered at the Archives nationales de France. By owning a printing works, the Ecole centrale was probably able to publish its textbooks at minimal cost and sell them to students at a low price. This hypothesis is sustained by the collection of handbooks found in the archives of François Vitale, who studied at the Ecole centrale between 1919 and 1921 (Vitale 1919–1925). This collection indicates that the 1921 edition of Arnaud's set of textbooks was a standard production of the Imprimerie des arts et manufactures except for its numerous illustrations and its sixth volume, a folio album of the size of 44 x 29 cm gathering 262 plates. The set of textbooks was sold along with other similar publications to all the students at the Ecole centrale.

On the other hand, it is not certain that students at the Ecole Nationale Supérieure des Beaux-Arts could use this set of textbooks in the same way that their peers at the Ecole centrale did. As the textbooks were printed by the Imprimerie des arts et manufactures, students outside the Ecole centrale may not have been able to purchase it in the same condition, although the journal *L'Architecture* mentions a larger edition in 1923 which met demand from both architects and engineers in and outside of the Ecole centrale and the Ecole des Beaux-Arts (»Bibliogaphie« 1923). Students at the latter may have borrowed the textbook, whether from the school's library or from their peers, as it was common for an atelier, a group of pupils studying architectural design at the Ecole des Beaux-Arts under the guidance of a patron to share books in the form of a small private library (Garric 2011). In this case, the first improvement envisioned by Edouard Arnaud may have been reduced.

Second, the textbook's organization and content reflected the global educational effort made by the teacher, as Arnaud himself declared in the introduction to the lesson:

»Pour rendre ce cours plus pratique, plus ordonné et plus utile pour vous [les étudiants], j'adopterai dans mon enseignement l'ordre suivant lequel le bâti-ment s'édifie.«

»To make this lecture more practical, more methodical, and more useful to you [students], I will follow in my teaching the sequence in which an edifice is built.« (Arnaud 1921a: 9)

In the 1921 edition, Arnaud divides the lesson into three parts. In »Opérations à envisager pour l'édification d'un bâtiment« he defines twelve operations leading from the program issued by a client to the completion of the building. Then, in »Technique du bâtiment«, he presents the different construction techniques available at the time in order of their execution, from groundwork to roofing. In »Application du cours de constructions civiles«, he finally shows how his method can be put to practical use through a case study based on one of his own realizations, a housing estate in Paris. The structure of this lesson serves three didactic purposes. First, it facilitates the understanding and learning of the lesson's content by presenting it in a logical, practical order that the student can observe in architectural practice. Second, this partition offers a progression from a comprehensive approach to the act of building, with general guidelines given in the first part, to detailed knowledge of construction techniques which are presented in the second part of the lesson. Finally, it offers an evolution from theory to practice by putting the theoretical knowledge presented in the first two parts to practical use in the case study in the final part of the lesson.

This didactic effort is also apparent in the third chapter of the first part of the lesson, which can be regarded as its most important moment, consisting of 80 out of 170 pages. In this chapter, Edouard Arnaud observes the same progression from theory to practice to thoroughly explain the notion of »composition« which he regards as »the key to success« (Arnaud 1921a: 2). After an almost philosophical introduction, he presents the main concepts and rules of his composition theory, followed by a precise description of the design process and work method, and he concluded with an illustrated application based on the program of the Ecole centrale (fig. 3), which is well known to the students of this school. This thorough explanation is both didactic and unusual. As Edouard Arnaud underlined in his introduction, the teaching of the Ecole centrale dedicated little to no time to composition, while the teaching of the Ecole des Beaux-Arts revolved around it (Arnaud 1921a: 2). Yet, even if this notion was a central part of the former, it was never explicitly taught. Students had to learn it through practice, first in the atelier under the guidance of their patron, a famous architect appointed by the school or chosen by the students to teach architectural design, then, by helping with older students' projects, and finally, by submitting their own work to competitions to earn prizes. Thus, Arnaud's lesson on composition can be seen as an attempt to improve both schools' pedagogy by clarifying this key notion for students.

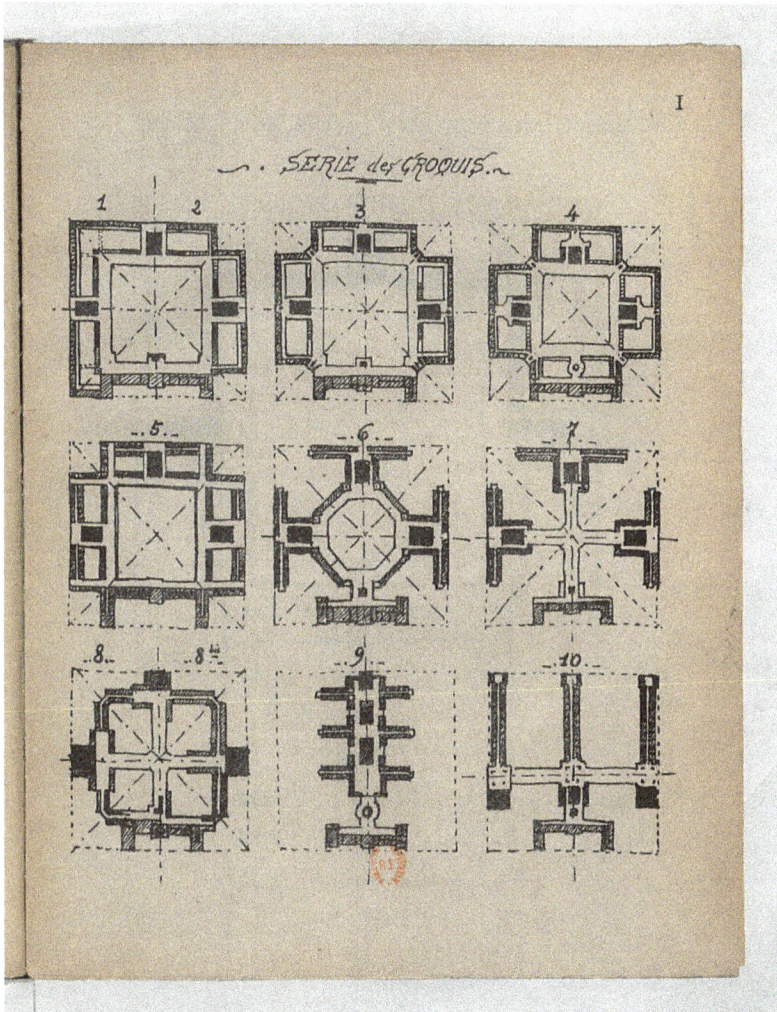

3.
Sketches illustrating the first steps of Arnaud's work method for composition (Arnaud 1921a: I). After designing multiple options that could accommodate the program (Arnaud 1921a: I), Source: Bibliothèque Nationale de France, Paris, France.

— 31 —

(40,83), comprenant, avons-nous vu, une partie tubulaire et une partie en forme de T supportant la poutre-ceinture. Depuis là, seule la forme tubulaire continuera.

Poteaux au droit des Bow Windows.

Les bow-windows font saillie sur l'alignement de la façade (fig. 17). La poutre-ceinture devra en faire autant (elle sera élargie) et pour la supporter on donnera en élévation, à la partie supplémentaire en forme de T des poteaux, un élargissement affectant la forme d'une console très allongée.

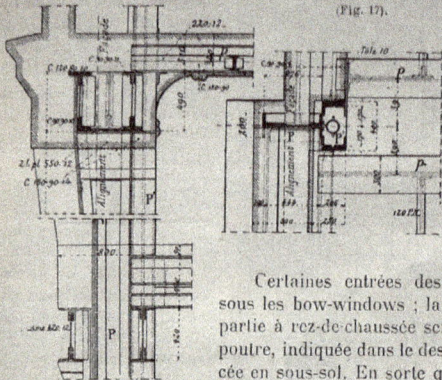

Certaines entrées des immeubles se font sous les bow-windows ; la maçonnerie de cette partie à rez-de-chaussée sera supportée par une poutre, indiquée dans le dessin (fig.17) en P placée en sous-sol. En sorte qu'en dessous de cette poutre, le sous-sol sera libre. La coupe verticale est faite dans l'axe du bow-window. La photographie (fig. 18) montre, dans les deux premiers poteaux, la forme de console support au droit des bow windows dont je viens de parler.

Je vous donne en façade (fig. 19) l'entrée d'un des immeubles située sous un bow-window. Ces entrées seront les seules liaisons de maçonnerie entre la façade supérieure suspendue et le sol, parce que ce sont les seules qui pourront être déterminées d'une façon immuable et obligatoire.

(Fig. 17).

(Fig. 18).

4.

Presentation of the metal frame of the housing estate »Rue des Italiens« (Arnaud 1921e: 31). Photographs of the construction site and sections on bow-windows illustrate Arnaud's description of the construction work. Source: Bibliothèque Sainte Geneviève, Paris, France.

Finally, Arnaud designed the application part of his textbook to replace visits to construction sites. Even if he claims that »practice is actually learnt on the construction site« the teacher argues that such visits are time-consuming, dangerous, and profitable to only a few students (Arnaud 1921g: 1). Therefore, he conceived of a paper alternative which offered both a comprehensive overview of the act of building and a concrete example of how his teaching could be implemented. Following the same course as the lesson, Arnaud presents the realization of the housing operation »Rue des Italiens« that he conducted for the company l'Urbaine-Vie in the 1910s. His presentation emphasizes the relationship between program, design, and construction and links every step of the project to the construction site. This relation is underlined by italicized remarks in the text and by the illustrations, mostly photographs taken on the construction site (fig. 4).

Textbook as a Professional Guide: Accompanying Practice
In the last part of his textbook, Edouard Arnaud declares, regarding operations such as »Rue des Italiens«:

> »L'Architecte, qui ne construit pas avec ses deniers et qui est responsable du bon rendement des capitaux qui lui sont confiés, a le devoir de sacrifier à l'utilité son sentiment de l'unité, de l'harmonie et son désir, en toute autre circonstance bien légitime, de faire une belle œuvre.«

> »The architect, who does not build on their own dime and is responsible for the good return of the capital they were given, has the duty to sacrifice their sense of unity, of harmony, and their desire, otherwise legitimate, to achieve a masterpiece to utility.« (Arnaud, 1921e: 8)

This statement clashes with the approach to architectural design presented in the previous part of the lesson. As a result, the author's view of composition in the application part of the lesson reveals the gap between the ideal program of the Ecole Centrale des Arts et Manufactures, which was used in the chapter dedicated to composition, and the reality of the trade for which Edouard Arnaud prepared his students. Arnaud's textbook can therefore not only be seen as a pedagogical device but also as a professional guide.

This aim was first expressed in the textbook's material form. The octavo format of 22 x 16 cm, and the relative slimness of the five first volumes made them easy to handle and carry around. This format was the same as most of the publications of the Imprimerie des arts et manufactures which may initially result from an economic and practical decision made by the Ecole centrale, which acted as a publishing house for all its textbooks. However, this format also served Edouard Arnaud's design as he conceived of his textbooks as a set of references which could be carried around by professionals and used on the construction site (Arnaud 1921g: 2). Plus, the division of the lesson's content into five volumes identifies the general guidelines to lead a project (Part 1: »Opérations à envisager pour l'édification d'un bâtiment« vol.1) from the set of references on building techniques (Part 2: »Technique du bâtiment« vol.2, vol.3, and vol.4), and the application of the lesson (Part 3: »Application du cours de constructions civiles« vol.5). This division facilitates the process of referring to the lesson and makes the more »didactic« third part able to be detached from the other two. This reflexion on the format is exposed when comparing the 1921 edition of the lesson printed by the Imprimerie des arts et manufactures with the 1931 edition published by the Librairie Polytechnique (Arnaud 1931). While the 1921 edition was designed for students, the 1931 edition is intended for a larger public as indicated by the content of the catalog of the Librairie Polytechnique that covers a large range of subjects from architecture to sports. This change in the target audience is further shown in the form and content of the 1931 edition. Adopting the standard format set by the Librairie Polytechnique for its publications, the 1931 edition of the »Cours d'architecture et de constructions civiles« is composed of two quarto volumes of around 30 x 22 cm of 600 and 755 pages each, covered in a crimson percale cotton engraved with the title of the lesson and the name of the author in silver letters (fig. 5). The first volume gathers the first part of the lesson and 27 chapters of the second part of the lesson, while the second volume covers the remaining 38 chapters of the second part of the lesson, leaving the third part of the lesson out. Those changes in the format and the content indicate that the 1931 edition of the lesson is not designed for students anymore, as it is likely to be expensive and it discards a major didactic part. For established professionals however, it can be included in their library and used as a reference point. Thus, this edition of the »Cours d'architecture et de construction civiles« loses its role as a pedagogical device and only serves as a professional guide.

This dimension is already underlined by Edouard Arnaud in 1921, when describing his textbook:

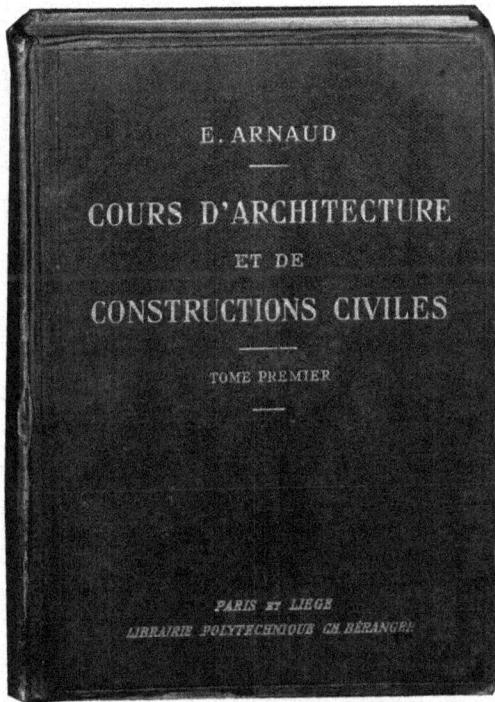

5.
Cover of the first volume (out of two) of the 1931 edition of Edouard Arnaud's textbook. Source: Personal archives of Françoise Boudon.
Photography: Gabriel Bernard Guelle.

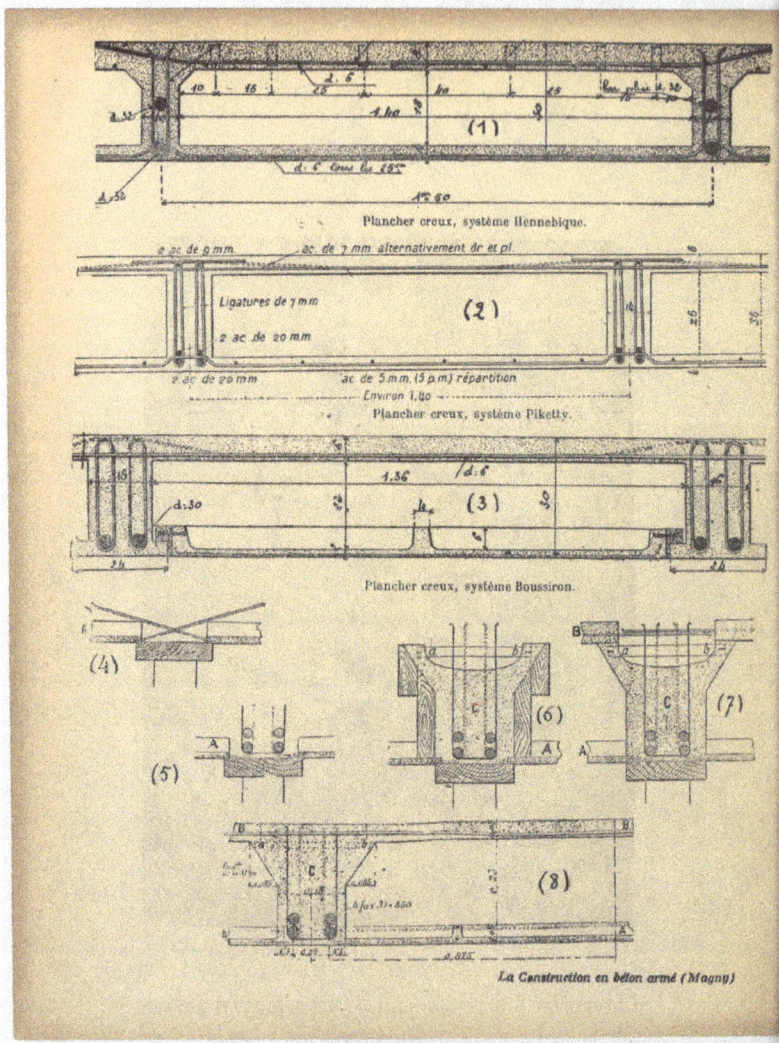

6.

Illustrations of foundation and reinforced concrete techniques from the second part of the lesson (Arnaud 1921b: 528). The inscriptions at the bottom right of p. 528 indicate it's pictures' source. On p.528, he numbered the graphics from (1) to (8) to refer to them in the text. Source: Bibliothèque Nationale de France, Paris, France.

»Il [L'élève] doit trouver dans cette documentation tous les procédés de construction et une expérience que sans cela il ne pourrait acquérir qu'à la fin d'une
longue carrière. «

»They [the student] must find in this documentation all the construction techniques and an experience that they would otherwise acquire only at the end of
a long career«. (Arnaud 1921g: 2)

While the »Cours d'architecture et de construction civiles« may serve as a
point of reference for established practitioners it is first meant to guide
young graduates' first steps into the professional world. This aim is evident
in the textbook by the position of mentor Edouard Arnaud adopts toward the
reader. At the age of 57, the teacher had been working on various projects as
an architect and an engineer for 25 years, among which included the first
reinforced concrete building realized by Hennebique. His nomination as
Architecte des bâtiments civils et palais nationaux (1919) distinguished him
as a knowledgable expert on construction matters who was recognized by
the state (cf. Teyssot 1982). Thus, Edouard Arnaud addressed his students as
a seasoned professional using first-person narration in the textbook and providing advice and remarks on various subjects, including professional policies and construction techniques. His expertise was shown not only in the
information he shared, but also by the multiple sources of the illustrations
that were presented in the second part of the lesson, among which were the
Encyclopaedia of Construction, edited by Planat, the architectural theory lesson
of Guadet, and technical booklets issued by firms (Arnaud 1931b: 737–738). To
better include those illustrations in his lesson, Arnaud annotated them (fig.
6) and combined them together with photographs of his own realizations to
depict the execution of the building techniques they illustrated (fig. 7). By
skilfully arranging his own professional knowledge with other references,
Edouard Arnaud offered a comprehensive professional guide for architects
and engineers.

Finally, the 1921 edition of this textbook addresses both the architect and
the engineer. Through its form, Arnaud's textbook combines the traits of architecture handbooks, which had a preponderant graphic dimension and
were often presented in the form of a folio album, and engineering handbooks, characterized by their thorough written explanations (Garric 2011).
Although it was printed by the Imprimerie des arts et manufactures, it was
probably used for lectures at both the Ecole centrale and the Ecole des Beaux-

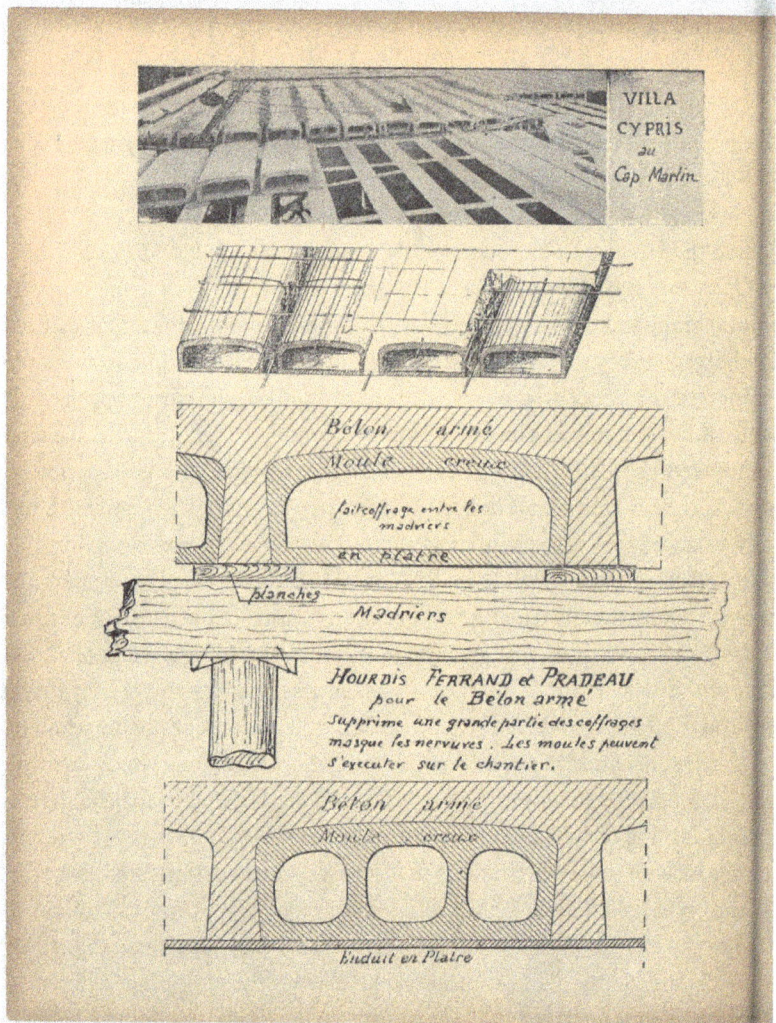

7.
Illustration of the hollow bricks system from »Ferrand et Pradeau« from the second part of the lesson (Arnaud 1921b: 534). Drawings illustrating the system are complemented with a photograph of its execution on the construction site of the Villa Cypris in Cap Martin, France, one of Arnaud's realizations. Source: Bibliothèque Nationale de France, Paris, France.

Arts, as it was available at the library of the latter and no Beaux-Arts edition can be found. This hypothesis of a double audience is also supported by the fact that, despite addressing second-year students at the Ecole centrale who are to obtain an engineering diploma, Edouard Arnaud makes several references to the architectural practice in the introduction. His description of the trade, mentioning composition and »public competitions«, his shift from the content of engineering studies to the professional role of the architect, and the repeated use of the term »constructeur« (Arnaud, 1921a: 4) when referring to his students' future careers shows that his lesson is relevant to both architects and engineers. In doing so, Edouard Arnaud reminds us that neither professional title was regulated at the time. In France, the »Loi sur les conditions de délivrance et usage du titre d'ingénieur diplômé« passed on July 10, 1934 and the »Loi instituant l'ordre des architectes et réglementant le titre et la profession d'architecte« passed on December 31, 1940 are the first to regulate the architect and engineer titles, even if both the engineering and the architecture diploma precede them. Prior to these laws, the distinction between architects and engineers was less clear than the division between the schools would have us believe which justifies the use of the same textbook in both schools.

The Teaching of Construction: A Key to the Definition of the Architects' Relationship to Technique and to Engineers

With his textbook, Edouard Arnaud answers both contemporary pedagogical and professional questions that his experience as a student, a teacher, an architect and an engineer allowed him to identify. As a pedagogical device the textbook improves on the material and didactic aspects of teaching construction at both the Ecole Nationale Supérieure des Beaux-Arts and at the Ecole Centrale des Arts et Manufactures. As a professional guide, it furthers the training of young professionals outside the school, therefore improving on the practice generally.

Furthermore, Arnaud's handbook demonstrates that the teaching of construction is key to the training and professional practice of architects and engineers. First, it connects education with the profession by organizing all the knowledge gathered in the training into a coherent sequence regarding the reality of the trade and puts it into practice using concrete examples. Second, it provides a body of architectural and technical solutions to which the student can refer once they have become a professional. Finally, it lays the groundwork for the professional relationship between architects and engineers, as it is part of both curricula. Regarding this last aspect, Edouard Arnaud's decision to use the same textbook at the Ecole centrale and at the Ecole des Beaux-Arts can be seen as a way to ensure that architects and engineers share a common language and culture and are informed by each other's professional habits, thus improving their collaboration.

This study of Edouard Arnaud's teaching of construction brings new light to the debate on the teaching of construction in architecture schools in France which has been revived by the latest reform of the European architectural curriculum (Voyatzaki 2002). For example, the growing popularity of the double architect-engineer curriculum first instituted in the 2000s and now offered within twelve out of twenty-two architecture schools in France according to the the Ministry of Culture illustrates the need for a reflection on the collaboration between architects and engineers which could be prompted through the teaching of construction. In this context, I hope that my research can be used as a basis upon which to reflect on the contemporary teaching of construction in architecture schools. It could either serve as a set of pedagogical references for teachers to design their lessons or reflect on their own pedagogy, or as a comprehensive study to help institutions deliberate on the role of current construction pedagogy in the architectural curriculum as it relates to the present social and professional situation in France.

References

Arnaud, Edouard (1921a): *Cours d'architecture et de constructions civiles: Première partie. Opérations à envisager pour l'édification d'un bâtiment*, vol.1, Paris: Impression des arts et manufactures

Arnaud, Edouard (1921b): *Cours d'architecture et de constructions civiles: Deuxième partie. Technique du bâtiment: Tome I. Edification du bâtiment. Béton armé – maçonnerie – plancher*, vol.2, Paris: Impression des arts et manufactures

Arnaud, Edouard (1921c): *Cours d'architecture et de constructions civiles: Deuxième partie. Technique du bâtiment: Tome II. Edification du bâtiment. Combles – couverture – escaliers*, vol.3, Paris: Impression des arts et manufactures

Arnaud, Edouard (1921d): *Cours d'architecture et de constructions civiles: Deuxième partie. Technique du bâtiment: Tome III. Edification du bâtiment. Serrurerie – installations diverses et décoration*, vol.4, Paris: Impression des arts et manufactures

Arnaud, Edouard (1921e): *Cours d'architecture et de constructions civiles: Troisième partie. Application du cours de constructions civiles*, vol.5, Paris: Impression des arts et manufactures

Arnaud, Edouard (1921f): *Cours d'architecture et de constructions civiles: Recueil de planches*, vol.6, Paris: Impression des arts et manufactures

Arnaud, Edouard (1921g): »Le Nouvel Enseignement de la Construction à l'Ecole Nationale et Supérieure des Beaux-Arts«, in: *L'Architecture* XXXIV, 3–5

Arnaud, Edouard (1931): *Cours d'architecture et de constructions civiles*, 2 vols., Paris/Liège: Librairie polytechnique Ch. Béranger

»Bibliographie« (1923): *L'Architecture* 36/10, 29

Brucculeri, Antonio (2006): »Renewal and Tradition in the Teaching of Building Construction at the Ecole des Beaux-Arts of Paris: The Course of Edouard Arnaud, 1920-1934«, in: *Second International Congress on Construction History*, 417–440

Diener, Amandine (2016): »La photographie au service de l'enseignement de la construction à l'école des Beaux-Arts. La démarche de François Vitale«, in: *Livraisons d'Histoire de l'Architecture* 31, 39–49

Epron, Jean-Pierre (1997): *Comprendre l'éclectisme*, Paris : Norma

Vitale, François (1919–1925): *Formation de François Vitale: Notes de cours et dessins d'école*. Paris: Centre d'archives d'architecture contemporaine. 186 IFA 35/1-2.

Vitale, François (n.d.): *Enseignement à l'Ecole nationale supérieure des beaux-arts. Cours de constructions civiles de E. Arnaud et F. Vitale: Hygiène de l'habitation*. Paris: Centre d'archives de l'architecture contemporaine. 186 IFA 404: SV-15-11-17-01

Garric, Jean-Philippe (2011): »Bibliothèques d'atelier«, in: *Bibliothèques d'atelier: Édition et enseignement de l'architecture*, Paris 1785-1871 [online]. Paris: Publications de l'Institut national d'histoire de l'art

Hassler, Uta/Meyer, Torsten/Rauhut, Christoph (2019): *Versuch über die polytechnische Bauwissenschaft*, Munich: Hirmer Verlag

Lichtenstein, Katrin (2012): »Modell oder Schule? Das ›Dortmunder Modell Bauwesen«, in: Klaus Jan Philipp/Kerstin Renz (eds), *Architekturschulen: Programm, Pragmatik, Propaganda*, Tübingen: Wasmuth, 219–232

Nègre, Valérie (2011): »Architecture et construction dans les cours de l'Ecole centrale de arts et manufactures (1833–1864) et du Conservatoire national des arts et métiers (1854–1894)«, in: Jean-Philippe Garric (ed.), *Bibliothèques d'atelier. Edition et enseignement de l'architecture*, Paris 1785–1871, Wavre: Mardaga, 42–59

Nègre, Valérie (2012): »Oral Transmission and the Use of Models in the Teaching of Architecture and Construction at the Turn of the 19th Century«, in: Robert Carvais/André Guillerme/ Valérie Nègre/ Joël Sakarovitch (eds), *Nuts and Bolts of Construction History*, Paris: Picard, 555–563

Pfammatter, Ulrich (2000): *The Making of the Modern Architect and Engineer: The Origins and Development of a Scientific and Industrially oriented Education*, Basel: Birkhäuser

Saint, Andrew (2007): *Architect and Engineer: A Study in Sibling Rivalry*, New Haven/London: Yale University Press

Teyssot, Georges (1982): »The Planning and Building in Towns: The System of the Bâtiments civils in France, 1795–1848«, in: Robin Middleton (ed.), *The Beaux-Arts and Nineteenth-century French Architecture*, London: Thames & Hudson, 3–49

Thevenot, Jean (1994): »Edouard Arnaud et l'enseignement de la construction«, Paris : Université Paris IV. Unpublished Master's thesis.

Thibault, Estelle (2017): »Les cours d'architecture de Gustave Umbdenstock dans le premier tiers du XXe siècle: Formes orales et documents imprimés«, in: *Histoire de l'Enseignement de l'Architecture au XXe siècle* 3, 25–32

Voyatzaki, Maria, (ed.) (2002): *The Teaching of Construction in Architectural Education: Current Pedagogy and Innovative Teaching Methods*, Thessaloniki: Aristotle University of Thessaloniki

Dimensions of Architectural Knowledge, 2022-03 &
https://doi.org/10.14361/dak-2022-0322

WEBSITE
Site-Reading Writing Quarterly

Jane Rendell

Abstract: Each solstice and equinox, for *Site-Reading Writing Quarterly*, a website I curate, I invite
contributors to exchange recently completed written works and provide a situated »review« of
each other's work. These acts draw on feminist theories and critical spatial practices to open
up different ways of »reading writing« differently, exploring the practice of »reviewing« from
situated perspectives. The ambition is to critique and experiment with the genre of the »critical review essay«. Paying close attention to the subject matter at hand generates modes of
response that create entangled and dialogic textualities – that I suggest we think of, following
Donna Haraway and Rosi Braidotti, as »feminist figurations«. In this article I provide an overview
of the approaches adopted by the contributors involved in the first 7 issues, interweaving presentations of the 14 books »reviewed« with theoretical reflections on the situated processes that
reader-writer-reviewers have engaged with so far.

Keywords: Site-writing; Re-viewing; Reading; Feminist Figuration; Situated Practice; Poethics.

December 21, 2019

Dear Friends,

As we approach the shortest day of the year in the northern hemisphere,
and the longest in the south, I am sharing the first issue of Site-Reading Writing
Quarterly, which will go live on December 21, 2019 (Rendell 2019).

Each solstice and equinox, I am inviting two writers to read each other's
work, hoping to help generate more interest in the amazing writing in our expanded field, explore ways of »reading writing« that critique the practice of »reviewing« from a situated perspective, and that re-write the genre and texture
of the »critical review essay«.

My massive thanks to Mona Livholts and Hélène Frichot who, with everything else they have going on, agreed to inaugurate this reading writing exper-

Corresponding author: Jane Rendell (Bartlett School of Architecture, UCL, UK); j.rendell@ucl.ac.uk;
https://orcid.org/0000-0001-6365-7075.

iment, and it is no surprise to discover that the theme of their dyadic reading writing emerged as »exhaustion«!

Perhaps I was drawn to the language of exhaustion because I was traveling to my doctor for a health control on November 4, the day when I read the book and made this first« diary note. Or maybe Frichot's book is so thought provoking in the way it unexpectedly awakens the reader's attention to the richness of theoretical language that exhaustion offers that it speaks to many readers who will feel that they have waited a long time for this book to be written? From »A Situated Reading Diary of Exhaustion as a Creative Methodology«, Mona Livholts reads Creative Ecologies (2019) written by Hélène Frichot.

Still, to recognize this precarity. To recognize this damaged world. To recognize our exhausted subjectivities, and to continue to work, but slowly, and with care. From »We apologise for the delay. Arriving into Nuremberg Main Station, 12:07, Saturday early afternoon, 23 November 2019«, Hélène Frichot reads Situated Writing as Theory and Method (2019) written by Mona Livholts.

And a big thank you to those who have recently sent new projects for https://site-writing.co.uk and https://criticalspatialpractice.co.uk; to Maryjane Orley and Martin Purvis for allowing me to use their *Solar Trajectories* and to Stuart Munro, the designer who makes these websites.

If you have a written work that you've recently completed and/or someone else's work that you'd like to read, please get in touch.

Site-Writing

Back in 2002, I introduced the term »critical spatial practice« as one which placed attention on how processes of engaging with sites varied across different modes of artistic and design practices in architecture and in urbanism (Rendell 2003; Rendell 2006; Rendell 2016). I defined these critical spatial practices as ways of questioning and transforming the social conditions of the sites into which they intervened, as well as testing the boundaries and procedures of their own disciplines, and their own subjectivities. I stressed three particular qualities of these site-specific projects: the spatial, the critical, and the interdisciplinary, discussing how distinct practices articulate differently the relations between the spatial and the social, and the aesthetic and the ethical, depending on position.

In writing »about« critical spatial practice, I began to consider how, since responses to art and architectural works happen *in situ*, we can understand them as taking place *somewhere*, and that thus criticism can itself be recog-

1.

Park bench before removal due to park restauration, 2019, Thora Dahls Park, Stockholm, Sweden. Photographer: Mona Livholts. https://site-readingwritingquarterly. co.uk/december-2019/

2.

»We apologise for the delay«. Arriving into Nuremberg Main Station, 12:07, Saturday early afternoon, 23 November 2019. Image: Hélène Frichot. https://site-readingwritingquarterly.co.uk/december-2019/

nized as a kind of critical spatial practice. The desire to work with variations in voice to reflect and create spatial distances and proximities between works and texts on the one hand, and writers and readers on the other, became the motivation for *Site-Writing*, a collection of essays and documentations of text-works produced between 1998 and 2008 which question and perform notions of situatedness and spatiality in critical writing (Rendell 2010). Here, I located site-writing as a feminist form of critical spatial practice, which, because of its interest in situation and situated knowledge could be connected to the ways in which, over the past 30 years, feminist philosophers and geographers had been articulating new ways of knowing and being through spatial terms, proposing conceptual and critical tools such as »situated knowledge« and »standpoint theory« for examining the relationship between the construction of subjects and the politics of location (Haraway 1988: 575–599; Flax 1991: 232; Benhabib 1992: 225–228; hooks 1989). I argued, following Donna Haraway, that objectivity is partial and knowledge is situated (Haraway 1988), and that one constructs one's viewpoint and performs one's critical attitude through writing in relation to one's lived and located experiences. Site-writing draws on the history of feminism, and like much feminist discourse and critical practice today, it returns to second-wave feminism, to rework the politicized yet also personal practices which emerged from that moment, especially Carol Hanisch's notion of »the personal is political« (Hanisch 1970).[1]

March 21, 2020

I hope you are well in these unsettled and unsettling times.

March 21, 2020 sees the second installment of Site-Reading Writing Quarterly, where Katja Hilevaara and Emily Orley read Mohamad Hafeda's *Negotiating Conflict in Lebanon: Bordering Practices in a Divided Beirut*, (2019) and Mohamad

---

[1] This phrase has been attributed to a paper by Carol Hanisch, originally titled, »Some Thoughts in Response to Dottie's Thoughts on a Women's Liberation Movement«, (February 1969) which deals with »therapy v. politics« and discusses the role of personal experiences in »therapy« or consciousness-raising groups as part of the Women's Liberation Movement. This paper was published in *Notes from the Second Year: Women's Liberation* (1970), edited by Shulamith Firestone and Anne Koedt, and Hanisch states that the title »The Personal is Political« was given to the paper by the editors. See http://www.carolhanisch.org/CHwritings/PIP.html.

Hafeda reads *The Creative Critic: Writing As/About Practice*, (2018), edited by Katja Hilevaara and Emily Orley (Site-Reading Writing Quarterly 2020a).

Already, we can see the impact of our current situation – of university strikes in the UK and the impact of COVID-19 globally – on reading and writing activities.

Take care everyone – of (y)ourselves and all (y)our loved and vulnerable ones!

If you have a written work that you've recently completed and/or someone else's work that you'd like to read, please get in touch.

Situated Practice

While the notion of situatedness allows us to address the particularities of a site and our relations to it, and may lead us to address the material, political, and emotional qualities of our own subjectivities from both spatial and temporal perspectives, there is still a need to consider in more detail what actually constitutes a change to a condition that can bring us into a situation of critical awareness. This is where feminist concerns with situated knowledge meet the history of politically conscious art.

In her 2014 investigation of the Situationist International (SI) concept of »constructed situations« as a methodology, art historian Frances Stracey describes how SI's theory and practice involved unitary urbanism, psychogeography, and the *derive*. She writes that »common to all these tactics was the transient, momentary temporality of constructed situations that the SI defined as ephemeral, without a future, mere ›passageways.‹« (Stracey 2014: 9) And as critic Ira Ferris has discussed, the SI aimed to allow »moments of life to be experienced in almost laboratory settings where they are highlighted and made obvious and where one can start to critically examine them«. (Ferris 2014).

In Sara Ahmed's *Living a Feminist Life* she refers to Lauren Berlant's elaboration of situation as »something which will perhaps matter« (Ahmed 2017: 12–13). And in »Thinking about Feeling Historical«, Berlant herself writes about two men »in the now«: »A situation has forced them to think. A situation has changed the ordinary into something they can no longer presume... A situation is a state of things in which something that will perhaps matter is unfolding amidst the usual activity of life«. (Berlant 2008) The phrase »perhaps matter« led me to wonder about the very process of taking notice and becoming aware, and how this is an embodied experience. Iris Marion

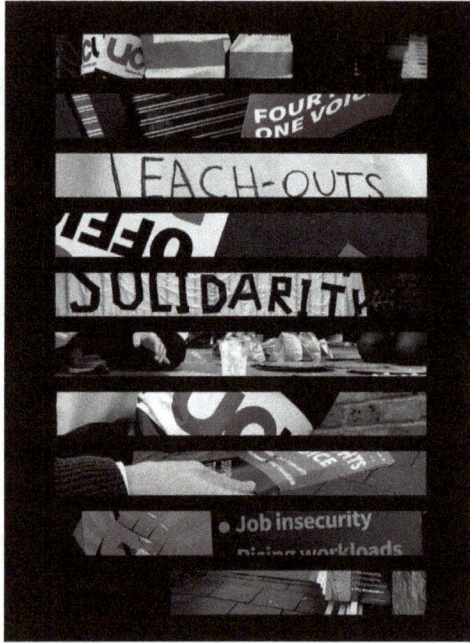

3.
Katja Hilevaara and Emily Orley, Responding to Negotiating Conflict in Lebanon: Bordering Practices in a Divided Beirut in Three Acts, Act 2. https://site-readingwritingquarterly. co.uk/march-2020/

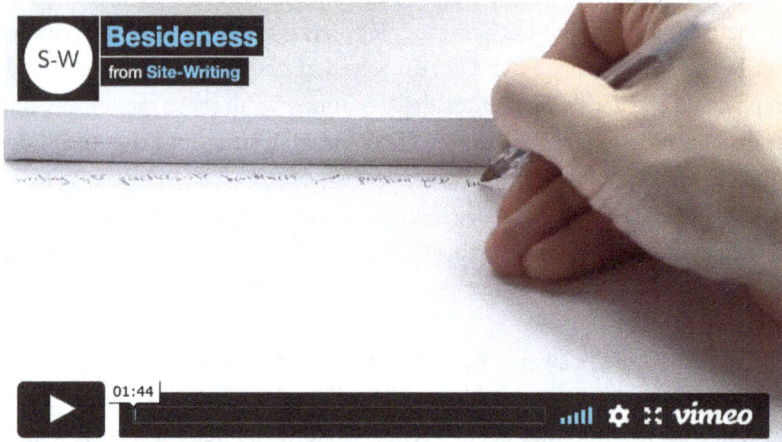

4.
Mohamad Hafeda, Besideness, 2020.
https://site-readingwritingquarterly.co.uk/march-2020/

Young, drawing on Toril Moi's work and existentialist philosophy, uses the term »body-in-situation« to argue that the lived body is a better concept for theorizing subjectivity than gender. Young writes, »The lived body is a unified idea of a physical body acting and experiencing in a specific sociocultural context; it is body-in-situation.« (Young 2005: 16)[2]

June 21, 2020

Dear Fellow Site-Writers and Critical Spatial Practitioners,
I hope you are well in these turbulent times.
June 21, 2020 sees the launch of the third issue of Site-Reading Writing Quarterly, where Marko Jobst, Hélène Frichot, Klaske Havik and Catharina Gabrielsson read Caroline Rabourdin's Sense in *Translation: Essays on the Bilingual Body* (2020) and Caroline Rabourdin and Matthew Chrislip read »Reading(s) and Writing(s), Unfolding Processes of Transversal Writing«, *Writingplace Journal for Architecture and Literature*, 3 (Site-Reading Writing Quarterly 2020b).
Already, we have seen how readers' experiences of recent situations – local, such as the university strikes in the UK of 2019–2020, and global, like the COVID-19 pandemic – have created writings made from intimate and located readings.
If you have a written work that you've recently completed and/or someone else's work that you'd like to read, please get in touch.

Ethopoiesis

One way of considering how the interpersonal and epistemological aspects of ethical practice are connected is through practices of »subjectivation«[3] as advanced by Michel Foucault. These »technologies of the self«, as Foucault describes them, place the practices of caring of oneself over practices of knowing oneself; these are the techniques through which subjects develop

---

2 Young also quotes Moi: »To claim that the body is a situation is to acknowledge that the meaning of a woman's body is bound up with the way she uses her freedom.« (Young 2005: 16; Moi 2001).

3 It is important to distinguish, as Frederic Gros does, subjectivation from subjection in Foucault's work. »The history of the subject, from the perspective of the practices of the self and the procedures of subjectivation, is completely separate from the project, formulated in the 1970s, of the history of the production of subjectivities, of the procedures of subjection by the machines of power« (Gros 2005: 697–708, 698).

5.
Group Image of the Transversal Writing Group in Kavala, Greece, 2-4 July 2018:
Klaske Havik, Catharina Gabrielsson, Kim Gurney, Naomi Stead, Marko Jobst,
Hélène Frichot, Robin Wilson and Anne Kockelkorn (photographer). https://site-
readingwritingquarterly.co.uk/june-2020/

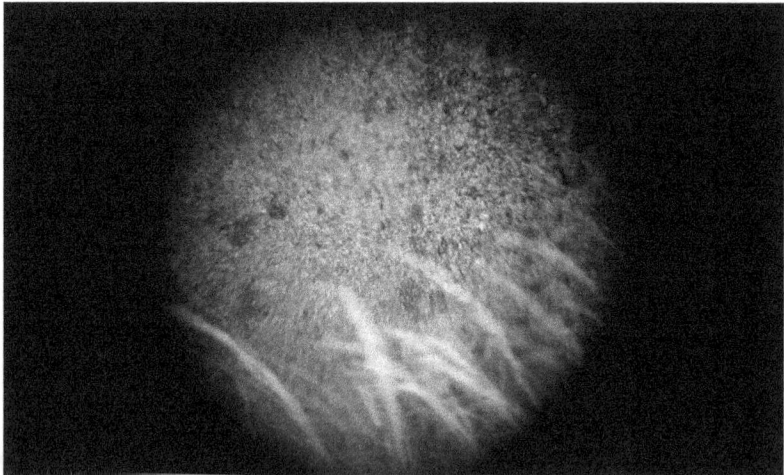

6.
Caroline Rabourdin and Matthew Chrislip, The Reader to the Authors, see http://
dowland.us/projects/thereadertotheauthors. https://site-readingwritingquarterly.
co.uk/june-2020/

themselves, establishing their relation to moral codes and norms with respect to their own lives. Foucault distinguishes between the rule of conduct, the conduct measured by the rule, and »the manner in which one ought to ›conduct oneself‹«: »that is, the manner in which one ought to form oneself as an ethical subject acting in reference to the prescriptive elements that make up the code«. These are concerned with what he calls the »*determination of the ethical substance*«; that is, the way in which the individual has to constitute this or that part of himself as the prime material of his moral conduct and »*the mode of subjection* (mode d'assujettissement); that is, with the way in which the individual establishes his relation to the rule and recognizes himself as obliged to put it into practice« (Foucault 1985).

»In his *Self Writing essay* from 1983, Foucault explains how the Stoics understood writing's relation to ethical practice: »As an element of self-training, writing has, to use an expression that one finds in Plutarch, an *ethopoietic* function: it is an agent of the transformation of truth into *ethos*« (Foucault 1983). He distinguishes between *hupomnemata* and correspondence as two modes of writing which differently address the self and the other as reader and writer. Where *hupomnemata* involves an »introspection« – »not so much as a decipherment of the self by the self as an opening one gives the other onto oneself«, in *correspondence* one »show[s] oneself«, – »project[s] oneself into view«.

September 21, 2020

I hope you are all as well as can be.

For the fourth issue of Site-Reading Writing Quarterly, Marsha Meskimmon and Penny Florence have decided to hold a virtual dialogue about their two new books, *Transnational Feminisms, Transversal Politics and Art: Entanglements and Intersections (2020) and Thinking the Sculpture Garden: Art, Plant, Landscape* (2020) (Site-Reading Writing Quaterly 2020c).

Talking across their two separate-yet-joined Zoom frames, their fascinating conversation stems from their shared interests in art, ecology, and feminist politics. They exchange thoughts about the highly practical events, as well as conceptual concerns, that have informed the realization of their book projects, as well as imagine together the alternative possibilities feminism offers for economics, knowledge, and life, that can be produced out of the challeng-

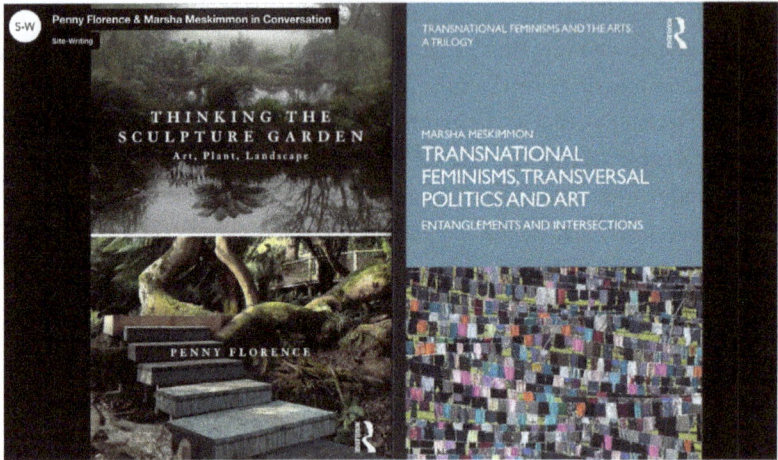

7.
Marsha Meskimmon reads Penny Florence's Thinking the Sculpture Garden: Art,
Plant, Landscape and Penny Florence reads Marsha Meskimmon's Transnational
Feminisms, Transversal Politics and Art: Entanglements and Intersections.
https://site-readingwritingquarterly.co.uk/september-2020/

8.
Penny Florence and Marsha Meskimmon in conversation.
https://site-readingwritingquarterly.co.uk/september-2020/

es posed by COVID-19 and the social-ecological crisis of which the virus is a symptom.

If you have a written work that you've recently completed and/or someone else's work that you'd like to read, please get in touch.

Geopoetics

The decision to set up *Site-Reading Writing Quarterly* was driven by a desire to balance the dominance of sole-authored achievements in the academy with opening the possibilities of reading and writing together, and to do this by creating a different type of reviewing – not the invisible point-scoring of the academic peer review, nor even the kind of judgment required by the journalistic book review which rarely acknowledges the positionalities of the re-viewers themselves. Situating the release of each issue at a solstice and equinox in correspondence with the movement of the earth was an attempt to connect a practice of reviewing to planetary patterns, and to forge a link, as Angela Last has done, from geopolitics to geopoetics: »At the same time, the proposal of the ›Anthropocene‹ has become linked with calls for a new 'geopolitics', characterized by notions of responsibility and care for the planet and planetary society« (Last 2017: 148).

While geographers have been developing new modes of place-writing, and artists and art critics connecting practice and criticism through art-writing; architectural and urban criticism has been slower to experiment with different writing forms. *Site-Writing* has been an attempt to explore the position of the critic, not only in relation to art objects, architectural spaces, and theoretical ideas, but also through the site of writing itself, to investigate the limits of criticism, and ask what it is possible for a critic to say about an artist, a work, the site of a work and the critic herself, and for the writing to still »count« as criticism. Site-writing has aimed to produce criticism as a form of situated practice that sets up different kinds of poetical, political, and ethical relationships with the works it encounters, while it also, as feminism has taught us, takes one's own life experience and responsibilities into account through the situated production of writing and reading. As Judith Butler argues in *Giving an Account of Oneself,* »the ›I‹ has no story of its own that is not also the story of a relation – or set of relations – to a set of norms« (Butler 2005: 8).

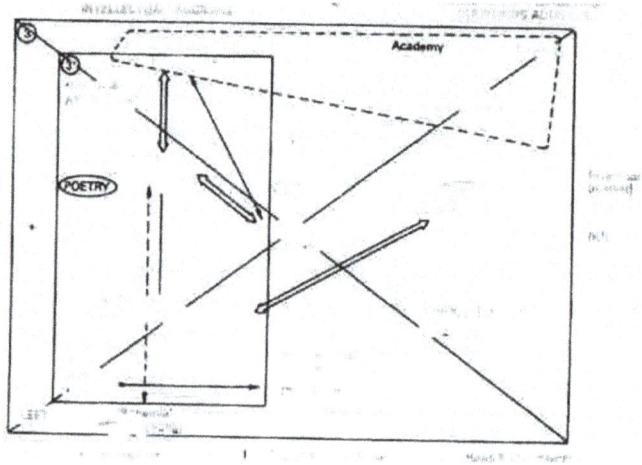

9.

Tim Cresswell, FIELD NOTES.
https://site-readingwritingquarterly.co.uk/december-2020/

10.

Kristen Kreider & James O'Leary, Media Archaeology (Maxwell Street I – IX) A set of
images to be read in sequence, (Maxwell Street II).

December 21, 2020

For this December 2020 solstice issue of Site-Reading Writing Quarterly I have invited geographer and poet, Tim Cresswell, and architect and artist-poet duo, Kreider and O'Leary, to respond to each other's books. Maxwell Street (2019), is Cresswell's historical and poetic investigation of a specific location in Chicago, while Kreider and O'Leary's, Field Poetics, (2018) explores how text and place intertwine through five of their site-related projects (Site-Reading Writing Quarterly 2020d).

2020 has been a year defined by the COVID-19 pandemic. Many have survived so far, but others have not. Lives have been lost. It has been a time of sadness and grief. But we have also shared many moments of kindness, laughter, and joy (perhaps more than usual?). The digital screen has brought people together, not only those who are usually physically close, but communities have been able to come together who are physically extended across the globe. As well as framing working life, we have eaten, cried, and laughed together in the time and space of the digital screen. Many talk of being exhausted by this »screen time«. For that reason, it is perhaps no surprise that Tim, and Kristen and James, decided independently to read each other's books by making images. The visual work they have produced demands no lengthy task of intense reading, line by line. Instead, they have put together a parallel series of intriguing combinations of letters and textures. Their compositions allow our eyes to wander around, to explore a bit, creating readings that unwind.

If you have a written work that you've recently completed, and someone you'd like to read it, please get in touch.

Sympoiesis

When Donna Haraway reconceptualizes the Anthropocene as the Chthulucene, as a »time of mortal compositions at stake to and with each other« (Haraway 2016a), she notes in *Staying with the Trouble*, that this epoch in which the human and nonhuman are inextricably linked is sympoietic not autopoietic. She takes the term sympoiesis from M. Beth Dempster, and writes that mortal worlds »do not make themselves« (Haraway 2016b: 33), but rather require a poiesis that thinks-with, makes-with, and becomes-with. This is what she calls SF, defined as »science fiction, speculative fabulation, string figures, speculative feminism, science fact, so far.« (Haraway 2016b: 2). For Haraway:

>>SF is practice and process, it is becoming-with each other in surprising relays; it is a figure for ongoingness in the Chthulucene.<< (Haraway 2016b: 3)

SF threads and traces, passes on and receives, makes and unmakes, and, rather than the self-producing generative systems Haraway associates with autopoiesis, is >>always partnered all the way down<< (Haraway 2016b: 33). But SF also, as I understand it, continues the practice, described initially by Haraway, and then by Rosi Braidotti, of >>feminist figuration<< (Haraway 1997: 11; Braidotti 1994: 4; Rendell 2017).

March 21, 2021

Dear Friends and Colleagues,

As we approach spring equinox in the north and autumn equinox in the south, night and day rebalance, and point to the need to restore equalities in the landscapes of deep social injustice that COVID-19 has brought into stark relief.

For this issue of *Site-Reading Writing Quarterly* I have invited artist Polly Gould and architectural historian Paulette Singley to respond to each other's books – Gould's *Antarctica, Art, and Archive* (2020) and Singley's *How to Read Architecture* (2019) (Site-Reading Writing Quarterly 2021a). Through careful acts of positioned observation these inter-connected readings of each other's writings encourage the need for a more ecological approach to criticism and practice – paying attention to how near relates to far.

Equinox greetings to you all!

Feminist Figuration

In looking into the history of feminist life-writing, I discovered a specific strand of work called >>auto-theory<<, where autobiography itself operates as a mode of theory, described by Lauren Fournier as >>the practices of engaging with theory, life, and art from the perspective of one's lived experiences<< (Fournier 2018: 643). The early history of such an approach can be located in the writing of second-wave feminists of color, such as Audre Lorde and Gloria Anzaldúa, as well as Adrienne Rich, as Stacey Young has done (Young 1997; Lorde 2007; Anzaldúa 1999; Moraga 1981). But it is also possible to consider how such feminist life-writing has taken shape through practices of feminist figuration, that Haraway considers to be about >>location and his-

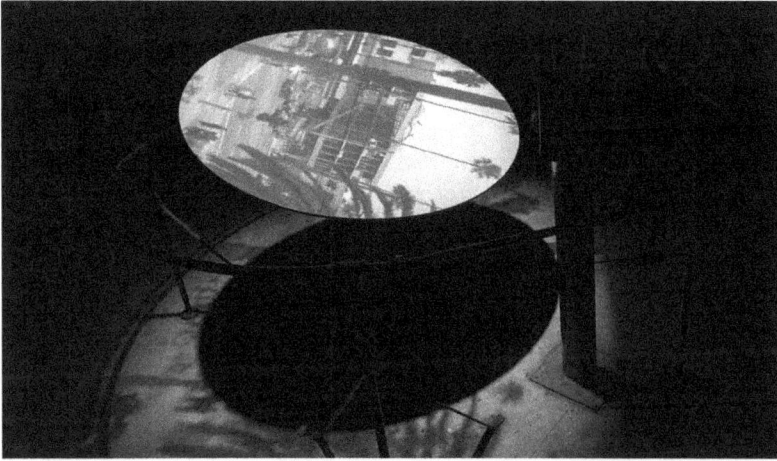

11.

Camera Obscura, Santa Monica California. Photograph by Lorie Shaull (2018).
https://commons.wikimedia.org/wiki/File:Santa_Monica_Camera_Obscura,_
Santa_Monica_California_(26357316558).jpg. https://site-readingwritingquarterly.
co.uk/march-2021/

12.

'Montage of illustrations', taken from Polly Gould, Antarctica, Art and Archive
(London: Bloomsbury, 2020) and Paulette Singley, How to Read Architecture: An
Introduction to Interpreting the Built Environment (New York: Routledge, 2019).
https://site-readingwritingquarterly.co.uk/march-2021/

torical specificity«, and »a kind of assemblage, a kind of connectedness of the figure and the subject« (Haraway 2004: 338), and Braidotti describes as »not mere metaphors, but rather markers of more concretely situated historical positions«. She writes:

> »A figuration is the expression of one's specific positioning in space and time. It marks certain territorial or geopolitical coordinates, but it also points out one's sense of genealogy of historical inscription. Figurations deterritorialize and de-stabilize the certainties of the subject and allow for a proliferation of situated or 'micro' narratives of self and others.« (Braidotti 2006: 90)

June 21, 2021

Dear Colleagues and Friends,

For this issue of *Site-Reading Writing Quarterly*, which marks the lightest day in the north and the darkest in the south, I have invited nonbinary researcher and theorist of embodied practice, Ben Spatz, and writer-artist, Emma Cocker, to review publications which explore practices associated with the laboratory. As a result of the pandemic this past year has seen a complete change to our usual operating conditions, and required a large degree of experimentation. (Site-Reading Writing Quarterly 2021b)

Composed of a trilogy of audio-recordings, Ben Spatz's *Making A Laboratory: Dynamic Configurations with Transversal Video* (2020) is a work to be listened to; while Ben Spatz's reading of *Choreo-graphic Figures: Deviations from the Line,* (2017), co-edited by Cocker, with Nikolaus Gansterer and Mariella Greil, takes a more conventional review essay form. Spatz explores the performative methods of artistic research practice presented in the volume, and in drawing attention to wit(h)ness—a playful combination of witness and withness—introduced in *Choreo-graphic Figures* – calls for whiteness to be taken into account in prac-tice-led artistic research.

That this public act of reading *Choreo-graphic Figures* has taken place four years after it was published, opens up for re-viewing how the gap between one writing and another reading is always framed by historical difference. Spatz's reading offers a stark reminder that despite an increased awareness of race is-sues in current academic and artistic practice over the past year—following the murder of George Floyd and the ways in which COVID-19 has laid social inequalities bare – white privilege largely remains invisible. This is a matter to address in future issues of *Site-Reading Writing Quarterly*.

Solstice greetings to you all!

Poethics

Writing that draws to attention to the relation between the poetic and the ethical, has been described by poets Seamus Heaney and Joan Retallack as »poethical«, and developed more recently by Denise Ferreira Da Silva through her »black feminist poethics«.

In the seventh section of Seamus Heaney's 2001 collection, *Electric Light*, entitled »W. H. Auden, 1907–30«, Heaney includes this sentence: »A pause for po-ethics« (O'Brien 2019). According to Eugene O'Brien, for Heaney, poetry and ethics are entwined and »Po-ethics allows for a slanted perspective, a swerve, which looks at the ethical demands on life from just such a different perspective«. And in her 2003 book, *The Poethical Wager*, Joan Retallack writes of this concept as »a poetics of the swerve« or in terms of »opportunities to usefully rethink habits of thought« (Retallack 2003: 1). For Retallack, poethics is a »distancing form of play« located in the »intermediate zone between self and world«, and it is in the distance »engendered by a poethical recognition of reciprocal alterity« that »curiosity and exploration« are stimulated (Retallack 2003: 7).

For Ferreira Da Silva, »black feminist poethics«, articulates, as Andrea Phillips has described, »a mode of living and thinking which apprehends and moves beyond the categories of slavery«. (Phillips 2018) For Phillips, »this call to the absolute unpicking of the bonds of the capitalist slave narrative of Black history, written through capital accumulation«, requires 'a total rethink of the temporal–spatial structures of what we serve to display and cherish in the name of poethics« (Phillips 2018). And for Da Silva herself, the Black Feminist Critical worksite is located both in the poet's intention that the Category of Blackness can be emancipated from the scientific and historical ways of knowing that produced it in the first place, and through the ethical as a mandate for »opening up other ways of knowing and doing« (Ferreira Da Silva 2014: 81–97).

It is this call by Black Feminism, for other ways of knowing and doing, that white feminism must now respond to, and find ways of figuring, actions

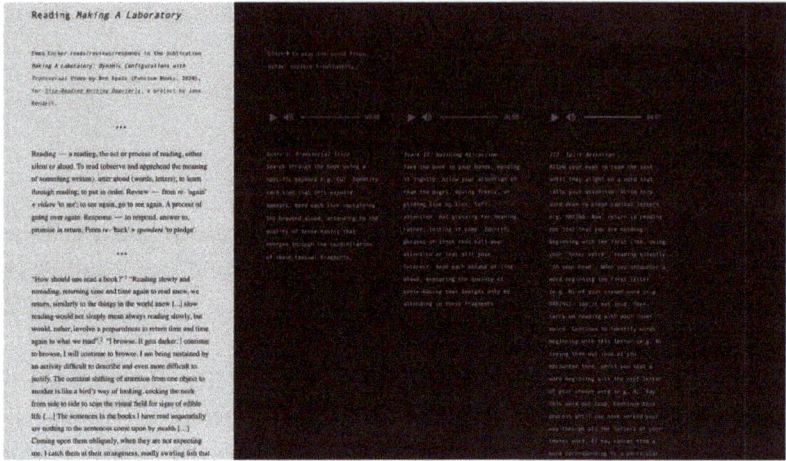

13.
Emma Cocker reads Ben Spatz, Making a Laboratory (New York: Punctum Books, 2020), https://www.researchcatalogue.net/view/1290573/1290574. https://site-readingwritingquarterly.co.uk/june-2021/

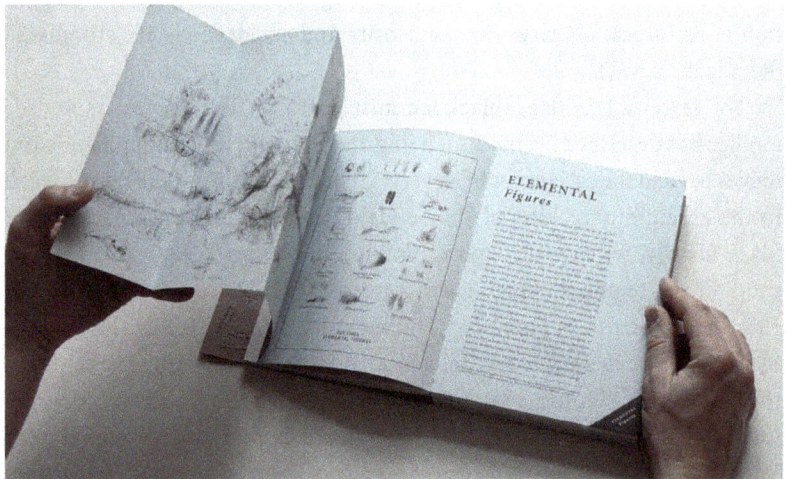

14.
Ben Spatz reads Emma Cocker, Nikolaus Gansterer, Mariella Greil, Choreo-graphic Figures: Deviations from the Line (Berlin: de Gruyter, 2017). https://site-readingwritingquarterly.co.uk/june-2021/

of resistance to racial injustice in this time of ecological crisis, ones that position poethics politically but also relationally.[4]

References

Ahmed, Sara (2017): *Living a Feminist Life*, Durham, NC and London: Duke University Press.

Anzaldúa, Gloria (1999 [1987]): *Borderlands: La Frontera – The New Mestiza*, San Francisco: Aunt Lute Books.

Benhabib, Seyla (1992): *Situating the Self: Gender, Community and Postmodernism in Contemporary Ethics*, Cambridge: Polity Press.

Berlant, Lauren (2008): »Thinking about Feeling Historical«. In: Emotion, Space and Society 1, October.

Braidotti, Rosi (1994): *Nomadic Subjects: Embodiment and Sexual Difference in Contemporary Feminist Theory*, New York: Columbia University Press.

Braidotti, Rosi (2006): Transpositions: *On Nomadic Ethics*, Cambridge: Polity Press.

Butler, Judith (2005): *Giving An Account of Oneself*, New York: Fordham University Press.

Ferreira Da Silva, Denise (2014): »Toward a Black Feminist Poethics«, in: *The Black Scholar*, 44/2, 81–97.

Ferris, Ira (2014): »Relational Art: An Arty Way to Twitter, with Nothing to Say?«. In: December, 21 at: https://artiris.wordpress.com/2014/12/21/relational-art-an-arty-way-to-twitter-with-nothing-to-say/.

Flax, Jane (1991): *Thinking Fragments: Psychoanalysis, Feminism and Postmodernism in the Contemporary West*, Berkeley, Los Angeles: University of California Press.

Foucault, Michel (1983): »Self Writing«. Translated from Corps *écrit* 5 (February), 3–23. See https://foucault.info/documents/foucault.hypomnemata.en/

Foucault, Michel (1985): *The History of Sexuality, Vol. 2, The Use of Pleasure.* Translated by Robert Hurley, New York: Vintage Books.

Fournier, Lauren (2018): »Sick Women, Sad Girls, and Selfie Theory: Autotheory as Contemporary Feminist Practice«. In: a/b: *Auto/Biography Studies*, 33/3.

Gros, Frédéric (2005): »Le souci de soi chez Michel Foucault, A review of *The Hermeneutics of the Subject: Lectures at the Collège de France, 1981–1982*«. In: Philosophy and Social Criticism, 31/5–6, 697–708.

Hanisch, Carol (1970) »The Personal is Political«. In: Firestone, Shulamith and Koedt, Anne, eds., *Notes from the Second Year: Women's Liberation*, New York: Radical Feminism.

Haraway, Donna (1988): »Situated Knowledges: The Science Question in Feminism and the Privilege of Partial Perspective«. In: *Feminist Studies*, 14/3 575–599.

---

4 See for example, Denise Ferreira Da Silva and Valentina Desideri's »Sensing Salon« project.https://www.artandeducation.net/announcements/308693/valentina-desideri-and-denise-ferreira-da-silvathe-sensing-salon

Haraway, Donna (1997): »Syntactics: The Grammar of Feminism and Technoscience«. In: Modest_Witness@Second_Millenium. FemaleMan_Meets_OncoMouse: Feminism and Technoscience, London: Routledge, 1–22.

Haraway, Donna (2004 [2000]): »Cyborgs, Coyotes and Dogs: A Kinship of Feminist Figurations and There are Always More Things Going On Than You Thought! Methodologies as Thinking Technologies: An interview with Donna Haraway conducted in two parts by Nina Lykke, Randi Markussen, and Finn Olesen«. In: The Donna Haraway Reader, London: Routledge, 2004, 321–342.

Haraway, Donna (2016a): »Chthulucene Manifesto from Santa Cruz«, revised from: »Donna Haraway and Cary Wolfe in Conversation«. In: Manifestly Haraway, Minneapolis: University of Minnesota Press, 2016. See https://laboratoryplanet.org/en/manifeste-chthulucene-de-santa-cruz/

Haraway, Donna (2016b): Staying with the Trouble: Making Kin in the Chthulucene, Durham, NC and London: Duke University Press, 2016.

hooks, bell (1989): »discussion of the margin as a place of resistance and hope«. In: Yearnings: Race, Gender, and Cultural Politics, London: Turnaround Press. See https://www.mdpi.com/2076-0787/8/3/138/htm

Last, Angela (2017): »We Are the World? Anthropocene Cultural Production between Geopoetics and Geopolitics«. In: Theory, Culture & Society 34/2–3, 147–168.

Lorde, Audre (2007 [1984]): »The Master's Tools Will Never Dismantle the Master's House«. In: Sister Outsider: Essays and Speeches, Berkeley, CA: Crossing Press.

Moi, Toril (2001): »What is a Woman?«. In: What is a Woman?: And Other Essays, Oxford: Oxford University Press.

Moraga, Cherríe (1981): This Bridge Called My Back: Writings by Radical Women of Color, Bath: Persephone Press.

O'Brien, Eugene (2019): »A Pause for Po-Ethics': Seamus Heaney and the Ethics of Aesthetics«. In:

Phillips, Andrea (2018): »Annotation« to Ferreira da Silva, Denise (2018): »Toward a Black Feminist Poethics: The Quest(ion) of Blackness Toward the End of the World«. In: https://www.visibleproject.org/blog/book/toward-a-black-feminist-poethics-the-question-of-blackness-toward-the-end-of-the-world-in-the-black-scholar-442/

Rendell, Jane (2003): »A Place Between Art, Architecture and Critical Theory«. In: Proceedings to Place and Location, Tallinn, Estonia, 221–233.

Rendell, Jane (2006): Art and Architecture: A Place Between, London: I.B.Tauris.

Rendell, Jane (2010): Site-Writing: The Architecture of Art Criticism, London: I.B.Tauris.

Rendell, Jane (2016): »Critical Spatial Practice as Parrhesia«. In: MaHKUscript, Journal of Fine Art Research 1.

Rendell, Jane (2017): »Figurations«. In: The Architecture of Psychoanalysis, London: I.B.Tauris.

Retallack, Joan (2003): The Poethical Wager, Berkeley: University of California Press.

Site-Reading Writing Quarterly 1 (2019): https://site-readingwritingquarterly.co.uk/december-2019/

Site-Reading Writing Quarterly 2 (2020a): https://site-readingwritingquarterly.co.uk/march-2020/

Site-Reading Writing Quarterly 3 (2020b): https://site-readingwritingquarterly.co.uk/september-2020/

Site-Reading Writing Quarterly 4 (2020c): https://site-readingwritingquarterly.co.uk/september-2020/

Site-Reading Writing Quarterly 5 (2020d): https://site-readingwritingquarterly. co.uk/december-2020/

Site-Reading Writing Quarterly 6 (2021a): https://site-readingwritingquarterly. co.uk/march-2021/

Site-Reading Writing Quarterly 7 (2021b): https://site-readingwritingquarterly. co.uk/june-2021/

Stracey, Frances (2014): *Constructed Situations: A New History of the Situationalist International*, London: Pluto Press, 9.

Young, Iris Marion (2005): »*Throwing like a Girl« and Other Essays*, Oxford: Oxford University Press, 16.

Young, Stacey (1997): *Changing the Wor(l) d: Discourse, Politics, and the Feminist Movement*, London: Routledge.

Dimensions of Architectural Knowledge, 2022-03 ᵃ
https://doi.org/10.14361/dak-2022-0323

WRITING-DRAWING
An Entangled Archival Practice

Emma Cheatle

Abstract: This article is based on a 2016 talk I gave to a drawing research group led by Lesley McFadyen, Huda Tayob and Sophie Read. In it I look back at my PhD research completed in 2013, with a view to trying to disentangle my complicated relationship with drawing as a practice of architectural research. Working through what drawing might and might not be, I propose that, hand in hand with writing, writing-drawing forms an entangled mode of doing architectural history and theory that draws out something more, or other, than each can do alone.* The mode of writing-drawing is particularly developed in the context of historical research on a building where archival material on the architect's intent, or evidence of the uses of the building once it was built, are missing. I argue two things: firstly, that the building itself can be read as an original archive, as a series of Lacanian part-objects; and that secondly, the writing-drawing research practice creates a further archive, a »living archive« that can be contributed to over time.† The article reflects on the roles of writing and drawing in the PhD whilst incorporating thinking developed in my recent research, chiefly drawn from ethnography, sociology, literary studies, and situated feminist and autotheory writing.⸸

Notes, indented, act as contextual asides.

Keywords: Drawing, Writing, Maison de Verre, Glass, Dust, Air, Archive, Autotheory

---

* The idea of entanglement is from Donna Haraway, where she suggests that »thinking with« allows us to entangle our relations in fruitful ways and see the inherent relationality of our existence. Donna Haraway (2016): *Staying with the Trouble: Making Kin in the Chthulucene*, Durham, NC: Duke University Press.

† See Emma Cheatle (2017): *Part-Architecture: The Maison de Verre, Duchamp, Domesticity and Desire in 1930s Paris*, London: Routledge, Chapter 3, 129–134 for this argument in full. A »living archive« is one that is contributed to in an ongoing way. On the part-object see Rosalind E. Krauss (1994): *The Optical Unconscious*, Cambridge, MA: MIT Press, and Jacques Lacan (2002): *Écrits: A Selection*. Trans. Bruce Fink, New York: W.W. Norton; on archival thinking see, Jacques Derrida (1996): *Archive Fever: A Freudian Impression*, Chicago: University of Chicago Press; Arlette Farge (2013): *The Allure of the Archives*, New Haven: Yale University

Corresponding authors: Emma Cheatle (University of Sheffield, UK); e.cheatle@sheffield.ac.uk; https://orcid.org/0000-0003-0675-157X

architectural	drawing	as architecture
site	drawing	as site
survey	drawing	
critical	drawing	as criticism
writing-	-drawing-	-writing
re-	drawing	
observational	drawing	
working	drawing	work
diagrammatic	drawing	
plan	drawing	
	drawing	out
on	drawing	on
methods of	drawing	methods
tactical	drawing	tactics
line	drawing	line
dust	drawing	dust
	drawing	the body
air	drawing	air
	drawing	the invisible
towards	drawing	towards
forensic	drawing	as forensics
archival	drawing	as archive
not	drawing	

†

---

† The making of this list-as-image *draws* inspiration from Georges Perec (2008): *Species of Spaces and Other Pieces*. Trans. John Sturrock. London: Penguin, 3–4. It reappears in sections later in the essay.

§

»(N.B. I'm saying writing-or-drawing, because these are often twin adventures, which depart to seek in the dark, which do not find, do not find, and as a result of not finding and not understanding, (draw) help the secret shoot forth.)« Hélène Cixous[**]

I have an ambivalent relationship with *drawing*: I am thinking of the verb and its meanings to draw forth, to draw out. As Hélène Cixous says, drawing seems to me an act of faith performed in the darkness. I find drawing to be fickle and capricious whereas reading and writing are courses of action I am happy to hold hands with. I am perplexed by the act of drawing. *The drawing* – as a noun, an object, a production, held in the hand, looked at – is not, with regard to my own practice, something I find easy to speak of. Drawings »do not find, do not find«. Indeed, when I began my doctoral research, which culminated in the book *Part-Architecture: The Maison de Verre, Duchamp, Domesticity and Desire in 1930s Paris*, I did not imagine I would use drawing as a practice at all.[††] As a practicing architect turned academic, I had hoped that I would no longer have a need for drawing, with its muteness that often failed to be turned into building, nor bring forth the hidden.[##] I would no longer feel the test of it, my lack of competency at it, the problematic of its aesthetic value, its questioned relationship to art or to artefact. I would no longer be exposed by what I had always felt was my and its deficiency.

And yet, my PhD research was born from a drawing: »the drawing is born«![§§] This drawing, or more specifically a set of four related drawings, had

---

Press; Carolyn Steedman (2001): *Dust: The Archive and Cultural History*, Manchester: Manchester University Press.

[*]   Also see Elizabeth Adams St. Pierre (2021): »Post Qualitative Inquiry, the Refusal of Method, and the Risk of the New«. In: *Qualitative Inquiry*, 27/1, January, 3–9.

[§]   The making of this list-as-image *draws* inspiration from Georges Perec (2008): *Species of Spaces and Other Pieces*. Trans. John Sturrock. London: Penguin, 3–4. It reappears in sections later in the essay.

[**] Hélène Cixous (2005): »Without end, no, State of drawingness, no, Rather: The Executioner's taking off«, in: Cixous, *Stigmata: Escaping Texts*. Trans. Catharine A. F. MacGillivray, London: Routledge, 17.

[††] Cheatle, *Part-Architecture*.

[##] See Robin Evans (1997): »Translations from Drawing to Building«, in: *Translations from Drawing to Building and Other Essays*, London: Architectural Association, 153–193.

[§§] Cixous, »Without end, no, State of drawingness, no, Rather«, 16.

been made many years before. These drawings responded to a 1992 visit as a student to the iconic modernist house and integrated gynaecology clinic, the Maison de Verre (Pierre Chareau, Paris 1928–1932). During the tour of the building, neither the words gynaecology nor clinic were mentioned; the room in which surgery had once taken place stayed locked and not spoken of. Instead, the house was glossed into the iconic, modern, mechanistic yet domestic space as written by 20th-century architectural historians. On our return to London I made drawings in response – drawings as an analysis of the gap, the absence of discourse on the history of the gynaecology clinic in the house. The drawings used architectural conventions of plan and section, and various scaled details of the building. Using the same architectural style they located and positioned the gynaecological body into the spaces, and explored her and the building's interior detail through her exposure and absent presence.

> I consciously describe here with writing rather than the images themselves, to experiment with the idea that Cixous's »writing-or-drawing« becomes the non-binary entanglement of writing-drawing. The idea of writing-drawing also takes reference from Walter Benjamin's »thought image« and Jennifer Bloomer's »[s]crypt«.*** The drawings I refer to in the text can be seen instead in the book *Part-Architecture*, or in my thesis online in the UCL library.

These drawings were hand-drawn with Rotring ink onto A1 tracing paper. Collage made from newspaper and magazine images, and Letraset lettering and texture were added. A full size photocopy was made onto thick cartridge paper then painted with acrylic color to a pick out a few key details in the drawing. The final four drawings were the most successful I had completed as a student. They stayed with me, as did the parallel conundrums of the Maison de Verre, and yet I cannot now write anything further about them. Although I talked about them at length in a public review, I am now not sure what I was thinking. They are drawing-without-writing. As Cixous states: »The drawing wants to draw what is invisible to the naked eye. It's very diffi-

---

*** See Walter Benjamin: »This is how the angel of history must look. His face turned toward the past. Where a chain of events appears before us, he sees one single catastrophe« from Walter Benjamin (1992): »Theses on the Philosophy of History«, in: *Illuminations*, London: Fontana Press, 257; Jennifer Bloomer (1993): *Architecture and the Text: the (S)crypts of Joyce and Piranesi*, London: Yale University Press, 3–23.

cult. The effort to write is always beyond my strength«.††† The drawings remain talismans I carry around with me – one of the tracing paper originals is framed and sits at the end of the bath in our bathroom – but they are mute objects heavy with their own beauty. And yet, they are part of the forming of my younger feminist self, and of my position in relation to architecture. And they later launched my PhD.

But as I said, I did not plan to draw during my long revisitation of the Maison de Verre.*** My intended analysis would instead be through the firmness of words, the incisiveness of theoretical and historical architectural analysis, with the clarity and criticality that writing could bring.

And yet, drawing, as it turns out, remained a necessary part of opening up and making explicit the building that I understood the Maison de Verre to be. In the PhD, and the subsequent book, drawing became a critical process to survey, observe, notice, and imagine what is there, might be there, and is no longer there.§§§ I became akin to a detective, an ethnographer of the absent; drawing became a forensic tactic aimed at speculating upon and drawing-out the formerly overlooked, the absent, the invisible.**** My assertion was that the then illegal abortion and contraception occurred in the house as well as a range of daily domestic, social, and sexual interactions, and yet none of this was archived in the traditional ways. To begin with, I sat in the Maison de Verre itself for long periods of time, in different spaces, and sur-

††† Cixous, »Without end, no, State of drawingness, no, Rather«, 20.

*** See Jenny Erpenbeck (2010): *Visitation*. Trans. Susan Bernofsky, London: Portobello.

§§§ The development of my drawing-thinking was particularly in the context of Jennifer Bloomer's practice of writing and drawing, see for example: Bloomer (1993): Architecture and the Text; Jennifer Bloomer (1992): »Abodes of Theory and Flesh: Tabbles of Bower«. In: *Assemblage*, 17, 6–29. It was also developed in conversation with, for example, the drawing practices of Roni Horn, Louise Bourgeois, and Diller and Scofidio, see in particular Elizabeth Diller and Ricardo Scofidio (1994): *Flesh: Architectural Probes*, London: Triangle Architectural Publishing; as well as the writing of Mieke Bal, see Mieke Bal (2001): *Looking In: The Art of Viewing*, Amsterdam: G and B Arts International; Mieke Bal (2001): *Louise Bourgeois' Spider: the architecture of art-writing*, London: University of Chicago Press; Jonathan Hill (2006): »Drawing research«, in: *Journal of Architecture*, 11, 329–333; W. J. T. Mitchell (1994): *Picture Theory: Essays on Verbal and Visual Representation*. Chicago: University of Chicago Press; Katja Grillner (2007): »Fluttering Butterflies, a Dusty Road, and a Muddy Stone: Criticality in Distraction«, in: Jane Rendell/Jonathan Hill/Murray Fraser/Mark Dorrian (eds.), *Critical Architecture*, London: Routledge, 135–142.

**** See Lauren Fournier (2021): *Autotheory as Feminist Practice in Art, Writing, and Criticism*, Cambridge, MA: MIT Press; Richard E. Ocejo/Brian Bond/Kyoichi Tachikawa (2012):

veyed. I used the conventions of measured architectural survey plans, with the addition of observational and analytic annotations and lines: lines of sight, lines of activity, lines of movement through the house. The lines were sketched in various colors and thicknesses, and dotted or dashed to form mappings of imagined, proposed, and guessed-at inhabitations. I also took notes in a diaristic mode, written onto the drawings themselves, as fictional or imagined, and made observational annotations. Then, when I returned to the studio, I redrew these, »drew them up«, transformed them, using mostly digital drawing. I made new plans inscribed with lines unfolding the views and trajectories that underpin the building's strange interior, and its correspondence with Marcel Duchamp's *Large Glass* (1915–23).[tttt] My aim was to situate and embody the inhabitants of the building. The drawing drew out their potential relationships using collage and line. I made folded paper drawings, books with drawn pages, drawings of the *Large Glass* itself, of the cracks and dust in its glass, and drawings of its later counterpart *Étant donnés* (1946–66).[####] Throughout the six years of research, I filled numerous A4 sketchbooks – 13 in total – which now sit in a box file gathering their own dust.

Throughout all of this work, the drawing line – line, collage, photocopy, print, paper fold – paralleled, no, entangled with, the written line. Informed by social and historical research on sexuality, gynaecology, and abortion, as well as art, culture, and literature of 19th and early 20th-century Paris, various forms of writing were used, both critical and creative.[§§§§] The writing line

---

Ethnography and the City: Readings on Doing Urban Fieldwork, London: Routledge; Giampietro Gobo (2008): *Doing Ethnography*, London: Sage.

[tttt] The *Large Glass* and *Étant donnés* are housed in the Philadelphia Museum of Art. The drawing and notational practices of Marcel Duchamp – full of homophones and puns – underpinned this practice. See for example, Marcel Duchamp (1994): *Duchamp du signe: écrits*, Paris: Flammarion; Marcel Duchamp (1973): »The Box of 1914«. Trans. Elmer Peterson, »À l'Infinitif«. Trans. Cleve Gray, in: Michel Sanouillet/Elmer Peterson (eds.), *The Writings of Marcel Duchamp*, New York: De Capo.

[####] Marcel Duchamp (1987): *Manual of Instructions for Étant donnés*, Philadelphia: Philadelphia Museum of Art.

[§§§§] The social theory and novels used were extensive: see for example, Shari Benstock (1986): *Women of the Left Bank: Paris 1900–1940*, New York: University of Texas Press; Alain Corbin (1990): *Women for Hire: Prostitution and Sexuality in France after 1850*, Cambridge, MA: Harvard University Press; Louis-Ferdinand Celine (1950): *Journey to the End of the Night* [1932]. Trans. John H. P. Marks, London: Vision Press.

rewrites the history of the building through sexuality and the gynaecological body. It is contiguous with – written through, alongside, in dialogue with – the drawing research I made while in the building.

Although Cixous suggests writing and drawing might be »writing-or-drawing«, she continues to prove them to be both inseparable yet partial: »twin adventures, which depart to seek in the dark, which do not find«. Cixous describes the sense in which writing-drawings are »expeditions« or »advance[s] into the unknown«, but also bound to failure: »we won't finish«; we »lose ourselves«.[*****] My drawing is a mode of forensics – a tactic for uncovering the absent but imagined or implied, for tracing clues to the past, seeking out a suggested inhabitation. Yet it is a melancholy mode, one bound up with loss and failure, as it fails to definitively find evidence, fails to fully demonstrate, fails to completely solve the mystery. Writing pulls it back from the failure – frames and tethers its ideas back down to the ground. The imaginary of writing takes us somewhere, along the path, to a logical conclusion. Even if we disbelieve the ending, we reach it.[†††††]

In my PhD research there are three entangled writing-drawing trajectories. These are framed through the three main chapters which identify and follow three materials present in the *Large Glass* and Maison de Verre.

Jacques Lacan's understanding of the part-object and his L Schema underpin my thesis. Lacan describes the outcomes of different parts of his schema enacting on each other, with the part-object as »like a bump in the fabric of something else«, a kind of present absence. The bumps can also be thought of as leftovers, which he associates as seeing (glass), waste products (dust) and speech (air). Part of my research reformulated the L Schema into a Part-architecture Schema as an index for the research practices. In the *Large Glass* and Maison de Verre, glass, dust, and air are: »intrinsic and connected materials. Glass predominates, forming a surface for dust collected intentionally on the surface of the *Large Glass* or as a by-product in the *Maison de Verre*; air, contained within the glass walls, both activates their interior life, whether metaphorically (the *Large Glass*) or literally (the *Maison de Verre*) and oxidises their materials causing

---

[*****]   Cixous, »Without end, no, State of drawingness, no, Rather«, 16.

[†††††]   On the construction of stories as history see Hilary Mantel's Reith Lectures »Resurrection: The Art and Craft«, at: https://www.bbc.co.uk/programmes/b08vkm52/episodes/player. Retrieved 23 November, 2021.

further dust. Each material variously signifies sexuality, domesticity and modernity […] glass signifies visual interaction, or the visuality of sexuality; dust suggests the past, bodies, unwanted matter, decay, cleaning and archiving; and air the breath of life and the carrying of sound and smell.«[*****]

1. **Glass**
    [observational drawing-
    -survey drawing-
    -plan drawing-
    -drawing out-
    -drawing tactics-]

Here, drawing is a form of ethnographic observation, creating knowledge through observation and close attention. I use architectural drawing to capture and represent what is materially present, to scale and with a level of rational accuracy. This could be described as Justine Clark, following Andrea Kahn, writes: »as an architectural object configuring architectural knowledge«.[§§§§§] These drawings are plans, always plans, with added sight-lines and arrowed, dotted, colored lines indicating routes, with sometimes additional annotations and collaged images. The directional colored lines follow, imagine, and index the spatial connections of several potential inhabitants of the building: the salon visitor; the gynaecological patient; Madame Dalsace (the owner of the house); and her husband gynaecologist, Dr Dalsace. They make (mark) possession of the private, domestic, and private/public gynaecological spaces in which events – gynaecological and sexual, familial, and public – must have taken place. Yet as Jacques Derrida writes, we are blind when we draw; drawing is blind.[*******] We do not know and cannot see these past inhabitations. They remain speculations.

[*****] See Cheatle, *Part-Architecture*, Chapter 3, 47, 50.

[§§§§§] See Justine Clark (2019): »Smudges, Smears and Adventitious Marks«. In: *Interstices: Journal of Architecture and Related Arts*, 1-8, and Andrea Kahn (1992): »Disclosure: Approaching Architecture«. In: *Harvard Architectural Review*, 8. I am indebted to Clark for some of the new references in this text.

[*******] Jacques Derrida (1993): *Memoirs of the Blind: The Self- Portrait and Other Ruins*, Chicago: University of Chicago Press.

2. Dust
[-drawing the body-
-drawing as archive-
-forensic drawing-
-drawing dust-
-drawing as archive fever-]

The bodies of the past have gone from the building. There is no record of their visitation or the activities that went on there; no archival remains. The glass drawings, despite being of material lines, merely map from the outside, failing to actually capture the real embodied presence of these past witnesses.[††††††] Dust as a material is composed substantially from human skin, hair, and clothing. Layers of it remain embedded in the corners and cracks of the building no matter how many times it is cleaned. Dust hence constitutes the leftovers of past inhabitations, fragments left behind from previous iterations of the body. Dust then is the only real archive. I became a cleaner in the house, and swept up its dust, from the nooks in the Nevada glass lenses to the crannies of the gynaecological surgery and its equipment. Departing from the drawing as line, the dust drawings are made from dust itself, re-presented through the old fashioned ink-dust-transfer method of photo-copying. The dust collections and their drawings attempt to get closer to the past body and archive its real presence. Yet the collecting of the dust became a painful corporeal experience in itself. It got inside me, up my nose, ingrained in my fingers. I ended up sneezing and ill with an allergic response. Even now though, I continuously return to dust, dirt, the ground: full of anomaly and contradiction they suggest both our presence somewhere, our history, and, with Haraway's thinking on compost and the »humusities«, our interdisciplinary kinships and relations.[§§§§§§] Dust is always a remainder worth looking at.[*******]

[††††††] On the materiality of lines see Catherine Ingraham (1991): »Lines and Linearity«, in: Andrea Kahn (ed.), *Drawing/Building/Text*, New York: Princeton Architectural Press, 73.

[******] Walter Benjamin (1992): »Paris – Capital of the Nineteenth Century«, in: *Illuminations*, London: Fontana Press. See also Teresa Stoppani (2007): »Dust Revolutions. Dust, Informe, Architecture (Notes for a Reading of Dust in Bataille)«. In: *Journal of Architecture*, 12/4, 437–447.

[§§§§§§] For Haraway, the humanities should be known as the humusities, to include all species, human and non-human. Haraway, *Staying with the Trouble*, 4.

[*******] Carolyn Steedman aligns dust with all history writing, see: Steedman, *Dust*.

3. **Air**
    [-drawing air-
    -drawing the invisible-
    -not drawing-
    -drawing-writing-sounding-]

The drawings of glass were made through visuality. Those of detritus and dust and the leftover body left something [else] to be desired. Dust is death. Vision is partial, tricksy. The building was also described by Dr Dalsace in the 1930s as a big sound machine. The sounds of the family, of the consultations with patients, of the weekly salon of notable avant-garde artists and writers drifted unconfined through the »free-plan«, mingling, and overheard.[†††††††] The doctor therefore had a soundproof telephone booth installed to have private discussions with his patients. Madame Dalsace fixed heavy sound-dampening velvet curtains and a thick piled carpet to her boudoir. The sounds and communications of the past are like ghosts that I try to grasp. Ghosts that won't go away because as Avery F. Gordon says, they have knowledges to tell us that we might have turned away from.[††††††] In the 1930s, air was pumped through the building via floor grilles, gently warming or cooling the spaces. The air of the past and the smells and sounds it carried are no longer visible materials but instead sounds in ghostly bubbles. How does one draw the invisible? By not-drawing. These not-drawings were instead audio pieces, performances of sound – of sweeping, of imagined past stories, of breath, of conversation – created on miniature sound chips and then embedded into tiny handmade books. They were neither drawing nor writing, but writing-drawing-sounding: I wrote creative pieces that imagined and followed the ghosts through the thresholds of the building's interior spaces. But can we avoid drawing? The final images in the PhD are plans showing where the books can be found in the building in an imaginary exhibition. The books themselves were lost in a house move several years later.

[†††††††] The weekly salon hosted the likes of Louis Arragon, Paul Eluard, Jean Cocteau, André Breton and Walter Benjamin, see Cheatle, *Part-Architecture*, 32, and Maria Gough (2002): »Paris, Capital of the Soviet Avant-Garde«. In: *October*, 101, summer, 55–61.

[††††††] See Avery F. Gordon (2003): *Ghostly Matters: Haunting and the Sociological Imagination*, Minneapolis: University of Minnesota Press.

On drawing, I am still uncertain. Drawing does not find, yet seeks blindly in the dark. It extends its line, its mark, meets its lack. Yet hooked through writing it continues to look, to hear, to smell. It potentially helps writing to present the formerly unseen »*living of life*«.[§§§§§§]

> My research after *Part-Architecture* has re-explored many of the positionings of the thesis, but also moved into new theoretical areas, particularly around embodying architecture and health. In recent work on the rise of maternity buildings and the materialization of the maternal body in the 18th to 20th centuries, I once again assumed that I no longer had a use for drawing, only to find I am reliant on 19th-century »found object drawings« that stand in for the »lost« 18th-century maternity buildings and their absent plans.[*********] Reading these requires a redrawing of them in order to analyze how their spaces were inhabited and how maternity, over time, becomes a spatialized social practice. I also redraw the plans of 20th-century maternity spaces in order to understand how the maternal experience is embedded differently in these spaces. Once learnt, drawing as writing-drawing seems to be a practice I cannot leave behind. »There is no end to writing or drawing. Being born doesn't end. Drawing is a being born. Drawing is born.«[†††††††††]

[§§§§§§] Cixous, »Without end, no, State of drawingness, no, Rather«, 21.

[*********] There are very few extant original 18th or 19th-century maternity buildings, and where they do exist, such as the Newcastle Lying-in Hospital of 1826 and the General Lying-In Hospital, York Road in Lambeth, London of 1830, their interiors are substantially converted. See Emma Cheatle (2024): *Lying in the Dark Room: Architectures of British Maternity*, London: Routledge.

[†††††††††] Cixous, »Without end, no, State of drawingness, no, Rather«, 16.

References

Bal, Mieke (2001): *Looking In: The Art of Viewing*, Amsterdam: G and B Arts International.

Bal, Mieke (2001): *Louise Bourgeois' Spider: the architecture of art-writing*, London: University of Chicago Press.

Benjamin, Walter (1992): »Paris – Capital of the Nineteenth Century«, in: *Illuminations*, London: Fontana Press.

Benjamin, Walter (1992): »Theses on the Philosophy of History«, in: *Illuminations*, London: Fontana Press.

Jennifer Bloomer (1993): *Architecture and the Text: the (S)crypts of Joyce and Piranesi*, London: Yale University Press.

Bloomer, Jennifer (1992): »Abodes of Theory and Flesh: Tabbles of Bower«. In: *Assemblage*, 17, 6–29.

Benstock, Shari (1986): *Women of the Left Bank: Paris 1900–1940*, New York: University of Texas Press.

Celine, Louis-Ferdinand (1950): *Journey to the End of the Night* [1932]. Trans. John H. P. Marks, London: Vision Press.

Cheatle, Emma (2024): *Lying in the Dark Room: The Architectures of British Maternity.* London: Routledge.

Cheatle, Emma (2017): *Part-Architecture: The Maison de Verre, Duchamp, Domesticity and Desire in 1930s Paris*, London: Routledge.

Cixous, Hélène (2005): »Without end, no, State of drawingness, no, Rather: The Executioner's taking off«, in: *Cixous, Stigmata: Escaping Texts.* Trans. Catharine A. F. MacGillivray, London: Routledge.

Clark, Justine (2019): »Smudges, Smears and Adventitious Marks«. In: *Interstices: Journal of Architecture and Related Arts*, 1-8.

Corbin, Alain (1990): *Women for Hire: Prostitution and Sexuality in France after 1850*, Cambridge, MA: Harvard University Press.

Derrida, Jacques (1993): *Memoirs of the Blind: The Self-Portrait and Other Ruins*, Chicago: University of Chicago Press.

Derrida, Jacques (1996): *Archive Fever: A Freudian Impression*, Chicago: University of Chicago Press.

Diller, Elizabeth and Ricardo Scofidio (1994): *Flesh: Architectural Probes*, London: Triangle Architectural Publishing.

Duchamp, Marcel (1994): *Duchamp du signe: écrits*, Paris: Flammarion.

Duchamp, Marcel (1973): »The Box of 1914«. Trans. Elmer Peterson, »À l'Infinitif«. Trans. Cleve Gray, in: Michel Sanouillet/Elmer Peterson (eds.), *The Writings of Marcel Duchamp*, New York: De Capo.

Duchamp, Marcel (1987): *Manual of Instructions for Étant donnés*, Philadelphia: Philadelphia Museum of Art.

Erpenbeck, Jenny (2010): *Visitation*. Trans. Susan Bernofsky, London: Portobello.

Evans, Robin (1997): »Translations from Drawing to Building«, in: *Translations from Drawing to Building and Other Essays*, London: Architectural Association, 153–193.

Farge, Arlette (2013): *The Allure of the Archives*, New Haven: Yale University Press.

Fournier, Lauren (2021): *Autotheory as Feminist Practice in Art, Writing, and Criticism*, Cambridge, MA: MIT Press.

Gordon, Avery F. (2003): *Ghostly Matters: Haunting and the Sociological Imagination*, Minneapolis: University of Minnesota Press.

Gobo, Giampietro (2008): *Doing Ethnography*, London: Sage.

Gough, Maria (2002): »Paris, Capital of the Soviet Avant-Garde«. In: *October*, 101, summer, 55–83.

Grillner, Katja (2007): »Fluttering Butterflies, a Dusty Road, and a Muddy Stone: Criticality in Distraction«, in: Jane Rendell/Jonathan Hill/Murray Fraser/Mark Dorrian (eds.), *Critical Architecture*, London: Routledge, 135–142.

Haraway, Donna (2016): *Staying with the Trouble: Making Kin in the Chthulucene*, Durham, NC: Duke University Press.

Hill, Jonathan (2006): »Drawing research«, in: *Journal of Architecture*, 11, 329–333.

Ingraham, Catherine (1991): »Lines and Linearity«, in: Andrea Kahn (ed.), *Drawing/Building/Text*, New York: Princeton Architectural Press, 73.

Kahn, Andrea (1992): »Disclosure: Approaching Architecture«. In: *Harvard Architectural Review*, 8.

Krauss, Rosalind E. (1994): *The Optical Unconscious*, Cambridge, MA: MIT Press.

Lacan, Jacques (2002): Écrits: A Selection. Trans. Bruce Fink, New York: W.W. Norton.

Mantel, Hilary (2017): Reith Lectures »Resurrection: The Art and Craft«, at: https://www.bbc.co.uk/programmes/bo8vkm52/episodes/player.

Mitchell, W. J. T. (1994): *Picture Theory: Essays on Verbal and Visual Representation*. Chicago: University of Chicago Press.

Ocejo, Richard E./Bond, Brian/ Tachikawa, Kyoichi (2012): *Ethnography and the City: Readings on Doing Urban Fieldwork*, London: Routledge.

Perec, Georges (2008): *Species of Spaces and Other Pieces*. Trans. John Sturrock. London: Penguin.

Steedman, Carolyn (2001): *Dust: The Archive and Cultural History*, Manchester: Manchester University Press.

Stoppani, Teresa (2007): »Dust Revolutions. Dust, Informe, Architecture (Notes for a Reading of Dust in Bataille)«. In: *Journal of Architecture*, 12/4, 437–447.

St. Pierre, Elizabeth Adams (2021): »Post Qualitative Inquiry, the Refusal of Method, and the Risk of the New«. In: *Qualitative Inquiry*, 27/2, January, 163–166.

CONTRIBUTORS

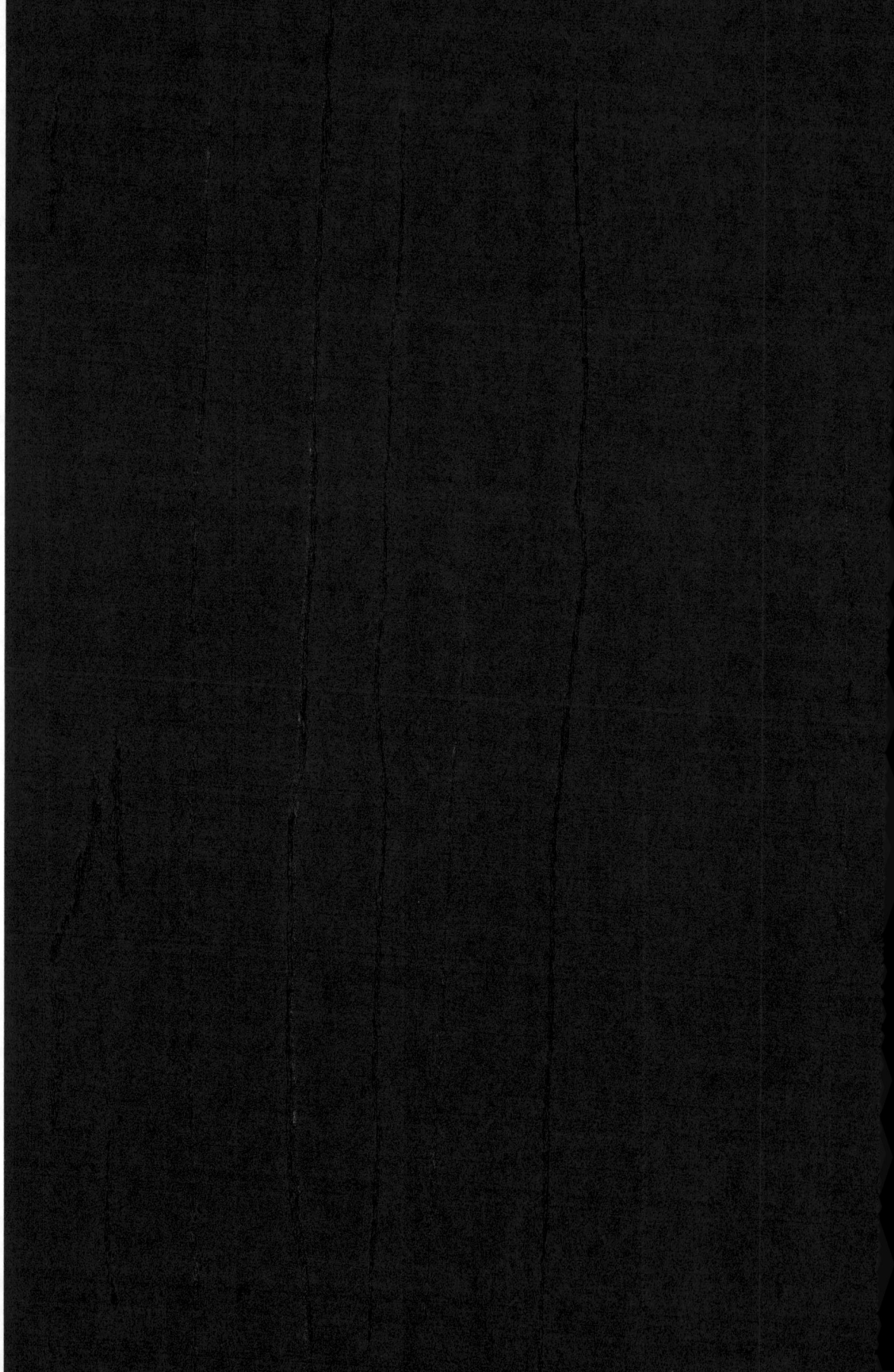

Biographies

Yara Al Heswani

is an architect, urban researcher, and teaching assistant at Damascus University. She is also currently pursuing doctoral research. She holds a diploma degree in architecture from Damascus University, awarded in 2013, and a master's degree in the theories and history of architecture from Damascus University, which was awarded in 2018. She is interested in urban research that studies the relations between humans and their urban environment, and spatial changes during conflicts. She has participated in many related workshops and visual exhibitions in Syria, Lebanon, Denmark, the Netherlands, and the United Kingdom. She is part of the Syrbanism network which connects to share knowledge.

Dirk Bahmann

is an architect and fine artist practicing in Johannesburg, South Africa. He lectures in the School of Architecture and Planning at the University of the Witwatersrand and oversees the s'Fanakalo makers space. He is pursuing arts-based doctoral research at the Wits School of Arts and his research interests center on investigating the psycho-spatial aspects of architecture and atmospheres. His practice is deeply embedded in a methodology of making and its processes that explore the agency and auratic quality of materials.

Jhono Bennett

is the co-founder of 1to1 Agency of Engagement, a design-led social enterprise based in Johannesburg. 1to1 was established in 2010 to support the multi-scalar work being done to redevelop post-apartheid South African cities in the face of systemic spatial inequality. Jonathan is currently enrolled at the Bartlett School of Architecture as a doctoral candidate in the TACK/ Communities of Tacit Knowledge: Architecture and its Ways of Knowing network. His practice-led research interests are driven by issues around inclusive design approaches, spatial justice, critical positionality, and urban planning in South African cities.

Emma Cheatle

is a senior lecturer at the University of Sheffield School of Architecture. Trained as an architect, her PhD (from University College London) received the 2014 RIBA President's Award for Outstanding PhD Thesis.Her interdisciplinary research examines the intersections of architecture, art, and urban space through the contexts of gender, health, and inequality. Her monograph *Part-Architecture: The Maison de Verre, Duchamp, Domesticity and Desire in 1930s Paris* (2017) weaves critical and creative writing and drawn analysis to understand the social, sexual and medical histories of the building and artwork. Her new book *Lying in the Dark: The Architectures of British Maternity* uses autotheory to examine historic and contemporary maternal spaces and practices.

Nicholas Drofiak

is an artist and researcher. He earned his doctoral degree at ETH in Zürich in 2016 with the thesis »Irúsan or, Canting for Architect« before taking up a Leverhulme early career fellowship in theatre and performance studies at the University of Warwick. He is interested in how repertoires of collective knowledge, memories, and attitudes toward identities are continuously and communally constituted, evolved, exchanged, and negotiated through ongoing and co-constructive relations between humans and agentive, non- or more-than-human actors. His research project Performing Indigenous Identities: Memory and Belonging in the Russian Far North explores these issues in collaboration with a multilingual villa community in Turukhansk rajon, the language of whose Ket indigenous residents is severely endangered.

Davide Franco

is an architect, researcher, and lecturer trained at the Politecnico di Bari. He developed research with TU München and DAM in Frankfurt and was particularly interested in the construction of architecture. He completed a doctoral thesis on industrial buildings in Berlin in the early 20th century, which focuses on the relationship between technique and the language of construction. In practice, he works as an architect in Italy and in Germany, mainly on the reuse and restoration of domestic buildings.

Hélène Frichot

is Professor of Architecture and Philosophy in the Faculty of Architecture, Building and Planning at the Melbourne School of Design at the University of Melbourne. Until 2019 she was Professor of Critical Studies and Gender Theory, and Director of Critical Studies in Architecture at KTH Stockholm. Her recent publications include *Creative Ecologies: Theorizing the Practice of Architecture* (2018) and *Dirty Theory: Troubling Architecture* (AADR 2019). She has collaborated on editing many anthologies, including: *Infrastructural Love: Caring for our Architectural Support Systems* (2022); *Architectural Affects after Deleuze and Guattari* (2021) and *Ficto-Critical Approaches* (2020).

Janina Gosseye

is Associate Professor in the Department of Architecture in the TU Delft Faculty of Architecture and the Built Environment. Her research is situated at the nexus of architectural history, urban design history, and social and political history, focusing particularly on the 20th century. Gosseye has authored and edited several books; most recently: *Urban Design the 20th Century: A History* (2021), *Activism at Home: Architects Dwelling between Politics, Aesthetics and Resistance* (2021), and *Speaking of Buildings: Oral History in Architectural Research* (2019).

Gabriel Bernard Guelle

is an architect and building engineer who trained at the École nationale supérieure d'architecture Paris-La-Villette and at the Ecole spéciale des Travaux publics. His ongoing doctoral research, funded by the French ministry of culture, links an interest in construction history and architectural education, and focuses on the teaching of construction to architects between the 1920s and the 1970s in France, and in the German cultural space. His research aims to understand the influence of this teaching on the architect's relationship to building techniques and the engineer. Alongside his research, Gabriel teaches morphology at the Ensa Paris-La-Villette and the Ensa Nantes, and architectural analysis at the Ensa Normandie.

Rachel Győrffy

studied architecture at the TU Munich and at the Arts University Bournemouth. After close to ten years of professional experience in Germany and Hungary, she began her PhD at Moholy-Nagy University of Art and Design in Budapest in 2019. Her doctoral research focuses on the spatial practices of identity construction and the layers of urban memory within the context of the current paradigms of architectural reconstructivism. Since 2021 she has been a research scholar in the New National Excellence Initiative (ÚNKP), examining the possibilities of cultural heritage digitalization. She is currently a research and teaching assistant at the Institute of Architectural Theory, History of Art, and Cultural Studies at TU Graz.

Walaa Hajali

is an architect and a research student at Manchester School of Architecture. She completed her master's degree in environmental design and engineering at UCL, UK in 2019 where she developed a multi-lens approach toward understanding architecture as an interdisciplinary science that requires collaboration among different parties to design and operate energy efficient, sustainable, and healthier buildings.

Jonathan Hill

is Professor of Architecture and Visual Theory at The Bartlett School of Architecture, UCL where he directs the MPhil/PhD architectural design program and tutors MArch Unit 12 with Elizabeth Dow. Jonathan is the author of *The Illegal Architect* (1998); *Actions of Architecture* (2003); *Immaterial Architecture* (2006); *Weather Architecture* (2012); *A Landscape of Architecture, History and Fiction* (2016); and *The Architecture of Ruins* (2019); editor of *Occupying Architecture* (1998); *Architecture—the Subject is Matter* (2001); and *Designs on History: The Architect as Physical Historian* (2021); and co-editor of *Critical Architecture* (2007).

Amina Kaskar

is a South African architect who obtained a master's in architecture from the University of the Witwatersrand, Johannesburg, and gained a master's in human settlements from KU Leuven, Belgium. Her work is predominantly informed by ideas regarding »soft architectures«, textiles, gender, and migration. She was awarded the Global Minds Scholarship to complete a PhD at KU Leuven. Her proposed PhD is entitled »Soft Architectures: Afro-Asian Spatial Practices«. She co-founded Counterspace (2014–2020), a collaborative architectural studio dedicated to architectural projects, exhibition design, art installations, public events curation, and urban design.

Anna Keitemeier

is conducting her PhD project as a cotutelle between the laboratory Architecture, Milieu et Paysage at École nationale supérieure d'architecture Paris-la Villette (École doctorale Abbé Grégoire at Conservatoire national des arts et métiers) and the Institute for Urban and Landscape Design at Karlsruher Institut für Technologie. Her research interests are the role of nature and landscape in late 20th-century urban design projects in Paris, Berlin, and Rome. Anna studied architecture and urban design at Technische Universität Dortmund, Università degli Studi in Florence and ENSA Paris-la Villette, and has built up a rich international and interdisciplinary portfolio through complementary activities, including working at the Kunsthistorisches Institut in Florence, and in different architecture offices.

Therese Keogh

is an artist and writer living and working in Naarm/Melbourne. Her practice operates at the intersections between sculpture, geography, and landscape architecture to produce multi-layered projects that explore the socio-political and material conditions of narrative and knowledge production. Therese works collaboratively through writing and research projects, including co-facilitating »Magnetic Topographies« and »Written Together«. Therese holds a bachelor of fine arts from Monash University, a master of fine arts from Sydney College of the Arts, and a master of arts in geography from Queen Mary University of London. She is currently undertaking a PhD at Victorian College of the Arts, the University of Melbourne.

Santosh Kumar Ketham

is a practicing architect, educator, researcher, and philanthropist. He is the founder and principal of the architectural office Ketham's Atelier Architects and the NGO, Thinking Hand, in Hyderabad. His ongoing doctoral research is on adaptive architecture and urbanism with a focus on flooding cities in the Global South, at the University of Innsbruck, Institute of Experimental Architecture. He has taught design, architecture, and urbanism at various universities in India and Austria. He has been interviewed about flooding cities on Deutsche Welle Documentary, 3Sat, ORF TV, and also on Architecture Live!, Shoutout DFW, The Hindu, TOI, and Eenadu.

Torsten Lange

is a lecturer in cultural and architectural history at Lucerne University of Applied Sciences and Arts (HSLU). His research focuses on modern and contemporary architecture with a special interest in the discourses and networks of architectural production in the (late) socialist world and, more recently, relationships between the built environment and gendered bodies. His publications include, among journal articles, the edited volume *Re-Framing Identities: Architecture's Turn to History, 1970–1990* (with Ákos Moravánszky), the special edition of the European Architectural History Network (EAHN) open-access journal *Architectural Histories*, »Architectural Historiography and Fourth Wave Feminism« (with Lucía C. Pérez-Moreno), and archithese reader: *Critical Positions in Search of Postmodernity 1971–1976*, as well as *gta Papers* no.7 »Care and Architecture« (both with Gabrielle Schaad).

Elena Markus

studied architecture at the Universität der Künste (UdK) (Berlin University of the Arts). Between 2011 and 2014, Elena was a curator at the Swiss Architecture Museum (SAM) in Basel. Since 2014, she has been teaching architecture theory at the TUM Technical University of Munich. Elena organized seminars and workshops on the subject of the »Theory of Siedlung« and curated exhibitions at the 5th Architecture Biennale in Moscow, and in the Lothringer13 art hall in Munich. In her PhD entitled »(Dirty) Realism: Analogue Architecture 1983–87«, she investigated the social and political significance of architectural production in regard to the dirty realism discourse in the art and architecture of the 1980s.

Anna Odlinge

is a doctoral candidate at KTH School of Architecture in Stockholm (KTH-A). She was trained in architecture primarily at KTH-A and SCI-Arc in Los Angeles, and in astrophysics at the universities of Umeå and Stockholm. For decades she has focused on creative processes, both as a senior lecturer within architecture, interiors, and spatial design, and in her own artistically driven research. She has taught at KTH-A and at Konstfack - University College of Arts, Crafts and Design in Stockholm, and within the field of computer game development in Gotland (Uppsala University). In 2009 she was a fellow/teacher at Oberlin College in Ohio. Besides her research studies at the KTH-A and her own drawing practice, she works with building permits in the municipality of Gotland.

Natalia Petkova

is a Paris-based architect who graduated from the University of Cambridge and the École des hautes études en sciences sociales, in Paris. Her ongoing PhD research, jointly funded by the French ministry of culture and the Caisse des Dépôts, employs ethnographic methods to explore what the structural use of stone does to contemporary architectural production. In practice, she has most recently worked for Barrault Pressacco in Paris and Caruso St John Architects in London. Alongside her doctoral research, Natalia is pursuing independent building projects and teaching diploma at the École nationale supérieure d'architecture Paris-Malaquais.

Andreas Putz

is Assistant Professor of Recent Building Heritage Conservation at TUM Department of Architecture in Munich. His research focuses on the history and theory of building conservation in the 20th century, and on options for the maintenance and repair of synthetics, fair-faced concrete, and curtain wall facades. He was employed as an architect in Basel and in Dresden, and from 2009 onward he was in charge of the conversion of Erich Mendelsohn's former Schocken department store in Chemnitz. His doctoral thesis at ETH Zürich (2015) was awarded the Theodor-Fischer-Prize. He is a member of several scientific boards and expert committees on building heritage conservation.

Jane Rendell

is Professor of Critical Spatial Practice at the Bartlett School of Architecture, UCL. She introduced the concepts of »critical spatial practice« and »site-writing« through her authored books: *The Architecture of Psychoanalysis* (2017); *Silver* (2016); *Site-Writing* (2010); *Art and Architecture* (2006); *The Pursuit of Pleasure* (2002), and her co-edited collections include *Reactivating the Social Condenser* (2017); *Critical Architecture* (2007); *Spatial Imagination* (2005); *The Unknown City* (2001); *Intersections* (2000); *Gender, Space, Architecture* (1999), and *Strangely Familiar* (1995). She currently curates a situated reviewing site – site-reading-writingquarterly.co.uk, and, with Dr David Roberts and Dr Yael Padan, www.practisingethics.org.

Meike Schalk

is Associate Professor of Urban Design and Urban Theory, and Docent of Architecture at the KTH School of Architecture in Stockholm. Her research focuses on contemporary shifts in welfare spaces and policies on housing in Sweden and in Vienna, which she explores through practice-oriented research in individual and collaborative projects. Currently, she is an Anna Boyksen fellow at the Institute for Advanced Study, Technical University Munich where she addresses themes relevant to gender and diversity in technosciences and institutional contexts, along with colleagues and students at TUM.

Tijana Stevanović

is a lecturer in architectural history and theory at the Bartlett School of Architecture, UCL (2015–) and an affiliated researcher on the AHRC (UK)/ FAPESP (Brazil) funded project »Translating Ferro/Transforming Knowledges of Architecture, Design and Labour for the New Field of Production Studies [TF/TK]«, 2020–2024. She was a postdoctoral research fellow at the School of Architecture, KTH Stockholm (2020– 2021). Tijana's research interests and publications span the fields of labor, technology, feminist architectural history, and the institutionalization of care. Her PhD thesis »Incorporating Self-management: Architectural Production in New Belgrade« (Newcastle University, 2019) explored the ways in which constitutionally established workers' self-management in post-war Yugoslavia influenced the organization of architectural techniques.

Rasha Sukkarieh

is a Beirut-based architect who trained in the Faculty of Architecture at Beirut Arab University and the Institute for Advanced Architecture of Catalonia, where she achieved a master's in advanced architecture II. She is currently a PhD candidate focusing on the intersection of architecture, technology, and biology, and investigates how new advances in material, digital fabrication, and computational design could lead to a more efficient and sustainable design-build process. Rasha teaches and leads multi-scalar workshops and seminars in computational design and robotics, and for the past year, she has contributed substantially to humanitarian work in Lebanon as the shelter project manager for the non-governmental organization Nusaned.

Anita Szentesi

is an architect, lecturer, and filmmaker who is based in South Africa and who trained at The University of the Witwatersrand (Wits). She also completed the Professional Practice and Management in Architecture course at The Bartlett School of Architecture, UCL. She is currently pursuing a doctoral degree at Wits. Her ongoing research is a balance between the two academic disciplines of architecture and film. Alongside her doctoral research, she teaches in the undergraduate design and design representation studios, and supervises master's students at the University of the Witwatersrand.

Meitar Tewel

is a Master's student at the Faculty of Architecture and the Built Environment at TU Delft, The Netherlands. Her work lies at the intersection of architectural research and design, with a focus on the evaluation of the agency of architecture in rebuilding Jewish communities in post-World War II Israel and Europe. Her ongoing Master's thesis deals with unearthing spatial and cultural layers of the historic city centre of Frankfurt am Main, Germany, focusing on the modern urban fabric which was built on the relics of the Judengasse, the centuries-old Jewish ghetto.

Ina Valkanova

is a doctoral candidate at the Institute for Landscape and Urban Studies at ETH Zürich. She completed her masters' degree in architecture at RWTH Aachen in 2010. During her studies, she was a guest student at UdK Berlin and the University of Granada. She has worked in many architectural offices, including Kadawittfeldarchitektur, Aachen, Paul Böhm, Cologne, and Benthem Crouwel, Amsterdam. Upon graduation she was awarded the Building Europe Scholarship for young architects which led to a collaboration with Alvaro Siza in Porto, Portugal. Ina has been the director of Architecture Week in Sofia, and the coordinator of the municipal initiative Vision Sofia 2050.

GPSR Authorized Representative: Easy Access System Europe, Mustamäe tee
50, 10621 Tallinn, Estonia, gpsr.requests@easproject.com

www.ingramcontent.com/pod-product-compliance
Lightning Source LLC
Chambersburg PA
CBHW081151030426
42335CB00033B/2676